KU-712-797

CONTENTS IN BRIEF

rei ned on or before

EXPLORING MASS MEDIA
FOR A CHANGING WORLD

LIVERPOOL JOHN MOORES UNIVERSITY
Aldham Robarts L.R.C.
TEL. 051 231 3701/3634

LIVERPOOL JMU LIBRARY

3 1111 01057 0115

EXPLORING MASS MEDIA FOR A CHANGING WORLD

RAY ELDON HIEBERT
UNIVERSITY OF MARYLAND, COLLEGE PARK

SHEILA JEAN GIBBONS
COMMUNICATION RESEARCH ASSOCIATES, INC.

2000

LAWRENCE ERLBAUM ASSOCIATES, PUBLISHERS
MAHWAH, NEW JERSEY   LONDON

Copyright © 2000 by Lawrence Erlbaum Associates, Inc.
  All rights reserved. No part of this book may be reproduced in any
  form, by photostat, microfilm, retrieval system, or any other means,
  without prior written permission of the publisher.

Lawrence Erlbaum Associates, Inc., Publishers
10 Industrial Avenue
Mahwah, NJ 07430

Cover design by Kathryn Houghtaling Lacey

Library of Congress Cataloging-in-Publication Data

Hiebert, Ray Eldon
Exploring mass media for a changing world / by Ray Eldon
Hiebert and Sheila Jean Gibbons.
    p.   cm.
  Includes bibliographical references and index.
ISBN 0-8058-2916-4 (pbk. : alk. paper).
1. Mass media. I. Silver, Sheila. II. Title.
P90.H478 1999
  302.23—dc21   99-28304
                                                        CIP

Books published by Lawrence Erlbaum Associates are printed on
acid-free paper, and their bindings are chosen for strength and durability.

Printed in the United States of America
10 9 8 7 6 5 4 3 2

CONTENTS

PREFACE

This book was written to introduce college students to the mass media, one of the most important areas of study in the curriculum today. Many introductory texts are on the market, so why would we want to enter into competition in such a crowded field? The answer is that we feel a different direction is needed from the one being taken by most other texts. Many texts have become overly large and detailed, filled with facts, graphs, charts, boxes, and pictures. Some look as if they were aimed at junior high and high school audiences in their attempt to make the subject flashy and colorful. To use an old cliché, they seem to have lost a clear view of the forest because of too many trees.

We have long felt that the time has come to step back from that approach. We have tried instead to produce a simpler, less cluttered, and less expensive book, one that emphasizes the simple basic elements essential to understanding the subject. We have not felt it necessary to engage in trivial pursuit of media programs and characters, nor to fill these pages with detailed data, statistics, and numbers. We have illustrated with examples and anecdotes only when needed to clarify principles and to support generalizations.

We have organized the book historically, because we feel that is the best way to comprehend the subject. Mass media have to be seen as evolving and constantly changing institutions. We start off by placing communication media in a historical context because that best demonstrates not only the changes in media but the effects of those changes on society.

The first seven chapters deal with broad, general, and theoretical issues that apply to mass communication and mass media. In each of these chapters, where necessary, we show differences in media, but our general purpose is to show commonalities among media in their historical development, definitions, processes, functions, political systems, economic considerations, internal controls, external laws and social responsibilities; their use by audiences; and their effects on individuals and society.

The next five chapters deal with specific media. We have presented these chapters in the chronological order in which the media they describe became mass media. Newspapers were the first to reach the masses, in our definition. Books and magazines were next, and we have included newsletters in this print media chapter for convenience. Movies, radio, sound recordings, and television became mass media in that order.

Chapters 13 and 14 examine two institutions that operate outside the media—advertising and public relations. But these two activities have become so essential to mass media and the way mass communication works in our society that one could never understand the media without a full comprehension of advertising and public relations.

We end by returning to a specific medium, in this case the Internet, the latest to develop as a mass medium. We discuss the Internet in the context of the technological changes that are producing many new forms of media. The Internet is by far the most important, and we feel it will revolutionize communication and the world as much as Gutenberg's printing press has from the fifteenth century on and as much as the electric age did in the nineteenth and twentieth centuries.

Two other themes run through this book. One is that technology makes the difference. We are not technicians, and we do not discuss the technical aspects of how a printing press works, or a vacuum tube, or a transistor, or a microchip, or the connection of millions of computers. But this book is based on the idea that the technology of a communication medium not only opens new possibilities but also places restrictions on what can be communicated, how it can be communicated, and how it will be received. Each new technology has created a new language for recreating human experience, and although we do not have to understand the technology itself, we have to understand its language in order to master mass communication.

Finally, this book is written by Americans from an American perspective, but we feel strongly that a more global view is needed. Communication is culture bound, and Americans have tended to be provincial about mass media, thinking that what works and is right in our culture should be the same worldwide. Media systems are different in each country and culture. We have tried to take that into consideration in looking at mass media as Americans. Many other books need to be written about world cultural differences in mass media and about American mass media influence on other cultures. In this book, we have been able only to acknowledge those concerns. We do acknowledge that mass media are becoming global, and the Internet will underline this fact more than any previous medium.

—*Ray Eldon Hiebert*
—*Sheila Jean Gibbons*

EXPLORING MASS MEDIA
FOR A CHANGING WORLD

1

DEVELOPMENT OF MASS MEDIA
AND SOCIAL CHANGE

We are overwhelmed by mass media. In the United States, more than 60 million copies of newspapers are printed every day, as well as millions of copies of magazines and books. More than 10 thousand radio stations fill the airwaves, giving the average listener 40 to 50 different choices of programs every minute of every day. Network television reaches audiences in the tens of millions every weekday evening, and most people have access around the clock, over the air or via cable or satellite, to dozens of non-network programs, achieving a total audience every day of more than 100 million viewers. Movies are rolling off the Hollywood assembly line at a greater rate than ever, attendance is increasing, and a blockbuster new movie can bring in $30 million to $40 million.

That's a bird's-eye view of the mass media scene in America at the beginning of the twenty-first century, the beginning of a new millennium. Much can be written about the overwhelming successes of mass media to inform us about the world around us; to interpret and explain its meaning; to entertain us; and to advertise the products, personalities, and ideas that make our world work. In the area of information alone, mass media provide much careful reporting on a vast array of issues and events that are necessary to our lives every day—the actions of our political leaders, the votes of our representatives, the attitudes and opinions of people, the daily performance of the stock market and many other indispensable financial and business transactions, health news, weather forecasts, scores of our favorite sports teams, critical appraisals of entertainment offered to the public, and products available in our stores. In fact, we have come to take for granted this cornucopia of important information provided every day by mass media, without which we could not exist as a civilized society in the twenty-first century.

If we look a little closer at this scene, we also see that mass media are overwhelming us with sales pitches and commercials—with persuasive messages urging us to buy things we don't need: to be as thin as fashion models, to measure our sexuality by the cars we drive or beverages we drink, to eat greasy fast food and go on diets, to equate success with body scent or biceps and quads. If we look at the information in mass media, we find we are often underwhelmed with news, much of which is sensational headlines and disappointing stories, tabloid and trash journalism filled with crime, sex, accidents, fires, and assorted violence. If we look at mass media entertainment, we too often find shallow dramas, sitcoms, and soap operas filled with gratuitous sex and violence. America is a country that prides itself on freedom of speech and freedom of the press. But if we look more deeply into our mass media, we can find many citizens who don't know the names of their congressional representatives or Supreme Court justices. We can find that the average citizen seldom has much of a voice and little real access to public expression through mass media. In fact, perhaps fewer voices were really being heard at the end of the twentieth century than were heard at its beginning, as mass media companies were merged into larger corporate giants presided over by ever smaller groups of executives. At the beginning of the twenty-first century, the catchword is *global media*, because the mass media giants now send their messages out worldwide and often control media in more than one country.

We count on the press to give us essential information we need to be informed citizens in control of our destinies in democracy. But in the last third of the twentieth century we learned that even democratic governments sometimes lied and misled in order to achieve their ends. We discovered that even the watchdog press and mass media, and thus the public, could often be deceived, even if only temporarily. We have relied on the press and mass media to give us essential information about our leaders, so we could vote intelligently for those who would lead us intelligently. But we learned that media can be managed and manipulated in political election campaigns, and perhaps even bought off with political campaign advertising worth hundreds of millions of dollars, leaving the public to be the hapless recipient of political propaganda rather than useful information.

What, then, should we be thinking about mass media as we begin a new century? Are we their victims, or do they serve us well? Can we take charge of the situation so that mass media will ennoble us as human beings, enrich our minds with essential information, make our lives easier with meaningful entertainment and delightful diversions, and help us achieve a society where the good of all will prevail? The answer is yes, but it will take knowledge, understanding, and effort. It will require bright young people with good motives to be attracted to careers in mass media. And it will require intelligent and educated audiences who understand the meaning of media, so they can make proper choices about messages they receive and demand that media work for them, not they for the media.

This book was written for that purpose. It is aimed at the college student interested in a career in mass communication. It provides the essential information needed to chart one's educational path and career choice to achieve one's goal as a journalist or mass communicator. We assume there are many specialties into which one can fit one's talents—writing, editing, producing, acting, announcing, reporting, illustrating, photographing, advertising copy writing, promoting, public relations advising, and many more.

This book is also written for all of us who will be audiences of mass media for the remainder of our lives. Only when we understand mass media can we demand that they be meaningful. Since media are so much a part of our everyday world and so influential, we believe that every educated person should read a book such as this one, or take a basic course on mass media to learn their essential facts and theories, their historical development, their impact on our lives, and ways in which they operate. This subject matter is as crucial as that in a course in civics, or art or music appreciation, or history, or politics, or economics. Figure 1.1 demonstrates at a quick glance the mass media we will be discussing in this book, including some basic figures about the numbers of media units in each category and the size of the audience or the reach of the media. More complete descriptions and definitions are developed in later chapters.

THE AGE OF MASS COMMUNICATION

We have just completed the mass media century. The twentieth century was the most populated, most warlike, most violent, most inventive, most technologically progressive, and also the most communicative century in human history. In 1900, newspapers were the largest mass medium, and they had just come into that role in the previous 20 or 30 years. In 1900, the amount of time the average person spent on what today we regard as mass communication was perhaps a few minutes a day. The twentieth century saw the development of motion pictures, radio, television, and the computer, and by the year 2000, the average American was spending more than half his or her leisure time (when not working, eating, or sleeping) on mass media, mostly on television. We now spend more time on mass media than we do on social activities, hobbies, active sports, travel, or any other single activity. Young people going to college at the end of the century were part of a more "mediated" generation than any previous generation in human history; they spent more time with mass media than with parents or teachers, family or friends; more time in front of a television set than in a classroom.

During the twentieth century, scholars tried to understand this new phenomenon of mass media and mass communication. Their work grew steadily, and our understanding increased accordingly. Many early efforts to research media questions were feeble by today's standards. But by the end of the century, we were in a much better position to use the theories and data of scholars to understand the processes and to make that understanding work for us. During the century, scholars frequently debated whether mass media were powerful or not; whether they had an impact on some individuals but not on others; whether they could be dismissed entirely as unimportant phenomena—trifling, frivolous, shallow entertainment, signifying nothing—or all-powerful juggernauts, capable of swaying the masses of the world.

Daily Newspapers
 Number—about 1,500
 Combined circulation (morning and evening)—56.7 million
 Readership—58.7% of U.S. adults (over 18) read a daily newspaper
Weekly Newspapers
 Number—about 7,200
 Combined circulation—70.3 million
Consumer and Business Magazines
 Number—about 18,000
 Circulation—368.6 million per issue
Consumer Newsletters
 Number—approximately 20,000
Books
 Number of new titles published yearly—about 40,000
 Consumer books sold in the U.S. annually—1 billion
Motion Pictures
 Number of feature films produced annually—about 400
 Movie audience— 1.4 billion annually
 Motion picture screens—32,000
Sound Recordings
 Quantity shipped—approximately 1.14 billion units annually (audio and music
  video)
 Music audience—Nearly 9 out of 10 adults accompany their leisure activities with
  music
 Sales—U.S. represents 30.5% of all recorded music purchases
Television
 Number of commercial stations—about 1,200
 Number of public television stations—350
 Average television viewing day—6 hours, 57 minutes
 Percentage of homes with television set—98%
 Percentage of homes passed by cable television—64%
 Average number of channels received—45
Radio
 Number of commercial AM and FM stations— about 11,200
 Number of noncommercial radio stations—about 1,900
 Average time spent listening per weekday—3 hours, 18 minutes
 Average time spent listening per weekend—5 hours, 45 minutes
Internet
 Number of users—about 62 million
 Percentage of population 16 and over with Internet access—30%
 Percentage of homes with Internet access—23%
 Average amount of time spent on-line daily—45 minutes

FIG. 1.1. A snapshot of mass media in the United States.

At the beginning of the twenty-first century, most scholars have come to believe that mass media have proved to be powerful agents in our lives, although their power is complex and subtle and not all people are affected in the same way. In this book, we summarize research that has led to these conclusions. We find that research has shown a difference between the short-term and long-term impact of mass media. This book's premise rests on the assumption that long-term effects are far more meaningful than short-term; that Marshall McLuhan was quite right, after all, and very perceptive when he reasoned that the medium is ultimately more important than the message. What he meant was that the content of a message sent by a mass medium might produce short-term effects, but the medium that carried the message affects the way we receive and perceive the message and the way we think about it over the long term. In sum, the medium itself affects the way we think, even the way our brain works, and that is the most powerful impact of all. We examine this and other theories about the impact of mass media at greater length later in the book.

MEDIA DEVELOPMENTS THROUGH HISTORY

This is a book that applies what has been learned about mass media in the past to the mass media of the twenty-first century. Throughout this book, we look ahead to where the mass media are going. For example, this new millennium begins at the threshold of an entirely new communication revolution—the Internet. As we analyze the ongoing development of mass media, we keep this forward-looking perspective always in mind.

To begin with, however, we want to take a quick cruise through history to see how changes in media have changed the way human beings think, and the way they organize their lives. By taking a long view and general look at history, we can see the power of media better than we could from a short or intimate view, where the clutter of detail might obscure the larger picture. By looking at the way previous changes in media have changed history, we begin to comprehend how the new world of computers, the Internet, and global mass communication will change the twenty-first century. You may want to refer to Fig. 1.2 throughout our discussion of the chronology of mass media.

Oral or Prealphabet Society

Imagine what our world would be like if our only means of communication were our conversation with family and friends. What would we talk about? We would know only those things that came immediately into our experience, what we saw, heard, felt, smelled, or tasted. We wouldn't have an explanation for these things, or for the changes in the weather, the lack or availability of food, the enemy encamped on the other side of our horizon. Since we would have no explanations, life would be mysterious, events would happen that we could explain only by calling them magic. We would probably concoct a world of spirits and demons, of gods who worked in inexplicable ways, and believe that these gods controlled the mysterious happenings around us. There would be no laws or rules of conduct except a commonly shared agreement about what pleased or dis-

A Mass Media Chronology

5000 BC—clay tablets and evidence of writing

3000 BC—Egyptian hieroglyphics carved into stone

2500 BC—papyrus, kept in scrolls

1500 BC—beginnings of phonetic alphabet

300 BC—24-letter Greek alphabet

150 BC—parchment

100 BC—23-letter Roman alphabet

150—codex binding for books, replacing scrolls

1450—movable type and printing perfected

1455—first printed book published, the Bible

1476—first print shop in England

1500s—rapid development of printing and book publishing in Europe

1600s—first newspapers in Germany, France, and Belgium

1638—first printing press in American colonies

1702—first daily newspaper in London, *The Daily Courant*

1810—first steam-powered press

1833—first penny press, *New York Sun*

1837—Daguerre develops photographic images

1844—telegraph links Baltimore and Washington; telegraph network established in France

1850s—news agencies begin operating

1866—transatlantic telegraph cable connects North America and Europe

1875—photoengraving permits pictures in newspapers

1876—telephone patents in Europe and America

1879—Edison patents electric light

1884—Eastman perfects roll film

1891—Edison perfects motion picture projection

1895—first wireless signals transmitted

1900—first broadcast of music and voice sounds

1910s—telephone in wide use in large cities

1920s—rapid development of private radio stations

1922—radio advertising begins

1923—radio networks develop

1926—television demonstrated in London

1927—Federal Radio Commission (FRC) established; transatlantic telephone service begins

1928—talking movies perfected

1934—FRC becomes Federal Communications Commission

1937—first digital computer

1938—technicolor comes to movies

1939—regular telecasts start in New York

1940s—radio becomes primary source of World War II news

continued on next page

1947—transistor developed to replace vacuum tubes

1949—network television starts in the United States

1950s—television surpasses radio audiences; movies decline, despite new 3–D and other new techniques

1962—first commercial satellite in use

1960s—television becomes primary source of Vietnam war news; color comes to television

1968—first portable video recorder

1970s—general interest and picture magazines die; network television reaches 95% of America at prime-time

1980s—cable-television wires a majority of American homes; network audiences decline; VCRs and video cassettes used in a majority of American homes; personal computer use becomes widespread

1982—birth of *USA TODAY*, new national newspaper

1990s—development of the Internet into a new mass medium; movie attendance starts to increase

FIG. 1.2. A mass media chronology.

pleased the mysterious gods who worked the magic. This agreement would be passed on by word of mouth among one another, from one generation to the next.

Anthropologists have studied primitive tribes that still live in oral, prealphabet societies, so we do not have to base our understanding completely on our imagination of prehistoric humans. There still are peoples who live in this kind of magical world of spirits, without any communication except the rudimentary oral language they have developed to carry out the simple tasks of living. We can study their thought patterns and understand the way their brains work. Anthropologists have concluded that primitive peoples' restricted means of communication has placed limits on and affected the way they perceive and think about the world around them.

Pictures and Tokens for Record Keeping

As we can already see, the manner in which people communicate has some obvious relationship to the way in which their society is organized and governed. In ancient oral societies, people were ruled by unpredictable gods who worked in mysterious ways. When human beings learned how to cast their messages and conversations into written language, they were able to begin to organize their lives in more rational systems. They could record history and discover patterns in the weather, their food sources, and the ways of their enemies. They could take more control of their lives, solve some of nature's mysteries, and become less dependent on the whims of their gods. This posed a severe challenge to those among them who were priests and holy men and women; obviously these leaders regarded writing as subversive, destructive, and sinful. It didn't take them long to realize that if they could control the writing, they could regain their power as emissaries of the gods.

The development of writing proceeded over thousands of years, from pictures and tokens to pictographs and hieroglyphs to letters and alphabets. The first known human depictions were created some 45,000 years ago. Humans began using tokens as record-keeping devices between 8000 BC and 3100 BC, primarily in the Fertile Crescent of the ancient Middle East, at a time when agriculture in that region was replacing hunting. As one expert put it, "the need for record keeping was related to particular aspects of human adaptation to food production" (Schmandt-Besserat, 1991, p. 27).

Sometime between 5000 BC and 3500 BC, record keeping was done on clay tablets, and an early form of writing, called *cuneiform*—wedgelike symbols etched into clay tablets that were baked—was developed by the Sumerians in what is now southern Iraq. By 3000 BC, a hieroglyphic system of writing was being developed in Egypt. A millennium and a half later, in 1500 BC, people in the Middle East began to use a phonetic alphabet that gradually, over hundreds of years, made its way to ancient Greece, carried by Phoenician traders and sailors plying the Mediterranean Sea.

Stone and Clay Tablets

Since writing was destructive to the mystery of prehistoric gods, it was quickly controlled by members of the power structure in society, lest it destroy their civilization. From the very first, according to some experts, writing was used to control people, not to free them from authority. "Writing was invented for the exploitation of man by man," wrote French historian Claude Levi-Strauss (qtd. in Crowley & Heyer, 1991, p. 26).

First of all, the original media for expressing writing were not available to the average human being. The production of clay tablets, and even tokens for that matter, was fairly complicated and could easily be controlled by authorities. Carving messages on stone was equally difficult, time consuming, and costly. The average human being was not capable of creating such messages. Furthermore, and most important, clay and stone gave the impression that these messages were permanent, immutable. One had to be powerful to create messages in these media, and one was powerless to change them once they had been created. Laws carved into stone were created to be in force forever, and the creator of laws on stone was considered almighty. Babylonian emperors had their laws carved into permanent stone pillars. Egyptian pharaohs created enormous stone pyramids as symbols of their immutable power and authority.

Papyrus and Parchment

About 2500 BC, a form of paper was developed from papyrus reeds that grew in ancient Egypt along the Nile River. Messages could be written in ink rather than carved in stone and when reproduced on papyrus were at once easier to create, easier to change, and easier to destroy; thus from the beginning, paper attacked the power and permanence of authority based on stone, and it caused a revolution in Egypt. Harold Innis (1950), an economic historian in the first half of the twentieth century, in a landmark study of the effects of communication media on society, wrote:

> The profound disturbances in Egyptian civilization involved in the shift from absolute monarchy to a more democratic organization coincided with a shift in emphasis on stone as a medium of communication or as a basis of prestige, as shown in the pyramids, to an emphasis on papyrus. (p. 29)

In order to maintain power in an age of the impermanent and more widely accessible medium of papyrus, Egyptian pharaohs restricted writing to a privileged profession of scribes. Innis points out that writing had long been confined to governmental, fiscal, magical, and religious purposes. The spread of writing on papyrus was harder to control and was accompanied by, and probably caused, the development of new religions. Scribes themselves became central to religious authority; their words were imbued with power. The Egyptian god Osiris was served by a sacred scribe, Thoth, lord of the creative voice, master of words and books, who made Osiris a powerful religious figure by using writing to instruct people about divine rights and duties.

American students are sure to be more familiar with Moses than with Osiris, so his story may be more instructive for us. Moses was born in Egypt during the age of papyrus, between 1200 BC and 1100 BC, of parents belonging to a Semitic tribe, the Israelites, enslaved by the Egyptians. The Egyptians, threatened by new religions and subversive politics, had declared that every Israelite's first-born had to be sacrificed, but the baby Moses was hidden by his family in the Nile's reeds in the hope he would escape the infanticide decree. He was found by the Pharaoh's daughter, who protected and raised him. Moses undoubtedly learned how to read and write and probably became a privileged scribe.

Ultimately, Moses led his fellow Israelites in their exodus from Egypt to their freedom in the Sinai peninsula. But they were an unruly group stranded in the desert, and Moses had to assert authority to organize the tribe into a cohesive unit. He went to the top of Mount Sinai where, according to scripture, God gave him the Ten Commandments engraved on two stone tablets. The medium was immutable; the authority of stone made Moses and his laws powerful. Moses the scribe, the writer, is often given credit for enlarging the laws into five books that would govern the Israelites, as well as provide the story of who they were and where they came from and the power of their one God. These five books, called the *Pentateuch* or the *Torah*, became the first five books of the Bible.

Scrolls

Although the Ten Commandments were carved into stone, Moses probably wrote the Pentateuch on papyrus. What he had to write was complex, the laws were many, and it would have taken far too long to carve them all onto stone, especially when the easier medium of papyrus was available. But papyrus was not a permanent medium; it could deteriorate easily or be changed quickly. Therefore to imbue his work with power and authority, Moses restricted its access to a privileged few—the high priests. The Israelites, wandering freely in the Sinai desert in search of a home, created a portable temple for their religious worship, the tabernacle, at the center of which was a sacred place—the inner sanctum, the holy of holies—and into that secret and inaccessible place the books of Moses were placed, to become the religious scriptures, to preserve their power over the people as the Law and the Word of God. Papyrus as a medium was so impermanent that it had to be given a carefully controlled sacred place to preserve it, to ensure that it would continue to have power over the people.

Papyrus was not handled as sheets of paper but rather as long, wide ribbons that could be wound around a wooden roller into a scroll. Papyrus was fragile, and scrolls were difficult to handle. Since there were no separate pages, there were no page numbers, and it was difficult to find specific laws or passages. Probably for that reason repetition was frequent. Explanations were not rational or logical or even linear; they were imaginative and creative and poetic. The Bible has continued over two or three thousand years to be one of the most powerful messages ever written. When we read it today, if we acknowledge that it was written for a medium of papyrus scrolls, it is easier to understand its imaginative metaphors, its poetic language, and its repetition. It may not have become a continuing source of religious power and authority if the ancient Hebrews had not made it into a mysterious document, accessible only by the powerful few, and imbued with supreme authority as the Word of God.

Papyrus scrolls made their way from Egypt to Greece as well, and about the first century BC, the Greeks developed a more durable form of paper by curing and stretching animal skins into thin sheets called *parchment*, adding further to the utility of writing.

The Alphabet

About 700 BC, the Greeks developed a 24-character alphabet, greatly simplifying the act of writing from the much more complicated ancient Hebrew, Arabic, Sanskrit, and the pictograph languages such as Egyptian hieroglyphics. Eric Havelock, former professor of classics at Yale, wrote that the introduction of this alphabet altered the character of human culture. "The Greeks did not just invent an alphabet," he wrote; "they invented literacy and the literate basis of modern thought" and what this "may have done in the long run was to change somewhat the content of the human mind" (qtd. in Crowley & Heyer, 1991, p. 57).

The experience with writing and media was much different for the ancient Greeks than it was for the Hebrews in ancient Israel. Whereas the ancient Hebrews made writing sacred and thus secret and powerful and a source of authority, the ancient Greeks made writing common and available, and this no doubt encouraged the development in ancient Athens of the first great democratic society. When people could learn to read and write, they no longer needed to depend on priests or scribes to tell them what they had to do. They could make up their own minds and take charge of their own lives. The alphabet and papyrus made it possible for the Greeks to publish codes of laws and constitutions to organize society with some logic and thus with more equal justice, reducing the power of despotic authorities and equalizing the classes. It also made possible academies in which people could learn to read what was being written. The academies, in turn, created scientists and philosophers, and libraries where learning could be accumulated and where a body of knowledge about the world could be stored. Indeed, the basis of our study today of drama, logic, ethics, rhetoric, and history all began with the ancient Greeks.

In time, Greek civilization declined, and power shifted to ancient Rome. Athens continued to be a center of learning, however, and it wasn't until the beginning of the sixth century AD that the freedom of teaching was curtailed in Athens. In 529 AD, the study of philosophy was forbidden by the edict of Justinian, which brought an end to ancient Greece and ushered in what came to be called the Dark Ages.

Codex Binding

Roman civilization was built on the foundation laid by Greek thinkers, writers, dramatists, poets, military strategists, philosophers, logicians, mathematicians, and politicians. The Romans, however, also made an important contribution to the development of communication that had far-reaching effects—the act of cutting scrolls of written laws into separate pages and binding those pages on one edge to form what, today, we call a book. It was termed codex at that time, because this form of binding was used for codes of law.

This might seem to be a minor development, but in fact it had enormous consequences. It allowed written communication to be organized in a way that was impossible for scrolls. With codex binding, pages could have numbers, a table of contents could show where different laws or passages were located, and an index could list passages on specific pages. This simple act further reduced the mystery of writing. It allowed laws to be studied, to be compared. It made changing the law easier.

One of the first pieces of writing to be bound as a book, aside from Roman laws, was the Bible, and having it in book form widened its study. However, during the Middle Ages, when the Christian Church, headquartered in Rome, became powerful in the secular as well as the religious world, its leaders feared that indiscriminate study of the Bible could lead to changes in interpretations, which might challenge the authority of the Church. So the Christian Church in Rome reacted as the ancient Hebrews had: Its leaders allowed only privileged priests to read the Bible, which was kept in sacred places within the Church to keep it from improper hands. Not until printing developed in the fifteenth century did the Bible reach many "unauthorized" readers.

Printing Press and Movable Type

It is important to understand that before the fifteenth century AD, all written material was actually hand copied, one page at a time. Thus, all written communication was highly personal, and we cannot apply many principles of mass communication to any medium until well into the nineteenth century. Some books became works of art, because copyists created intricate designs, often in color, to accompany a text, and much of the work was done on parchment for permanence. Paper, as we know it today, made from wood or cloth pulp, was created in China and introduced in Europe by Arab traders in the eighth century AD; but the more durable parchment continued to be used for important works, most of which were religious and were copied by monks who devoted their entire lives to this work.

This practice began to change in the fifteenth century, when, about 1450, a German printer, Johannes Gutenberg, used a wine press to impress a sheet of parchment onto inked blocks of carved wooden movable type, enabling multiple impressions of a printed page. Although printing did not reach a mass audience for almost another 400 years, we can say that Gutenberg's invention marked the beginning of mass communication. This new means of communication spread rapidly among the elite of Europe, developing almost as fast as radio, television, and the computer developed in the twentieth century. Yet those early books should not yet be considered a mass medium; they were produced for an elite, literate few who could afford them and knew how to read them.

Printing was first used to reproduce books such as the Bible, then works of literature, philosophy, and natural science from the Greek and Roman classics. Within a generation of Gutenberg's invention, more than 50,000 different titles had been printed and bound, most in the original Latin or Greek, but translations into more common languages for the common people developed slowly.

The availability of books in one's native tongue stimulated an interest in reading and literacy and was certainly a factor in moving Europe from the Dark Ages into the Renaissance and the Age of Enlightenment. Indeed, one can easily hypothesize that printing was responsible for one of the greatest revolutionary transformations of society in human history.

In Western Europe, scholar–priests such as Martin Luther soon were translating the Latin Bible into common languages, enabling new access to the Word of God that had previously been available only to a privileged few. When greater numbers of common people could read the Bible, their questioning of the absolute power of the mother Church led to a revolt against the Church of Rome, what we know as the Protestant Reformation. At the same time, the availability of books containing observations about the natural world led to the development of science, perhaps the most significant impact of early printing. Just slightly more than one generation after Gutenberg's invention, Columbus proved that the world was not flat but round. Without books to reproduce accumulated wisdom and logic, the New World may never have been discovered.

Newspapers and the Rise of Democracies

The revolution in religion and science caused by books also affected economics and politics in Western Europe. With information available in books, middle classes began challenging the aristocracy and the divine right of kings. Information in books, and later in magazines and newspapers, led to the rise of commerce, of a mercantile class, and eventually to an entrepreneurial economy based on free-market competition, or capitalism. All this happened even before the printed word had become a mass medium.

It did not take long for authorities—monarchies and the Church in Rome—to realize that printing could be highly subversive, encouraging religious reformations and political and economic revolutions. So those in charge often increased burning, banning, and censoring books and writings, usually restricting publication to those with official licenses. But printing was hard to control; the cat was out of the bag, so to speak. People began to believe they had a right to know, and the understanding grew in society that information was essential to fulfill one's own destiny rather than to live one's life to serve the needs of king or pope or aristocracy.

Newspapers and magazines began to appear in the seventeenth century, at first reaching only a relatively small audience of elite readers. These publications were licensed by monarchical authorities, and they could be shut down if they displeased the authorities. Nevertheless, they often contained information that informed and influenced communities, providing facts and raising questions that challenged those in authority. They became essential to a process that democratized the western world. They helped stimulate the revolutions in America in 1776 to 1783, and in France in 1789. Because they were less expensive than magazines and books, newspapers made knowledge and information available to a much larger percentage of the population. They made it possible for more people to think about governing themselves, a process that finally produced democracies in the Western world, the first since the Athenian democracy of ancient Greece.

Indeed, the rise of newspapers and the rise of Western democracy occurred at the same time, making it easy to speculate that newspapers caused democracy, not the other way around. The Harvard historian, Arthur Schlesinger, Sr. (1957), wrote that the weekly newspapers of the 13 colonies in America were the chief reason for the break with the British monarchy that lead to the American Revolution. And another historian, Allan Nevins (1978), credited the newspapers of the new republic with the spread of ideas that led to the adoption of the Constitution and a representative form of government. The writers of the Constitution, realizing how crucial newspapers were to democracy, declared in the First Amendment that Congress should never pass any law that would prohibit freedom of speech or the press.

The Penny Press and the Rise of Mass Media

Not until the nineteenth century, with additional technological developments, did public communication become truly mass communication. Industrialization starting in the early nineteenth century—the use of machines and of assembly-line techniques (later of automation) for mass production—was necessary for mass communication. Steam engines, rotary presses, and paper in rolls rather than in sheets, allowed large quantities of printed materials to be produced at low cost, making them affordable to a mass audience. But mass communication also required a content that a mass audience would find desirable to buy.

These two factors came into being in the 1830s, with the rise of the *penny press* in New York City, the first newspapers that sold for one penny and were thus affordable to the average citizen. Even though it was the smallest denomination of coin, a penny was worth a good deal more in 1833 than it is today; a few pennies could purchase a full meal. The penny newspapers were printed using the latest technology for the fastest reproduction, and, equally important, they contained the kind of information and gossip people were interested in reading. These newspapers also carried advertising, without which the newspaper could not have survived, since the low customer price did not cover the entire cost of production.

The penny press ushered in the age of news, as opposed to the essays and editorials of earlier newspapers; it started journalism as we now define it, based on reporters going out into society and finding facts that interested their readers. It ultimately gave rise to objective journalism; before the penny press in America, newspapers were usually owned or subsidized by political parties or had some political agenda. Now newspapers were in business more to make a profit than to influence political decisions. Because they printed objective rather than politically slanted news, the penny newspapers appealed to a larger and more general audience. They had become market oriented, another characteristic of mass communication.

Within a few years, the penny press was followed by the nickel magazine and the dime novel. Inexpensive production and popular content made mass media out of many forms of printed matter. Daniel Boorstin, professor of history at the University of Chicago, wrote, "The industrialization of book-binding was perhaps the most important step in the democratization of the book in America" (qtd. in Crowley & Heyer, 1991, p. 169). This could be said of the technologies that came to the newspaper and magazine media as well. Most of the features that characterized the early print version of mass media, in general, have become essential to the mass communication process, no matter what the medium.

Photography

The scientific revolution caused by the printing press speeded the process of invention and technological development. By the mid-nineteenth century, the discovery of one new technology was followed rapidly by the discovery of another, a process that has continued to our day. By 1837, many scientists and inventors were experimenting with ways to record reality artificially. Until that time, all pictures were artists' conceptions of reality. Their work was time consuming and based on personal, highly subjective interpretations, influenced by individual skills and talents, or by patrons who commissioned the work. Some artists were good, others not so good.

Photography changed that. It allowed a photographer to capture on film and paper a representation that was claimed to be an exact depiction of reality. It seemed that a photograph could not lie or distort. The photograph also opened a world that humans had never seen before. When Matthew Brady and his colleagues took their cameras to the battlefront in the Civil War, their pictures provided the first depiction of real war—an ugly view of real human beings suffering, wounded and dying in the mud—unfiltered by the idealism or patriotism of an artist's painting of a battle scene done after the fact, on commission from the winning government.

Thus photography, like the news story of the penny press, ushered in an era of objectivity in the representation of reality. We could trust the photograph, apparently, because it seemed to tell the truth. More than ever, today, photography brings us information about the world most of us would otherwise never know, about exotic lands and peoples, strange animals and insects, life that exists in a drop of water, or what earth looks like from outer space. We can stop action and catch reality on film in slow motion, showing things the eye could never see. We can visualize an automobile accident, a child starving to death in Ethiopia, and celebrities on a nude beach in southern France.

By the end of the twentieth century, however, we were less confident about the truth and objectivity of photography, because we had learned that the photographer's eye as well as the lens, the camera angle, the type of photo development and paper on which the photo was printed all could affect the way reality was portrayed. And we also had learned that the computer can play all kinds of tricks with photographs to change reality. And yet photography, without any doubt, has permanently altered the way we think about the universe and the way our minds deal with information.

Wired Media: Telegraph and Telephone

At nearly the same time that photography was developed, telegraphy was added to human communication. This invention made use of electricity to send a signal through a wire. When in 1844 Samuel F. B. Morse strung a wire between Washington and Baltimore to send the message, "What hath God wrought," he removed geographic distance from human communication. Until that time, human messages had to be delivered in person, either by way of the human voice or by delivering a printed sheet of paper by hand. Suddenly messages could quickly span large distances, another critical step toward mass communication. Today, our minds simply assume the possibility that information can be communicated instantaneously from anywhere in the world.

Within months of Morse's demonstration, a telegraph network was established in France connecting 29 cities. By the 1850s, news agencies in France, England, and the United States were getting organized to send information by telegraph to far-flung newspapers. The telegraph was used as a military instrument in the war in Crimea in 1854, as it was in the 1860s in America's Civil War. In that war, the telegraph was also used by reporters to send their dispatches from the front to their newspaper offices.

In 1856, the Western Union Telegraph Company was established, and 10 years later, a cable was laid under the ocean between Newfoundland and Ireland to allow instantaneous communication between two continents. The move toward worldwide instant mass communication had achieved yet another important milestone.

Ten years later, in 1876, Alexander Graham Bell received the first patent for the telephone, an instrument that could send the human voice and sounds other than the dots and dashes of the telegraph over wires across both lands and oceans. The vast telephone system that developed has become an essential part of mass communication, not only for the production of information but for the delivery of it as well, including the use of telephone lines for cable television and the enormous Internet.

Motion Pictures

Photography and electricity ultimately connected in a new medium of great power. In 1879, Thomas Edison won the patent for the electric light bulb. Five years later, in 1884, George Eastman perfected photographic film on a roll, enabling a series of pictures to be taken in rapid succession. When displayed in rapid succession, because of the anatomical phenomenon of persistence of vision, these pictures gave the viewer an impression of moving images. By 1891, Edison had perfected a way of shining his electric light, using lenses, through a moving strip of film to project a moving picture. He had given birth to movies.

Edison and other early motion picture pioneers thought moving pictures would become an important new educational medium, to assist in teaching by depicting natural phenomena that could not be reproduced in printed matter nor seen by the natural eye. But entrepreneurs more concerned with making a profit than educating the public quickly found a new market for dramatic productions projected on a screen in a theater. From the beginning of the twentieth century to the end, movies were almost exclusively a market-oriented entertainment medium.

Radio

Many scientists and inventors in the 1890s experimented with sending sound through the airwaves without the use of wires, and Guglielmo Marconi is usually given credit for achieving that feat in 1895. Over the next 25 years, from 1895 to 1920, dozens of technological developments enhanced the wireless transmission of sound—called *radio*—but radio did not become broadcasting, did not become a mass medium, until the early 1920s. Companies such as Western Union, which maintained the business of sending messages over telegraph wires, used wireless transmission simply to increase the speed of and traffic in messages, rather than to provide a new means of mass communication.

One American electric company, Westinghouse, experimenting with wireless transmission in 1918 and 1919, accidentally discovered that an audience, a market, existed for news and entertainment broadcast over the airwaves. By 1920, regular programs were being scheduled. As soon as entrepreneurs discovered a large market for radio, they rushed to establish radio stations and to mass produce radio equipment. By the end of the 1920s, radio was already big business, with national networks and a mass audience. By the 1930s, radio had developed a full schedule of programs, with music, drama, comedy, news, and advertising.

World War II has been called the *radio war* because much of the world listened to news of the war over the radio, since radio news was faster, more realistic, and more dramatic than news in printed form. With the advent of television after the war, radio shrank into a medium primarily for broadcasting music between commercials. Some called it *narrow*casting. By segmenting radio audiences into different demographic groupings or audience interests, by the end of the twentieth century radio had helped cultural diversity become a fact in America, with almost every cultural or ethnic entity represented on radio frequencies.

In most homes in America 40 or 50 different radio programs can be received at any given time. We have been conditioned to think that at an instant's notice, we can switch on our portable transistor radio and receive the latest news about some significant development anywhere in the world. Because it has become so simple to produce an inexpensive radio, radio is the most widely used mass medium worldwide. Tribes without written languages in remote regions can connect with the world through simple, inexpensive radio sets.

Television

Of all the electronic media, television is the king. Perhaps later in the twenty-first century, it might be eclipsed by the Internet, but for now it stands alone as the most dominant mass medium worldwide, a position it held for the last half of the twentieth century. Television became a reality in the 1920s, and many countries claim it was their scientists who invented it. For several decades, it was far too expensive for the average person to buy, and thus no candidate for mass communication. Television needed its version of the penny press to reach a mass market.

World War II helped provide that. Although scientists turned their attention to creating electronic weapons for war rather than for mass communication, the electronics industry grew large as a result of the war. When the war ended and war production ceased, it was easy to retool the assembly lines to mass produce television sets for ready consumers. The price was lowered, and the average household was able to acquire a TV. By 1950, television was a mass medium, quickly surpassing radio and movies in audience size and attention.

The early age of television was dominated by three national networks; but throughout its first half-century, television expanded and changed, its technology improved enormously, and its reach grew. Most important, it changed the world. It revolutionized our institutions as much as movable type and the printed book had done in the fifteenth and sixteenth centuries. It changed the way we see things and the way our minds work. Its coverage of the war in Vietnam forever changed the nature of warfare. Its coverage of political elections forever changed the way democracy works.

Just as Christopher Columbus needed the printed word to discover the new world, so we can hypothesize that NASA might never have been able to land a space rocket on the moon with men aboard without television. Many observers feel that it was television, especially video recordings, that brought down the Soviet Empire and breached the Berlin Wall. Ted Koppel, in his documentary "Revolution in a Box," suggests that television is democratizing the world, as early newspapers had democratized Western civilization. It may be doing that, but it also has changed the very nature of democracy.

Computers and the Internet

Television revolutionized the world in just half a century, and we know now that we are at the beginning of yet another revolution—this one brought about by computers. Computers have gone through a development and marketing process similar to other media. Each new electronic development—from vacuum tubes to transistors to silicon chips—brought the computer closer to a mass market. The first workable computers, from the 1950s and 1960s, were as large as a house, cost millions of dollars, and used thousands of vacuum tubes that constantly blew out. By the 1980s, computers using microchips instead of vacuum tubes were reduced to the size of a typewriter, cost a few thousand dollars, and were faster and more reliable than their enormous and expensive ancestors. By the end of the twentieth century, computers were small enough to hold in your hand, were affordable for the average person, and had become part of the mass market.

Computers have changed every aspect of the mass communication process itself. They have changed the way news is gathered, edited, processed, and produced. They have changed printing and broadcasting processes. Many of the processes of mass communication can now be automated. For example, radio stations can use computers to program the music that will attract the right type of audience. Perhaps the most significant impact of computers has been on the marketing process, allowing the communicator to identify with much greater precision the market for the message as well as the feedback that results.

Without doubt the most significant development for the computer as a mass medium was the Internet, the connection between personal computers and a worldwide web of computers through telephone lines. The Internet began to reach a critical mass by the mid-1990s. The Internet allows individuals to tap into the resources of giant computers storing trillions of bits of data and information. It allows users to put together the precise kinds of information that best serves their needs. The audience can be in greater control of the communication. And it is already, within a few years of its development, so large that it has been estimated one can spend a lifetime on the Internet and sample only 3 percent of what is already available.

A key principle to remember in all our discussion of mass media throughout this book is that technology cannot produce mass media until it is easily used and inexpensive, and thus available to the masses. The Internet became a mass medium only when user-friendly computers became affordable and widely available, and software and on-line services such as American Online (AOL) became easy to operate and inexpensive. AOL joined forces with Netscape in late 1998 to form the largest and easiest access to the World Wide Web. That development and others like it will likely prove as important to the Internet revolution as the rise of the penny press in 1833 was to the development of newspapers as mass media.

THE EXAMPLE OF COMMUNICATION IN CHINA AND THE ORIENT

So far, we have looked at the development of mass communication primarily from a Western point of view. Not all countries and cultures have developed in a similar way. As mass media have made the world smaller and closer, it is important for us to have a larger view of the world. China and the Orient are examples of cultures with a different kind of language structure, a different kind of alphabet, and which the regions' media develop quite differently. When we look at developments in the Eastern world, we can confirm the hypothesis that the dominant medium has an effect on culture and society; because of the different language structure in the Orient, media development there has been significantly different from that of the Western world.

It is important to note that printing, without the alphabet, could not have produced the revolution that it created with the alphabet. It was the Chinese who invented movable type to make a printing press, but because of the vast difference between the alphabet of the Western world and the characters of written Chinese, the printing press was not used for any important communication in China until changes were made in the Chinese language in the twentieth century. And in many ways China and much of the Orient did not develop politically and technologically the way the West did, until the mid-twentieth century.

The alphabet of the Western world allows a connection between sound and letters. Different combinations of letters make different sounds. Chinese language, however, for thousands of years has been based on ideograms that evolved from earlier pictograms. In its purest form, these ideograms exist almost without sound, although once one is conversant in Chinese, there are some clues as to how a character might sound since it would share common elements with other characters.[1]

To be fluent in written Chinese, a person needs a basic vocabulary of about 3,000 characters, in their various combinations. Also, one needs to memorize the tone associated with each character. Each character consists of one or more elements that compound into more complex meanings. An ear, heart, and eye together mean *to listen*. A woman under a roof means *peace*. A pig under a roof means *home*. Two women under a roof mean *discord*. One tree is a *tree*. Two trees are a *glade*. Three trees are a *forest*.

It was the creation of these characters thousands of years ago that gradually produced a unified China. However, there are still hundreds of dialects in China, and people often cannot understand each other when speaking, even though they might communicate perfectly through writing. For example, a person in Guangzhou could look at a character and pronounce it *lok* whereas a person in Mandarin might pronounce it *hua*, and yet they would both give the same meaning to the written character.

Imagine what kind of problem we would have today with national radio or television in America if we had one written language but hundreds of different ways of speaking that language. Radio and television as mass media would not be possible. When the Communist party came into power in China, its leaders realized that the Chinese language itself could prevent China from becoming a powerful unified nation in an age of mass media. So the party leaders developed a simplified version of Chinese writing, hoping to improve mass literacy and mass communication. They stripped strokes from many characters to make them easier to remember and to say. According to purists, they removed a lot of meaning from the words. But to make Chinese a language of mass communication in the twentieth century, that change was essential.

Today, in order to type on the computer in Chinese, one has to use Mandarin, or the national language, as the communists called it. To use Word Perfect for Chinese, one types in the romanized version of the word (*sho, xiang, feng,* etc.). After the first letter comes up, the computer starts anticipating the various choices of characters and their most common combinations. The more letters one inputs, the more likely an exact hit. It can be faster to type on a computer than to write Chinese in longhand, because a complex character might require 18 strokes by hand, but might be accessed in three or four computer keystrokes. Changing the language in China and the Orient to make mass communication and computer use possible has already, in less than half a century, caused the greatest revolution in China's long history.

THE LONG VIEW OF HISTORY PROVES MEDIA'S POWER

Thus, as we can see by taking a long view of human history, the way in which people communicate affect the way human beings organize their lives and their societies. Stone media reinforced a highly authoritarian social structure, as did papyrus and parchment media when they were kept secret and made sacred. But because papyrus and parchment were more readily accessible to a wider variety of people, it was also more difficult to keep such a medium secret, which helped pave the way to the world's first democratic society in Greece.

Written materials bound in books rather than wound on scrolls helped organize and codify Rome into a society based on laws, rather than on gods, superstitions, or mysticism. But papyrus, parchment, and even paper were still limited to relatively few until the printing press began to make it possible for the average person to gain access to information and knowledge, with cataclysmic results for Western society.

Printing made possible the age of science and discovery, reformations in religion, economic upheavals giving power to a mercantile class rather than to the aristocracy, and the transfer of power to the people through democracy. Electronic media revolutionized the twentieth century. One can argue that electronic media have made the world less democratic and more authoritarian by centralizing information in the hands of a powerful few in a media oligarchy. Or one can argue that electronic media have given more people more information than ever, and thus human beings are more in control of their own destiny than ever before. The jury is still out on this debate, and it needs much further discussion in class and research in libraries and laboratories. One thing is certain—electronic media, especially television and computers, have changed democracy and the way the world is today. Now, in the twenty-first century, we stand on the threshold of the Internet revolution, which could just as easily change everything that has gone before.

Further Reading

Boorstin, Daniel. (1962). *The Image*. New York: Atheneum. Also in David Crowley and Paul Heyer (Eds.). (1991). *Communication in History: Technology, Culture, and Society* (pp. 168–175). New York: Longman.

Carpenter, Edmund, and McLuhan, Marshall. (1960). *Explorations in Communication*. Boston: Beacon Press.

Crowley, David, and Heyer, Paul. (Eds.). (1991). *Communication in History: Technology, Culture, and Society*. New York: Longman.

Czitrom, Daniel J. (1982). *Media and the American Mind: From Morse to McLuhan*. Chapel Hill: University of North Carolina Press.

Havelock, Eric. (1982). *The Literate Revolution in Greece and Its Cultural Consequences*. Princeton: Princeton University Press. Also in David Crowley and Paul Heyer (Eds.). (1991). *Communication in History: Technology, Culture, and Society* (pp. 57–62). New York: Longman.

Innis, Harold. (1950). *Empire and Communications*. Toronto: University of Toronto Press.

McLuhan, Marshall. (1964). *Understanding Media: The Extensions of Man*. New York: Signet.

Nevins, Allan. (1978). The Constitution Makers and the Public. *Public Relations Review, 4*, 3.

Schlesinger, Arthur Meier. (1957). *Prelude to Freedom: The Newspaper War on Britain*, 1764–1776. New York: Knopf.

Schmandt-Bessart, Denise. (1986). Tokens: Facts and Interpretation. *Visible Language, 20*, 3. Also in David Crowley and Paul Heyer (Eds.). (1991). *Communication in History: Technology, Culture, and Society* (pp. 20–28). New York: Longman.

Ward, Hiley H. (1997). *Mainstreams of American Media History*. Boston: Allyn & Bacon.

Note

[1]For our discussion of Chinese language and communication, we are indebted to Michelle Foster, Vice President of market development, Newspaper Division, Gannett Co., and an expert on China.

2

PROCESS AND FUNCTIONS

Intrapersonal, interpersonal, small-group, large-group, mass-audience—what is the difference? If we write articles for a school newspaper, or talk over a two-way radio system, or take family pictures with a videocamera, are we engaging in mass communication? When does *personal* become *mass*? Technologies are essential for the process, but using a technology itself does not guarantee mass communication. We need to set our parameters with some definitions. We also need to know why humans communicate on a mass basis, and the purposes or functions mass media fulfill in society.

Communication is an act shaped largely by the medium that carries the message. Changing the medium transforms content and meaning. Think of what often happens to our inner thoughts when we try to utter them aloud to another person. Almost always, we are surprised that our *intra*personal musing takes on different dimensions when we give voice to them. The message changes again when we address those thoughts to a small group and yet again when the group is large. And if the group is very large, we need to interpose some technology—a microphone and public address system, for example, or paper and a printing press—and these technologies further change the way we express ourselves and the way our audiences receive and process our message.

This book introduces students to mass media and what happens in the process of making messages massive. If we can understand how and why mass media process messages, each in their own way, we will be in a better position to use mass media effectively and to interpret more properly the messages we receive from them. Each medium codifies reality differently, because each uses its own codes and languages. This book explains and interprets those codes and languages.

DEFINITIONS

We should make a distinction between the *medium* and the *process* of mass communication. This book is about both. Media are instruments of the process. Any instrument that makes *mass* communication possible is a **mass medium**. (Please note: *medium* is singular; the plural word is *media*. When we write about media, we are referring to more than one medium.)

In the 1950s, as television grew into a national medium, mass communication became the focus of much study and research, and sociologists attempted to define it as a social process. One important work in creating usable definitions was *Mass Communication: A Sociological Perspective*, by sociologist Charles R. Wright (1986), which first appeared in 1959 and has been revised twice since then. Wright's definitions, widely accepted and standard in the field, divide the process into three parts.

1. Message or Content

In mass communication, the message is *public*, put into the stream of communication for no one in particular but for everyone who wants it. The process is *rapid*, produced in a relatively short period of time and intended to reach audiences quickly, even simultaneously. And it is *transient*, meaning that the message is produced for immediate consumption. The permanence of a medium is relative, of course; a daily newspaper lasts one day before it is replaced by the next day's edition; a weekly lasts a week, a monthly a month; news on radio or television might only last an hour before the next update. A book, on the other hand, may be relevant for years; a few, forever.

2. Communicator

The mass communicator is *well organized*; many people have to operate with a high degree of teamwork to make mass communication possible. Dozens of people must work together each day to produce a daily newspaper, a television program, a sound recording, a movie, a magazine, or a book; radio and newsletters can be produced with fewer people; and the Internet alone offers the possibility of the individual communicator reaching a mass audience without the support of a large organization. (Please note: In this book we consider the Internet a new mass medium, although it still defies some of the categorizations we normally apply.)

An important distinction between mass and personal is the *competitive nature* of the mass communicator, especially in a free-market society. Whenever one engages a mass audience, others will be competing for the attention of that audience. Although the number of cities with competing dailies has declined, newspapers are in competition with other media, local and national, including alternative papers, local magazines, and local radio and television news shows; and all are in competition with one another for our time. There are still only 24 hours in a day, and if we spend time on one medium, it will have to be taken away from another. Look at the array of magazines at any newsstand, the lineup of newspaper boxes, the number of books or recordings in any book or record store, the 40 or 50 different radio stations we can choose to listen to, the 50 or 60 different television channels we can watch, or the dozens of movies being shown at the local cineplex.

And finally, mass communicators are shaped by the enormously *expensive* operation in which they work. In every case, mass communication requires complex technologies. A daily newspaper is printed on a giant printing press that has thousands of moving parts and requires many skilled mechanics to keep it running. Such a press can cost hundreds of millions of dollars. The broadcast equipment for an average television station is not as expensive as the printing press of a daily newspaper, but you would still have to pay hundreds of millions to buy many existing stations, whose worth, because of the value of their licenses, exceeds the total value of their physical plant and equipment. (Later, in the media chapters in this book, we discuss the economics of individual media and examine the high costs involved.)

3. Audience

Audiences of mass media must be relatively *large*, best defined as a group whose members are so numerous they could not be gathered together in any one place for personal interaction with the communicator at any point in time. Mass media's audiences are usually *heterogeneous*, meaning that the message is not aimed at a narrow, exclusive group. Rather, it could be received by anyone. And the relationship between audience and communicator is *anonymous*, meaning that members of the audience usually are not known personally to the communicator. Later in this book we devote a chapter to mass media audiences, focusing particularly on their use of and reactions to mass media.

MASS MEDIA

The media we usually regard as making mass communication possible are books, magazines, newsletters, and newspapers (the print media), and radio, television, motion pictures, sound recordings, and the Internet (the electronic media). In free-market societies, these institutions make up a complex system that can be divided into four parts.

The industry defines the broad categories of each mass medium into **media products**. Newspapers are divided into dailies, weeklies, and Sunday supplements; magazines into weeklies, monthlies, and quarterlies; books usually into consumer books, textbooks, and professional books; radio into AM and FM; television into UHF, VHF, DBS, and cable; and both radio and television can also be classified as commercial or educational. Sound recordings are usually divided into products classified by format—rock 'n' roll, classical, country, and so forth; movies are usually classified as feature films or informational documentaries, or by the type of feature films—dramas, horror, comedy, and so forth. For the Internet, the product is the individual message or document a user puts online and the level of intractivity that is offered.

Basic media units are the entities legally responsible for the messages or content they carry. Examples are, for newspapers, *The New York Times, Baltimore Sun, Denver Post*, and *San Francisco Chronicle*; for broadcasting, the stations—WTOP–AM in Washington, DC, WBAL–FM in Baltimore, WNBC–TV in New York; for magazines, the individual titles—*Cosmopolitan, People, Sports Illustrated*. The titles of specific books, recordings, and movies are the basic units for these media, but book publishers, record companies, and studios are held legally responsible for the content of all the individual titles they produce. On the Internet, the basic media unit, and the entity legally responsible, is the individual who puts the message online.

Media service units are an important element of the system, but for the most part they are not owners of basic media units. Instead, they provide content or other services, and the unit using this content accepts the legal liability for doing so. Service units include news agencies, associations such as AP and UPI, which are able to provide more extensive news coverage (and analysis and entertainment content, too) than individual media units can supply. Service units also include broadcast networks such as ABC, CBS, NBC, and Fox (although these companies also own some basic media units, or individual stations). Other service units include distribution companies, such as motion picture theaters and chains, and publication and record distributors; manufacturing services, such as printers and paper makers; broadcast and printing equipment producers; and representational services, such as talent agencies and labor unions. On the Internet, companies such as AOL and Erols are service providers, as are such search engines as Yahoo and Alta Vista.

Media associations include institutions that serve media owners, such as the National Association of Broadcasters; media professionals, such as the American Society of Newspaper Editors; and service organization owners and professionals, such as the American Association of Advertising Agencies. All of these have to be considered when we look at the total mass media system.

MASS MEDIA CONTINUUM

One should avoid making too many sweeping generalizations about the massiveness of media, because their size is quite relative. We can create a continuum for media that places each medium at some point between two extremes of personal and massive, as Fig. 2.1 shows. By doing so, we can get a generalized picture of different media and the extent to which the principles of mass communication might apply to each medium.

On this continuum, global television would probably be the most massive medium, but national TV should be considered to be nearly as massive. Television was, at the end of the twentieth century, the only medium with the potential for a truly national (or in some instances a worldwide) audience at any given moment; examples of such a moment are the moon landing in 1969, and the funeral of Princess Diana in 1997. About 52 million Americans got up early in the morning to watch Diana's funeral, and an estimated 2.5 billion people saw some part of that event worldwide.

FIG. 2.1. The media continuum.

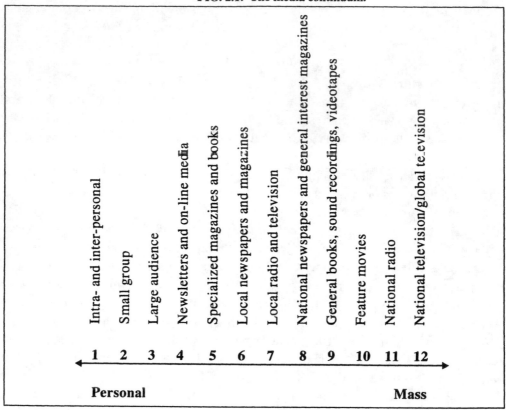

National newspapers, such as *USA TODAY* and *The Wall Street Journal*, and national news magazines, such as *Time, Newsweek,* and *U.S. News & World Report,* technically are available to everyone in the nation at approximately the same time and thus have many of the characteristics of massive media, with some exceptions. *The Wall Street Journal,* for example, although national in circulation, is aimed at a relatively homogeneous audience of people with strong business interests; even so, technically, anyone who wants that newspaper can receive it.

Most motion pictures usually try to reach national and increasingly global audiences, but of course their reach is not as instantaneous as television or radio. On the other hand, most newspapers and radio stations are aimed at local or regional audiences. Some books are published for general audiences, but most are targeted for narrower niche markets. Newsletters are most often produced for a small and select public. The Internet is evolving; at first it was a highly personal medium, but in the last few years of the twentieth century, it became a true mass medium, as we explore later in this book. Yet it defies easy categorization: Information posted on the Internet might reach no one, but, technically, it could also be received by millions.

Most important, the process of communication changes as it becomes more massive or more personal. On the media continuum in Fig. 2.1, as you move from the left (from intra- to interpersonal) to the right (from national to global television), four things happen to the communication process:

1. The Message Becomes More General.   The larger the audience, the less the message can be specialized or personalized. The language used must be common, with a smaller vocabulary. Fewer specific details can be added. Complex ideas must be simplified and abstract or highly technical messages avoided.

2. The Relationship Between Communicator and Audience Becomes More Remote. As the audience grows larger, the communicator has less personal contact, may not know any individuals in the audience, and may not even know the kinds or the number of people receiving the message. Any feedback the communicator gets is delayed, so there can be little immediate change resulting from communicator–audience interaction.

3. The Audience Becomes More Heterogeneous.   As the audience grows larger, of course, it includes a greater diversity of receivers; ultimately a national or international audience can have every type of living individual, all age groups, sexual classifications, racial and ethnic distinctions, religious differences, political affiliations, and more.

4. The Medium Becomes More Technology Driven and Costly.   Even the Internet, although it might not require much equipment or money for an individual to go online, requires a vast and global array of expensive and powerful linked computers.

The changes that take place as the message is aimed at larger and larger audiences affect all aspects of communication, an idea that is further developed throughout this book.

MASS COMMUNICATION PROCESS

We can best understand communication as a process if we realize that it is not static, fixed in time or space, but dynamic, in constant movement. It involves an exchange of messages that transfer meaning, transmit social values, and provide a sharing of experiences. A *process* means a series of actions or operations, always in motion, directed toward a specific goal. If we examine mass communication as a process, then, we can study its component parts and see how they work together. We have already seen that the parts include communicator, message or content, media, and audiences. But how do these parts fit into the entire process?

Since the dawn of the mass media age in the twentieth century, the thinking of social scientists has steadily evolved in an attempt to answer that question. Harold Lasswell (1948) proposed an early model defining a linear process, with five basic questions that had to be answered:

Who? (communicator)
Says what? (message)
In which channel? (medium)
To whom? (audience)
With what result? (effects)

Others realized this formula was too simplistic to picture all essential components, and too linear. Communication should be seen as a two-way process, they said, as in *commune* (to talk together) or *communion* (a sharing of thoughts or emotions). Wilbur Schramm (1954) wrote: "In fact, it is misleading to think of the communication process as starting somewhere and ending somewhere. It is really endless. We are switch-board centers handling and rerouting the great endless current of information" (p. 8).

Schramm and his colleague C. E. Osgood created a new model that showed communication as a circular rather than a linear process. They added the important features of *encoding* and *decoding*. Messages must be put into codes (such as language); the sender has to encode the message; and the receiver must be able to understand or decode it. They also realized that the process must work in reverse as well—the message must be encoded by the receiver and sent back to the sender who decodes the feedback—all in order for communication to take place as a sharing or two-way process. Although difficult to measure in the mass communication process, feedback is a crucial component, as we see later on in the book.

In the 1960s, scholars began to see that physical, emotional, and psychological factors also influenced the communication process—that self-image, personality, environment, and organization of both sender and receiver are important, as well as pressures or constraints on those involved. Melvin DeFleur (1970) created a model that added the idea of *noise* to the process, which refers to any distraction or barrier—physical, emotional, psychological, technological, political, economic, cultural—that interferes with or alters the message flow between sender and receiver.

In the early 1970s, Ray Hiebert, Donald Ungurait, and Thomas Bohn (1991) developed the HUB model, as shown in Fig. 2.2, showing the mass communication process as a series of concentric circles with the communicator at the center. They suggest that the content or message of mass communication, which starts with a communicator, has to go through a series of steps before it reaches the audience. It has to be encoded, pass internal gatekeepers, and be put into a medium, which in turn must meet the requirements of regulators, then match the filters (physical, emotional, psychological, cultural, or other frames of reference) of the audience before it can be received by an audience. Hiebert and his colleagues suggest that feedback has to travel from the audience back to the communicator, and that at any point in the process, the message or content can be amplified by the media or suffer distortion and noise.

In the 1980s, Denis McQuail and Sven Windahl (1993) depicted the media organization as the central aspect of mass communication, in which many factors make demands or bring constraints to the process. The McQuail model further expands on and explains some important aspects of the HUB model, especially regulators. McQuail's model shows regulators in a more complex form as government or laws, advertisers, pressure groups, sources, and owners or investors, as we explain further on.

The evolution of the attempt to depict the component parts of mass communication as a process will no doubt continue. But for now, we have a good road map to help us define and understand the process. We have already defined mass message or content, mass communicators, mass media, and mass audiences. We need to complete the pic-

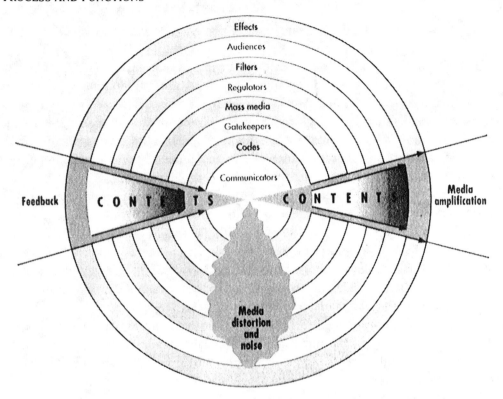

FIG. 2.2. The HUB model of mass communication. From Hiebert, Ungurait, and Bohn (1991).
Mass Media: An Introduction to Modern Communication (6th ed.). New York: Longman.
Reprinted with permission of Addison Wesley Educational Publishers.

ture by explaining codes, gatekeepers, regulators, filters, distortion, amplification, and feedback.

Codes and Grammars of Mass Media

Edmund Carpenter (1960), a Canadian anthropologist, argued in the 1960s that each medium has its own way of expressing ideas, and the code each medium uses gives unique shape to that idea. Carpenter wrote:

> English is a mass medium. All languages are mass media. The new mass media—film, radio, TV—are new languages, their grammars as yet unknown. Each codifies reality differently; each conceals a unique metaphysics. Linguists tell us it's possible to say anything in any languages if you use enough words or images, but there's rarely time; the natural course is for a culture to explore its media biases. (p. 218)

Harold Innis (1950), who influenced Carpenter and McLuhan, wrote about the *biases* of communication. He meant that each medium has its own preferences for, or puts its own stamp on, its content. And, as we pointed out in chapter 1, McLuhan (1980) summed up this idea in his well-known phrase, the medium is the message, meaning that, in the long run, the language, or grammar, or bias of the medium is ultimately more important than the message itself.

To illustrate this point, suppose you go to a neon sign shop and commission a sign to carry a specific message. The neon sign, as a medium, has limitations regarding its grammatical possibilities, and thus has preferences or biases for very simple messages. It can say, "Buy Hot Dogs," or "Drink Beer," but you would have an impossible task if you tried to communicate the Declaration of Independence using a neon sign. If you tried to use neon to convey Thomas Jefferson's thesis, it would have to be condensed into something like "Power to the People" or "End Tyranny."

Each mass medium codifies reality according to its own biases or preferences. *The New York Times* can publish a detailed analysis of the President's annual budget, but it probably cannot do a good job of communicating a doctoral dissertation on nuclear physics, which could be better handled by a scientific journal. On TV, the "CBS Evening News" can do a good job of showing the President's impassioned defense of his budget in a press conference on the annual budget, but it cannot do a good job of dissecting the economic and mathematical aspects of the budget.

Another way of looking at the differences in the grammars of mass media would be to compare a movie with the printed novel on which it was based. In most instances, the movie has to be significantly different, simply because it encodes messages differently from the printed word.

If we get all our messages, all our information, from any one medium, we will almost certainly have a skewed view of reality, biased in the sense that we will only perceive the reality of those messages from the point of view of that medium. If all our political knowledge comes to us from neon signs, for example, we will have a very simplistic and distorted notion of politics.

One can hypothesize that in this age, when television has become the dominant medium of our time, when most people get most of their information from television, our view of reality will of necessity be biased by the preferences of television for certain kinds of information presented in television's own codes. For example, in today's mass media world, politics has been reduced to television sound bites, photo ops, and 10-, 20-, or 30-second advertisements.

To be a mass communicator, one must master the grammar and the codes of a mass medium. To be an educated consumer of mass media, one must understand these grammars. Perhaps the most important purpose of this book is to help you master and use these codes. It is meant both for those who will go on to become mass communicators, and for those who will be lifelong users of mass media.

Gatekeepers

In spite of freedom of the press, mass media are full of rules and regulations, and it would be absurd to think that anybody can say anything they want in the mass media. For one thing, an owner of a medium cannot be forced to put something into that medium he or she didn't want. Therefore, owners have the first freedom, and they can decide what goes in and what stays out. In large and corporate-owned media, day-to-day decision making is usually left in the hands of employees—editors, publishers, producers, managers, directors, and other executives. But if these executives fail to follow the orders of their superiors, they can be dismissed.

These internal decision makers are called **gatekeepers**, and we can think of them as people who open and shut the gates on what gets into print or goes out over the airwaves. Four main functions are served by gatekeepers. They can decide:

> What goes in or is kept out of the medium.
>
> The context or order in which it is placed.
>
> How important any item is in relation to other items.
>
> How the prominence of any item should be increased or decreased.

At newspapers, editors make assignments for writers and reporters and decide what the day's news is and how much space and prominence each item should be given. Copy editors carefully review the work of writers and reporters for grammar and accuracy, but they might also check to make sure the newspaper's policy is being followed in the story. Most media have their own internal policies, some more complicated than others, and these must be followed by all staff members. When television coverage of politics and elections started to become a major concern because its audience had reached a critical mass in the 1960s, CBS News, for example, produced a lengthy manual, hundreds of pages long, detailing many aspects of how CBS News staffers were supposed to handle political issues and election coverage. This process is followed in one way or another by every medium, with the possible exception of the Internet, where one can get into the stream of mass communication without a gatekeeper; this, of course, poses new and interesting problems, which we deal with in a later chapter.

Regulators

Regulators are those external forces that provide a gatekeeping role for what can and cannot get into mass media and how material will be presented. As we mentioned, McQuail's (1993) model shows five different kinds of external regulators, each one worth examining in some detail: government and law; sources; advertisers; audiences; and pressure groups. (McQuail added owners and investors, but they are more properly considered internal gatekeepers.)

Government and Law. In one way of looking at it, at least in the United States, governments and laws are not significant regulators of mass media. The First Amendment to the American Constitution says that "Congress shall make no law respecting an establishment of religion, or prohibiting the free exercise thereof; or abridging the freedom of speech, or of the press; or of the right of the people peaceably to assemble, and to petition the government for a redress of grievances." Most of the time that has been interpreted to mean absolutely *no law* should restrict free speech or the press.

But clearly even the American government is involved in the mass communication process in many ways, and it is important to understand just what that involvement includes. Over the years, of course, government has had many temptations to pass laws curbing the press and has given in to those temptations from time to time. The Supreme Court must then decide whether the law is constitutional; does it violate the First Amendment, for example? Throughout most of the more than 200 years of our constitutional history, the Supreme Court has ruled more often in favor of the media than the government.

Sources.   *Sources* are the people or institutions (now usually in public relations offices) outside the media who have the information and data which mass media use to create content. It is important to understand that in any free, democratic society, everyone has an equal right to influence mass media. No one has to reveal any information to anyone else unless ordered to do so by legal authorities, and such an order can be given only in a few specific circumstances. In other words, control over information rests not with the media so much as it does with the originator. Some information is in the public domain, but it often is so only because the owner of the information voluntarily made it public.

Suppose you are involved in an automobile accident, and the accident is observed by a newspaper reporter. In this case, the reporter is a witness and thus owns his or her observations and can use them as he or she desires. But suppose the reporter didn't see the accident and comes to the scene after the fact and starts asking questions. "What happened? How do you feel?" A citizen is not obligated to answer any questions from a reporter, or anyone except certain legal officials, including police in certain circumstances. If one answers questions from the police, and they put those answers into their official report, that report is a public document, in the public domain, and only then can a reporter use it without risk.

In other words, external forces can control to a large extent what gets in or stays out of the public stream of mass communication. Increasingly, those external forces are guided by principles and techniques of public relations. In later chapters, we discuss the legalities of withholding information and the ways in which sources and public relations practitioners can influence mass communication through strategic withholding or releasing of information or staging events to attract media attention and to gain news coverage.

Advertisers.   *Advertisers* also have a great deal of opportunity to regulate or control mass media content. If an advertiser owns a medium, it can certainly control what is said in that medium and how it is said. If an advertiser owns a billboard on a highway, it can put anything on that billboard it wants. Usually an advertiser buys only a portion of time or space in a mass medium and can control only that specific portion. However, advertisers who buy a lot of time or space in the media obviously can exert considerable influence. Since advertising is the sole means of support for commercial radio and television and provides the lion's share of revenue for print media, it seems logical to assume that such financial support is highly influential.

Even newspapers, which get roughly one third of their support from subscribers, nevertheless sometimes face pressures from their advertisers. In the mid-1990s, the *San Jose Mercury-News* published some investigative reports on questionable practices of auto dealers. Local dealers, who were heavy advertisers in the newspaper, all decided to withdraw their advertising in protest, causing severe financial strain on the newspaper. Only when the newspaper published some positive articles about the business of selling cars did the dealers resume their advertisements.

This is not normal procedure because most mass media are concerned about their public credibility. To protect their credibility, most mass media have adhered to a principle many regard as sacred—keeping editorial or programming content separate from advertising content or influence. And they usually provide clear labels for advertisements, to distinugish them from news or editorial or program content.

However, the blurring of lines between ads and editorial and program content had become a major issue for mass media by the end of the twentieth century. For example, a weekly syndicated TV program that started in 1994, called "Main Floor," took viewers into department stores to show them the latest fashion and beauty trends. It appeared to be an informational program, but in fact it steered its audience to specific merchandise that sponsors had paid to promote on the show. This type of approach has been especially controversial when it has involved children's television programming. One example is "Mighty Morphin Power Rangers," a TV program that was really a long commercial for toy action figures.

Audiences.   *Audiences*, or consumers of mass media, of course, provide the ultimate control over mass media in a competitive system. In a free market, the product that sells is a success, the one that doesn't is a failure. Thus the manufacturers of media content are most likely to produce messages that can find a market, an audience. Of course, market interest is no guarantee of truth or quality; and what audiences want may not always be good for society as a whole. As the twentieth century came to a close, audience acceptance of sex and violence in media had been borne out by favorable ratings. The impact of this on society has become the subject of considerable debate.

Audiences also exert some control over the communication process through the courts, by being able to sue mass media for libel or invasion of privacy. These are not situations in which government takes action against media, but in which citizens take action through civil courts. Both these issues are of increasing concern; more libel suits are being filed against media than ever before, with juries awarding ever larger judgments to plaintiffs, resulting in a **chilling effect**, the phrase used by journalists to describe their reluctance to deal with certain problems because of the fear of libel suits. Invasion of privacy is not so well defined by the courts, but it is an area of increasing concern.

Pressure Groups.   *Pressure groups* can exert control over mass media when large numbers of people join forces on a particular issue. Group pressure has become a popular way to influence media content; some groups are political, some religious; some organize around specific consumer issues. Most of the efforts have been aimed at television, for the simple reason that TV has the most powerful impact on the public. For example, the Center for the Study of Commercialism is a nonprofit consumer advocacy organization that attempts to alert citizens to advertising that is parading as programming. This group called public attention to the TV program "Main Floor," mentioned previously.

Some groups make an effort to police children's programming on television. For example, the Center for Media Education is a Washington-based pressure group critical of children's TV. This group tried to get the federal government to make sure children's TV serves the needs of children rather than of advertisers. It was instrumental in the Federal Communications Commission's (FCC) adopting a regulation that every television station must provide at least 3 hours of educational programming every week.

The American Family Association is a group that seeks to protect the public from obscenity in the media. It pushed the U.S. Justice Department to investigate Calvin Klein ads to see if an advertising campaign using models appearing to be children in provocative poses violated federal child pornography laws; the investigation did not find any violation, because the models were all adults, but the wave of public criticism of the Calvin Klein ads resulting from the pressure group's publicity prompted the company to withdraw the ads in that campaign. These are just a few examples of the many pressure groups that have been formed to seek some kind of control over mass media.

Filters

Filters are the frames of reference we bring to the communication process, and they may be cultural, psychological, and physical. Filters are a more difficult part of the process to describe definitively, because they deal with an infinite variety of individual differences. But social scientists have been increasingly concerned with this aspect of the process.

Hiebert, Ungurait, and Bohn (1991) describe the individual frames of reference that communicators and audiences bring to the process of communication as a filtering system affecting all messages, the sender's as well as the receiver's. These filters allow some messages to pass through, or they might keep some out, and they can change or distort messages in the process. Only when the sender's and receiver's filters are identical will message and feedback pass between them without problems.

Obviously, this is most likely to happen in personal communication. Two people, known to each other, with similar backgrounds, similar moods, similar age and sex, will be most likely to achieve perfect understanding in their dialogue. As the size of the audience and complexity of the communicators increase, and differences grow between sender and receiver, it is obvious that chances for misunderstanding grow as well. In mass communication the problems of achieving understanding are many, and to be successful requires not only technology but skill and talent with the language of the mass medium.

Simplifying, stereotyping, and *framing* are often mass media's way of reducing the problems of differences in filters or frames of reference. Because mass media are aimed at vast audiences of people with enormous differences—in cultures, in psychological and physical conditions—they must reduce most messages to their simplest elements. Usually mass media are also confronted with a highly limited amount of time or space in which to deliver a message. It is surprising that anything complex can ever be communicated by mass media. And if you were to ask scientists or experts, they probably would say that mass media never communicate anything about their specialties that is remotely adequate to their needs.

In addition, mass media must often resort to easily identifiable stereotypes and readily understood formulas and themes for quick recognition by all types of people in the mass audience. For example, mass media often portray individuals as caricatures of groups, exaggerating characteristics for quick identification, rather than offering careful delineation of individual characters with all their own traits and personalities.

Mass media are also highly stylized in structuring or framing content in order to facilitate comprehension across vast audience differences. Each print medium—newspaper, magazine, book, and newsletter—has its own stylized way of presenting information or content. The same is true of each electronic medium. Different kinds of content within a medium will also be presented in a structured way, to facilitate communicating across audience differences. A news story has a specific structure; so does an editorial or an editorial column; the same is true of different radio and TV formats, from sitcoms and soap operas to MTV, or from country rock to adult contemporary to talk radio programming.

Distortion and Amplification

Throughout the process of communication, as the message travels through the various stages from communicator to audience and back, it is subject to the elements of amplification or distortion. **Distortion** can obviously come from the mismatch of filters that each person brings to the process.

Take the automobile accident, for example. Suppose the reporter did not witness the accident but interviewed both parties involved. Even though he or she tried to be fair to both sides, neither side feels the reporter gave the true version of what happened. Somehow the editor distorted the story in the writing. Furthermore, the copy editor, who is not supposed to change the facts of the story, nevertheless decided that the accident story was too long and shortened it, and in the process left out important elements, further distorting the "real" story. Several auto accidents happened on the same day, so your accident story got lumped in with the others in a general accident story summary, further reducing what got told and making it harder to determine the truth of what happened in your case.

When the elements of a communication are much more complex than a simple auto accident, the chances for distortion are all the greater. Distortion can also happen through no fault of the communicators or gatekeepers. Static on radio, "snow" in a television picture; poor quality of paper or printing in a newspaper, magazine, or book; a cheap sound system in a movie theater; and many other factors can cause distortion or noise.

Amplification is one form of distortion. The media can take an auto accident and make it into an enormous event by amplifying it through repetition, placement, and enhancement. On a quiet Saturday night in late summer of 1997, an auto accident occurred in Paris. It was one of several dozen accidents that occurred in Paris that night. But within hours, mass media had amplified the story of that accident to such an extent that it became the most widely covered auto accident in history. That accident, of course, was the one in which Princess Diana lost her life. The story of her accident was played and replayed on the front pages of the world's newspapers, on the covers of magazines, on prime-time television to such an extent that few people in the world could have been unaware of it.

Feedback

Finally, **feedback** is a response to a message, and it is essential for communication to take place. If two people are talking but one doesn't hear the other, there has been no communication. If two people are talking but each speaks a different language, so they do not understand each other, they have both heard sounds but they have not communicated. There is no feedback between them. In mass communication, feedback is very difficult to measure or interpret for a variety of reasons.

First of all, since there is no direct contact between senders and receivers of mass messages, feedback is delayed, diffused, indirect, and imprecise. It may take days or weeks or even months for the communicator to find out who has received the message and how audiences have responded to it. For print media, feedback is most often measured in terms of copies sold—how many newspapers, magazines, or books were purchased. Numbers of sales are used to determine the worth of the product; even the quality of a book is judged by whether it made the bestseller list. Sales and circulation figures, however, do not measure whether the newspaper, magazine, or book has been read, or understood, or liked, or disliked; whether it is honest or dishonest, of high or low quality. Letters to the editors or authors might provide a small measure of response, but such response is by no means a valid indication of the general or average reaction.

Radio and television feedback is usually measured in ratings made by organizations that sample the mass audience to determine what was heard or watched and by whom. These ratings, measured by organizations such as Nielsen or Arbitron, are extremely important in determining the success or failure of a station or its programs and are used to set all-important advertising rates, which are crucial for income. These ratings can become crucial in determining program content and policy. Yet they, too, are not really indicative of what was liked or disliked, what was understood or misunderstood, what was of good or poor quality. Nevertheless, feedback is an essential part of the mass communication process, however it is gathered.

FUNCTIONS OF MASS MEDIA

Mass media perform a variety of roles in American life, but we can identify five that are most important: They *inform, interpret, entertain, educate,* and *sell.* We tend to think of some media as news and information oriented (i.e., newspapers), and others as entertainment oriented (i.e., radio, television, sound recordings, and motion pictures), but to varying degrees, all media inform and entertain, analyze and interpret, socialize and educate, advertise and sell.

One of the sacred precepts of American journalism is the notion that some of these functions should be kept separate from others, much as we believe in the separation between church and state. The distinction between advertising and other content should not be blurred. News should not contain analyses and interpretations that are merely opinions of the writer, editor, or news organization. News might be used to entertain, to some extent, but it should not be used to advertise and sell. Editorials can be informative and entertaining, but they should not be disguised advertisements, nor should they contain news, which more properly should be put into a news story.

Information and News

Many thoughtful people regard news and information as the most important function of mass media, but news is neither the most common nor the most popular content. Yet most would agree that news and information are essential to life in a complex democratic society in which citizens have a right to know what is going on and should have the opportunity to exercise informed judgments by voting for the best candidates to govern and buying the best products in a competitive market. For that, people need information, and mass media came into existence primarily to serve such need.

Information is a set of facts about reality that is not necessarily news. **News** is the set of facts selected by journalists from all the information available and put into the news format of a given medium. Information doesn't become news until a news medium presents it as news. Each medium has its own format for news.

Newspapers have always been the primary news medium, and their news format is the most familiar: a headline, a lead of one or two paragraphs that summarize the main elements of the story ("who, what, where, when, why, and sometimes how"), and the remaining details written not in chronological form as they might be in drama or fiction, but in the **inverted pyramid** form, meaning the most important details are placed at the top and the least important at the bottom of a story. In other words, news is information that has been selected, structured, and framed in a certain way by a journalist. It is structured differently for each medium.

Obviously, there are many aspects to news, and, it seems, an increasing number of issues and problems surround it. We raise here only a few: objectivity, accuracy, fairness, and impartiality versus bias, sensationalism, overkill, emphasis on violence and conflict; the public's right to know versus an individual's, institution's, or even government's right to privacy and secrecy; the right to freedom of the press versus the right to a fair trial. We expand our discussion of some of these issues in later chapters.

Interpretation, Analysis, and Persuasion

The tradition in American journalism is that a news story is supposed to give readers, viewers, and listeners the facts, "just the facts, ma'am." Audiences are supposed to interpret these facts for themselves and to develop their own opinions about their meaning. This "objective" journalism is a tradition not shared in many other, especially European, systems, in which journalists usually write the news from their own perspective, putting in their own opinions, interpretations, and analyses. In the American tradition, however, factual news and opinionated interpretation and analysis are supposed to be kept separate, with opinion and analysis clearly labeled as such.

Yet Americans need to have the facts explained, put into perspective, analyzed, and judged as right or wrong, good or bad, evil or righteous. Newspapers, magazines, television, radio, and the Internet offer many opportunities for individuals, inside and outside the media, to offer their explanation of current events. Here are some common ways:

Staff-written **editorials** are labeled as reflections of the views of their medium's owners, or, if the owner prefers, as the consensus of an editorial board, usually composed of staff members who debate the issues and reach a position on them. Newspapers have had a long, vigorous tradition of taking stands on the issues of the day on the editorial page. Many magazines also express editorial opinions. Broadcast editorials have practically vanished with the abolition of the Fairness Doctrine, an FCC concept that once required broadcasters to present citizens' responses to a station's editorial stance.

Regularly produced essays, or **columns,** can be produced by individual writers who may or may not be members of a periodical's staff. **Op-ed pieces** are often contributed by writers outside the newspaper. They appear opposite the editorial page on which the newspaper's editorials appear, hence the name. The broadcast version of op-eds are public affairs programs such as "Meet the Press," "This Week," "Face the Nation," "Crossfire," "The McLaughlin Group," and "To the Contrary" (a program with an all-woman discussion panel), and radio call-in programs such as those hosted by Rush Limbaugh and Diane Rehm.

Editorial cartoons use art and caricature to cleverly make powerful visual statements. **Letters to the editors** and various **talk-back** departments give concerned citizens an opportunity to comment on the issues and also to critique the periodical's performance in reporting on and analyzing those issues.

All these mechanisms are intended to provide opportunities to analyze and interpret current events and to persuade others to consider different points of view. They represent the public forum that originated in the newsletters and newspapers of colonial times, in which citizens made detailed, impassioned calls to action on matters of widespread importance.

Entertainment

Entertainment, although perhaps not mass media's most important role, has nevertheless become its dominant function. Today's mass media are saturated with entertainment in order to attract readers, viewers, and listeners. Entertainment is not news, but news is often entertaining.

All mass media, even most newspapers, are probably used by audiences more to entertain than anything else. All can inform and educate, and whereas some do this more than others, all of them act as diversions for us. The person who curls up with the weighty Sunday *New York Times*; the hoop fans parked on their couches for the duration of the NCAA Final Four and their football and baseball counterparts glued to the Super Bowl and the World Series; the Book-of-the-Month Club member eagerly opening the latest shipment; the youngster playing an interactive game of "Tomb Raider" with competitors over the Internet—all of them use media to supply diversions.

Never have there been more choices for people who want to amuse themselves. Not all represent quality fare; television and motion pictures offer some of the most compelling entertainment, but they also receive the lion's share of criticism for violence, exploitation, and stereotyping.

Even advertisments, both print and electronic, have often become more entertaining than informative. The Super Bowl is a prime occasion when many new, clever commercials debut. Their rollout is hyped in advance and critiqued the day after the game by major media as if they were regular television programming. The one-liners they contain often become part of everyday lingo. As Neil Postman (1985) said, "Americans no longer talk to each other, they entertain each other." Our mass media and our culture are nearly one.

Socialization and Education

Mass media can play an important role in the education and socialization of media consumers. With some exceptions, they play a minor role in **formal education**, by which we mean structured programs of learning within an institutional framework. The exceptions are books, of course, without which formal education would probaby be impossible. Academic journals, too, play a key role, as does the Internet, which opens vast storehouses of data that can be used in research. But books, journals, and databases used in education could hardly be considered mass media; they are highly specialized.

On the other hand, most popular books, magazines, radio, television, motion pictures, and sound recordings play only a minor role in formal learning. All print and electronic media can be adapted for instructional purposes, however, and nearly every type of medium has been used to further learning, whether for a classroom setting, an individual programmed endeavor, or distance learning.

Perhaps the most important nonbook medium for formal education has been video recordings, which increasingly can be used in a manner similar to books; they can be stored, retrieved, and reviewed to serve a scholar's needs. And some educational programming, such as "Sesame Street," has proved useful in using television for more formal learning processes of children. The National Information Center for Educational Media in 1998 had more than half a million educational items in its database of nonprint instructional media, covering all subject areas that apply to learning. These include titles from preschool through professional, including vocational and technical education, management and supervisory training, health and safety, history, psychology, fine arts, engineering, literature, and drama. The formats catalogued include not only videotapes but also film, videodiscs, audiotapes, filmstrips, CD-ROMs, software, slides, transparencies, and sound recordings.

However, mass media's real educational function is in **informal education**, or **socialization**, the process by which people come to identify themselves as members of a social group and to learn group norms. Mass media hold up a mirror to society and show its members how they relate to each other, what is socially acceptable, what is normal and abnormal, what is good and evil, what is true and false. In fact, in most ways, mass media are the greatest teachers of all. Children now spend more time with television than they do with parents, teachers, or religious leaders. It is television that now teaches most children their values, and as they grow up, it is television's values that will prevail, that will become the teacher of us all.

Advertising and Selling

Mass media, especially in a free market economy, also serve the function of promoting and selling, of telling us what is for sale, and of convincing us to buy, usually through advertising. By doing so, media keep the wheels of industry turning and the free-market economy prospering, while also earning revenues that make them viable businesses. Most mass media couldn't operate without advertising income. Many media owners depend on income they receive from advertising, but advertisers depend on mass media to distinguish their products from their competition and to get their message out to the potential customers.

Advertising has been a part of mass media from its earliest days. From colonial newspapers to the present day, notices of merchandise for sale, services for hire, and emerging business opportunities have characterized American newspapers and magazines and were essential to broadcasting from its very beginning.

Since mass media in American society receive no support from government (with the exception of educational broadcasting), they must earn income either from subscribers or from advertising. Newspapers and magazines, on average, get more than two thirds of their income from advertising and could not operate without it. Radio and telelevision (excluding cable) receive all their income from advertising. Cable gets considerable revenues from subscribers, but money from advertising is growing as well. Only books, motion pictures, and recordings get most of their income from individual buyers, whereas the Internet, free at first, is now reaching out to advertising to support a rapidly growing online business.

Further Reading

Baran, Stanley J., and Davis, Dennis K. (1995). *Mass Communication Theory: Foundations, Ferment, and Future*. Belmont, CA: Wadsworth.
Carpenter, Edmund. (1960). The New Languages. In Edmund Carpenter and Marshall McLuhan (Eds.), *Explorations in Communication* (pp. 218–223). Boston: Beacon Press.

DeFleur, Melvin L. (1970). *Theories of Mass Communication* (2nd ed.). New York: McKay.

DeFleur, Melvin L., and Ball-Rokeach, Sandra. (1975). *Theories of Mass Communication* (3rd ed.). New York: Longman.

Hiebert, Ray Eldon, Ungurait, Donald, and Bohn, Thomas. (1991), *Mass Media: An Introduction to Modern Communication* (6th ed.). New York: McKay; Longman. (Originally published 1974)

Innes, Harold. (1950). *Empire and Communications*. Toronto: University of Toronto Press.

Lasswell, Harold. (1948). The Structure and Function of Communication in Society. In Lyman Bryson, (Ed.), *The Communication of Ideas* (pp. 37–48). Chicago: Institute for Religious and Social Studies.

McLuhan, Marshall. (1980). *Understanding Media: The Extensions of Man*. New York: McGraw-Hill. (Originally published 1974)

McQuail, Denis, and Windahl, Sven. (1993). *Communication Models* (2nd ed.). New York: Longman.

Postman, Neil. (1985). *Amusing Ourselves to Death: Public Discourse in the Age of Show Business*. New York: Viking Penguin.

Schramm, Wilbur. (1954). How Communication Works. In Wilber Schramm (Ed.), *The Process and Effects of Mass Communication* (pp. 3–26). Urbana: University of Illinois Press.

Severin, Werner J., with Tankard, James W., Jr. (1988). *Communication Theories*. New York: Longman.

Wright, Charles R. (1986). *Mass Communication: A Sociological Perspective*. New York: Random House. (Originally published 1959)

3

POLITICAL SYSTEMS:
NATIONS AND CULTURES

When Vice President Albert Gore visited China in 1997, news stories in American media were full of criticism of much of what the Vice President said and did. They criticized him for appearing to appease the Chinese, for not speaking out about jailed dissidents or China's record on human rights, for not being tough enough on arms sales and nuclear arms control negotiations. And when the Vice President made a few negative comments, the American news media quoted many sources critical of him for endangering the delicate balance in Chinese–American diplomatic relations. Some American news photos even appeared to depict Gore squirming in his seat as he was trying to figure out what to say to the Chinese. According to his country's news media, it seemed Vice President Gore could not get it right.

When the Chinese President, Jiang Zemin, came to the United States a few months later, the Chinese mass media dealt with his visit in a far different manner. The Chinese President was followed by demonstrators (mostly Chinese Americans) for much of that visit, protesting China's human rights violations and the jailing of political dissidents. These demonstrations were never shown on Chinese television or written about in Chinese newspapers. Instead, Chinese headlines praised Zemin and President Bill Clinton for strengthening and promoting relations. Flattering pictures were shown of Zemin, laughing with Clinton, walking with the American President past the honor guard, arriving at the White House in a limousine. The Chinese TV newscast showed the complete U.S. Navy Band rendition of the two countries' national anthems, the 21-gun salute, and the two leaders walking into the White House. In the Chinese media not one critical word was said nor one negative image shown of Zemin's entire visit.

WHAT ACCOUNTS FOR MEDIA SYSTEM DIFFERENCES?

Why these two different ways of treating a similar news event in two different countries? One answer is that they hold very different philosophies about the role of mass media in society. This chapter explores those differences in worldwide media systems.

Until recently, mass media have not operated on a global basis. Each country has had its own media system, evolving from many factors, including economics, politics, technologies, and cultures. Media content for the most part has been based on local languages, local interests, local subjects, and local events. News is different from one country to the next, and it is treated differently.

In England, for example, many newspapers are national, not local, and many are full of gossip, sensationalism, and even nudity. Television in most of Europe contains far fewer commercials than in the United States, and rarely one that will interrupt a program. One can watch an entire tennis match and never see a sales pitch between games! In the former Soviet Union, commercial advertising was not permitted at all. In Spain, much television advertising and programming contains full nudity, something that would never be seen in the Middle East. There and in Africa, newspapers tend to have few pages, with very little advertising, and news is dominated by the country's leaders, often with their pictures on the front page. Television will almost always have prominent news stories showing the president meeting various dignitaries. But these brief examples do not fully explain the differences in the world's mass media systems; we need a broader analysis to understand them.

THE MEDIA SYSTEMS PARADIGM

In every country of the world, a variety of factors interact to create a national media system. In 1974, Hiebert, Ungurait, and Bohn created a *media systems paradigm* to illustrate those factors and show their relationships. They depicted a model of media systems with three circles representing (1) social factors or natural forces essential to the creation of (2) media institutions (print and electronic) that (3) perform certain functions for the society (news and information, analysis and interpretation, education and socialization, persuasion and public relations, sales and advertising, and entertainment). These three circles, however, interact and to some extent influence, modify, or change each other. Figure 3.1 illustrates this paradigm.

We discuss media institutions and functions elsewhere in this book, but we need to take a closer look at social factors and natural forces to better understand the differences in the world's media systems:

Political Philosophy.   Perhaps the most obvious social factor is a country's political philosophy. Capitalism, communism, fascism, monarchism, religious fundamentalism—each political system, whichever dominates, views the role of media differently.

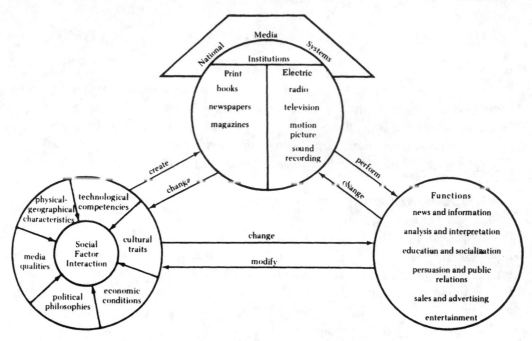

FIG. 3.1. The media systems paradigm. From Hiebert, Ungurait, and Bohn (1991). *Mass Media: An Introduction to Modern Communication* (6th ed.). New York: Longman. Reprinted with permission of Addison Wesley Educational Publishers.

Economic Conditions. These also affect media systems. Less-developed economies will not be able to sustain the quantity or quality of media that a highly developed economy can produce. A society with an undeveloped economy will probably have controlled media, no matter what the political philosophy. However, if there are wealthy people within a poor economy, they might be able to gain access to outside mass media that cannot be controlled by their own governments, and that could weaken the communication power of their governments. However, the wealthy are usually the ones in power in any case, so the threat is rarely real.

Technological Competencies. These are extremely important in determining the orientation of a society's mass media, simply because mass media require sophisticated printing presses, broadcasting equipment, and production and distribution facilities. Some countries are more technologically advanced than others, and that will be reflected in their mass media. A society without sophisticated technology will probably have government-owned or -controlled media, although again the wealthy could have a way, in this new age, to subvert government's power by establishing their own private access to high technology, such as computers and the Internet. Technical competency in an educational sense is also crucial, since those societies with professional mass media education are probably the only ones that will develop meaningful professional standards.

Physical and Geographical Characteristics. These characteristics can also affect mass media. Mountainous terrain can alter a country's broadcast capabilities; tropical climates can make paper production prohibitively expensive. The availability of highways, railroads, and air transport can all affect a country's media system.

Cultural Traits. Languages, traditions, social norms, mores, values, and attitudes all can influence the way mass media operate in any society, especially as to the kinds of content the media provide and the extent to which the media are free.

Media Qualities. The qualities of media themselves can be predictors of a country's media system. For example, since print media require literacy, countries with a high level of illiteracy are more inclined to concentrate on developing electronic media. Radio, which is perhaps the least expensive medium to send and receive, is most likely be dominant in less developed countries with high rates of illiteracy.

THE CLASSIC FOUR SYSTEMS OF THE PRESS

In the mid-1950s three American scholars, Frederick Siebert, Theodore Peterson, and Wilbur Schramm, in a book called *Four Theories of the Press* (1963), made the first comprehensive effort to describe different media systems. Although their work is now sometimes regarded as a biased cold-war view of the world's media politics, it has been widely influential and is certainly a first step in understanding the subject. Siebert and his coauthors divided the world into four main media systems based primarily on political philosophy, media ownership, media freedom, and media control.

According to the four theories concept, the world's media were either authoritarian or libertarian. If authoritarian, their role was to support the central authority of the state. If libertarian, their role was to serve the needs of individuals, usually to protect them from the authority of the state. Siebert, Peterson, and Schramm (1963) also described two other systems: Soviet (or communist) totalitarianism was an authoritarian system of the most restrictive kind; social responsibility was a libertarian system with a social conscience. Each one of these four systems needs a bit more description. (Since strictly speaking, Siebert, Peterson, and Schramm were not really describing theories, we prefer to use the term *systems*.)

Authoritarian Systems. Authoritarian systems might be privately or publicly owned but basically media have to serve a central authority—state, king, dictator, government, religion, or whatever. If privately owned, media are subject to close scrutiny, through licensing or other legal controls to ensure they serve the needs of the central powers.

Authoritarian systems certainly prevailed under monarchies where kings had absolute power, under fascism in the 1930s in Germany and Italy, in military dictatorships such as have existed in Central and South America, or in economically less-developed countries (sometimes called the Third World, meaning not third class but rather nonaligned with the Western or old Soviet power structure). Those countries typically have a vast underclass and a small ruling class that exercises most authority, including

control of mass media. Authoritarianism also prevails in societies that have one official or national religion, where God is invoked as the supreme authority and his representatives on Earth have absolute power, as in the Catholic Church in Europe's Middle
Ages or in fundamentalist Muslim countries in the modern world.

Communist Systems.   For supposedly ideological reasons, communist systems are
authoritarian. (With the demise of the old Soviet Union, we can no longer meaning-
fully use the term *Soviet-totalitarianism* except for historical purposes.) In the communist societies that remain in the world, primarily China and Cuba, one political
ideology is vested in one political party that dominates government and controls all
means of public and sometimes private communication. Government and the Communist Party (really one and the same) own all media, in the name of the people. Public
communication outside party apparatus is limited, and any public (or sometimes even
private) criticism of party or government is not well tolerated. The purpose of media
under this system is to serve the needs of society, as interpreted by the Communist
party, in order to bring about Karl Marx's idea of a new social utopia, in which peace
and brotherhood and economic equality would be prevailing social values, rather than
the aggressive, acquisitive, and self-centered competition of capitalism.

China's mass media philosophy has been guided by communist principles, among
them that the good of the state and society is more important than individual freedom.
In China, mass media are publicly owned and controlled by the Communist party and
serve to advocate the government's and the party's positions. In the old Soviet Union, the Communist party, particularly under Stalin, became very repressive, admin-
istering harsh punishment for anything seen as a threat. China, at the end of the
twentieth century, was less Stalinistic, although dissidents were still jailed for speaking out too loudly or publicly in defiance of the state, as were the Tiananmen Square
demonstrators in 1989. There simply has been no free political expression in China
under communism.

Libertarian Systems.   Libertarian systems are based on the idea that individual
rights are more important than rights of the state or society as a whole. This notion
grew out of the thinking of political philosophers such as John Locke, Thomas Hobbes,
John Milton, Thomas Jefferson, and John Stuart Mill in the seventeenth, eighteenth,
and nineteenth centuries. Two of the most important features of libertarianism are that
truth is most likely to emerge from a free and open discussion, expressed most elo-
quently by the poet Milton in his essay *Areopagitica*, and that government properly exists only to serve the needs of the people, not the other way around, an idea given its
most powerful expression in Jefferson's Declaration of Independence. To assure a free
marketplace of ideas and a government that serves the people, the libertarian philosophy maintains that public media should not be owned, operated, or controlled by government but be completely free and in private hands. The purpose of the press and mass
media in this system is to serve the needs of their owners, but also to be a watchdog on
behalf of the people against possible corruption or concentration of power in govern-

ment. To assure this kind of media function in a democratic society, the framers of the American Constitution, in their very first amendment, stated that "Congress shall pass no law abridging the freedom of speech or of the press."

American media are guided by the First Amendment and by the principle that government should protect the rights of individuals, who are free to say, print, or broadcast almost anything they want. The privately owned media in America have assumed an adversarial role, believing that criticism and exposure of government problems are entirely justified because people have a right to know what government is doing, or not doing, to serve their interests.

Social Responsibility.   This system poses the idea that media need to serve both individual and society, and if media should fail to serve the public, then people have a right to take action against them. Even though privately owned, mass media have responsibilities to society, and, if they fail in the exercise of those responsibilities, society can through legal means exercise some control. For example, if commercial broadcasters do not produce educational programs because they do not attract enough advertising, the public has a right to use public property—its airwaves—to establish public broadcasting to serve educational needs; using exactly that rationale, the U.S. government in the 1960s established National Public Radio (NPR) and the Public Broadcasting Service (PBS) to provide educational and other socially useful programs on radio and television that were not being produced by profit-making enterprises.

Social responsibility ideas grew out of the "clear and present danger" doctrine of the early twentieth century, when philosophers (such as Chief Justice Oliver Wendell Holmes and philosopher W. E. Hocking) began to realize that in the modern age, powerful mass media could in fact bring about grave harm to society in their pursuit of gain for a few individuals. After World War I, Holmes declared in an important Supreme Court ruling that the government could prosecute individuals for their statements during the war if their public expression hurt the nation's war effort. Philosopher Hocking, in a number of essays, argued that freedom was not an inalienable right but a moral responsibility that required accountable behavior.

America's mass media system for the last half of the twentieth century was really a dual system: primarily libertarian for print and film media, and social responsibility for broadcasting. In the 1920s and 1930s, through establishment of the Federal Radio Commission first, then the Federal Communications Commission, and through various regulations passed by Congress and rulings by the Supreme Court, broadcasting was made a socially responsible system. The original rationale was that broadcasting was potentially too powerful to be left entirely in the free hands of a few individuals and, furthermore, that it made use of public, not private, property—the airwaves—which belonged to the people. Basically the laws provided that a broadcaster's license could be taken away if he or she had not broadcast in the public interest.

In many European countries, broadcasting was originally placed in the hands of public commissions or government agencies, to ensure social responsibility and to operate for the good of society rather than for the profit of its owners. In America, private

LIVERPOOL JOHN MOORES UNIVERSITY
LEARNING SERVICES

broadcasters originally had to have a government-issued, time-limited license to operate, which might not be renewed if the broadcast station failed to meet the needs of its audience. Ownership was limited to prevent broadcasting from falling into the hands of a powerful few, and equal time provisions and a Fairness Doctrine were written into law to ensure political and social responsibility. But much of that has been changed by deregulation, as we discuss later in this book.

FOUR THEORIES' CRITICISM AND ALTERNATIVES

Although *Four Theories of the Press* (Siebert, Peterson, & Schramm, 1963) was widely influential for nearly half a century, it has attracted increasing criticism from contemporary communication scholars for being oversimplified and incomplete. Perhaps a more realistic analysis would simply use the classic political-economic labels that have developed over the past 200 years: capitalism, fascism, socialism, and communism. We could add two more labels that describe existing political-economic policies: national capitalism, and national socialism.

Capitalism.   Countries in which the mass media system exists purely to make a profit for its owners are known as capitalist. In modern capitalism, ownership has largely shifted to corporate bodies, owned by shareholders from the general public, most of whom are interested in receiving dividend payments for their investments rather than in doing social good. This approach to a large extent characterizes the systems of North America, Western Europe, Australia, and New Zealand.

Fascism.   Fascist countries can have privately and publicly owned mass media, but their purpose is to support the nation and the dominant ethnic, cultural, or religious cohort. Nazi Germany and fascist Italy from the 1930s and early 1940s are historic examples, and Iran, Iraq, and some other fundamentalist Muslim countries and some small African nations are modern examples.

Communism.   As we have seen, communist countries have media whose sole purpose is the support of the Communist party, are usually owned exclusively by the party and the government in the name of the people, and are strictly controlled by party leaders. The former Soviet Union is the prime historic example, and in contemporary times China and Cuba still maintain this political philosophy.

Socialism.   Socialist countries have publicly or privately owned media, but government can own and operate them where needed to serve society, and all media's primary purpose is to serve society rather than to make a profit. The best contemporary examples are probably Scandinavian countries.

National Capitalism.   This is a capitalist system in which media are privately owned, primarily to make a profit, but the owners are in such close collaboration with government leaders that the media serve to support the government, which, in turn, can exercise some control over media. Examples are Japan and many newly industrialized nations, primarily in Southeast Asia, such as South Korea, Indonesia, Singapore, Taiwan, and Malaysia.

National Socialism.   This is a socialist system, with privately and publicly owned mass media whose purpose is to serve both society and the government in power. Best examples are many countries of Central and South America, and developing countries in Africa and Asia, including India. In these systems, national development is often used as a rationale for controlling mass media.

Systems in Transition.   Also characteristic of much of the world today are countries in which media systems are in transition. Russia, the other countries of the former Soviet Union, and other former communist countries of Eastern Europe are the best examples. It is still too soon after the 1989 revolution to state categorically which system will ultimately take hold in many of these countries. Many at first wanted to embrace the American way, but in fact are evolving into systems unique to their own cultures and political traditions. Many countries around the world are in a state of transition toward multiparty politics, free-market economies, and democratic structures that will make mass media freer than they have been.

THE FREEDOM VERSUS CONTROL CONTINUUM

If we reduce the world's mass media systems to their simplest differences, perhaps we should describe their levels of freedom and control. A number of institutions track freedom of the press around the world, among them the World Press Freedom Committee, The Freedom Forum, and Freedom House. Other efforts have been made by the United Nations, UNESCO, The European Union, and other similar agencies. Of course, these institutions and agencies each bring their own biases about freedom and control to the task. However, we can summarize most of their findings and place each country or philosophical and political system at some point on a continuum from absolute freedom on one end to absolute control on the other, as Fig. 3.2 illustrates.

Although such generalizations can be risky, they can also provide a helpful way to place a society or culture on a freedom versus control continuum, showing that such placement is relatively fluid, with lots of shadings, unlike the more rigid black-and-white formulations of the "four theories." Obviously, no country has absolute freedom within media, but print media in the United States probably comes as close as any, although some countries may be more sexually open in their media than is the United States. At the same time, no country exerts absolute control, but Stalin's repressive Soviet Union, where millions of people were exterminated to enforce and maintain one political system, probably asserted more control over mass media than any other society in modern history. At the beginning of the twenty-first century, communist China comes the closest to the control end of the continuum.

FIG. 3.2.   Mass media freedom versus control continuum, some typically suggested placements.

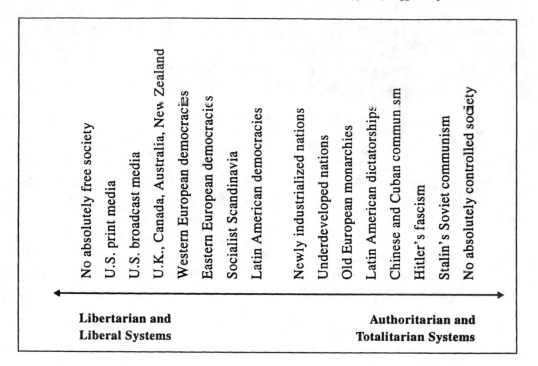

NEW GLOBAL REALITIES

Over the past 50 years, media systems of the world have changed, sometimes drastically, because of technology, political climate, and national leadership. And our understanding of these systems has also changed as we have become better informed about the world and the way it works. Three developments have been primary agents of change in media systems: new communication technologies; increasingly effective techniques of public relations; and global media companies that have emerged, crossing boundaries of politics, economics, culture, and even language.

New Technologies.   In the last few decades of the twentieth century, new technologies—especially satellites, microwave relays, fiber optic cable, videocassette cameras and recorders, fax machines, cell phones, and particularly the Internet—were bringing yet another revolution to the world's communication processes. Ted Koppel's 1990 ABC documentary "Revolution in a Box" showed how new technologies are spurring deomocracy in every corner of the globe, especially with camcorders and VCRs that have become so inexpensive and ubiquitous that almost anyone can use them to achieve mass communication through television. Add the introduction of the Internet as a new mass medium and by the beginning of the twenty-first century most individuals now have the means to send messages to the masses without much government interference.

The new communication technologies are difficult for central authorities to control. Over-the-air radio and television cannot be contained by borders, "iron curtains," or Berlin walls. Satellites can beam messages almost anywhere on the globe. And the Internet is almost unstoppable, although some authoritarian governments are trying. (The military dictatorship in Burma, for example, has forbidden the use of computers and Internet communication.)

William E. Halal (1990), professor of management at George Washington University, and Alexander I. Nikitin, scholar at the Russian Academy of Sciences in Moscow, wrote in a recent collaboration, "The biggest event of our time is that unprecedented advances in computerization, telecommunications, and other forms of information technology are relentlessly integrating the world into a unified whole" (p. 9).

Public Relations.   Public relations has also changed the relationship of individuals and groups to the power structures of society. (For a complete description of public relations and its role, see chap. 14.) The effective use of sophisticated public relations techniques can allow almost anyone with some resources and professional know-how to achieve mass communication.

In the postcommunist world of inexpensive technologies and sophisticated public relations, the power to control the source of information is no longer likely to come from a central authority, or from any one government, organization, institution, political party, or religion. It may no longer even be possible for the mass media in democracies to keep governments from communicating directly with citizens, which in the past was frowned on in libertarian and free-market democracies. In sum, it seems, almost no one can be stopped from communicating almost anything to anybody. The only question is the effectiveness of the message.

Global Media Companies.   These have emerged rapidly in the last decade of the twentieth century. Ben Bagdikian's (1992) book, *The Media Monopoly*, showed that in the early 1980s, 50 firms had come to dominate U.S. mass media. Later, he predicted that by the end of the century five to ten corporate giants will control most of the world's important newspapers, magazines, books, broadcast stations, movies, recordings, and videocassettes. The mergers he predicted began speeding up in 1992 and by 1997, according to Robert W. McChesney, nine global media firms had come to dominate the world. (We expand on ownership and control in chap. 4.)

These media giants do not have to pay much heed to political ideologies other than those that further their enterprise. Their main concern is not promoting national patriotism, generating religious spirit, educating the public, or creating a better society. Their primary goal is simply to make a profit for their shareholders, and they support almost any business ventures that will further that end. It should be noted that making a profit need not preclude serving the public. As long as there is competition, profit will go to those who best fill the public's needs and desires.

THE NEW LIBERTARIAN REALITY

Changes are taking place in all the traditional systems, including the libertarian. In those countries in which libertarian ideas have prevailed, politics and culture have been undergoing great changes, no doubt partly or wholly caused by the threat of communication revolution. In America, for example, where the people once abhorred any direct public communication from the government, such intrusion is now more widely accepted. Americans have come to expect lots of government messages, even though government still does not own or operate any mass media. In fact, government is a major mass communicator, with tens of thousands of public relations specialists from the White House down to the smallest mayor's office using public relations techniques to get government's messages into mass media. And the government now uses a variety of Web sites to put its messages into the public domain via the Internet, unhindered by the analysis of journalists or the judgments of media gatekeepers.

Some other libertarian countries have taken the very unlibertarian stance of adopting stricter government controls on some parts of the communication process that were formerly unregulated. In Canada, Australia, and the United Kingdom, for example, post-World War II laws have been created to keep official secrets from the press in the name of national security, and in the United Kingdom to limit photographic access to the royal family to assure royal security. In Japan, the free and privately owned press is so culturally synonymous with government that reporters rarely ask tough or embarrassing questions of their public officials.

Even in the United States, private ownership that has given way to corporate ownership is creating media oligarchies much more inclined to join forces with government to serve their own ends rather than to be the watchdog of government. Some critics have proposed that a media-government complex could develop, making so-called libertarian media as much a tool of government as the Communist media were a tool of the Kremlin.

However, other factors serve as a counterbalance. The new technologies and public relations techniques have also allowed more nongovernment organizations, groups, and individuals to enter the stream of mass communication. Among other things, this has increased multiculturalism. Today we accept the fact that there are many different cultures in society. We accept that special interest groups can communicate with the public and that they may have any number of motives including self-expression, objective presentation of information, the making of profit, the spread of a particular cause or point of view—even one antagonistic to the power structure or prevailing public opinion—or even the spread of disinformation.

THE NEW SOCIAL RESPONSIBILITY REALITY

Two developments in the 1980s greatly reduced the socially responsible role of mass media, especially within the large corporate media entities: the acceptance in the early 1980s of Ronald Reagan's philosophy of deregulation in the marketplace and the demise of the Soviet Union in 1989. These developments spurred a free-market economy in which the social responsibility of all businesses, especially mass media conglomerates, has declined considerably. The responsibility to make a profit seems to have superseded most other social concerns.

The end of the Soviet Union removed the threat of communist world dominance, fear of which was a major cause for corporate responsibility during the cold war. But deregulation's effects can best be seen in American broadcasting, which was originally intended by law to be less free but more socially responsible. Deregulation has meant that licenses can be renewed almost without question, restrictions on ownership have been loosened, the equal-time provision has been eliminated, and the Fairness Doctrine, after a long battle, has disappeared. These changes opened the door to consolidation and centralization. (See chapters 5 and 12 for more details.)

Even in Europe, where broadcasting was traditionally public rather than commercial and was charged with the exclusive purpose of serving the public interest, much broadcasting has been privatized, supported by advertising rather than taxpayers, and given almost as much freedom as print media.

THE NEW COMMUNIST REALITY

In the old Soviet Union, in the 1970s and 1980s, people began to discover that they could obtain access to information and communicate publicly, even though their system was opposed to such activity. Private printing presses and even photocopy machines were illegal, but an underground press flourished. Rock 'n' roll was outlawed, but teenagers got records on the black market. International broadcasts were jammed, but the Soviet government couldn't stop illegal trading of American videotapes and VCR machines. In addition, dissidents learned how to use public relations techniques to achieve public communication. They knew how to stage events to capture the world's media attention. The protestor who set himself on fire in Prague and the Chinese student standing in defiance of a tank rumbling toward him in Tiananmen Square became world news.

In the 1980s, Soviet leaders, particularly Mikhail Gorbachev, began to admit that the control of information was not transforming society into the utopian ideal of communism. In fact, it had become clear to the Soviets that communism could only survive with new communication policies, such as *glasnost* (openness) and *perestroika* (restructuring). These policies gave the people more access to news and information, ultimately even to a form of free press, to the unjamming of foreign broadcasts, and to greater access to computers. The result, as we know, has been the development of a multiparty system, and the people, given information and political options, often voted the communists out of control.

In China, where communism still prevails, there has been a steady relaxation of the controls formerly exercised by the Gang of Four in the Cultural Revolution. And although China at the beginning of the twenty-first century is still far from the open society that Russia has become, it has moved further toward the middle in many respects. China is more willing to open its doors to new technologies, including computers, and free-market business practices seem to be developing.

NEW REALITIES IN THE AUTHORITARIAN DEVELOPING WORLD

In the so-called Third World, too, governments can no longer depend on their ability to control the communication process. Even in countries too poor to afford much variety in media, cheap radio receivers and satellite dishes hooked up to community TV sets are bringing in news and entertainment from around the world, giving people access to information—and power—they never had before.

Many now question the developmental policies that some Third World leaders used to rationalize their control of public media. In some of these countries in the last decade of the twentieth century, their former "lifetime" presidents were removed from office, often charged with corruption that had been hidden by the controlled mass media. Development, these countries and their peoples are coming to understand, is not likely to take place in the absence of the free flow of information.

ONE GLOBAL MEDIA SYSTEM?

What we are describing here sounds as if all media systems of the world have been stood on their heads, so to speak. Everything is upside down and topsy-turvy, and certainly much is changing. It may be that the new technologies and public relations techniques, and the rise of global media companies, will ultimately produce one kind of media system, although still with many variations from country to country, for the reasons already explained in the media systems paradigm section. As long as countries have different physical and geographical characteristics, different technological competencies, different cultures, politics, economics, and media qualities, their media will be different. At the beginning of the twenty-first century, political ideology has become far less important than it was in the twentieth. The world seems to be moving toward the acceptance of a more scientific or pragmatic and less political model of mass communication.

MEDIA SUBSYSTEMS

Since many societies seem to be organizing their media systems in new ways, it might be useful to find new classifications for these systems by focusing on subsystems. Seven different subsystems seem to be growing in power in highly developed societies:

1. **Commercial media**—where the goal is to do whatever makes a profit.
2. **Professional media**—where professionals, for whom making a profit is not so important, adhere to some agreed-on standards and values.
3. **Public media**—where citizens use public taxes and donations to operate for the public good, whether profitable or not.
4. **Government media**—where national interests can be furthered by the party in power.
5. **Political media**—where all political parties can promote their ideologies, whether in power or not.
6. **Organizational media**—where specific needs of a nongovernmental body—tribes, ethnic groups, religions, corporate or business entities—can be served.
7. **Individualized media**—where individuals can freely express themselves without organizational support, made possible primarily by the emergence of the Internet.

Increasingly, many nations have multiple subsystems, and few any longer have one or even a dominant subsystem. It would seem logical that the more highly developed the economic, technological, and educational capabilities of a society, the more subsystems would exist and the more powerful each would be in competition with the others. In addition, the more varied the media subsystems, the better the chances for all citizens to benefit, to have options and choices, and to fulfill individual needs.

A COMPREHENSIVE MASS COMMUNICATION MODEL

Perhaps the only real model of mass communication is the model developed by social scientists in the middle of the twentieth century. The social scientists, as we saw in chapter 2, proposed that communication does not exist unless the message has an effect, no matter what the source, medium, or content. Harold Lasswell's "who says what to whom with what effect" remains the basic definition. The message has to have an effect, or to be effective. But we need to make Lasswell's model more comprehensive for the new world of the twenty-first century.

We propose that such a model as illustrated in Fig. 3.3 can be used to describe the media systems of most nations. This model shows that no matter what the nation, there are various sources of communication, various purposes, media, content type, audience type, results, and methods of measuring feedback or results. It assumes that any person or agency that is a source of communication will communicate in order to achieve a particular result. From the variety of media and types of content available, the source decides how to communicate to achieve those results and then receives some feedback about the effectiveness of the message and uses this to confirm or refine the message for subsequent communication.

FIG. 3.3. A comprehensive mass communication model.

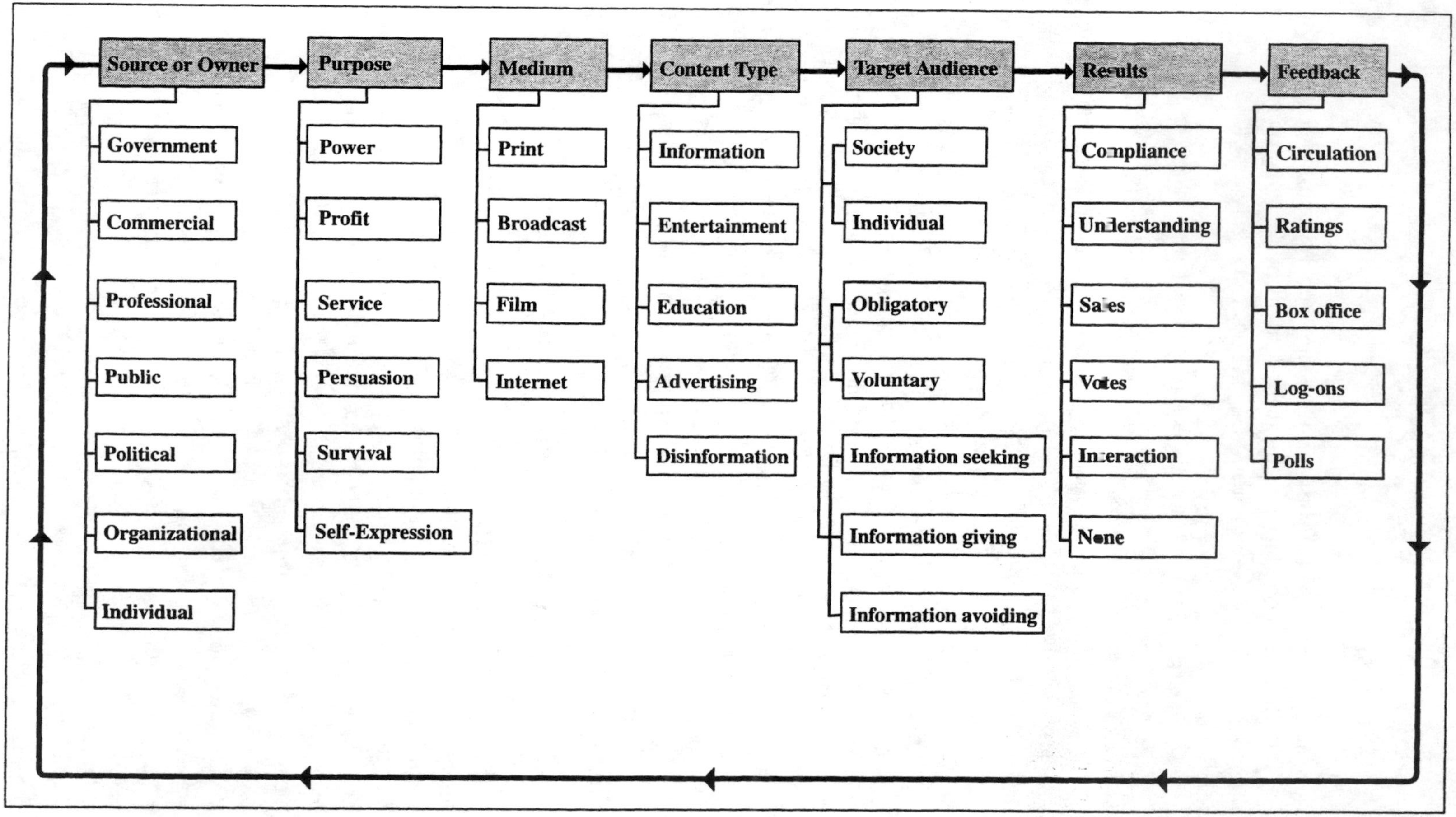

Source or Owner	Purpose	Medium	Content Type	Target Audience	Results	Feedback
Government	Power	Print	Information	Society	Compliance	Circulation
Commercial	Profit	Broadcast	Entertainment	Individual	Understanding	Ratings
Professional	Service	Film	Education	Obligatory	Sales	Box office
Public	Persuasion	Internet	Advertising	Voluntary	Votes	Log-ons
Political	Survival		Disinformation	Information seeking	Interaction	Polls
Organizational	Self-Expression			Information giving	None	
Individual				Information avoiding		

Some societies obviously utilize more parts of this model than others, but all fit into this paradigm. The more developed the society, the more elements of this model are available to all communicators.

This model also suggests that all sources of information are basically in competition with each other for their target audiences. Given the new technologies and the techniques of public relations, it is now much more difficult for any one source to monopolize or control the process of communication. Even governments, or the dominant coalition, or the corporate leadership must compete in the communication marketplace to achieve the desired results.

In short, the comprehensive mass communication model can be characterized in the following way: *A variety of sources of communication, for a variety of purposes, can use various media to produce a variety of content aimed at various target audiences to achieve a variety of results, as demonstrated by various kinds of feedback that in turn, affect the way the original source of communication continues to produce messages.*

Given the new technologies and the decline in the power of political ideologies and central authorities, any individual, or group, or institution, or business endeavor, or government agency, either by owning media or by using public relations techniques, can place messages into the stream of mass communication aimed at target audiences to achieve a desired result. That process will change the world's communication systems of the twenty-first century.

Further Reading

Altschull, J. Herbert. (1984). *Agents of Power*. New York: Longman.

Bagdikian, Ben H. (1992). *The Media Monopoly* (4th ed.). Boston: Beacon Press. (Originally published 1983)

Frederick, Howard H. (1993). *Global Communications and International Relations*. Belmont, CA: Wadsworth.

Goban-Klas, Tomasz. (1994). *The Orchestration of the Media*. Boulder, CO: Westview Press.

Habermas, Jurgen. (1989). *Structural Transformation of the Public Sphere*. Cambridge: MIT Press. (Originally published 1963)

Hachten, William A., and Hatchen, Harva. (1989). *The World News Prism*. Ames: Iowa State University Press.

Halal, William E., and Nikitin, Alexander I. (November–December 1990). One World: The Coming Synthesis of a New Capitalism and a New Socialism. *The Futurist, 24*(6), 8–14.

Herman, Edward S., and McChesney, Robert W. (1997). *The Global Media: The New Missionaries of Global Capitalism*. London and Washington, DC: Cassell.

Hiebert, Ray E., Ungurait, Donald, and Bohn, Thomas. (1991). *Mass Media: An Introduction to Modern Communication* (6th ed.). New York: Longman. (Originally published 1974)

Hocking, William E. (1947). *Freedom of the Press: A Framework of Principle*. Chicago: University of Chicago Press.

Martin, L. John, and Chaudhary, Anju Grover. (1983). *Comparative Mass Media Systems*. New York: Longman.

McChesney, Robert W. (1997). *Corporate Media and the Threat to Democracy*. New York: Seven Stories Press.

Merrill, John C. (1995). *Global Journalism: Survey of International Communication*. New York: Longman.

Merrill, John C., and Lowenstein, Ralph L. (1971). *Media Messages and Men*. New York: McKay.

Nerone, John C. (Ed.). (1995). *Last Rights: Revisiting* Four Theories of the Press. Urbana: University of Illinois Press.

Siebert, Frederick S., Peterson, Theodore, and Schramm, Wilbur. (1963). *Four Theories of the Press.* Urbana: University of Illinois Press. (Originally published 1956)

4

ECONOMIC REALITIES:
OWNERSHIP AND CONTROL

When Frances Cerra was a reporter covering Long Island for *The New York Times*, she believed the billion dollar investment in the construction of a Long Island nuclear power plant was a matter of public concern. She began writing investigative reports about construction delays and cost overruns that might amount to hundreds of millions of taxpayer dollars. Her editors at *The Times* disagreed with her and took her off the story. Unhappy with being second-guessed and reassigned, Cerra left the newspaper.

Michael Kelly, then editor of *The New Republic,* was fired in 1997 by the magazine's owner, Martin Peretz, because Peretz thought Kelly's columns about President Bill Clinton and Vice President Al Gore were too critical. Similarly, that same year, *New York Daily News* editor Pete Hamill lost his job after clashing with owner Mortimer Zuckerman, who disagreed with Hamill about news values. Zuckerman also owns *U.S. News & World Report* and in 1998 fired its editor, Jim Fallows, a widely respected journalist. When an owner and an editor disagree, the owner's views prevail, Fallows later said.

And when a longtime correspondent for ABC News, Bob Zelnick, told his bosses in 1997 he'd been offered a contract to write a book about Vice President Gore, they at first agreed to allow him to proceed with the project. In September of that year they reversed themselves, saying they thought the book project might bias his ABC reporting about Gore. They told him he would have to break his book contract and return his advance if he wished to continue to report for ABC News. Zelnick refused to abandon the book project and reluctantly left the network.

These examples are just a few of many that illustrate the reality of mass media in America: The owner is the source of media control in a libertarian system. As A.J. Liebling once tartly observed, "Freedom of the press is for those who own one" (quoted in Stephens, 1988, p. 211). *The New Republic*, *The New York Times,* and the American Broadcasting Company (ABC) are all privately owned businesses, and as such, their owners are entitled to have complete and final authority over all aspects of their enterprises, including staffing, editorial content, programming, and policy.

To comprehend the influence of mass media on America's culture and economy, one must understand who owns and operates them. Mass media consumers probably don't spend much time contemplating who or what is behind the media they use. Their primary concern is being satisfied with the product. If they are unhappy, few go to the trouble to complain, and, for most, ownership of media for which they are the audience is of little consequence. But for the informed citizen, the serious student of mass media, and anyone contemplating a career in the field, an understanding of the ownership and control of mass communication is absolutely essential.

CHANGING OWNERSHIP PATTERNS: TYPES OF ENTREPRENEURSHIP

Over the two centuries of America's history as a nation, ownership patterns have changed for all businesses, including mass media. What usually begins with a single owner of a small shop grows into a family-run business, then into a large company with nonfamily executives, then into a corporation, which then becomes public and sells stock to shareholders, finally merging with other corporations into global conglomerates. These changes often seem to come naturally as the result of growth, success and failure, and economic conditions.

Small-Business Entrepreneurs. America's first media owners were small business owners, not writers or editors. They were colonial printers who produced legal documents and commercial notices, and, sometimes as a sideline, also published small four-page sheets of local news and summaries of information from abroad. In the nineteenth century, newspapers developed into influential and then profitable businesses. As that happened, an owner often stopped being merely a printer and instead became a newspaper publisher.

Magazine and book production followed a similar pattern. Because magazines and books are not produced as frequently as newspapers, their owners often do not have to own expensive printing equipment. In fact, almost all manufacturing aspects of books and magazines can usually be contracted to other firms, providing the ideal business situation for the small operator or individual entrepreneur.

Partisans. The printed word has always attracted those who would use it to influence readers about causes in which they passionately believed. Many early printers and newspaper owners were unapologetically partisan, passionately devoted to a political cause. In the 13 colonies, the cause was usually independence from Great Britain; that idea fired up the printers' zeal, and they filled their pages with one-sided editorials. For most of them, income from their publications was marginal anyway and profit secondary to the issues they promoted. That partisan role of newspapers continued into the mid-nineteenth century.

Magazines and book publishing often were started by individuals more devoted to special interests and causes, literary, political, or otherwise, than to objective reports. Even though in the late nineteenth and twentieth centuries many magazines reached mass circulations and many books have become best sellers, the vast majority throughout history, even to the present day, have been aimed at small, specialized audiences and are produced by specialists devoted to their fields or interests. Their publishers have usually felt that partisanship was more important than the presentation of objective fact, which they left to the province of newspapers.

Family Businesses. In the eighteenth and nineteenth centuries, before inheritance taxes made it more difficult, successful entrepreneurs passed their businesses on to their families. Many newspaper, magazine, and book publishing enterprises became the property of children, grandchildren, and great grandchildren of their founders. Family ownership even characterized early radio, television, and motion picture businesses, too, and a few founding family members are still prominent in some mass media. But family control will not typify much media ownership in the twenty-first century, partly for tax reasons.

By the beginning of 1998, of more than 1,500 daily newspapers in the United States, only 305 were family-owned, one-newspaper operations. The largest of these was the newspaper in Ohio's state capital, the *Columbus Dispatch*. Other newspapers typical of those totally family owned were *The Bakersfield Californian*, the Fredericksburg, Va., *Free-Lance Star*, the *Daily Herald* in Arlington Heights, Ill., a Chicago suburb, and *The New Mexican* in Santa Fe. Family ownership is a dying tradition.

Press Lords and Media Moguls. Media owners who were powerful individuals began to appear in the eighteenth century but did not really become important until the mid-nineteenth century. Benjamin Franklin was perhaps the first. Before he became a great statesman, scientist, and patriot, he was a successful printer who started a chain of newspapers in the large cities of the 13 colonies, using local printers as his partners to form an early version of a media conglomerate, becoming wealthy in the process. Franklin's periodicals displayed his wit, intelligence, and fine eye for graphic design. It is interesting to note that throughout their early history, many American mass media expressed the individual personalities of their owners.

With the rise of mass circulation newspapers and magazines and best-selling books after the Civil War, a number of important and influential newspaper owners—often called press lords—emerged. Among them were individuals such as Horace Greeley, William Randolph Hearst, Joseph Pulitzer, and Adolph Ochs, all personally involved with running their businesses to further their interests. Greeley used his *New York Tribune* as a tool in his crusade against slavery, liquor, and political corruption. Hearst used his *San Francisco Examiner* and *New York Journal* to further his political agenda, even to instigate the Spanish-American War and to promote himself as a presidential candidate. Pulitzer organized newspaper stunts that achieved circulations of millions of readers for his papers, the *New York World* and *St. Louis Post*. Ochs used *The New York Times* to establish his personal standards of news as a "newspaper of record."

In the twentieth century, many media owners applied their authority behind the scenes, but some powerful new public personalities emerged early in the century as "media moguls" by developing new media into big business. They included people like Louis B. Mayer, the motion picture czar, who built movies into a national medium and for a time controlled much of Hollywood; and David Sarnoff, who developed commercial radio and, with William Paley, established network broadcasting.

The chief magazine patriarch was probably Henry Luce, who started the concept of a news magazine with *Time*, the picture magazine with *Life*, the business magazine with *Fortune*, and the sports magazine with *Sports Illustrated*. Each magazine was personally crafted by Luce and reflected his political and business philosophy, and until his death he remained involved in much of the operation of the magazine empire he had inspired.

Cable television helped create another kind of media godfather, Ted Turner. In the 1960s, he inherited a failing billboard business, rebuilt it, and began buying television stations and libraries of old TV programs and feature films. His creation of a 24-hour TV news channel, Cable News Network (CNN), made him one of the great media innovators of the late twentieth century, and when he ultimately merged his companies with and became vice chairman of Time Warner, he became a prime example of the new multimedia baron.

Certainly the biggest mogul of global multimedia at the beginning of the twenty-first century is Rupert Murdoch. An Australian by birth, he inherited his father's newspaper and from it built a global communications empire, with newspapers, magazines, radio, and television in Australia, Europe, Asia, and North America. Murdoch became an American citizen so he could buy television stations in the United States, where only citizens can own majority stock in broadcast properties. Murdoch is the type of owner for whom news publishing and mass media operations are a significant contributor to a core business in which the owner's social and political views are vigorously expressed.

Inventors and Creators.   For the most part, people who have invented the technologies that have made mass media possible, and those who create the content of mass media, even though they might originate products and claim patent rights and copyrights, rarely become the owners of mass media. Likewise, the eventual owners rarely started as inventors or creators, or writers or journalists.

A good case in point is Thomas Edison, whose experiments with electronics, sound waves, light, and film helped give birth to the recording and motion picture industries. Edison established and controlled many businesses that used his patents, but he did not have the vision to organize companies devoted primarily to mass media. Alexander Graham Bell won patents for the telephone and was able to control the business for a time, but never as a creator of consumer mass media. Guglielmo Marconi, whose experiments contributed much to the development of radio, used the device only for sending business messages. It was David Sarnoff who later had the vision to create radio as a public medium.

At times inventor or creator types have sought to gain control of their media. In 1919, actors Mary Pickford and Douglas Fairbanks, actor and director Charlie Chaplin, and director D. W. Griffith, upset at seeing their artistry taken over by business people, formed their own movie studio, United Artists. Nevertheless, the artists were not good enough at business to keep it going for long, and it came under the control of business executives (today it is part of Metro Goldwyn Mayer [MGM]).

Some artists, such as Walt Disney and actress Lucille Ball, managed to control successful companies that produced their work and programs. But the companies they started ultimately were managed by professional executives, not artists or actors. Steven Spielberg, one of the most creative directors in the history of Hollywood motion pictures, is a contemporary example of a creator who has become major owner of a production company, Dreamworks SKG. But these examples are few and far between in mass media industry.

The newspaper industry has had few owners who started as journalists or writers, but magazines and newsletters have sometimes been an exception to the rule. They have often attracted creative people, perhaps because they can be started and successfully built with little money. In the nineteenth century, *Frank Leslie's Illustrated Weekly* and the muckraking magazine *McClure's* were both successfully created and owned by former journalists for whom they were named.

Examples from the twentieth century of creative people with little money but a new idea, who were able to become successful magazine owners, include Harold Ross (*The New Yorker*), Lila and Dewitt Wallace (*The Reader's Digest*), David Lawrence (*US News & World Report*), Hugh Hefner (*Playboy*), and Martha Stewart (*Martha Stewart Living*). Newsletters require even less starting capital. Willard M. Kiplinger, a struggling young Associated Press reporter in the early 1920s, was able to build a successful newsletter empire on the strength of his creative ideas.

Another example of blending creativity and inexpensive technology is the mid-1990s emergence of the *zine*, a magazine of sorts, aimed at a specialized audience, usually produced by one person, often using photocopying production (sometimes circulated on the Internet, where they are known as *e-zines*). *Plotz*, for example, was a photocopied zine produced by a young New Yorker about her experience of Jewishness. It was 24 pages long, reproduced in about 2,000 copies, some of which were sold in stores, with a subscription price of $1 and two first-class stamps. But zines were usually not produced to become mass media or make anyone rich.

By the beginning of the twenty-first century, we can see creative genius again coupled with new technologies—computers, desktop publishing, and of course the Internet—to form inexpensive yet sometimes successful media. A number of Internet Web sites, developed by one creative person, have become financially successful. The "Drudge Report" has become one of the more famous. (For more on this, see chap. 15.)

Investors. With the rising financial success of mass media, a new type of owner—the investor—began to appear in the twentieth century. Building a new medium into a mass medium almost always requires money and business know-how, which inventors and creators often lack. They often turn to outside investment for the needed cash. These outsiders and their business partners often invest until they own a majority of the media company and thus acquire control.

Electronic media, requiring large amounts of money for complex and expensive equipment, were often the first to turn to outside investors. Radio, television, motion pictures, and the sound recording business have for the most part been organized as investment companies. In the early 1920s, when regular radio broadcasting began, its investors not only owned controlling stock in stations that transmitted programming, but some also owned majority shares in companies that manufactured the radio sets over which people could hear the broadcasts, an early form of vertical integration. As the twentieth century progressed, the investor-as-owner characterized much of the print media as well. In the twenty-first century, most mass media are owned and controlled by businessmen concerned about their investments rather than by partisan zealots, artists, creators, writers, or journalists.

Professionals, Executives, and Managers.   To manage the emerging mass media companies, investors concerned more with money than with the product itself ultimately turned to business managers rather than to inventors or creators who had started the businesses. Managers represent and serve at the pleasure of owner–stockholders. They tend to be business school graduates with MBAs, or lawyers, accountants, and investment bankers. One of the exceptions to this is the Gannett Company, the largest newspaper publisher in America; its chief executive officers (CEO) from its inception have been journalists who have worked their way up the ranks as reporters and editors, including its most famous CEO, Allen Neuharth, who created *USA TODAY*. However, chief executive officers of most newspapers and other mass media businesses are increasingly more likely to come from the business side of a company, such as sales, law, or accounting, or from outside the news business and media altogether.

TYPES OF MEDIA FIRMS

Mass media organizations are either privately owned by a single person or family or a partnership or privately owned by a public corporation. In the United States, a publicly owned company is not owned by the public at large or owned and controlled by the government; *public corporation* means that the company's stock can be purchased by the general public and is not under anyone's exclusive control.

Private Companies

Privately held companies are owned by individuals outright who do not offer shares in the company to anyone outside their group. Often in the media field, these have been family-owned concerns, such as The Hearst Corporation, publisher of magazines, newspapers, and books, and operator of radio and television stations, a news service, television programming, and production facilities. The Hearst Corporation is owned by The Hearst Family Trust and has been administered under the terms of founder William Randolph Hearst's will since his death in 1951.

Advance Publications, Inc., which owns newspapers and magazines and is controlled by the Newhouse family, is another example of private ownership of multiple media properties. Included in the category of private businesses would be the family-owned newspapers described earlier. But private mass media companies are declining. In 1997, of the top 25 newspaper companies in the United States, only nine were privately held. See Table 4.1 for examples of newspaper companies and their ownership status.

Corporate Ownership

By far the largest category of mass media company type by the beginning of the twenty-first century is the publicly owned corporation. How these corporations came to be is an instructive lesson for anyone concerned with mass communication. It is a story of mergers and consolidation, expansion and acquisition. Figure 4.1 illustrates this point. A few corporate profiles might best illustrate the twentieth-century history of corporate ownership. These profiles are separated into media categories, because each medium has developed somewhat different structures, although consolidation has been the primary thrust for all of them.

Newspaper Industry Examples.   The largest newspaper company in the United States, in terms of circulation (average number of copies sold daily), is Gannett Co., Inc. The company traces its origins to 1906, when founder Frank Gannett bought a half-interest in the *Gazette*, in Elmira, N.Y. Gannett eventually bought out his partners and purchased other daily newspapers, mostly in the northeastern United States. Gannett also acquired radio and television stations and started a news service in Washington, D.C., to supply his news organizations with reports from the nation's capital. His successors continued expanding both newspaper and broadcasting holdings to all sections of the United States.

Frank Gannett started his company with just $3,000 in savings, $7,000 in loans, and $10,000 in notes. In 1997, Gannett Co., Inc. had revenues of $4.7 billion. Its 80-plus newspapers, including *USA TODAY*, had a combined daily circulation exceeding 6.5 million—more than 10 percent of the total U.S. newspaper circulation. The company's 20 television stations reached 16 percent of the U.S. market.

Knight Ridder, the second-largest newspaper company, was formed in 1974 through a merger of Knight Newspapers, Inc., and Ridder Publications, Inc. As had Frank Gannett, both Charles Knight and Herman Ridder started out with single newspapers. In 1903, Knight purchased the *Akron* (Ohio) *Beacon Journal*. The Knight Newspapers company was founded by his son, John S. Knight, who inherited the *Beacon Journal* from his father in 1933. Knight Newspapers went on to make acquisitions such as *The Miami Herald* in 1937, the *Detroit Free Press* in 1940, *The Charlotte* (N.C.) *Observer* in 1955, and *The Philadelphia Inquirer* and *Philadelphia Daily News* in 1969.

TABLE 4.1

Type of Ownership / Top 25 U.S. Newspaper Companies

		Type	Circulation
1.	Gannett	Public	5,953,284
2.	Knight Ridder	Board	3,894,711
3.	Advance Publications	Private	2,780,364
4.	Times Mirror	Traded	2,347,515
5.	Dow Jones & Co.	Traded	2,347,115
6.	New York Times Co.	Traded	2,236,091
7.	MediaNews Group	Private	1,385,800
8.	The E. W. Scripps Co.	Traded	1,353,799
9.	The Hearst Corp.	Private	1,325,973
10.	Thomson Newspapers	Traded	1,309,678
11.	Tribune Co.	Board	1,241,863
12.	Cox Newspapers, Inc.	Private	1,123,627
13.	Hollinger International	Traded	1,060,696
14.	McClatchy Newspapers	Traded	964,131
15.	Freedom Newspapers	Private	961,320
16.	A. H. Belo Corp.	Traded	899,055
17.	Washington Post Co.	Traded	830,626
18.	Media General	Traded	816,711
19.	Central Newspapers	Traded	800,440
20.	The Copley Press, Inc.	Private	790,014
21.	Morris Communications	Private	739,144
22.	Donrey Media Group	Private	709,182
23.	Chronicle Publishing	Private	643,672
24.	Lee Enterprises	Public	643,241
25.	Pulitzer Publishing	Traded	573,276
		TOTAL	37,758,328*

Companies in which newspaper is dominant form of business, although the company may own other types of businesses as well, ranked by total newspaper circulation as of September 1997. Public: Single type of voting stock, all publicly owned. Board: Public owns majority of voting stock, but family members continue on board of directors. Traded: Two classes of stock; publicly traded stock has limited voting rights. Private: Founding family controls the company outright.

*Total U.S. average daily paid newspaper circulation in September 1997 was 56.7 million.

Source: Condensed and adapted with permission from "U.S. Newspaper Ownership Trends," *Presstime* magazine April 1998, p. 29.

In 1892, Herman Ridder bought the *Staats-Zeitung*, the leading German-language newspaper in the United States. In the 1920s, Ridder Publications began a string of acquisitions that included *The Journal of Commerce,* the *St. Paul Pioneer Press,* and *St. Paul Dispatch* and majority ownership stakes in newspapers in Aberdeen, S.D., and Grand Forks, N.D. The Ridders acquired seven more newspapers and launched the Commodity News Service before merging with Knight Newspapers.

After the merger, Knight Ridder continued to grow by acquisition, entering the television and cable businesses, flirting with online financial information services, and continuing to buy newspapers. From two newspapers owned by two different families, the Knights and the Ridders, grew a company whose 1997 revenues were $2.9 billion. Both Gannett and Knight Ridder had first offered their stock for sale to the public in the late 1960s—Gannett in 1967, Knight Ridder in 1969.

Broadcast Industry Examples. The Columbia Broadcasting System (CBS) is one of many broadcast operations that have been acquired by larger nonmedia companies. CBS traces its roots to United Independent Broadcasters, Inc. (UIB), a radio group founded in 1927. William Paley bought UIB in 1928, changed its name to Columbia, and pioneered the idea of stations grouped together into networks to increase their access to program content. His CBS network produced various programs, including news, for its affiliated network stations. The company started television broadcasting in the late 1940s and expanded the network to include TV programs for its own and its affiliated TV stations. The company also acquired recording and magazine businesses and studios for television and movie production.

In 1995, CBS became part of Westinghouse Electric Corporation, until then a venerable American company known for its refrigeration units, power generators, energy systems, and other industrial components. The acquisition represented a return for

---

- Knight Ridder acquired four newspapers from Walt Disney Company's ABC unit for $1.65 billion.

- A. H. Belo Corporation acquired The Providence Journal Company for $1.5 billion.

- McClatchy Newspapers purchased Cowles Media for $1.4 billion.

- Media General bought Park Communications for $710 million.

- Pulitzer Publishing bought Scripps League Newspapers for $214 million.

- Seagram (MCA) purchased Multimedia Entertainment from Gannett for $45 million; Brillstein-Grey Communications for $100 million; 50 percent of Interscope Records for $200 million.

- Gaylord Entertainment acquired Word Record Music Group for $110 million.

- Alliance Entertainment purchased Red Ant Entertainment for $45 million.

FIG. 4.1. Selected media acquisitions, 1996–1998.
(From Veronis, Suhler, & Associates, Inc.; press reports.)

Westinghouse to its broadcasting roots, which had been in radio. Westinghouse had owned KDKA, the Pittsburgh radio station that transmitted the first commercial radio broadcast in 1920. After buying CBS, Westinghouse proceeded to sell off its other businesses and focused exclusively on broadcasting, even changing its corporate name from Westinghouse to CBS. In addition to its television holdings, the company controlled the largest group of radio stations in the United States. Its 1997 revenues were $5.4 billion. (For more on Westinghouse and CBS, see chap. 11.)

From the mid-1960s to the mid-1980s, most mergers and acquisitions of media companies had been by other media companies. The Westinghouse transaction shows how media ownership was changing in the 1990s. It was no longer uncommon for media companies to be acquired by a nonmedia company. The National Broadcasting Company (NBC) went through a similar process when its parent company, Radio Corporation of America (RCA), was purchased by General Electric in 1986. Other nonmedia companies, such as groups of business investors, bought media properties: For example, Hicks, Muse, Tate, & Furst, a Dallas investment group, purchased large shares in dozens of radio stations and many of the nation's motion picture theaters in the 1990s.

Entertainment Industry Examples.   Time Warner, the largest media corporation in the world, devoted primarily to entertainment, was formed in 1989 through the merger of Time Inc. and Warner Communications. It includes *Time*, *Fortune,* and *Sports Illustrated* magazines; CNN, Warner Brothers, Castle Rock Entertainment, and New Line Cinema; the Book-of-the-Month Club; Cinemax and Home Box Office (HBO); and the Atlantic, Warner, and Elektra recording labels.

Time Inc. was the magazine and book publishing empire that started with *Time* magazine in 1923 by Luce and Briton Hadden. Warner Communications grew out of Warner Brothers, a motion picture studio started in the 1920s. As Warner Communications, it became an entertainment giant with interests in movie production, motion picture theaters, and recorded music. The 1996 acquisition of Turner Broadcasting's powerful cable channels and huge motion picture library added to Time Warner's own cable channels and cartoon library. This global media giant, a major player in nearly every medium worldwide, had 1997 revenues of $24.6 billion.

The Walt Disney Company, with 1997 revenues of $22.5 billion, is second only to Time Warner in the size of its annual revenues. The legacy left by its founder includes a brand recognition unparalleled in the global entertainment industry. Disney and his brother, Roy, started it all when they opened the Disney Brothers Studio in 1923 on the strength of a contract Walt had received to produce a series of animated short subjects called the "Alice Comedies." Five years later, in 1928, Walt produced his first animated film with sound effects and dialogue and introduced the character whose persona remains the company's emblem three-quarters of a century later, Mickey Mouse.

During his lifetime, Disney produced animated films and feature-length movies, opened Disneyland, the theme park in Anaheim, Calif., and launched a weekly television series that aired, under various titles, for an astounding 29 seasons. Disney himself controlled the various companies he had started for his different entertainment and amusement businesses, but he also began offering public stock in Walt Disney Productions in 1940. By the time of his death in 1966, the company was perhaps the primary source of family entertainment in America. And though there were still some Disney family members involved in the company, it became a corporate giant managed primarily by nonfamily business executives.

Disney's successors started new divisions, modernized and expanded older ones, and made acquisitions such as Capital Cities/ABC (which gave Disney control of a television network) and Miramax Film Corporation. Through acquisition and expansion, Disney executives molded a vertically integrated company that created content, managed its distribution, exhibited it on Disney-owned broadcast and cable television channels and home video, published it in Disney-owned magazines and books, and sold it in Disney stores. See Fig. 4.2 for a list of Disney holdings.

Another vertically integrated entertainment giant is Viacom, whose operations include Blockbuster Video, MTV Networks, Paramount Pictures, Paramount Television, Showtime Networks, and the Famous Players and United Cinemas International theater chains. Viacom also owns a film library that includes "Cheers," "I Love Lucy," and "The Honeymooners"—a lucrative source of syndicated programming for cable channels.

Viacom is essentially controlled by its chairman, Sumner Redstone. He had been chairman of the board, chief executive officer, and majority shareholder of National Amusements, Inc. (NAI), a closely held corporation operating movie theaters. When NAI bought a controlling interest in Viacom in 1987, Redstone became Viacom's controlling shareholder, meaning he could influence policy and product development across a broad spectrum of entertainment media. In 1997, Viacom's revenues were $13.2 billion.

Advertising and Public Relations Industry Examples.   Advertising agencies also have gone through much consolidation. Large ad agencies often look for acquisitions of smaller agencies that will help them fill gaps in expertise and experience and equip them to take on clients from industries they haven't worked with or from new regions or countries. More important, owning a number of different advertising agencies eliminates the appearance of conflict of interest among competing clients, since each client can be represented by a different agency within the parent advertising company.

An example of a large advertising company that has grown by acquisition is Interpublic Group of Companies, Inc. Its beginnings date to the turn of the century, with the birth of the Alfred W. Erickson agency in 1902 and the H. K. McCann Company in 1911. In 1930, the two agencies merged to form McCann Erickson, and in 1954 they acquired the Marschalk and Pratt Agency. Interpublic was officially created in 1960 as a holding company for its two wholly owned subsidiaries, McCann Erickson and Marschalk and Pratt. Interpublic offered its stock to the public in 1971 and began a long series of acquisitions throughout the United States and abroad that by 1997 made it into the biggest advertising company in the world, with revenues of $3.13 billion.

The Walt Disney Company

Motion Pictures

Walt Disney Pictures

Touchstone Pictures

Caravan Pictures

Hollywood Pictures

Miramax Films

Buena Vista Pictures Distribution

Home Video and Interactive Products

Buena Vista Home Entertainment

Theater/Stage

Walt Disney Theatrical Productions

Broadcast and Cable Television

ABC Television Network

10 television stations reaching nearly 25% of U.S. households

Buena Vista Television (syndicated programming)

The Disney Channel

Classic Sports Network

Joint ventures in cable

 Lifetime Television (50% ownership)

 ESPN, ESPN2, and ESPN International (80% ownership through ABC)

 A&E Television Networks (37.5% ownership)

 E! Entertainment Television (34.4% ownership)

The History Channel (37.5% ownership)

Walt Disney Television

Walt Disney Television International (pay television programming abroad)

Walt Disney Television Animation

Touchstone Television

Radio

26 radio stations

ABC radio networks with 2,900 affiliates reaching 140 million listeners weekly

Music

Hollywood Records

Mammoth Records

Walt Disney Records

Magazines

Fairchild publications, which publishes *W, Jane, Los Angeles,* and nine other fashion and retail trade publications

continued on next page

Books

Disney Press

Hyperion Books

Recreation

Disneyland and Disneyworld Theme Parks and Resorts

Disney Cruise Line

Anaheim Mighty Ducks (National Hockey League franchise)

Anaheim Angels (Major League Baseball franchise)

Retail

636 Disney Stores

ESPN—The Store

**FIG. 4.2. A snapshot of The Walt Disney Company's vertically integrated businesses.
(From 1997 Annual Report of The Walt Disney Co.)**

Advertising agencies have also sought acquisition of public relations firms, to complement their advertising and marketing expertise with public relations services, including issues and image management and media relations. For example, Young & Rubicam, Inc., well known for its advertising and marketing work, also owns Burson-Marsteller, a large American public relations firm. Similarly, WPP Group, a marketing and advertising powerhouse, owns Hill and Knowlton, a sprawling public relations agency with 51 offices in 28 countries.

Types of Stock

Publicly owned corporations can have two different forms of publicly owned stock, and these differences can be important to our understanding of media ownership and control.

    Stock With All Shares Having the Same Voting Rights.   CBS, the Interpublic Group, and Gannett Company, Inc., are examples of corporations with one type of stock, common stock; each share has equal weight in voting on the company's directors who set the policies. The more shares you own, the more power you could have within the company. This kind of stock allows anyone with enough money to buy stock until they can control the company. Money is the ultimate power.

    Until the late 1960s, the Gannett Company had two kinds of stock, voting and nonvoting, and, until his death, either Frank Gannett or the Gannett Foundation, which he controlled, owned all the voting stock. Employees owned shares of nonvoting stock. No one outside the company could purchase shares. This meant he had absolute control of the company, even though others might own part of it. When the Gannett Company offered its stock to the public in 1967, Gannett went to a single form of stock, where each share has an equal vote. (Of course, those owning the most shares have the most power.) Employees who had owned shares of the old nonvoting stock were allowed to trade their shares for the new common stock. When they did so, they immediately had more power within the company in the sense that their shares could be used to vote for the company's directors.

No members of the Gannett family still serve on Gannett's board. But some public corporations started or owned by families do still have family members on their boards. Knight Ridder is an example. It also has only one kind of stock, but members of the founding family continued to serve on the company's board of directors after the company went public, P, Anthony Ridder, serving only at the pleasure of the directors, was elected chairman of the board and chief executive officer of the company.

Two Tiers of Stock With Different Voting Rights.   Viacom, New York Times Company, Dow Jones, and the Washington Post Company are examples of corporations with two classes of stock. One, Class B stock, is traded publicly but has limited voting rights. The other, Class A stock, has preferential voting rights that effectively give its owners complete control of the company. Usually that stock remains in the hands of a few individuals, often the founding family, and rich outsiders cannot take over the company by buying stock.

The Washington Post Company is a good example. Although it offered shares of its stock to the public in 1971, the Graham family retained most of the voting stock. Katharine Graham inherited *The Washington Post* newspaper from her father, Eugene Meyer, who had bought it in 1933 when it was in bankruptcy. Meyer built it up, and his son-in-law, Phil Graham, helped make the newspaper into a profitable journalistic enterprise, including *Newsweek* magazine and broadcast properties. After her husband's death in 1963, Katharine Graham took over management of the company, which became financially successful and politically influential.

Ownership of Class B stock, although having little power over policy in the company, can still be a good investment. The Washington Post Company stock was priced at $20 a share when the company went public; that stock has split two-for-one twice and had risen in value at one time to more than $600 a share. A person who bought 100 shares in 1971 for $2000 by the mid-1990s could have sold those shares for about $240,000.

GLOBAL MEDIA CONGLOMERATES

Consolidation of newspaper ownership that started in the nineteenth century steadily increased through the twentieth. Centralization of news processing started with the development of news agencies in the mid-nineteenth century. Centralization and nationalization of broadcast news and programming began with the development of networks in the 1920s and continued to the end of the century.

The biggest impetus toward centralization of ownership, content, and control, however, came during the Ronald Reagan administration in the 1980s, when the philosophy of the free-market economy was more enthusiastically embraced than ever before. The free-market concept was applied even to many areas that the government had long regulated, including broadcasting. The deregulation of broadcasting was a major factor in the development of global media conglomerates.

Ben Bagdikian (1992) pointed out that by 1989, 29 corporations in the United States controlled most of the business in daily newspapers, magazines, television, books, and motion pictures. By 1996, according to Robert McChesney (1997), nine of those firms held the dominant share of American media, and only about 50 firms worldwide controlled the overwhelming majority of the world's mass media.

At that time the nine firms were Time Warner, Disney (ABC), Bertelsmann (a German firm), Viacom, Murdoch's News Corporation, Sony (counting media only), Tele-Communications Inc. (TCI), Thomson Corporation (a British company), and General Electric (counting NBC media only). Immediately following the top nine were Advance Publications (Newhouse), Westinghouse (CBS media only), and Gannett Company, Inc. Table 4.2 is a more recent list of the world's top 25 firms.

GOVERNMENT REGULATION OF OWNERSHIP

If ownership of mass media becomes a matter of public concern, we need to ask ourselves, What role should the government play in regulating it to protect the public? As chapter 5 shows, the Constitution, which guarantees freedom of the press—as interpreted by the courts over the years—restricts government authority over mass media. Except for limits on monopoly ownership, the government has never regulated ownership of any print media.

When broadcasting developed, however, it was perceived as a medium that could be far more powerful than print, and it used public property, the airwaves. Because the broadcast spectrum is of finite size and cannot accommodate an unlimited number of users, and because the airwaves belong only to the people of the United States and not to individual licensees, the FCC historically has restricted how much broadcast spectrum any one individual or company could control. It was reasoned that government could and should exercise more authority over broadcasting, especially over ownership, in order to prevent a powerful medium using public property from falling into the hands of just a few people. That philosophy was not held to be in violation of the First Amendment of the Constitution, according to rulings by the Supreme Court, and broadcast regulations were written into law.

It is important to note that broadcast regulations apply primarily to questions of ownership, not to content. The Supreme Court has always been wary of any law that would interfere with content, with some exceptions, such as pornography. Content rights and limits are considered further in chapter 5. Of course, all media owners are subject to all the other laws that apply to any business, including environmental laws; fair-labor statutes; federal, state and local laws; and regulations related to the operation of a business, including public disclosure of information about their financial performance for publicly owned companies. Here we want to examine ownership rights and limitations that have raised some special concerns for mass media in three categories: broadcasting, monopoly ownership, and taxation.

TABLE 4.2

Top 25 Media Companies Ranked by 1997 Media Revenues

1.	Time Warner
2.	Walt Disney Co.
3.	Tele-Communications Inc.
4.	News Corp.
5.	CBS Corp.
6.	NBC TV (General Electric Co)
7.	Gannett Co.
8.	Advance Publications
9.	Cox Enterprises
10.	New York Times Co.
11.	Hearst Corp.
12.	Knight Ridder
13.	Viacom
14.	America Online
15.	Times Mirror Co.
16.	Tribune Co.
17.	MediaOne
18.	Comcast Corp.
19.	Cablevision Systems Corp.
20.	Washington Post Co.
21.	DirecTV (General Motors Corp)
22.	Dow Jones & Co.
23.	Thomson Corp
24.	Reed Elsevier
25.	A.H. Belo Corp.

Source: Reprinted with permission from the August 17, 1998, issue of *Advertising Age*. Copyright © 1998 by Crain Communications, Inc.

Broadcast Regulation and Deregulation

The Federal Communications Commission was organized to oversee broadcast regulations, especially the question of ownership. It was given the power to license broadcasting and to award licenses to individuals or to take them away. Limitations on ownership were applied from the beginning, in 1934. No owner could own more than seven radio stations, and only one in any given listening area. A license existed for a limited time—only 3 years—after which a new license had to be applied for.

With the development of FM radio and television, these limits were also applied to those areas of broadcasting, becoming the famous 7–7–7 rule. No owner could own more than seven AM, seven FM, and seven TV stations, and only one of these in a listening or viewing area, still only for a 3-year period at a time.

That rule continued until the Reagan administration's first attempt at deregulation. In 1983, ownership potential was expanded to 12 TV stations (reaching no more than 25 percent of U.S. households) and 12 AM and 12 FM radio stations. The new regulations also extended the life of a license to 5 years for TV licenses and to 7 years for radio, and made it easier to renew a license.

The 1996 Telecommunications Act loosened ownership controls even further. It raised the cap on households that could be reached from 25 percent to 35 percent, and removed most restrictions on the total number of stations that could be owned (although some limits remained on the number of stations owned in a single market). The act also extended the term of a broadcast license to 8 years.

The result of these changes was a flurry of buying and selling of broadcast properties, particularly radio stations, as corporations formed larger and larger groups. In radio, for example, by the end of 1998, four multibillion-dollar corporations had gained control of nearly one third of the U.S. radio business. The corporations were CBS; Hicks, Muse, Tate, & Furst; Jacor; and Clear Channel Communications.

The FCC still has a rule that prohibits *cross ownership*, in which an individual or corporation owns both a newspaper and a broadcast station in the same market. The rule, adopted in 1975, grandfathered in some newspaper-broadcast combinations existing at the time. The FCC waived the cross-ownership rule in a few cases in which enforcement of the rule would have jeopardized the operations of one of the properties or would have forced a sale of one of the properties at a depressed price. The purpose of the cross-ownership prohibition is to promote diverse, separately owned voices in a community, much as the Newspaper Preservation Act (see further on) is intended to do.

Not surprisingly, large media groups would like to see the cross-ownership ban eliminated. They contend that proliferation of media, such as cable television and the Internet, creates more competition, and that the Telecommunications Act frees cable and telephone companies to enter each other's businesses in the same markets, making the local-market newspaper-broadcast ban unnecessarily selective and unfair.

Anti-Monopoly Laws

Technically, no regulations similar to the FCC's have limited how large a print media company can be or how many print media properties it can own. However, the United States has anti-monopoly laws that are invoked when a corporate owner becomes so powerful, so dominant, that competition becomes nearly impossible. These laws are codified in the Sherman Antitrust Act of 1890. The U.S. Department of Justice is responsible for its enforcement. It evaluates unusual competitive situations and prosecutes companies it believes are violating antitrust laws. The Justice Department also is responsible for monitoring congressionally sponsored solutions to competitive challenges.

For example, the Newspaper Preservation Act of 1970 was passed by Congress in response to changing competitive situations in the newspaper industry. If two separately owned newspapers in a city could show that the cost of competing is actually damaging them to the point that one can be considered a failing newspaper, the Newspaper Preservation Act permits them to combine their business operations but not their newsrooms so that two separate editorial voices can be preserved. The Justice Department must approve applications for such *joint operating agreements*. JOAs, as they are known, have a mixed record of success in their communities: Of the 28 JOAs in existence or established since 1970, only 13 were left by 1999. Among the cities with JOAs are Detroit, Cincinnati, Honolulu, and San Francisco.

If companies do not agree with the Justice Department's decisions on antitrust matters, they can initiate a lawsuit through the U.S. court system. They can also prevail on Congress to enact laws that will recognize problematic competitive situations—such as it did with failing newspapers—and help to remedy them.

The Newspaper Preservation Act is just one example of congressional legislation designed to assist media owners in special circumstances. Media companies employ lobbyists and work through industry trade associations (such as the Newspaper Association of America, the National Association of Broadcasters, the National Cable Television Association, the Motion Picture Association of America, and the Recording Industry Association of America) to take their concerns to the attention of members of Congress and press for favorable legislation to mitigate problems.

Taxation

The *free* in *free press* does not extend to paying taxes. Like individuals and other corporations, owners of mass media must pay taxes on their income and their records are subject to review and audit by the U.S. Internal Revenue Service. However, media cannot be singled out for special taxes in order to limit their operations.

In 1936, the U.S. Supreme Court expressly ruled against a special newspaper advertising tax that Louisiana Senator Huey Long's political machine had sought because newspapers had been critical of him. Periodically, other states have considered taxes on income from advertising, but these efforts have not succeeded. The First Amendment has been interpreted to mean that media cannot be required to pay special taxes that other businesses do not have to pay.

The federal government and many states also collect inheritance taxes when people die. Properties that pass from one generation to the next have sometimes had to be sold to pay these taxes. Such sales are usually to corporations, causing some critics to say that the tax is part of the media consolidation problem. But family media sales to corporations have sometimes also been caused by disagreement among family members.

CONCERNS ABOUT MEDIA CONSOLIDATION

Have government statutes and regulations such as are described here kept freedom of speech and of the press in balance with media owners' accountability to society at large? Has the increasing consolidation of media ownership decreased the quality, fairness, responsiveness, and diversity of voices and opinion? Do fewer companies controlling more media result in an unhealthy concentration of influence over important cultural development? Naturally there are opposing views on these questions.

Corporate owners of mass media answer that their very size enables them to take risks a smaller company cannot afford. They can be more innovative and provide more service and greater value simply because economies of scale work in their favor. They argue that they can protect freedom of the press better, because they are able to pay high costs of defending libel and other lawsuits brought by those who seek to silence the press. A large and successful media company can better resist advertiser pressures on critical editorial content, the corporations say. A big company can more efficiently promote and protect the talents of its writers and artists than a little one can, they say.

Media watchdog groups who monitor behavior and output of media corporations feel it is a mistake to ignore the implications of media ownership, since mass media have such enormous impact on society. They say it seems obvious that the rise to dominance and control of the world's media by a few companies should be a matter of much public debate and concern. They argue that antimonopoly laws of the twentieth century seem to have failed to make communication ownership as widely dispersed as possible. Complacency about these concerns among readers, viewers, and listeners will ensure declining quality in publishing and programming. They contend that continuing consolidation among media companies will eliminate independent voices, fostering conformity and threatening democracy. Here is an analysis of the main concerns.

Conflicting Interests and Influencing News

The most serious charge by critics is that consolidation of ownership makes corporate executives more concerned with profit than with public service. The most serious result is that conflicts of interest are more likely to affect the company's news handling and judgment. Corporate control of news organizations could mean news might be selected to benefit the parent company. Critics cite accounts of journalists delaying a story to benefit a political or business objective, soft-pedaling accusations about deceptive practices that might offend an advertiser, killing a story that makes the company or a business ally look bad, and "puffing" a story to flatter corporate executives or allies or to pillory enemies.

Media scholar Mark Crispin Miller (1997) described some examples of such inherent conflicts:

> Glance at the ownership charts ... and see why, say, Tom Brokaw [of NBC News] might find it difficult to introduce stories about nuclear power [a key business of NBC's parent, General Electric.] Or why it is unlikely ABC News will ever again air an exposé of Disney's practices, as "PrimeTime Live" did in 1990 [Disney acquired ABC in 1996]; or, indeed, why CNN [now part of Time Warner]—or any of the others—will not touch the biggest story of them all: the media monopoly itself. (p. 4)

When journalist Ted Koppel, anchor of ABC's "Nightline," asked his network for comment on a report on the 1996 Telecommunications Act, he got nowhere with ABC or, for that matter, with any of the other networks. In his on-air introduction, Koppel said:

> It's possibly the most important communications bill in history, and here's what the networks had to say about it. NBC said, "No comment." ABC suggested that we talk to CBS, who also told us, "No comment." And Fox? They said, "No comment." (qtd. in Triano, 1997, p. 19)

This illustrates critic Den Bagdikian's (1992) point that "dominant corporations can, through their control of news and other public information, postpone public awareness for dangerously long periods" (p. x).

To be fair, it must be acknowledged that attempts to influence news reporting did not begin with corporate ownership of media. Individual media moguls, whose companies were private, also appropriated news columns of their publications, as well as editorial pages, to advance their agendas, favor friends, and cultivate advertisers. William Randolph Hearst was famous for altering or omitting facts to make a story support his world view.

Losing Public Trust

Critics say the general public perceives inherent conflict of interest between business owners and journalists to be real. A January 1997 nationwide survey on public attitudes toward news media found that 88 percent of respondents believed corporate owners improperly influenced news reporting (54 percent said they believed this occurred often, 34 percent sometimes). The same number said they also believed advertisers did so. Ninety-one percent said they believed news reporting is improperly influenced by media's desire to make profits (63 percent often, 28 percent sometimes).

But the public does not appear to be hostile to the idea of media mergers themselves. A 1995 poll found that 37 percent thought media mergers were good for consumers, 43 percent thought they were bad, and 6 percent thought they had no effect on consumers. The rest of those surveyed were undecided (Gitlin, 1996).

Declining Quality

Critics argue that quality declines when a corporation acquires a family-controlled, locally owned medium—a newspaper or broadcast station—or when one media conglomerate absorbs another. They say consolidation results in increased profits at the expense of quality. When higher profit goals and greater efficiencies are imposed, staff size is often reduced through layoffs, and professionalism declines when senior staff members retire and are replaced only with the youngest, least experienced, and cheapest labor, or not replaced at all, with the consequent decline in quality. Corporate owners answer that staff training often increases after an acquisition, and that other resources are made available to the staff that prior owners may have been unable to afford.

Critics say an emphasis on profit makes employees reluctant or unable to spend funds on projects that sustain or raise the quality of their work. Corporate owners disagree, saying they have no incentive to underinvest in quality projects; if underinvestment takes place, that decision is most often made by local or division executives. However, critics respond, local executives must account for their budget decisions to corporate superiors and may be intimidated by those above who must approve the expenditures.

Critics say the shift of personnel that takes place when one company acquires another also causes quality to decline. New executives often lack local knowledge and sensitivity to local needs. The departure of long-term employees contributes to the erosion of "institutional memory" inside the news organization. For their part, corporations reply that critics undervalue the fresh perspective of new executives, and that sometimes fair judgment of their capabilities is lost in the critics' nostalgia for the good old days, whether the old days were superior or not.

Controlling Access to Advertising

Corporate chieftains can influence news reporting, but they also can control access to advertising. When News Corporation's Twentieth Century Fox unit tried to purchase advertising time for its animated film *Anastasia* during ABC's "Wonderful World of Disney" program in 1997, Disney-owned ABC refused. ABC's official reason was that there might be confusion between the Fox film and the Disney images, but the denial was interpreted to indicate that Disney was using its television network to block advertising by its competitors.

Increasing Vertical Integration

Perhaps critics' key concern is a global media conglomerate's ability to control all aspects of the market, through vertical integration of media enterprises. Vertical integration characterizes a company that owns the content, the distribution process, and the delivery system that presents the information to the consumer. Vertical integration allows the organization to control multiple types of media and, within each type, to control many individual media units.

Earliest media companies owned one media unit, or at most a few, in one medium. This meant they had to compete with other units and other media, and their competition provided some check and balance through reporting and critical review and commentary. Vertical integration, on the other hand, takes place when one media company buys other media units—for example, a newspaper company buys magazines and book publishing units, radio and television stations, perhaps movies and recorded music as well. Such a company can use its various media to promote each other, without critical comment.

Media owners say it is common sense to control the key components of the communication process that would help distribute the product and secure the market. It has always been important to achieve economic efficiencies to offset the high start-up costs of investing in media. In the early years of electronic media, it was never unusual for owners to try to control many or most elements of the communication process, from content to consumer. RCA's simultaneous control of radio stations and radio set manufacturing enhanced its ability to deliver an audience, because RCA controlled two key pieces of the communication process—distribution of broadcast content and manufacture of the device by which an audience could listen to it.

Government has seldom regulated and restricted vertical integration of the media industry. One instance, however, happened in the early movie industry. Movie studios in the 1920s, 1930s, and 1940s managed to own the three key pieces of their communication process. The studios not only made films but owned distribution companies and the theaters where they were shown. This link in ownership of production, distribution, and exhibition was declared to be monopolistic, and the three activities were separated by government.

Critics say vertical integration protects a conglomerate's business interests at the expense of smaller independent media companies, particularly nondaily newspapers, book publishers, and magazine publishers. They still flourish in the United States, but because they are small, with special, narrow, or regional appeal, their reach and influence are also small. Occasionally, a book from a small press will attract the attention of a TV talk show and become a bestseller. Or an article from a small-circulation publication will be noticed by a reporter for a wire service or a big daily and achieve publicity that will bring it to the attention of a larger public. But this happens only rarely.

A vertically integrated media corporation, on the other hand, can release a book through its own publishing subsidiary, promote it on its television and cable channels, make it into a movie, have its own film distributor place it in its theaters, and sell and rent copies of the film through its home video division. The small press can only take a book to publication, but a vertically integrated company can make that book into a major media event and ensure its market. That is one reason smaller companies sell out to bigger conglomerates, which can obtain greater profits from a single work by adapting it for different media within their control, and marketing and promoting it through their different subsidiaries, to achieve a vast and sometime global market.

LOOKING AHEAD

As we begin the twenty-first century, many small independent media companies continue to serve regions or special-interest markets, but the dominant form of ownership is the media conglomerate, in which large transnational corporations control substantial holdings in publishing, broadcasting, cable, motion pictures, and sound recording.

More consolidation seems probable in the years ahead. But more new players will also enter the field, such as software developers, cable and satellite television, and telephone companies. These companies will also form new alliances to procure content from existing organizations, and they are positioning themselves to produce content on their own. These emerging capabilities will change mass media for both owners and customers. It will be important for all mass communicators and informed citizens to track the meaning and impact of those changes in the future.

The Internet, perhaps, poses one of the most interesting challenges to the future, because for the first time in human history, individuals, without large resources or massive organization, can become owners of messages that can reach mass audiences with very little control.

Further Reading

Auletta, Ken. (1991). *Three Blind Mice: How The TV Networks Lost Their Way*. New York: Random House.

Bagdikian, Ben H. (1992). *The Media Monopoly* (4th ed.). Boston: Beacon Press.

Barnouw, Erik, et al. (1997). *Conglomerates and the Media*. New York: The New Press.

Bingham, Sallie. (1989). *Passion and Prejudice: A Family Memoir*. New York: Knopf.

Bogart, Leo. (1996). What Does It All Mean? *Media Studies Journal, 10*(2–3), 15.

Brandt, J. Donald. (1993). *A History of Gannett: 1906–1993*. Arlington, VA: Gannett Co.

Compaine, Benjamin M. (1979). *Who Owns the Media: Concentration of Ownership in the Mass Communications Industry*. New York: Harmony Books.

Felsenthal, Carol. (1993). *Power, Privilege and The Post: The Katharine Graham Story*. New York: Putnam.

Gitlin, Todd. (1996). Not So Fast, *Media Studies Journal, 10*(2–3), 1–6.

Graham, Katharine. (1997). *Personal History*. New York: Knopf.

Herman, Edward S., and McChesney, Robert W. (1997). *The Global Media: The New Missionaries of Corporate Capitalism*. London: Cassell.

Leapman, Michael. (1985). *Arrogant Aussie: The Rupert Murdoch Story*. Secaucus, NJ: Lyle Stuart.

Mazzocco, Dennis W. (1994). *Networks of Power: Corporate TV's Threat to Democracy*. Boston: South End Press.

McChesney, Robert W. (1997). *Corporate Media and the Threat to Democracy*. New York: Seven Stories Press.

Miller, Mark Crispin. (1997). Free the Media. In Don Hazen and Julie Winokur (Eds.), *We the Media: a Citizen's Guide to Fighting for Media Democracy*. New York: New Press.

Neuharth, Allen H. (1989). *Confessions of an S.O.B.* New York: Doubleday.

Schiller, Herbert I. (1970). *Mass Communications and American Empire*. New York: Kelley.

Schiller, Herbert I. (1989). *Culture, Inc.: The Corporate Takeover of Public Expression*. New York: Oxford University Press.

Squires, James D. (1993). *Read All About It! The Corporate Takeover of America's Newspapers*. New York: Times Books/Random House.

Stephens, Mitchell. (1988). *A History of News*. New York: Penguin.

Triano, Christine. (1977). The Telecommunications Act: An Overview. In Don Hazen and Julie Winokur (Eds.), *We the Media: A Citizen's Guide to Fighting for Media Democracy* (p. 4). New York: New Press.

Whited, Charles. (1988). *Knight: A Publisher in the Tumultuous Century*. New York: Dutton.

5

LEGAL CONCERNS: RIGHTS AND RESPONSIBILITIES

Paparazzi chase Princess Diana to her death! Reporters rush to get the latest rumor at the White House! Newspapers reveal military's war plans for Iraq! Journalists report new secrets about the President! More murders on the evening TV news. Sex! Crime! Rumors! Gossip! Celebrities! Violence! Secrets!

That's the way many people see mass media, and many more ask why the press should be free to wallow in the sleaze. Mass media have more freedom in America than in most other nations on earth. And some people ask, Are they too free? Why should we have freedom of the press? What are the limits of mass media? What rights do the people have in protecting themselves from the press? What authority does the government have to control the press or to protect the public? These are questions that must be answered fully if we are to understand the way mass media work in a free society and why they have what seems to be such extraordinary freedom.

THE FIRST AMENDMENT

Certainly the single most important document for mass media in America is the First Amendment to the Constitution. It says simply:

> Congress shall make no law respecting an establishment of religion, or prohibiting the free exercise thereof; or abridging the freedom of speech or of the press; or right of the people peaceably to assemble, and to petition the Government for a redress of grievances.

For more than 200 years, that amendment has been the prevailing standard against which all questions of press freedom and control have been judged. The courts over those 200 years have interpreted all laws affecting public communication in light of that amendment, and for the most part, the judicial branch has held that the First Amendment gives the press a great deal of latitude. The press is the only institution in the country that enjoys such constitutional protection.

Why was this amendment added to the Constitution in 1789? The founders of the country and drafters of the Constitution agreed, ultimately, that democracy could prevail only with the guarantee of a free press. In part, they were reacting to the absolute and despotic power of European monarchy, and they wanted to prevent any such concentration of power in the new democracy. They designed a government with three branches—executive, legislative, and judicial—each to be a check and balance on the other so that no single branch could ever become all powerful.

They also believed that ultimate power should reside in the hands of the people; as Jefferson had written in the Declaration of Independence, the people should not serve the government, rather the government should serve the people. And if the government failed in its service, citizens should have the right to throw the rascals out and vote in a new government. That would only work if the people had unfettered access to information about government. If government could block that access, then it could control what people know and be able to assume awesome powers.

Thus, the press was seen as the people's representative, to be able to report freely on government and on everything else people needed to know in order to control their own destinies. In the nineteenth century, the press in England was called the fourth estate of the realm, meaning that it had become equal in power to the political, financial, and religious authorities. In twentieth-century America, historian Douglass Cater called the press the fourth branch of government, meaning that it had become a force of power equal to the other three—the executive, legislative, and judicial branches—responsible not to government but only to the people, to provide a check and balance on the other three branches.

All questions about press and public rights flow from those philosophical premises. In most cases where legal questions have been raised about those rights over more than 200 years of U.S. history, the courts' interpretations of the Constitution have tended to side with press and public rather than with government.

PUBLIC RIGHTS IN CONFLICT

Inevitably, of course, rights guaranteed to the press by the Constitution have come into conflict with other public rights, and the courts have had to sort out the winners in such disputes.[1] What rights do American citizens have when public communication is involved? And what rights do journalists and mass communicators have when dealing with the public? The following discussion explains those rights that are crucial to our concerns.

The Right to Know

The right to know may be the most important right of all. Certainly it is at the heart of the First Amendment. For most journalists, it is the most sacred right, and, as we will see, ethical standards are sometimes breached in the name of the public's right to know.

But does the public have an absolute right to know everything? Can individuals protect themselves from a prying press or from damaging information made public? Can the government make some things secret in order to protect national security? These questions and many more have been raised in judicial proceedings in which the courts have had to decide who has the ultimate right. The public's right to know may be the most essential right for a democracy, but where rights conflict the courts have to redress any grievances.

The Right to Protect One's Reputation

The right to protect one's reputation has been a long-revered principle in almost every society throughout history. **Defamation** of one's reputation or character has been considered especially onerous by courts and governments everywhere. Defamation has been defined as a communication that exposes persons to hatred, ridicule, or contempt, which lowers them in the estimation of their peers, causes them to be shunned, or injures them in their business or calling.

Defamation comes in two forms: published or broadcast defamation is **libel**; oral defamation is **slander**. Libel is considered far more damaging than slander because a published or broadcast defamation potentially reaches so many people. Libel is considered such a serious breach of a person's rights that he or she may sue, not only to recover actual damages, such as loss of wages, but punitive damages as well. Sometimes punishment can cost millions of dollars.

Libel can be an expensive proposition for mass media and mass communicators, even when they have a defense for publishing or broadcasting libelous material. In a biography written about newspaper columnist Drew Pearson, a Washington columnist who often dealt in gossip about political and governmental figures, the author maintains that Pearson was sued about 275 times, for a total of more than $200 million dollars; he won all the suits except one, which he settled out of court for $40,000. However, he did have to pay hundreds of thousands of dollars in legal expenses, enough to have a chilling effect on even the most responsible journalist.[2]

One of the most significant libel cases was *New York Times v. Sullivan* in 1964. In that case, an Alabama county commissioner by the name of L. B. Sullivan sued the *Times*, charging he had been libeled by an advertisement which had numerous small errors, taken out by a civil rights group criticizing Alabama officials by name, including Sullivan. Sullivan sued based on the fact that the ad's charges against him were basically false. He won a $500,000 judgment. But the Supreme Court reversed that decision, saying that the *Times* did not run the ad maliciously and that the mass media have special rights to express critical thoughts about political figures and public officials, an idea that has also extended to some extent to celebrities.[3]

One important element highlighted by this case is the role of malice in libel. If a medium of mass communication purposely defames a person with false information, the court has long held that such maliciousness is particularly wrongful, and punishment accordingly can be particularly severe. And in the case of political leaders, public officials, or celebrities, according to *New York Times v. Sullivan*, malice must be proved for a libel suit to be won by the plaintiff. The absence of malice, such as inadvertent use of false damaging information, can mitigate punishment for libel, but it does not completely relieve the medium of its responsibility to protect reputations.

It is important to make a distinction here between criminal and civil libel. In many parts of the world, libel is a crime, and a person found guilty of it can be fined or sentenced to prison. In the United States many states have criminal libel laws on their books (Louisiana's law says that "whoever commits the crime of defamation shall be fined not more than $3,000 or imprisoned for not more than one year or both"). But conviction of criminal libel charges is extremely rare in the United States, where the courts prefer for government not to be involved in punishing communication for any reason. Pressing charges of libel is left to individuals bringing suits in the civil courts as a remedy for public defamation. In some states, criminal libel laws have been written to protect the reputations of the dead who cannot defend themselves in civil actions, but actionable cases have been rare.

In regard to *defenses for libel*, one can defend the publication or broadcast of defamatory material, no matter how damaging it might be, if one can prove its truth. By and large, courts in the United States regard *truth* as an absolute defense. That is, if one can prove in court the truth of what has been published or broadcast, a plaintiff cannot recover damages, no matter how severe the hurt might have been. That is not the case in many countries, where defaming someone, especially a public official or a religious figure, is a crime, even if it is based on the truth.

In addition, *certain documents are privileged*; a fair and accurate report about police records, court transactions, or legislative proceedings can be published or broadcast without causing liability for a libel suit. Most of the potentially libelous news each day is based on information from such privileged documents or proceedings, so actionable libel is never a question. Without such privilege, much of the news would go unreported for fear of libel suits.

The concept of *fair comment* can also be a defense for publishing or broadcasting words that might be considered defamatory without resulting in a libel suit. This long-standing precedent permits journalists to express opinions on matters of public interest, as long as those opinions have some basis in truth and are not published or broadcast with malicious intent to injure. For example, a newspaper article criticized the poor performance of a college football coach and his team. The coach said he had been libeled, but the court held that the newspaper had a right to evaluate the coach and the team because they were performing in public. Critics can say that the coach couldn't coach, but they couldn't say that he was a lousy father, without the facts to prove it. Truth and fair comment are usually matters for the court and juries to decide, while privileged documents usually require no further interpretation by the court.

The Right to Privacy

The right to privacy is a newer concept in the history of legal matters, and it is much harder to define than libel. Invasion of privacy can result in legal action against the invader in four instances.

1. The use of an individual's name or likeness for commercial purposes without first getting consent.
2. The intrusion on a person's solitude.
3. The publication of private information about a person.
4. The publication of false information about a person, or putting someone in a false light.

In the first instance, using a person's name or likeness without consent for commercial purposes—in an advertisement, for example—is always an actionable offense. There is never a defense for it. All advertisements must have prior written permission for use of any person's name or picture in the ad.

In the other three instances, newsworthiness is usually a complete defense. That is, the courts regard the public's right to know about a newsworthy situation as more important than the privacy of the people involved. A person who becomes part of a newsworthy incident loses the right to privacy if the information is deemed by the court to be essential to the news. For example, a newspaper can publish the name of a person involved in an auto accident, together with a picture of that person in the accident, but the paper could not use that as an excuse to write about that person's sex life unless it was somehow pertinent to the accident.

The publication of false information might even be defensible if that information became public in the pursuit of news and if the publication or broadcast of such news was not motivated by malice, whereby the communicator knew the facts were false, or where the communicator recklessly disregarded the truth or falsity of the matter. Of course, it remains for the court to determine newsworthiness or maliciousness or recklessness in each individual situation. If the court rules that privacy has been breached illegally, the plaintiff can recover actual and sometimes punitive damages.

In 1993, ABC's "PrimeTime Live" used a hidden camera to record conversations secretly between two self-described psychics in the office of a telephone psychic hotline service. These conversations were broadcast as part of an exposé. The men sued, and one of them won a $1.2 million award for damages, claiming that his loss of privacy had driven him to alcoholism; the verdict was later overturned by an appeals court, ruling that the man did not have a reasonable expectation of privacy, because he worked in an open room with other employees. Obviously, each case in almost all areas of communication civil action has to be decided on its own merits by the courts.

The Right to Access

The right to access has come into serious question as mass media have grown larger, more expensive, and available to fewer individuals. Who has a right to communicate publicly? Who has a right to freedom of the press? Is it just the wealthy few who can afford to own and operate mass media? By and large, in the United States the courts have answered Yes to that question, with some exceptions.

In many countries, laws require mass media to give space or time for rebuttal to those criticized in mass media. Some of those laws require mass media to give equal time or space and equal emphasis to rebuttal. Some countries have laws requiring corrections or retractions to be published or broadcast. Some countries have laws mandating that sources being quoted in mass media be given the right to check their quotations before they are published or broadcast.

In the United States, however, such laws have been rejected as a violation of First Amendment rights, at least as applied to print media. In the landmark case *Miami Herald Co. v. Tornillo* (1974), the U.S. Supreme Court found that a Florida statute was unconstitutional when it required a newspaper to publish free of charge any reply by political candidates who had been criticized in the paper. Chief Justice Warren Burger wrote:

> Press responsibility is not mandated by the Constitution and like many other virtues it cannot be legislated.... It has yet to be demonstrated how governmental regulation of this crucial process [editorial control and judgment] can be exercised consistent with First Amendment guarantees of a free press.[4]

Broadcast media have not been awarded such sweeping freedom. In the classic case *Red Lion Broadcasting v. Federal Communication Commission* (1969), the Supreme Court unanimously held that radio stations could be required to provide free response time to individuals attacked on the air, arguing that allowing replies enhanced First Amendment values by providing communication of both sides of an argument.[5] The main reason for the distinction between print and broadcast media is that print media use private property whereas broadcast media use the public airwaves, a point we discuss more thoroughly later.

Licenses for cable systems are usually awarded with the proviso that the system owners will provide a local access channel, even with studio and production facilities, where citizens from the cable community can develop programs to express themselves and local concerns.

The Right to Fair Trial

The right to fair trial, guaranteed in the Sixth Amendment to the Constitution, can come into direct conflict with the rights in the First Amendment when news media coverage might jeopardize the fairness of judicial proceedings. Can you have a fair trial, for example, if jurors are getting information about the trial from the press as well as from the court proceeding? Many countries have been more concerned with judicial fairness than press freedom. The United Kingdom, for example, has an Official Secrets Act that prevents publication of news about court actions until the case has been decided. Once a person has been arrested, no news about the legal proceedings can be published or broadcast until the court has rendered its verdict.

One reason such a practice has not prevailed in the United States has been the fear of secret trials. Americans have long held that trials must be held in public, that persons being tried must have the opportunity of having their case judged by a jury of peers, and that free-press coverage is the best protection against corruption or politicization of the judicial process.

However, within the boundaries of press freedom, court officials can do some things to help ensure the fairness of a trial. They can request a change of venue, for example, moving a trial to a different city in which people may not have been exposed to media coverage that would prejudice their objectivity; or they can request a continuance, which can delay a trial until media interest has died down. The judge can admonish the jury not to read newspapers or watch television, or in cases of unusual media interest, such as the O. J. Simpson trial, the judge can sequester the jury, so they will have little or no access to mass media or outside influences during the trial. In grand jury proceedings, which are meant to be preliminary hearings and closed to the public, judges can issue *gag orders*, preventing those in the hearings from discussing the matter with news media. In rare instances, judges have issued gag orders to prevent reporters from attending or covering a public trial in order to prevent prejudicial publicity.

The Right to Protect Sources of Information

The right to protect sources of information is an area where journalists and their sources may come into conflict with courts seeking information in legal proceedings. Some of the most important information journalists get comes from sources who may not want to be publicly identified. Some journalists say they should not accept any information unless they can publicly name their sources. Other journalists say the use of anonymous sources is justified by the public's right to know. *Anonymous information*, often called **leaks**, can raise a host of difficult issues: Can the information be verified? Whose interest is being served? What are the motives of the leaker? How can you respond if you don't know who is making the charge?

Nevertheless, leaks have become an important part of news, primarily because journalists sometimes feel getting information anonymously is often the only way much important information can be obtained, and getting such information in any way serves the public's right to know. In the O. J. Simpson murder case and the Clinton–Lewinsky sex scandal, for example, much information came to reporters in leaks from unnamed sources, but reporters sometimes felt the information was vital to the public, even though they could not name the source. Obviously, this practice can be abused by those who spread false information anonymously. Clearly, the reporter must be able to trust such sources and to verify the information. Most legitimate news organizations require at least two independent sources to confirm all information.

However, what happens if anonymous information becomes essential to a case in court? This question became the basis of a Supreme Court case in 1972 when a reporter for the *Louisville Courier-Journal* wrote a story about two Kentucky youths converting marijuana into hashish. The reporter was allowed to observe the drug operation by promising not to name the youths in his story. After his story was published, the reporter was called before a grand jury and asked to reveal the names of the young drug dealers. He refused and was held in **contempt of court**. This case and several others were heard by the Supreme Court (*Branzburg v. Hayes*, 1972) which ruled 5 to 4 against reporters withholding names of sources needed in a criminal case. The Court's ruling established that journalists do not have an absolute constitutional right to resist subpoenas as protection for their sources; but it did lead to recognition in many lower courts that journalists do have a qualified (or partial) constitutional right to withhold unpublished information and sources' identifies in certain situations.[6]

Contempt of court has been used fairly frequently as a threat to reporters protecting their sources of information. A number of journalists have spent time in prison on contempt charges, without having to go to trial. Reporters can also be charged with contempt for violating a judge's gag order. As of 1997, 29 states and the District of Columbia had passed **shield laws** to provide some degree of protection for journalists in shielding their sources from court scrutiny. The scope of these laws varies widely from state to state, but they provide a more dependable form of protection than is available from the federal Constitution, as a result of the Branzburg ruling.

The Right to Ownership of Intellectual Property

The right to ownership of intellectual property is important for everyone who produces creative work, be they journalists, creative writers, artists, musicians, composers, or photographers. **Copyright** is the legal instrument used to protect one person's intellectual property from other persons who would exploit it for their own gain. Current copyright law states that authors can protect ownership of their work for their lifetime, plus 50 years. Facts cannot be copyrighted, but the style in which one organizes the facts can be. Freedom of the press does not give journalists and mass communicators the right to violate copyright nor, for that matter, the right to violate any law. It should be noted that the government does not pursue violators of copyright to bring them to justice. As in most other areas of public communication, individuals are responsible for protecting themselves through civil cases in the courts.

The 1976 revision of the copyright law permits some **fair use** of copyrighted material for such purposes as criticism, comment, news reporting, teaching, scholarship, or research.

The Right to Free Trade and Consumer Choice

The right to free trade and consumer choice also poses a potential conflict between a free press and public rights. The public has a right to exercise free trade and free choice in the marketplace, and neither journalists nor advertisers nor any other mass communicators have the right to restrain trade through activities that could be promoted by mass media, such as monopolistic practices, price fixing, or predatory pricing.

LIMITATIONS ON GOVERNMENT

Ownership, operation, and control of public mass media are not government functions in the United States. Because American constitutional democracy is based on reduced powers of central authorities, the tradition has long prevailed that governments should not be in direct communication with citizens. All government pronouncements traditionally have been filtered through privately owned news media to keep government from unduly propagandizing the public. With the advent of broadcasting, it has been easier for government officials, especially the President, to subvert media gatekeepers by going directly on radio and television. But the media have occasionally been able to say no, even to the President. Some of Reagan's addresses to the nation were rejected by the TV networks, because they were seen as too political. Mutual Radio rejected Clinton's Saturday radio broadcast simply because it lost listeners for the network.

Traditionally in the United States, news and information about public affairs have come from private businesses to prevent government from controlling communication for its own gain. For that reason, unlike in many other societies, American government does not own or operate newspapers, consumer magazines, radio or television stations, or motion picture studios that produce commercial feature films. The government does contribute funds to public broadcasting, but it does not own NPR or PBS. The federal government does produce some specialized publications, scientific journals and books, training films, and the like, but these are generally not available on the newsstands or in book stores, nor are they readily available to the general public except through one's congressional representative or through the Government Printing Office.

There are exceptions. For example, the federal government owns and operates an international broadcast station, the Voice of America (VOA), established after World War II to provide international transmission of news about the United States and an explanation to the world of America's policies and practices. The VOA was also useful in the propaganda battles of the cold war. The government undertook this role partly because there was no incentive for private enterprise to make it into a profitable proposition. However, in authorizing the VOA, Congress specifically denied the government the ability to direct its transmissions to the American people. In fact, it remains against the law for the federal government to make its international broadcasts or international publications available to American citizens.

Another exception is military media. The military establishment is permitted to publish newspapers or broadcast radio and television programs on military bases, posts, and ships at sea, based on the idea that military personnel, especially those overseas, cannot get easy access to privately published American newspapers and commercial radio and television broadcasts. Since it was started in World War II, *Stars and Stripes* has become an important newspaper published by the government, available only at military installations, and the Armed Forces Network has operated broadcasting facilities overseas for the benefit of military personnel.

Censorship or Prior Restraint

Censorship or prior restraint has been limited or even denied to the federal government from the earliest days of the new democracy. The framers of the Constitution and its advocates ever since have been strongly influenced by the tradition inspired by John Milton, as we saw in chapter 3. In a number of cases the courts have ruled that any censorship, or prior restraint, is unconstitutional. Some landmark cases illustrate how far the courts will go to protect media from government censorship.

In the 1920s, the Minnesota state legislature passed a law to prevent the publication of "public nuisances"; the law was aimed at a particularly scurrilous racist newspaper being published in Minneapolis by a man named J. M. Near. In the landmark case *Near v. Minnesota* (1931), the Supreme Court said even if something is racist it can't be censored. That decision has been called the single most important judgment formalizing the doctrine against prior restraint. Chief Justice Charles Hughes, writing for the majority, wrote:

> Liberty of the press, historically considered and taken up by the Federal Constitution, has meant, principally although not exclusively, immunity from previous restraints or censorship .... The fact that for approximately one hundred and fifty years there has been almost an entire absence of attempts to impose previous restraints upon publications relating to the malfeasance of public officers is significant of the deep-seated conviction that such restraints would violate constitutional rights....[7]

In the most famous incident of all, the Pentagon Papers case, *The New York Times* and *The Washington Post* received copies of secret documents taken from the Defense Department that detailed hundreds of mistakes being made by the U.S. military in the Vietnam War. When the newspapers decided to publish articles based on these highly secret but very damaging documents, the Nixon White House asked for a court injunction to prevent their publication as state secrets; the Supreme Court was asked to rule on the case, and the justices voted six to three against the government. Justice Potter Stewart, in a concurring opinion, wrote that he didn't think disclosure of the Pentagon Papers would result in "direct, immediate, and irreparable damage to our Nation or its people."[8] This suggested that censorship might not be absolutely forbidden if government could prove a "clear and present danger," an idea we will discuss further shortly.

In 1979, *The Progressive* magazine in Wisconsin planned to publish an article describing in detail the design and operation of a hydrogen bomb. The U.S. District Court in Wisconsin, referring to Justice Stewart's opinion in the "Pentagon Papers" case, said that in this instance the article met the test of grave, direct, immediate, and irreparable harm to the United States and issued a preliminary injunction to restrain publication. The magazine decided to challenge the court and proceeded to publication, and articles began appearing in newspapers describing the content of *The Progressive* article. As a result, the preliminary injunction became pointless and the court dropped its case.

Political Commentary

Political commentary has also been specially privileged in American media, and throughout most of U.S. history, government has been constrained from hampering public political communication. An early effort by the government, the Alien and Sedition Act, was passed in the 1790s during John Adams' administration. The act allowed government to charge editors with sedition (or criminal libel) for publishing critical commentary about political officials. The law was aimed at the followers of Thomas Jefferson, in an attempt to silence their criticism of Adams, and they were the only ones ever charged under the law. When Jefferson became President he allowed the law to lapse, and it has never been revived.

The *New York Times v. Sullivan* ruling in 1964 confirmed that mass media have considerable leeway in commenting on politicians and public officials, even if their comments are libelous, as long as the comments are made in good faith, concern only public rather than private matters, do not recklessly disregard the truth, and are not made with actual malice. This ruling and others like it over the years have emphasized the notion that political commentary is especially privileged in American mass media. They have also reinforced the idea that criminal or seditious libel should be rare in America, where freedom of political expression is the basis of democracy. One person may charge another with libel in a civil court, but government cannot make libel into a political crime, punishable by fines or prison sentences.

Clear and Present Danger

Clear and present danger rulings in the twentieth century have established the precedent that government can take action against mass media if and when it can prove that the welfare of society is seriously threatened. During World War I, Congress passed the Espionage Act of 1917, which said in part that "whoever, when the United States is at war, shall willfully cause or attempt to cause insubordination, disloyalty, mutiny, or refusal of duty, in the military" could be fined or imprisoned.

When some antiwar socialists published articles during World War I urging Americans not to go to war if drafted, they were charged with treason under the Espionage Act and found guilty. Their appeal was heard by the Supreme Court, in *Schenck v. United States*. Chief Justice Oliver Wendell Holmes, in the majority opinion, wrote that there were legitimate times when the government could step in to protect society. He wrote:

> When a nation is at war, many things that might be said in time of peace are such a hindrance to its effort that their utterance will not be endured so long as men fight and that no Court could regard them as protected by any constitutional right.[9]

Holmes also understood the sensitivity of this issue and urged that the free marketplace of ideas was better protection for the public than government action. In both World Wars I and II, however, Congress passed laws that made censorship possible during wartime, using the clear and present danger justification, and the Supreme Court did not rule these laws unconstitutional. The laws were allowed to lapse when the wars ended and they have not been reinstated at any time since World War II.

Government Secrecy

Government secrecy has become the alternative to government censorship. Though the courts have been reluctant to allow prior restraint or censorship, even in cases of clear and present danger, they have permitted government to censor itself to protect national security. During World War II the government established a system of classifying information according to the level of its danger to national security if revealed to the public. *Confidential*, *secret*, and *top secret* are some of the classifications used, and an elaborate machinery has been established by law to allow government officials to declare certain information classified to protect national security.

It is important to note that secrecy regulations apply to government officials, not to mass media. In other words, it is government officials who are legally responsible for protecting government secrets, not mass media. If journalists find out these secrets and decide they should be published, generally they could not be punished for doing so, but the officials who allowed the secrets to become known could be penalized. Again the American system is different from many other societies in this respect. In Great Britain, for example, the Official Secrets Act is binding on mass media as well as on officials, making the publication or broadcast of any official government secret a crime. That is not the case in the United States.

Unfortunately, since World War II, and especially in the atmosphere of the cold war that followed it for more than 40 years, U.S. government secrecy has mushroomed. Millions of documents are classified every year, and the extent to which most of them, if made public, would endanger national security, has been the subject of great public and media speculation.

The Freedom of Information Act

The Freedom of Information Act (FOIA), first passed in 1967, was an effort to control rampant government secrecy. The FOIA applied to every agency, department, regulatory commission, government-controlled corporation, and any other establishment in the executive branch of the federal government, but not to Congress or to federally funded state agencies. The act stated that all information from those agencies should be available to the public, but it also named nine exemptions and thus established in law the government's right to withhold certain kinds of information. The exemptions, or information that government can legally keep secret, are matters concerning (1) national security, (2) internal agency rules, (3) information specifically exempted by other federal laws already on the books (the so-called catch-all exemption), (4) trade secrets, (5) internal agency memoranda, (6) personal privacy, (7) law enforcement records, (8) bank reports, and (9) oil and gas well data.

Although this appears not to leave much that is available to the public, nevertheless since 1967, journalists and members of the public have made use of the FOIA to get much information from government that otherwise would have been hidden. The law establishes strict penalties for government officials who withhold information that is not exempt. In addition, the Federal Open Meetings Law requires most government meetings to be open to the public and to journalists, and many states have adopted similar open meetings and records laws at the state government level.

WHERE GOVERNMENT HAS AUTHORITY

There are areas of public communication in which government has some direct and some indirect authority over public communication. Government can exercise some control over broadcasting, advertising, and pornography, and it can provide protection for ownership of intellectual property. In each case, Supreme Court rulings have indicated the parameters within which government can exercise some control without violating the First Amendment.

Broadcasting

Broadcasting is of course the most important area of mass media regulation. Radio, television, and to some extent cable TV must have government licenses to operate, must meet certain technical standards, and as we saw in chapter 4, must be subject to some ownership limitations. For the most part, however, government does not have the right to interfere with program content and cannot censor programming.

The Radio Act of 1927 and the Communications Act of 1934 were not perceived by the courts to be in violation of the First Amendment primarily because of the principle of *spectrum scarcity*. Because broadcast frequencies are not infinite, not everyone can broadcast without chaos overwhelming the system. It was in the public interest to prevent chaos by setting up a system that assigned specific frequencies to specific broadcasters. In addition, since the airwaves were public property, the public had a right to oversee the assignment of frequencies by holding elected representatives responsible for creating laws that would allocate frequencies in a way that would serve the public interest.

Congress created the Federal Radio Commission in 1927 (renamed the Federal Communications Commission in 1934, as mentioned in chapter 3) to carry out government's responsibility in broadcasting, "as *public convenience, interest, or necessity* requires." The FCC is headed by seven commissioners, each appointed by the President for a 7-year term. Political balance is attempted by not allowing more than four commissioners from the same political party to serve at any one time. The Telecommunications Act of 1996 made important changes in many of the FCC's policies and practices but did not alter its essential role as the government's regulator of broadcasting.

A key regulatory power of the FCC is *licensing*; everyone who broadcasts must have an FCC license to do so. The granting of that license is based on spectrum availability, but most important on audience needs. A potential licensee must demonstrate that its station will broadcast in the public interest of the community it will serve. And before they renew that license, the FCC must *ascertain* that the station has indeed been broadcasting in the interests of the public it serves.

Deregulation, which started in the 1980s and continued with the Telecommunications Act of 1996, changed the limitations on ownership and equally important *license renewal policies*, as we saw in chapter 4.

Although the FCC cannot exercise prior restraint over broadcast program content, it can exercise some authority over certain aspects of content, such as the *equal time* and *equal opportunity* provisions for political discussion. These provisions simply try to ensure that broadcasters will not favor one political side over the other by requiring that any amount of time given to one candidate should be given equally to other candidates in the same political election and that no candidate can be prevented from gaining access to the airwaves. News is an exception to equal time and opportunity. That is, political candidates mentioned in bona fide newscasts, interview programs, news documentaries, and on-the-spot coverage, including debates, do not raise the requirement for stations to give equal time or opportunity to candidates not mentioned in the news.

The purpose, of course, is to allow as much political debate as possible, without placing limits on news programs, which would seem to violate First Amendment rights.

The **Fairness Doctrine**, as refined in the 1940s, was also designed to promote broadcast of a full range of viewpoints. The doctrine required broadcasters to devote a reasonable amount of programming to controversial issues of public importance and to provide contrasting views on those issues. Many broadcasters felt this was a limitation of First Amendment rights and fought to repeal the doctrine, which was abandoned by the FCC in 1987, although considerable sentiment has been expressed to reinvigorate it at some future time.

The Children's Television Act of 1990 adopted some specific rules with respect to **children's programming**, including limitations on the number of minutes of commercial time during children's programs. It also made license renewal subject to ascertainment of the extent to which a broadcaster has served the educational and informational needs of children.

Other content controls require that all paid broadcast messages identity the sponsor, prohibit broadcasting false information concerning a crime or catastrophe if it is foreseeable that such broadcast could cause substantial public harm, and control pornography or indecency to some extent. In 1978, the Supreme Court issued a ruling banning seven "filthy words" from broadcasting, in *Federal Communications Commission v. Pacifica*. And in 1987, the FCC adopted a tough standard on indecency and issued formal warnings to three stations, including stations airing "The Howard Stern Show," a call-in radio program featuring sex-oriented humor.

Cable TV

Cable TV also comes under the jurisdiction of the FCC, but since spectrum scarcity is no longer an issue in cable, there is greater question whether FCC oversight is a violation of First Amendment rights. In 1994, in the case of *Turner Broadcasting v. FCC*, the Supreme Court held that cable TV regulations should be scrutinized under the same First Amendment standards applicable to print media. Justice Anthony Kennedy, writing for the majority, said:

> Cable television does not suffer from the inherent limitations that characterize the broadcast medium. Indeed, given the rapid advances in fiber optics and digital compression technology, soon there may be no practical limitation on the number of speakers who might use the cable medium.[10]

The Telecommunications Act of 1996 was a step toward total deregulation of cable.

Advertising

Advertising has never enjoyed the full First Amendment privileges accorded to news, editorial comment, artistic, or personal expression. In the 1942 case of *Valentine v. Chrestensen*, the Supreme Court unanimously upheld a city ordinance prohibiting the distribution of commercial leaflets on the streets. The court's ruling said it was "clear that the Constitution imposes no such restraint on government [such as the First Amendment] as respects purely commercial advertising."[11]

LIVERPOOL JOHN MOORES UNIVERSITY
LEARNING SERVICES

As we discuss later in chapter 13, Congress established the Federal Trade Commission (FTC) in 1914 with a wide mandate to protect the public from fraudulent and monopolistic practices, including the policing of advertising. However, it should be pointed out that the FTC does not systematically monitor advertising. The FTC can respond to and investigate public complaints about deceptive advertising, and if it determines deception has occurred, it can ask for voluntary compliance in withdrawing the offensive ad. If a voluntary settlement cannot be reached, the FTC can issue a cease and desist order to stop the deceptive advertising, with a lengthy review and appeals process. The FTC can also require corrective advertising. If the advertiser has continued the deceptive advertising without correction, the offender can be fined a maximum of $10,000.

One law that has increasingly been watched carefully by the FTC in this era of antismoking sentiment has been the regulation of tobacco advertising aimed at children. In a 3 to 2 vote by the commissioners in June 1997, the FTC ruled that R. J. Reynolds' cartoon character Joe Camel was in violation of that law and required the tobacco company to cease and desist from using Joe Camel in future advertising.

In other words, the regulation of advertising is a sometime thing. Neither is the U.S. government a vicious watchdog of fraudulent ads nor is its bite very punitive, even after it has pursued an advertiser and finds continued deception. Rather, as in most other areas of public communication, the tradition prevails of allowing the marketplace to decide what is acceptable. Advertisers have a wide latitude in freely expressing their commercial messages.

Pornography, Obscenity, and Indecency

Pornography, obscenity, and *indecency* are much more difficult First Amendment issues. For most of its history, the United States has been puritanical in its public morals, but as attitudes toward sexuality began to change in the twentieth century, questions about public rights became more complex. Various courts had ruled on obscenity issues (for example, in a New York court, D. H. Lawrence's *Lady Chatterley's Lover* was ruled obscene in 1944), and whereas government shied away from direct censorship of pornography, it allowed local governments the right to restrict its sale and distribution, allowed the U.S. Customs Bureau to restrict its importation, and allowed the U.S. Postal Service to restrict its distribution through the mail.

Pornography did not merit Supreme Court attention until 1957. In *Roth v. United States*, the Court held that the First Amendment did not apply to obscenity, which opened the door for prior restraint of pornographic materials.[12] That decision ultimately allowed the FCC to develop some regulations on indecent programming. However, with some exceptions, the federal government has not actively censored obscenity (one exception being child pornography), leaving most regulation, except for broadcasting, to local jurisdictions. And local jurisdictions, instead of exercising prior restraint, have tended instead to regulate the sale or display of obscene material.

In *Paris Adult Theater I v. Slaton* in 1973, the Court by a 5 to 4 vote ruled against the First Amendment rights of two adult movie theaters in Atlanta, where an ordinance had been passed against public showing of obscene movies. "Nothing in the Constitution," wrote Chief Justice Warren Burger, "prohibits a State from reaching such a conclusion [against showing obscene films] and acting on it legislatively simply because there is no conclusive evidence or empirical data [that obscenity is dangerous for society]."[13]

Also in 1973, the Supreme Court accepted a definition of obscenity that has continued to be used, called the Miller test, in *Miller v. California*. Using this test, material can be considered obscene if:

(1) the average person, applying contemporary standards, would find that the work taken as a whole appeals to the prurient interest,

(2) the work depicts or describes in a patently offensive way sexual conduct specifically defined by the applicable state law, and

(3) the work, taken as a whole, lacks serious literary, artistic, or scientific value.[14]

All three aspects of the test must be proved in court before content can be labeled obscene, with the subsequent loss of First Amendment protection. As society's definitions of sexuality have changed in the last third of the twentieth century, finding content that would meet all three aspects of the Miller test has become increasingly questionable.

Internet and Online Media

Internet and online media are raising a whole host of new issues about the authority of government. The Internet is such a new opportunity for everyone to communicate publicly that much debate is ongoing as this book goes to press. We deal more with this issue in the final chapter. For now, a summary of rights and responsibilities issues on the Internet includes such things as pornography, privacy, and encryption (see further on). The possibilities for libel and copyright violation are obviously multiplied by online media to the point where special concern has been raised.

Invasion of privacy is a key issue, because much information about individuals is already stored in many databases. A series in *The Washington Post* in March 1998 revealed that "data warehouses" are growing in size and reach. One example is Info-Space Inc., a free look-up service on the World Wide Web that stores more than 100 million residential and commercial listings. To test what was available, *Post* reporters selected a willing subject and were able to find reams of private information about him. As of the date of that series, few laws restrict data warehouses.[15]

One way to protect privacy is *encryption*, software programs that embed electronic communications with secret codes effectively locking their data away from professional hackers or amateur snoops. However, the federal government has raised concerns about encryption, because it wants the ability to monitor electronic communications for law enforcement.

Pornography, too, has become an issue of greater public concern. In 1996 Congress passed the Communication Decency Act as part of the Telecommunications Act. It provides that using interactive computer service to display "indecent" communication "in a manner available to a person under 18 years of age" can lead to a fine of up to $25,000 or imprisonment up to two years, or both. But the act was challenged in court and a Supreme Court ruling declared it unconstitutional.

FREEDOM VERSUS RESPONSIBILITY

In all these legal decisions concerning the First Amendment and the role of mass media in society, it is clear that the courts have tried to protect freedom, but not absolute freedom that would allow the press to do anything it wishes. Mass communicators must abide by all the laws of the land. It is also clear that the courts regard freedom as serving a social purpose, not merely the whims of the communicator. Some philosophers have felt that freedom, as guaranteed by the First Amendment, is an absolute right, a position held by organizations such as the American Civil Liberties Union. Others have felt that freedom exists to preserve democracy, not to protect absolute individual rights, the whims of journalists, or the owners of mass media.

The latter philosophy was stated clearly by a public policy philosopher, Judith Lichtenberg (1990), who argues that there is a distinction between freedom of speech and freedom of the press. Freedom of speech should be nearly unconditional, she reasons, but freedom of the press should be measured by "the degree to which it promotes certain values at the core of our interest in freedom of expression generally … an instrumental good (p. 104)" that should be protected only if it furthers such social values as diversity of opinion and informing the people about the government.

In her exhaustive study of all the Supreme Court decisions concerning public communication from 1931 to 1996, Elizabeth Blanks Hindman (1997) concludes that the justices "almost always rationalized" media freedom. They wrote that "the media are free to educate the public, to be a steward, to tell the truth, to serve the political system" (p. 50). But she concludes that "media freedom is never seen as an unconditional or natural right" (p. 51). She writes that it is apparent in almost every court case that media freedom is seen as crucial to the functioning of democracy. "Media freedom is protected not because of its own intrinsic value, but because it has a larger purpose. The media were granted freedom so they could provide citizens with needed information" (p. 155). She concludes that media freedom has not been seen by the courts as an end in and of itself, but merely as a means to an end—democracy. And because of that, she feels, the Court meant that media could be "held accountable for their actions and to their purposes" (p. 155).

Hindman found, after her review of its decisions, that the Supreme Court has not been concerned about the rights of individuals to express themselves freely. Rather, it has guarded the collectivist goal of serving organized society. She quotes Justice William Brennan, who wrote that the First Amendment protects the communications industry only "to the extent the press makes [the existence of democracy] possible (p. 157)," but no further. She suggests that the Court leaves open the possibility that if the media are not responsible, they could have their rights taken away to ensure the rights of society.

WHAT ARE MEDIA'S RESPONSIBILITIES?

Oftentimes owners of mass media say their primary responsibility is to make a profit, because if they don't make a profit they can't stay in business, and if they don't stay in business they can't serve the public. Two centuries ago, the first prototype of those future press lords, Benjamin Franklin, owner of several newspapers in the 13 colonies, expressed a similar attitude when he said that unless one could make a profit, one couldn't be free. There is much truth in Franklin's homespun philosophy, but as the press and mass media have become powerful instruments, there is growing concern that profit be made honorably.

Is it enough to let the marketplace decide what is right and honorable? That has been the traditional rationale. But in an age of mass society and mass media, the marketplace is no longer so simple. Life has become complex, facts are infinitely varied and subject to many interpretations. What is true for one person may not be true for another. The mass media have the power to interpret facts to achieve certain ends. Throughout the Clinton–Lewinsky scandal, for example, conservative media interpreted the facts to mean that Clinton should be impeached, whereas more liberal media interpreted the facts to mean that the President should be censured but not impeached. As we mentioned previously, photographs, once considered true representations of reality, can now be "doctored" by graphic artists and computers to manipulate the reality they represent. Even unadulterated facts can sometime be dangerous (information about troop movements during wartime, for example); that is why we allow government to keep certain things secret.

During World War II, the power and danger of communication became clear to many observers. Nazi propaganda caused normal people to acquiesce to a holocaust. Soviet propaganda turned the masses into automatons. The American government's information apparatus turned a peaceful nation into a military power. Science had produced the ultimate weapon that could destroy mankind. If information fell into the wrong hands, the world could have been destroyed. With these thoughts in mind, a group of philosophers formed a Commission on Freedom of the Press and spent three years analyzing the news media and their obligations to the American people. It was known as the Hutchins Commission for its chairman, Robert M. Hutchins, chancellor of the University of Chicago.

In its final report, *A Free and Responsible Press*, the Commission on Freedom of the Press (1947) concluded the press had become large and powerful, that fewer people could participate in the media as they have grown, that the relatively few decision makers, mass communicators, and gatekeepers had often failed to serve the best interests of society, and that continued failure would eventually bring about outside control of the press and mass media. The five basic points the Commission set forth still form a basis for what the mass media should do in order to be responsible to society and remain free. They are shown in Fig. 5.1. Those principles are still seen as valid by all thoughtful observers who want to preserve freedom and democracy.

FIG. 5.1. Freedom and responsibility of mass media. From *A Free Responsible Press* (1947),
Commission on Freedom of the Press.

Five basic points for what mass media should do in order to be responsible to
society and remain free:

• Provide a truthful, comprehensive, and intelligent account of the day's events
in a context which gives them meaning.

• Provide a forum for the exchange of comment and criticism.

• Provide a means for projecting the opinions and attitudes of the groups in the
society to one another, to project a representative picture of the constituent
groups in society.

• Develop a method of presenting and clarifying the goals and values of the society.

• Provide a way of reaching every member of the society with full access to the
day's intelligence, with information, thought, and feeling.

ETHICAL AND MORAL CONSIDERATIONS

Since the First Amendment gives mass media wide latitude, being responsible is still
an ethical or moral act, not a legal one, and most questions for mass communicators are
ethical rather than legal. Ethical and moral decisions are personal, and they vary from
person to person based on personal values, whereas laws are applied equally to every
individual. Ethical and moral considerations are by definition not mandated by law but
are accepted and acted on as a matter of personal choice.

For example, it is not against the law to publish or broadcast a lie (unless it causes
damage), but doing so would be regarded by most people as unethical, and yet in certain circumstances, the lie might serve a larger purpose for society (for example, telling the world that America was not flying spy flights over the Soviet Union, because to
admit the truth at the moment in 1959 might have brought about World War III). Many
journalists, for example, consider some unethical behavior to be justified to serve the
larger purpose of the public's right to know. For example, using stolen documents in
the Pentagon Papers case was considered totally justifiable by many journalists, because they felt the public had a right to know what the Defense Department was doing
in Vietnam.

Similar cases can have different consequences. ABC's "PrimeTime Live," in an investigation of improper food handling at a Food Lion supermarket, used hidden cameras and deceptive practices (including having ABC employees obtain jobs at the
stores). ABC thought it was serving a higher purpose by informing the public about
conditions the public had a right to know. But Food Lion filed a lawsuit for breach of
contract and won. In a similar case, a *Wall Street Journal* reporter, Tony Horwitz, took
a job at a chicken-processing plant. He did not tell his employers he was a journalist.
He later wrote a story about food-handling violations, poor hygiene, and Dickensian
working conditions in the plant and won a Pulitzer Prize.

Ethical and moral considerations for the mass media can be complex issues, and many treatises have attempted to address the subject of whether the ends ever justify the means, or who should say what is ethical and moral, whether there is a higher authority or whether the marketplace should determine morality.

We feel that all these discussions can be reduced to two types of ethical considerations, both involving the exploitation of the privilege and responsibility of mass communication. One is exploitation of others for one's own gain. Lying, exaggerating, and sensationalizing in order to sell more copies, to get more listeners or viewers, to make more money is exploitation; it may not be illegal, but most would say it is unethical. Exploiting situations such as grief or agony or personal disaster in order to sell is not illegal, but most would say it is unethical. Exploiting the public by manipulating information, by not revealing sources of information, by hiding the facts in order to distort information for one's own purposes may not be illegal but most would say it is unethical.

The other kind of exploitation takes place when mass communicators allow others to use themselves without explaining to readers, viewers, and listeners the real source of the communication. To be a mass communicator in a complex, concentrated, and highly expensive operation is to hold a public trust, and that trust involves clearly identifying the sources of information and the interests that are served. Journalists who use press releases from outside interests as a news story, without explaining whose purpose is being served, are not acting illegally. But by allowing their audiences to think that something is an objective news account when it has been written solely for the purpose of furthering someone's cause is a violation of trust. It is not illegal, but most would say it is unethical. To accept free lunches, free drinks, free entertainment, free books, free airplane tickets, free lodging from those who would influence is not illegal, but most would say it can be unethical if it influences the mass communicator's public judgment.

CODES OF PROFESSIONAL CONDUCT

Most professional organizations of mass communication have adopted codes of conduct that establish voluntary guidelines for ethical behavior on the part of the profession and its members. These guidelines are not legally binding, and it is rare for organizations to take any action on members who might defy the rules. Because of the First Amendment, these professional codes would probably be held unconstitutional as absolute regulations. In other countries, however—Sweden, for example—journalists can be removed from their profession for breaking journalistic codes of conduct.

Organizations and associations that have such codes include the Society of Professional Journalists (the oldest code); the American Society of Newspaper Editors; the Radio Television News Directors Association; the National Association of Broadcasters (separate codes for radio and television); the Public Relations Society of America; and the American Association of Advertising Agencies. There are many others. These codes are all written in noble language, expressing honorable thoughts, and although they may not be legally binding, they are good models for individual members and good public relations for the profession.

RIGHTS OF OWNERS AND EMPLOYEES

Individual media organizations can also develop their own internal rules and guidelines. Every major newspaper, magazine, and broadcast entity maintains such internal rules. Broadcasting networks, for example, have developed complicated and lengthy guidelines for political coverage to demonstrate not only that they are abiding by FCC rules but also acting in good faith. Many organizations have rules about accepting gifts, something that was unlikely 20 or 30 years ago.

It is not uncommon for news employers to require their employees to sign an annual statement pledging that they will observe a corporate ethics policy. These policies typically include rules about accepting or giving gifts (generally prohibited for journalists); managing relationships with suppliers, advertisers, and distributors; and, in general, complying with company policies requiring honest dealings in all business matters in which an employee represents the company. Companies whose stock is traded publicly usually also ask employees likely to have privileged, confidential information about the company to sign a statement in which they pledge to refrain from insider trading, which is illegal.

Courts have ruled that these internal rules are not violations of individual rights. Even student journalists must abide by the rules of the school if it is the owner of the student media. In 1988, in *Hazelwood School District v. Kuhlmeier*, the court upheld censorship by a high school principal in Missouri.[16] That same rule has not been applied to public colleges, which cannot censor student media without violation of First Amendment rights, according to many court rulings.

In the end, the ultimate responsibility and freedom usually belong to the owners of mass media. As we saw in chapter 4, media ownership has become more concentrated, and thus the responsibilities of those powerful few have become greater. Any irresponsibility, although not against the law, can threaten mass media freedom, for many believe that freedom is not an absolute right, that it exists to promote democracy, and if freedom is exercised irresponsibly, democracy cannot be served.

Further Reading

Clark, David G., and Hutchison, Earl R. (Eds.). (1970). *Mass Media and the Law: Freedom and Restraint.* New York: John Wiley.

Commission on Freedom of the Press. (1947). *A Free and Responsible Press.* Chicago: University of Chicago Press.

Cullen, Maurice R., Jr. (1981). *Mass Media and the First Amendment.* Dubuque, IA: Brown.

Emord, Jonathan W. (1991). *Freedom, Technology, and the First Amendment.* San Francisco: Pacific Research Institute for Public Policy.

Garry, Patrick M. (1994) *Scrambling for Protection: The New Media and the First Amendment.* Pittsburgh: University of Pittsburgh Press.

Hindman, Elizabeth Blanks. (1997). *Rights vs. Responsibilities: The Supreme Court and the Media.* Westport, CT: Greenwood.

Lichtenberg, Judith. (1990). *Democracy and the Mass Media: A Collection of Essays.* Cambridge, England: Cambridge University Press.

Kaplar, Richard T., and Maines, Patrick D. (1995). *The Government Factor: Undermining Journalistic Ethics in the Information Age.* Washington, DC: Cato Institute.

Middleton, Kent R., and Chamberlin, Bill F. (1989). *The Law of Public Communication*. New York: Longman.

Owen, Bruce M. (1975). *Economics of Freedom of Expression: Media Structure and the First Amendment*. Cambridge, MA: Ballinger.

Pember, Don R. (1977). *Mass Media Law*. Dubuque, IA: Brown.

Schmidt, Benno C., Jr. (1975). *Freedom of the Press vs. Public Access*. New York: Praeger.

Schwarz, Ted. (1996). *Free Speech and False Profits: Ethics in the Media*. Cleveland: Pilgrim Press.

Taitte, W. Lawson. (Ed.). (1993). *The Morality of the Mass Media*. Dallas: University of Texas.

Notes

[1] We wish to acknowledge the special work of several communication law scholars whose research on specific court rulings concerning mass communication issues has been essential to our interpretation in the chapter. Key among them are Bill F. Chamberlin, Maurice R. Cullen, Elizabeth Blanks Hindman, Don R. Pember, and John D. Zelezny.

[2] Quoted in Pember, Don R. (1977). *Mass Media Law* (p. 97). Dubuque, IA: Brown.

[3] *New York Times v. Sullivan*, 376- U.S. 254 (1964).

[4] *Miami Herald Publishing Co. v. Tornillo*, 418 U.S. 241, 256, 258 (1974).

[5] *Red Lion Broadcasting Co. v. FCC*, 395 U.S. 367 (1969).

[6] *Branzburg v. Hayes*, 408 U.S. 665, 682 (1972).

[7] *Near v. Minnesota*, 283 U.S. 697, 718-719 (1931).

[8] *New York Times Company v. United States*, 403 U.S. 730 (1971).

[9] *Schenck v. United States*, 249 U.S. 47, 52 (1919).

[10] *Turner Broadcasting System v. FCC*, 129 L.Ed. 2d 497, 514 (1994).

[11] *Valentine v. Chrestensen*, 316 U.S. 52, 54 (1942).

[12] *Roth v. United States*, 354 U.S. 476 (1957).

[13] *Paris Adult Theater I v. Slaton*, 413 U.S. 49, 60 (1973).

[14] *Miller v. California*, 413 U.S. 15 (1973).

[15] Chandrasekaran, Rajiv (1998, March 8, 9, & 10). Eye at the Keyhole: Privacy in the Digital Age. *The Washington Post*.

[16] *Hazelwood School Dist. v. Kuhlmeier*, 795 F.2d 1368 (8th Cir. 1986).

6

AUDIENCES: USE OF MASS MEDIA

Have you ever stopped to think how much time you spend each day with mass media? It would be a useful exercise to keep a diary of your media activities for several weeks, to time your reading of newspapers, magazines, and books, your viewing of movies and television, and your listening to radio and recordings. If you are an average American, you spend most of your free time watching television, but if you are a college student you spend a lot less TV time than average, and less than you used to as a high school or elementary school student. A careful look at who uses mass media, how they are used, and why, is essential to our understanding of the entire process.

For a number of years in the mid-twentieth century, scholars of mass media neglected serious study of the role of audiences in the mass communication process, largely as a result of their thinking that individual interaction with media was the more important aspect. Producers of media always knew that audiences were key; without an audience, *mass* communication was not possible. Audiences made media into commercially successful enterprises. In the 1980s and 1990s, more serious study was focused on audiences, primarily because of the concern of students of popular culture and the cultural impact of mass media.

MASS MEDIA'S AUDIENCE

If we examine our habits, we can quickly see that mass media have become our main activity. We spend more time on them (about 3,400 hours a year, or 38.8 percent) than we do on working (about 2,000 hours a year, or 22.8 percent), or sleeping (about 2,900 a year, or 33.1 percent). That leaves only about 460 hours a year for everything else (5.3 percent). Television watching alone translates into 67 straight 24-hour days of watching for the average American—more than three months' worth of time. See Table 6.1 for a breakdown on time spent.

TABLE 6.1

How We Spend Our Time

	Hours per Year	*Hours per Day*	*Percentage*
Media	3,400	9.3	38.8
Sleeping	2,900	7.9	33.1
Working	2,000	5.5	22.8
Other	460	1.3	5.3
Total	8,760	24	100.0

Source: Veronis, Suhler, & Associates, Inc., 1996. Used with permission of Veronis, Suhler, & Associates, Inc., Wilkofsky Gruen Associates.

These figures come from Veronis, Suhler & Associates, an investment company that has been developing these statistics for a number of years.[1] Their figures show a steady increase in time spent on mass media over the years. They predicted an increase of 119 hours a year per person spent on mass media between 1996 and 2000; that's the equivalent of three work weeks, and since the number of hours in a year does not expand, the additional time spent on media means time taken away from something else.

If we divide our time by individual media, television takes up almost half, according to 1997 statistics: 1,595 hours a year (4.4 hours a day, or 47 percent of our media time). We spend 1,058 hours a year listening to radio (2.9 hours, 32 percent), 273 hours listening to recordings (45 minutes, 8 percent), 164 hours reading newspapers (27 minutes, 5 percent), 103 hours reading books (17 minutes, 3 percent), 85 hours reading magazines (14 minutes, 2 percent), and 122 hours on other media, including movies and online activities (20 minutes a day, 3 percent). See Table 6.2 for a breakdown of time spent with media.

These are national averages and probably do not represent most readers of this text. In addition, time estimates are derived from many sources and are subject to different interpretations. Also, some human activities overlap, especially some media activities. Thus Robinson and Godbey (1997), using the diary method to obtain data on media behavior, found a good deal more free time devoted to nonmedia behavior, as Fig. 6.1 illustrates. The diary method allows respondents to account for secondary activities, those that are being done simultaneously with primary activities. Robinson and Godbey found that some mass media behavior is secondary, especially watching television and listening to radio and records, whereas reading is usually a primary activity. Even walking and jogging is done these days with earphones and a Walkman. The Veronis, Suhler firm counts that as radio or record listening; Robinson and Godbey count it as recreation. Robinson and Godbey's picture of the way we spend our free time is probably more in line with our own perceptions.

Mass media consumption is in fact a fairly inexpensive way to spend time. The biggest expenditure is for the TV set, radio, VCR, or record player, but those costs have declined sharply and can be averaged out over many years of use. After initial purchase of the media device, all over-the-air broadcasting is absolutely free to the audience. The average consumer spends a little more than $500 a year on mass media, including $133 for cable TV; $175 for newspapers, magazines, and books; $83 for home videos; $25 for theater movies; and about $85 for other media such as online and Internet activity. The average American spends more on telephone and postal communication each year than on mass media.

TELEVISION AND THE AUDIENCE OF CHILDREN

Television has acquired a particularly captive audience. It grew rapidly as a mass medium, with receivers in 98 percent of all U.S. households within a few years of television's becoming a mass medium in the 1950s. By the 1990s, 67 percent of U.S. households owned two or more receivers; 63 percent received 30 or more channels, with the set on for 6 hours and 57 minutes a day in the average home; and television had become the main source of news for 70 percent of the U.S. public.[2] Poverty is no longer the reason for the 2 percent of American households not having a TV; more homes in

TABLE 6.2

How We Spend Our Media Time

Medium	Hours per Year		Hours per Day		Percentage	
	1996	1999	1996	1999	1996	1999
Television[1]	1,595	1,565	4.37[2]	4.29	47	46.4
Radio	1,058	1,066	2.90	2.92	32	31.6
Recordings	273	261	.75	.71	8	7.7
Newspapers	164	156	.45	.42	5	4.6
Books	103	95	.28	.26	3	2.8
Magazines	85	81	.22	.22	2	2.4
Home video	—[3]	53	—	.14	—	1.6
Video games	—	42	—	.11	—	1.3
Internet	—	39	—	.10	—	1.2
Movies	—	13	—	.03	—	0.4
Other[4]	122	—	.33	—	3	—
Total	3400	3371	9.30	9.30	100.0	100.0

Source: Veronis, Suhler & Associates, 1996, 1999. Their figures are based on data from Wilkofsky Gruen Associates, Nielsen Media Research, Simmons Market Research Interactive Digital Software Association, Paul Kagan Associates, Motion Picture Association of America, Recording Industry Association of America, Newspaper Association of America, Book Industry Study Group, Magazine Publishers of America, Software Publishers Association. Estimates of time spent were derived using rating data for television and radio, survey research and consumer purchase data for recorded music, newspapers, magazines, books, home videos, admissions for movies, and consumer online services. Adults 18 and older were the basis for estimates except for recorded music, movies in theaters, and video games, where estimates included persons 12 and older. Used with permission of Veronis, Suhler, & Associates, Wilkofsky Gruen Associates.

[1]Includes network affiliated stations, independent stations, and cable.
[2]Hours and fractions of hours, not hours and minutes.
[3]Blanks indicate data not provided in 1996.
[4]Blanks here indicate data not provided in 1999.

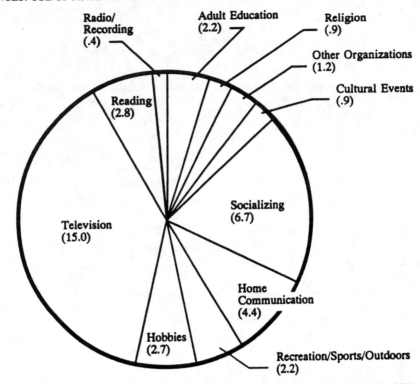

FIG. 6.1. How we spend our free time/total weekly hours in 1985: 39.4, up from less than 35 hours in 1965. (From Robinson, John P., and Godbey, Geoffrey, 1997, *Time for Life: The Surprising Way Americans Use Their Time.* University Park: The Pennsylvania State University Press, 1997. Reproduced by permission of the publisher.)

America have TV sets than bathrooms. The 2 percent of TV-free households conform to no particular pattern, cutting across every cultural division, including not only religious groups, such as Amish and Mennonite families, but also some conservatives, liberals, "new age" parents, and home-schoolers.

As television viewing has increased over the past 40 years, newspaper reading has decreased. Newspaper readership as a percentage of the total U.S. population has declined steadily since television became an important medium. In 1970, 77.6 percent of Americans read a daily newspaper. By 1998, that figure had declined to 58.8 percent.[3]

Preschool children seem to be particularly vulnerable to television at a time when they are in their most formative years. This may be happening because more children live in homes where both parents work, or in single-parent homes, and television is often used as a pacifier or babysitter, even in many day-care centers. According to A. C. Nielsen data, children ages 2 to 5 average 24 hours and 42 minutes per week watching TV, and this figure declines only slightly as children go to school; those aged 6 to 11 average 21 hours and 30 minutes per week, as Table 6.3 shows.

Newton Minow, former FCC chairman, wrote that by first grade, most American children have spent the equivalent of three school years in front of the TV set (Minow & LeMay, 1995). By the time they are 18 years old, they have spent more time in front of the television set than they have spent in school and far more time than they have spent talking with their teachers, their friends, or even their parents. An American

TABLE 6.3

Television Use by Gender and Age

Gender and Age	Hours
Women 55 and older	44 hours, 11 minutes
Men 55 and older	38 hours, 38 minutes
Women 25 to 54	30 hours, 55 minutes
Men 25 to 54	27 hours, 13 minutes
Women 18 to 24	26 hours, 23 minutes
Children 2 to 5	24 hours, 42 minutes
Men 18 to 24	22 hours, 41 minutes
Male teens	21 hours, 59 minutes
Children 6 to 11	21 hours, 30 minutes
Female teens	20 hours, 20 minutes

Source: Nielsen Media Research, copyright 1995. Reproduced with permission.

Academy of Pediatrics study in 1990 concluded that by the time today's child reaches 70 years old, he or she will have spent approximately 7 years watching TV.

MEASURING MEDIA AUDIENCES

Before the development of broadcasting, audiences for print media were estimated solely from the number of copies sold, that is, from their circulation. That was an easy statistic for publishers to get, but it did not provide information about which part of the newspaper, magazine, or book was read, if any, or whether readers liked or understood what they were reading. In broadcasting, there weren't even any sales figures comparable to publication circulation, so early broadcasters had little idea who was listening to what.

As we saw earlier, feedback is essential to the communication process; the communicator must get some kind of response from the receiver. The needs of broadcasting made audience measurement an important part of the mass media business. In the mass communication process, the measurement of audience response is still delayed, diffused, and indirect, and many aspects are still imprecise, but much progress has been made.

In 1936, Arthur C. Nielsen Sr. started Nielsen Media Research, one of the first companies devoted to measuring audiences for the rapidly developing radio and advertising industry. The Nielsen rating system is similar to other audience measuring processes. It still does not tell us much about what was liked or understood but only who and how many listened or watched. It is based on a representative sample of about 5,000 households, using metering equipment on TV sets, VCRs, cable boxes, and satellite dishes in each sampled household, all connected to a small central computer and modem that in the middle of each night automatically calls in the recorded data of that day to central computers. Nielsen can track commercials as well as programs, and it tracks more than 1,700 TV stations and 11,000 cable systems to identify specific pro-grams and coordinate that information with the data from the black boxes in the 5,000-household sample.

In an effort to go beyond the simple data about which programs were watched and to get feedback on whether what was seen or heard was liked or understood, Nielsen pio-neered the *people meter* system, a box the size of a paperback book assigned to each person who lives in a Nielsen sample household. The people meter allows individuals to record their TV use and response, thus providing data on age, gender, and other de-mographic factors. Nielsen also uses the diary method, booklets in each sample house-hold in which viewers can record their viewing during a measurement week. These diary measurements are recorded four times a year, in February, May, July, and No-vember, the so-called sweeps months in which Nielsen conducts a complete diary mea-surement in 211 television markets across the nation.

Nielsen was one of the first and largest audience-measuring companies, and most of its competitors use similar techniques. Now many companies compete in the media measurement business. Such careful measurement is no longer confined to broadcast-ing. For print media, the Audit Bureau of Circulations came into existence in 1914 as a private, independent agency to verify circulation and sales figures of newspapers and magazines, primarily to set advertising rates. Now all mass media businesses, includ-ing book, magazine, and newspaper publishers, and movie and record producers, en-gage in extensive market research to learn what people want, how they use their products, and what they think of them.

Each medium keeps careful statistics on its audiences and tracks them continually as a matter of good market research. Newspaper publishers, for example, know that newspaper readership increases with education, job responsibility, and home value. They know which section of the newspaper is read most by readers in various catego-ries, including sex, age, and race. They know their readers' average age and income. They even know when and where you are apt to buy a single copy if you are not a daily subscriber.

PREDICTING AUDIENCE BEHAVIOR

Audience measurement and market research can help communicators predict what au-diences prefer in media and contents, how they use media, when they use media, and with what effect. Audience research can categorize individuals into convenient groups or bodies that can be analyzed and counted. Audience research allows communicators to shape their messages to fit the needs of particular groups, since it would be impossi-ble to fill the needs of individuals. It allows marketers to put people into group profiles that can then be sold to advertisers, perhaps the most important reason of all for audi-ence measurement.

Audience research shows that much communication behavior is predictable. Sur-veys confirm, for example, that the hour of the day for radio listening and television watching follows standard patterns. Most radio listening increases sharply at 5:00 A.M. each weekday and peaks at 7:00 A.M., when the audience for radio is far greater than television, and then it declines over the rest of the day, with a little bump in the chart during evening rush hour. *Drive time* in radio is those hours in the morning and evening when commuters are most apt to be in their cars and listening to the radio while they drive to and from work, and it is the time most advertisers want to put their message on radio.

Television starts getting a larger audience about 10:00 A.M., and the audience continues to grow steadily until 5:00 P.M., when it rises sharply to *prime time* between 8:00 P.M. and 10:00 P.M. (Eastern Standard Time) each evening, falling off sharply after 10 P.M. as people start to go to bed.

The evenings on which people watch TV also varies according to a predictable pattern. Monday nights see the heaviest television viewing, with 98.2 million people watching, followed by Tuesday with 94.6 million, Thursday with 92.7 million, Wednesday with 91.7 million, and Sunday with 91.3 million. Friday and Saturday nights are the lowest viewing nights, with 79.7 million and 78.2 million people watching, respectively. TV viewing also varies according to season, with people watching most in the winter and least in the summer. These data vary slightly when age and gender are considered.

Movie attendance is most erratic month to month but still predictable. Highest attendance is in mid-summer, with a sharp decline in audience numbers when school starts in the fall and spring, during school exam times, and before the Christmas holidays, although attendance peaks again right after Christmas, before school starts in January. Among other things, these figures indicate how important young people are to the movie business. All these data are used in the marketing of movies, deciding when to release new movies, and, in fact, in all mass media marketing endeavors.

Audience participation in media activity is also greatly affected by events that capture public attention. The more an event has consequences or entertainment value for people, the more likely it will be to get audiences. Far more people read newspapers and magazines and listen to radio and watch television during war or a national emergency than when all is peaceful and calm. Sensational news events such as the O. J. Simpson trial, the death and funeral of Princess Diana, and the Bill Clinton–Monica Lewinsky scandal brought great masses of viewers, listeners, and readers to the mass media and much profit to the mass media industry.

THE MASS AUDIENCE

One of the most important questions about mass media audiences is whether or not there really is a *mass* audience. Most scholars now say no, not in the usual sense, except for such rare and unusual circumstances as the events mentioned in the previous paragraph. Momentous instances in history sometimes have brought together so many people of the nation or the world to constitute a mass audience: the funeral of President Kennedy in 1963, the landing on the moon in 1969, the wedding of Prince Charles and Princess Diana in 1981, the funeral of Princess Diana in 1997. These were moments when hundreds of millions of people worldwide participated simultaneously in the viewing of one event.

With the rise of industrialism starting in the nineteenth century, bringing about worldwide population growth and the massing of great numbers of people in urban centers, philosophers began to use the term *the masses*. Communist leaders used the concept of the masses to distinguish ordinary people from *aristocrats* and *wealthy capitalists*. In the twentieth century, as we have seen, national and international movements have used mass media in massive propaganda campaigns to sway the masses. In the late nineteenth and early twentieth centuries, psychologists began to move beyond the study of individuals to the study of groups and crowds. Crowd psychology became an important subtopic of psychology. Like a herd of cattle, a crowd could acquire its own instincts and be moved to operate as a unit. Strikes by union workers against their bosses, in which strikers might gather in a crowd in front of the factory and become unruly, were seen as examples of the crowd instinct, bringing about the psychology of crowd control.

Another important question involves *public opinion*. Our society today is constantly measuring public opinion through survey polls and market research, and as a result, public policies, political actions, and commercial decisions are almost always based on public attitudes and opinions. But we must remember that these polls do not represent an enduring public view. In fact, public opinion is constantly shifting. An opinion poll is only a snapshot that can register, one moment at a time, varieties of attitudes and opinions and determine who holds them and how dominant they are. The snapshot could be different a few moments, or days, later.

Careful measurement of media audiences indicates that for most of what gets communicated on a mass basis, audiences are not really massive but much more diverse. The terms *audiences* or *publics* are probably better for characterizing users of mass media than is the concept of one public or one mass.

AUDIENCE DIVERSIFICATION

Distinct publics have varied definitions. Most of us still think of audiences in one of three ways: as individuals, as a group, or as a mass. Historians say that in the eighteenth century, an elite public dominated the public sphere, or the public dialogue. The nineteenth century was characterized by a public of groups, whereas the twentieth century has seen publics as audiences. Cultural critics have divided audiences into highbrow, middlebrow, and lowbrow. Sociologists, anthropologists, demographers, and market researchers have increasingly divided audiences by demographic factors such as age, gender, race, ethnicity, socioeconomic status, political leaning, religion, and nationality. In fact, it seems that audiences can be divided into dozens of different types.

Perhaps the most important reason for varied audiences has been the diversification of media. Mass media are made up of many parts, and each new technological development seems to give birth to yet another new method of public communication. In authoritarian societies, as we have seen, the central authorities often attempt to control the media to sway the masses, but the new technologies have also made it more difficult to control all media, and electronic media and the Internet are almost impossible to control, although efforts to do so will continue.

McQuail (1997) defines four types of audience:

The Audience as Group or Public.   This occurs when media exist to serve a particular collection of people who have something in common: for example, a political newspaper that serves a political group, a religious magazine for members of a particular church or religion, a newspaper or radio station that serves a community. Such media can establish identity and increase cohesion in a group or public. But McQuail warns that group character may be weak if its members also have a disparity of other attributes and get their information from a wide variety of sources.

The Gratification Set as Audience.   This occurs when media exist to serve the particular interests or needs of readers, listeners, and viewers. In many ways, this type of audience has become much more prevalent, largely because of the ability to produce and market a vast array of specialized media to serve almost any interest group. Thousands of specialized magazines now create audiences with particular interests. Dozens of radio stations in any listening area can specialize in different kinds of music—such as rock, country, urban contemporary, and classical—to form loyal audiences who prefer one type of music.

The Medium Audience.   This occurs when people identify themselves as users of a mass medium: for example, television viewers, book readers, and moviegoers. Much effects research is based on this concept of audience, such as research on the effect of television on television users, the level of information of newspaper readers, and the influence of advertising on radio listeners. This way of looking at audiences, however, does not take into account such things as the differences in television programs and stations, newspaper differences in content and layout, and differences in radio station formats.

An Audience Defined by Channel or Content.   This is probably the best way to define media users. The people who watch a particular program on television, who read a particular issue or type of magazine or book, for example, would be better units to study, since they contain the least overlap with other types of audiences. Most market research, as well as media ratings, are based on this type of audience. The Nielsen ratings, for example, measure audiences for individual programs.

By looking at the demographic characteristics of audiences of individual programs, for example, we can see the homogeneity (or similarity) of audience members for a specific program. In general the audiences of the three major networks, ABC, CBS, and NBC, are very *heterogeneous* or different from one another. The audiences of cable television in general are less heterogeneous, and within cable networks some channels have very homogeneous audiences: for example, Nickelodeon (obviously mostly children), Financial News Network (mostly business people), and MTV (mostly teenagers and young adults).[4]

DEMOGRAPHIC DISTINCTIONS

It is also important to understand the demographic character of media audiences. When we use demographic factors in looking at the audiences of mass media, it becomes evident that people's use of mass media is often driven by who they are. In other words, there are differences in the way people use media according to such factors as age, sex, race, ethnicity, and socioeconomic status. For examples, see Table 6.4. We provide here only a few examples of the hundreds of statistical data available:

Age and Gender.   Television provides many examples of the extent to which the age and gender of a viewer makes a difference in what they view, and how much television they use.

One interesting study of teenage use of online media indicates particular ways in which they use the Internet (Webber, 1997). Since they have been trained by years of watching television to be zappers, to flip channels without hesitation, they tend to be more restless on the Web, roaming from site to site with greater frequency than adult users.

Children make up an important audience for mass media. Sleeping takes the most amount of their time, but television watching consumes the next most time, and schoolwork is third. For children, television viewing and book reading are the only two activities that remain constant in time of use. Through the preschool, elementary school, and secondary school years, children watch about 2 hours of TV per day and read books for about 1 hour a day.

Young people don't believe there is a lot of good television for them. Only 23.7 percent of the youth in one survey felt there were many good programs for children; even fewer parents (12.5 percent) thought so. Parents believe public broadcasting offers the best shows for children, but young people say the best shows are on cable.

Socioeconomic Status.   Media use varies by gender and age but also by education and income. Mass media as sources of information are different for all demographic groupings but more so for education and income than for other categories. The higher the education, the less likely the person depends on television as a source of information and the more likely to use newspapers, radio, and magazines. Nearly the same shift occurs as income gets higher.

Class.   Class also makes an important difference in media use. British sociologist David Morley (1980) examined differences in viewing a British television magazine called "Nationwide" and found that groups of students from different classes had distinctly different interpretations of the program; one group viewed the program as informational, the other as entertainment, and thus each reacted to the program in dramatically different ways.

Andrea Press's study (1991), *Women Watching Television*, found that middle-class and working-class women watched TV quite differently. For working-class women,

TABLE 6.4

Use of Mass Media as Primary Sources of Information, by Variations in Gender, Age, Education, Race, Income, and Computer Use (in Percentages)

	Tele-vision	News-papers	Radio	Maga-zines	Online	Other[1]	Total
General Public	56	24	14	1	1	4	100
By Gender							
Men	49	29	16	2	1	3	100
Women	62	20	13	1	0	4	100
By Age							
18–29	59	19	13	2	2	5	100
30–49	56	23	16	1	1	3	100
50+	53	30	13	1	0	3	100
By Gender and Age							
Men under 30	53	22	12	3	3	7	100
Women under 30	65	16	14	1	*	4	100
Men over 30	47	32	16	1	1	3	100
Women over 30	61	21	13	1	1	3	100
By Education							
High school graduate or less	61	21	14	*	1	3	100
Some college	57	23	12	1	1	6	100
College graduate	43	31	19	3	1	3	100
By Computer Use							
Goes online	41	29	19	1	6	4	100
AOL member	42	29	21	2	3	3	100
By Race							
White	52	26	16	1	1	4	100
Non-White	72	12	10	1	1	4	100
By Income							
Under $30,000	66	16	11	1	*	6	100
$30,000–$50,000	53	28	16	*	*	3	100
Over $50,000	49	26	17	3	2	3	100

Source: RTNDF, Profile of the American News Consumer, Washington, DC, 1997. Reproduced with permission.

[1]"Other" includes people, other media, and those giving multiple answers or unable to cite a particular source of information they rely on most.

*Less than 0.5%.

television presented a realistic portrayal, but middle-class women were much more skeptical of the realism of what they saw. Press suggests that "working-class women are particularly vulnerable to television's presentation of the accoutrements of middle-class life as the definition of what is normal in society" (p. 138).

Ethnicity and Race.   Various ethnic and racial groups also produce differences in mass media use. One national survey of fourth graders conducted by the U.S. Department of Education's National Center for Education Statistics shows that Hispanic children watch more television than white children, and African American children watch far more television than the other two groups. The study, repeated for two years, shows the comparisons in Table 6.5. Social scientists have not been able to say with certainty what causes this variance in TV viewing, or why it is so wide, but most believe it reflects poverty and other socioeconomic conditions in less advantaged communities.

TABLE 6.5

Percentage of Fourth-Graders Who Say They Watch 4 or More Hours of TV a Day

	1992	*1994*
White	35.7	36.6
Hispanic	48.9	49.9
African American	63.4	68.7

Source: National Center for Education Studies.

In another study, Jacqueline Bobo (1995) examined different perceptions of the movie *The Color Purple*. She found that black activists, black males, and black male critics regarded the film as racist, with stereotypical images of black men. On the other hand, black women identified with the main characters and felt a sense of empowerment from the portrayal of black women as strong lead characters.

Generational Differences.   These are being studied more carefully by demographers and sociologists, who have found common groupings and characteristics in certain age groups. One study, by the advertising agency BBDO Worldwide, found generational differences more important than race for certain categories of TV viewers. The agency found that a significant disparity continues to exist between the prime-time preferences of blacks and other viewers, except for young people ages 12 to 17. In that age group, 14 of the top 20 programs are the same for black teens and all teens, whereas for viewers 18 to 49, only 2 programs out of the top 20 are the same for both groups. Perhaps young people of all ages sense a kinship with one another that older generations do not share.

One popular typology divides the generations into four groups: *generation X*, born 1965 to 1976 (about 44.6 million in the U.S.); *baby boomers*, born 1946 to 1964 (about 77.6 million); *matures*, born before 1946 (about 68.3 million); and *others*, a generation still to be named, born after 1976 (about 72.4 million). Each generation group is an audience with different media behavior. For example, matures might prefer "The Golden Girls" and "Masterpiece Theatre"; boomers probably would choose "The X-Files" and "M*A*S*H" reruns; while generation Xers go for "America's Funniest Home Videos" and "The Simpsons." In general, generation Xers are more television-oriented, read fewer newspapers, and are quicker to turn to new media such as the Internet.

COMMUNICATOR ENCODING–AUDIENCE DECODING

As we have seen earlier in this book, the messages of mass communication must be put into the codes, or languages, of each medium. Communicators, gatekeepers, and audiences each bring their own experiences, perceptions, and languages to the process of encoding and decoding messages. Mass communicators are influenced by their personal experiences and by requirements of their media. Those receiving messages are also influenced by their own personal experiences as well as by their expectations of media. Thus, an audience may not understand what the original messengers meant to say.

For example, a white middle-aged male, with a postgraduate education in sociology writing for a scholarly journal might write the previous two sentences: "Decoding is the process whereby audiences use their implicit knowledge of both medium-specific and broader cultural codes to interpret the meaning of a medium's text. Thus, different types of groups within a general audience may decode the medium's message in line with the preferred meaning of the communicator or negotiate oppositional meanings." A young script writer trying to make the same point in a movie might have a young street-wise kid say, "Hey, if you have to use sign language, there's no way I can get your meaning, so I'll just have to make up something."

AUDIENCE–COMMUNICATOR RELATIONSHIPS

Perhaps the most important distinction about mass media audiences is the degree to which the relationship between communicator and audience is one-way or two-way. That is, are audiences passive recipients of messages or are they active participants in the mass communication process? As we will see in chapter 7 on media effects, passive audiences are less likely to be affected by mass media. So it is important to understand the difference. McQuail (1997) described three kinds of relationships: the audience as spectator (or passive), the audience as target or commodity (passive-active), and the audience as participant (active).

Passive Spectator Audiences

The *passive spectator audience* theory is perhaps the most common way we think about mass media audiences. Russell Neuman (1991) called this the *helpless audience* and shows how it derives from many arguments:

1. The *information overload* concept states that we are so overwhelmed by the quantity of mass-mediated messages that we are hypnotized by them.
2. The *audience segmentation* argument suggests that messages are targeted to exploit our weaknesses and prejudices.

3. The *medium-is-the-message* concept says that media technology determines the way we think about the message.
4. The *communication flow* notion posits that an increasingly global communication flow is breaking down national, regional, and local boundaries and cultures.
5. The *addiction* thesis argues that use of mass media becomes habitual, and that we use media without thinking or processing its messages.
6. *Cultivation analysis* or *spiral of silence* concepts suggest that the increased subtlety and sophistication of persuasive communication makes audiences into hapless victims.

We describe most of the theories mentioned in the previous paragraph further in chapter 7, but it is useful to discuss another media behavior, **habitual media use**, separately here. Although mass media are certainly not drugs like heroin, cocaine, or tobacco, many observers note that we do develop media habits, suggesting that we passively engage in media activities without making deliberate choices. For some of us such habitual behavior might be reading a newspaper every morning at breakfast. For others it might be watching every episode of a TV soap opera or sitcom, the evening news before or with dinner, late evening news before bedtime, or late-night talk shows to induce sleep.

Mass media companies encourage habitual use of their products for obvious marketing reasons. Subscribing to newspapers and magazines is an example of making a decision to use a medium on a regular basis; and once the subscriber is "hooked," subscription renewal is easier than was the first purchase. For one thing, we grow accustomed to the way in which "our" newspaper or magazine organizes its information, or to the way "our" TV station presents the news, or schedules "our" programs. Media that are produced serially, such as newspapers, magazines, and radio and television programs, have a better chance of success in developing repeat users than do individually sold media such as books, movies, and sound recordings. Efforts to build habitual behavior into these latter media have included monthly book and record clubs and books and movies that are produced serially, such as *Batman* and its sequels, the *Star Wars* trilogy and its "prequel," as well as detective or romance novels or other book genres in series. Sometimes these use the same cast of characters in book after book, fostering the habit of turning to media products we know and like and feel comfortable with.

The passive nature of the audience is also demonstrated by the phenomenon called **inheritance effects**. This term refers to the unusually high percentage of overlap in audiences from one program to the next, even when the content of successive programs is very different. Television audience surveys show, for example, that of those who watch TV at 7:00 P.M. each weekday evening, 74.4 percent will be watching at 8:00 P.M., 66.9 percent will be watching at 9:00 P.M., and 50.2 percent will still be engaged with televison at 10:00 P.M. A popular program aired early in the evening will bring in audiences and then keep them watching television for much of the evening. Social scientists have found few satisfactory explanations for inheritance effects other than laziness and passivity.

Many studies and examples exist supporting the passive spectator notion of mass media's audiences, some of which are identified elsewhere in this book, especially in chapter 7. In spite of this, a growing number of researchers argue that mass media use is an active, not merely a passive, activity.

Active Participant Audiences

The *active participant audience* theory suggests that audiences are made up of individuals, with their own lives and histories and social networks, and much recent research focuses on active interpretation of individual meaning. This research suggests three ways in which audiences are increasingly seen as active.

1. *Individual interpretation* is required for communication to be complete. This idea suggests that meanings of mass media messages are not fixed but constructed by audience members through an active engagement of audience member with audience text. Only in the context of audience interpretation do media messages take on meaning.
2. *Collective interpretation* takes place because audiences do not usually read, listen, or watch in a vacuum. Mass media are part of our social lives, and we often engage them in social settings, or we discuss their messages and meanings with other people. Turning to media reviews is another way of seeking collective interpretation of a book, a movie, a TV program, a magazine, a newspaper article, or an editorial column.
3. *Collective action* quite often occurs where audiences take formal and public stands on media productions, both positive and negative, making demands or seeking corrections or additions.

Even the notion of information overload, the overwhelming avalanche of messages with which we are faced, is increasingly being questioned. Neuman (1991) points out that audiences "have developed considerable skill in organizing, filtering, and skimming information through coping strategies or partial attentiveness." He suggests that most people do not feel bombarded by the expanded array of choices. For the most part, he says, audiences "seek out more media and respond enthusiastically to expanded choices. Media behavior is voluntary behavior. People [actively] choose to be exposed" (p. 90).

Target or Commodity Audiences

The *target or commodity audience* is probably the view of most producers of mass communication. They are interested in targeting their products to a market of buyers. It is the model for most advertising and public information campaigns, as well as for much education. The most massive media—newspapers, magazines, radio, and television—rarely, if ever, produce content as a work of art, for the beauty of creation alone. Almost always they are manufactured as products to be sold and are in search of a market to which they are targeted. Mass media not only sell their products to buyers, they sell audiences to advertisers as well. The audience is seen as an entity, a package, and a price is placed on that package depending on its size, its quality, and the quality of the media content that creates the audience in the first place.

AUDIENCES OF NEWS

In the chapter 2 discussion of functions, we explained *why* audiences use mass media. Here, as an example of function, we look at audience variations in the use of news. Of most concern is that general audience consumption of news has declined over the past 2 to 3 decades. In 1990, The Times Mirror Center for the People and the Press released a study showing the number of people who had "read a newspaper yesterday" had declined from 71 percent of the total population to 44 percent from 1965 to 1990. The overall decline was even greater for people under 35. Those who "watched television news yesterday" declined in that same period from 55 percent to 53 percent, with greater decline for those under 35 years old. Those who "listened to radio news yesterday" declined from 58 percent to 53 percent, but the decline was less for those under 35.

According to a "Profile of the American News Consumer" (Anon., 1997), television has become the primary source of information for most audiences, 56 percent, whereas newspapers are primary sources for only 24 percent and radio for 14 percent. Audiences for news also vary by demographics. More men use newspapers as their primary source of information (29 percent) than do women (20 percent), whereas more women use television (62 percent) than men (49 percent). Gender, education, race, and income also make a difference in the way people use mass media as their primary information source. See Table 6.4 on p. 114.

Furthermore, when audiences can demonstrate their choices of news content within a news medium, the content itself finds its audiences according to demographics.

AUDIENCES FOR SPECIALIZED AND NEW MEDIA

As mass media become more specialized—especially the proliferation of specialized magazines and books, cable television, and particularly the Internet—audiences for these media are naturally far more diverse. Going online, using the Web, and getting news regularly online are still activities in which only a few engage, although percentages will certainly increase in the years ahead. More important, those who go online, use the Web, and get news online regularly are much more likely to be young, male, educated, and higher-income audiences.

In other words, these media are *differentially available*. Their use depends a great deal on education and financial resources. Specialized magazines and books are obviously aimed at audiences with special training and education or interests. They are generally more expensive and often reflect expensive interests. Cable TV, with its rising rates, may not be readily available to a fairly large poverty-level segment of the population. Computers and online services are still fairly expensive for the average consumer. They certainly aren't as inexpensive as radio, network television, and daily newspapers. Two outcomes are important to be considered here.

Audience fragmentation is one predicted result of the rise of new and specialized media. Cable television provides a good example of the fragmentation of the television audience. In the 1970s, before cable TV became widespread, the three major networks during weekday evening prime-time hours were watched by about 95 percent of all U.S.

households. In the 1990s, after the advent of cable and other new media, the three networks had a household prime-time penetration rate of less than 60 percent. The average household can now receive more than 30 channels at any given time. Some cable systems are capable of carrying 70 or more channels. Audiences with satellite-receiving dishes are technically capable of receiving up to 500 different channels (but there are far fewer different programs available at any one time without overlap and repetition).

Television audiences have thus been fragmented into dozens, hundreds, even thousands of different audiences for programming. Magazines have fragmented their audiences even more. One might say that book, record, and movie audiences have always been fragmented. Each title finds its own unique audience. Online media will have an audience that is even more fragmented, since the production of messages and content will be available to almost anyone who can receive messages.

Audience polarization is another key outcome of proliferation and specialization of new media. New media that appeal to specialized interests and audiences also create new audiences, thereby, new publics, new groups. These audiences can become polarized in their own special groups. Instead of becoming part of a larger heterogeneous public, they can become part of a smaller homogeneous group. Many examples of polarization have already become apparent in American culture, for example, distinct cliques in high school.

Fragmentation of radio has had an interesting polarizing effect on many Americans. Before radio stations adopted specialized music formats, most radio broadcast "middle-of-the-road" programming—a little jazz, a little classical, a little country, a little top forty, and so on. The radio audience was a general, heterogeneous audience that listened to a great variety of different music forms. With the adoption of special formats, radio listening began to specialize as well. One small segment (mostly older, better educated, higher income categories) listens primarily to classical music. Other segments (even smaller) listen only to jazz. A much larger segment listens only to country, or oldies. Young segments of the population might listen only to rock, and within that category are demographic groups who listen only to album-oriented rock or other categories of rock music. It didn't take long for classical audiences to know nothing about rock, and vice versa. Audiences for music have become polarized.

This same phenomenon can occur for many categories of the population: business people polarized by specialized business media, workers polarized by labor media, liberals by liberal media, conservatives by conservative media, feminists by feminist media, male chauvinists by male chauvinist media.

AUDIENCE ATTITUDES TOWARD MASS MEDIA

Finally, we need to examine how various audiences react to mass media. For the last 50 years or more, systematic studies of public opinion have attempted to provide answers to these concerns. Of course, the main response comes from audience media selection in the marketplace and media use; those on which we spend time and money must be serving a useful purpose in our lives. And yet, in spite of our heavy use of and dependence on mass media, wrote Elizabeth Kolbert (1995), many studies show that Americans have a "starkly negative view of popular culture, and blame television more than any other single factor for teen-age sex and violence (p. 23)."

Her conclusions are based on a *New York Times* nationwide survey showing that a majority of adults felt TV was "a lot to blame" for sexually active teenagers (52 percent) and for teenage violence (56 percent), that 84 percent had forbidden children to watch certain TV programs, 64 percent had forbidden certain movies, and 42 percent certain musical recordings. The vast majority also favored content ratings for television (84 percent), for video games and tapes (79 percent), and for music (72 percent).

Other studies indicate a decline in public trust of the mass media. A *USA TODAY*/CNN/Gallup Poll in 1997 indicated that public trust in news media had fallen from 68 percent to 53 percent in the preceding 25 years. A Gallup poll rating journalists on honesty and ethical standards found that only 32 percent rated TV reporters high or very high in 1990, and the percentage had fallen steadily to 23 percent by 1996. Newspaper reporters fared even worse, falling from 24 percent in 1990 to 17 percent in 1996.[5] Meanwhile, another study of 515 journalists and 2,000 members of the general public showed that journalists did not fully understand or appreciate the "cultural divide" between them and the public. Only 10 percent of the journalists thought media sensationalism was a serious matter, but twice as many nonjournalists thought so (Kurtz, 1995).

Audiences divide into fairly discrete categories in their attitudes about media. Another Gallup survey completed in 1986 showed that the public divides into six distinct groups, three critical and three supportive of the press:[6]

Vociferous critics represent only about 5 percent of the public, but they are most outspoken in questioning press morality. Many believe the media actually harm democracy. Vociferous critics tend to be the heaviest news consumers and are most likely to have been in the news themselves. They tend to be affluent, college-educated, conservative men. Unlike most of the public, they think the news media can stand up to the power structure. They just wish the press would not stand up so often. An example might be someone like Rush Limbaugh.

Main Street critics make up about 15 percent of the population. They tend to be conservative, middle-Americans in small towns who regard the press as biased and uncaring but still see it as highly professional.

Embittered critics are about 10 percent of the population. They tend to be non-white, lacking a high school diploma, and over age 50. They see the press as immoral and unprofessional, but they also tend to have negative attitudes toward other institutions, except for the military.

Reflexive supporters constitute about 21 percent of the population. They find little to criticize in the press but know little about news. They tend to be older, pro-labor, and female, with only a grade-school education.

Empathetic supporters are about 26 percent of the public. They appreciate the press's watchdog role and believe its failures are caused by outside pressures. They tend to be upper-income, college-educated, female, and more liberal than the general public.

Ambivalent supporters are about 23 percent of the public, and they appreciate the press yet question its practices.

Without doubt, public attitudes toward the press and mass media are complex, making quick and easy interpretations of data often misleading. In addition, fragmentary survey results usually reflect instant snapshots of public opinion rather than well-thought-out views or deep-seated beliefs. At one time or another, all of us have been angry with mass media, yet all of us have trusted and depended on them as well.

Even the great father of press freedom, Thomas Jefferson, who, as we mentioned, authored the First Amendment guaranteeing press freedom, had his moments of doubt and disgust. In 1819, long after he had left the presidency, he wrote in a letter that he had become so dismayed with American journalism that he was now reading only one newspaper, the *Richmond Enquirer,* "and in that chiefly the advertisements, for they contain the only truths to be relied on in a newspaper."[7] Clearly, we all have our moments of doubt about mass media, but we also need to see that we are members of various media audiences. Understanding that is essential to understanding the process.

Further Reading

Anon. (1985). *The Media and the People: Americans' Experience With the News Media, a Fifty-Year Review.* New York: Gannett Center for Media Studies.

Anon. (1997a). *Changing Channels: Young Adults, Internet Surfers and the Future of the News Audience.* Washington, DC: Radio Television News Directors Foundation.

Anon. (1997b). *News in the Next Century: Profile of the American News Consumer.* Washington, DC: Radio Television News Directors Foundation.

Ball-Rokeach, Sandra J., and Cantor, Muriel G. (Eds.). (1986). *Media, Audience, and Social Structure.* Thousand Oaks, CA: Sage.

Becker, Lee B., and Schoenbach, Klaus. (Eds.). (1989). *Audience Reponses to Media Diversification: Coping With Plenty.* Mahwah, NJ: Lawrence Erlbaum Associates.

Bobo, Jacqueline. (1995). *Black Women as Cultural Readers.* New York: Columbia University Press.

Croteau, David, and Hoynes, William. (1997). *Media/Society: Industries, Images, Audiences.* Thousand Oaks, CA: Pine Forge.

Dennis, Everette E., and Pease, Edward C. (Eds.). (1996). *Children and the Media.* New Brunswick, NJ: Transaction.

Ettema, James S., and Whitney, D. Charles. (1994). *Audiencemaking: How the Media Create the Audience.* Thousand Oaks, CA: Sage.

Hornblower, Margot. (1997, June 5). Great Expectations. *Time,* pp. 58–68.

Kent, Raymond. (Ed.). (1994). *Measuring Media Audiences.* London and New York: Routledge.

Kolbert, Elizabeth. (1995, August 20). Americans Despair of Popular Culture. *The New York Times,* p. 23+.

Kurtz, Howard. (1995, May 22). Study Suggests Cultural Divide Separates the Press, the Public. *The Washington Post,* p. A6.

Levy, Mark R., and Gurevitch, Michael. (Eds.). (1994). *Defining Media Studies: Reflections on the Future of the Field.* New York: Oxford University Press. (See especially the section "Audiences and Institutions.")

McQuail, Denis. (1997). *Audience Analysis.* Thousand Oaks, CA: Sage.

Minow, Newton, and Lamay, Craig. (1995). *Abandoned in the Wasteland: Children, Television, and the First Amendment.* New York: Hill & Wang.

Morley, David. (1980). *The "Nationwide" Audience.* London: British Film Institute.

Neuman, W. Russell. (1991). *The Future of the Mass Audience.* New York: Cambridge University Press.

Press, Andrea. (1991). *Women Watching Television: Gender, Class, and Generation in the American Television Experience*. Philadelphia: University of Pennsylvania Press.

Robinson, John P., and Godbey, Geoffrey. (1997). *Time for Life: The Surprising Ways Americans Use Their Time*. University Park: Penn State University Press.

Spigel, Lynn. (1992). *Make Room for TV: Television and the Family Ideal in Postwar America*. Chicago: University of Chicago Press.

Strasburger, Victor C. (1995). *Adolescents and the Media: Medical and Psychological Impact*. Thousand Oaks, CA: Sage.

Times Mirror Center for the People and the Press. (1990, June 28). The Age of Indifference: A Study of Young Americans and How They View the News. Los Angeles: Times Mirror, Inc.

Webber, Thomas E. (1997, October 24). Where the Boys and Girls Are: Teens Talk About the Web. *The Wall Street Journal*, p. B1+.

Webster, James G., and Phalen, Patricia F. (1997). *The Mass Audience: Rediscovering the Dominant Model*. Mahwah, NJ: Lawrence Erlbaum Associates.

Zukin, Cliff. (1997). *Generation X and the News*. Washington, DC: Radio Television News Directors Foundation.

Notes

[1]Veronis, Suhler statistics are derived from a variety of sources, including the Newspaper Advertising Bureau, Magazine Publishers of America, Gallup, Motion Picture Association of America, Television Bureau of Advertising, Leo Shapiro and Associates, Wilkofsky Gruen Associates. They are estimates derived using data for television and radio, survey research and consumer purchase data for recorded music, newspapers, magazines, books, and home video, and admissions to movies. Adults 18 and older were the basis for estimates except for recorded music and movies in theaters, where estimates included persons 12 and older.

[2]"TV Industry Issues, Fast Facts and Resources," a continually updated reference source of the National Association of Broadcasters, 1998. The NAB is a good source for information about broadcasting and its audiences.

[3]These facts come from the *Facts About Newspapers*, 1997, an annual publication of the Newspaper Association on America, also a good source of information about newspapers.

[4]A. C. Nielsen has created an "audience homogeneity index" based on data from the Nielsen Homevideo Index: Cable Network Audience Composition Report (first quarter 1989), which divides the audience into 11 age–sex categories (children 6–11, teens 13–17, men 18–34, women 18–34, men 35–49, women 35–49, men 50–64, women 50–64. Men 65+, women 65+). The index was computed following these steps: (a) The number of persons in each of these categories who viewed each of the networks was converted into a percentage; (b) the number of persons in each of these categories included in the total people meter sample was converted into a percentage; (c) for each category, the percentage of persons who viewed the network was subtracted from the percentage in the total sample; (d) the absolute value of these differences were summed for each network to yield the index for that network,.

[5]See Benedetto, Richard. (1997, June 17). 25 years After Watergate, Public Trust Has Plunged, *USA TODAY*, p. 4A.

[6]See Radol, Andrew. (1986, January 25). The Vociferous Minority. *Editor & Publisher*, p. 13A.

[7]Quoted in Hentoff, Nat. (1985, May 2). Would You Buy a Used Typewriter From a Journalist? *The Washington Post*, p. 27A.

7

IMPACT: EFFECTS OF MASS MEDIA

In 1995 in a Woody Harrelson–Wesley Snipes movie thriller, *Money Train*, a sadistic pyromaniac named Torch squirted gasoline on clerks through the money-changing opening in a New York City subway toll booth and then set the booth on fire, creating an instant crematorium. Some weeks after the movie was shown in New York, two men poured a highly flammable liquid on a New York City toll booth clerk, setting him on fire inside his burning coffin.

In 1996, a court in Maryland convicted a man in a triple murder-for-hire case. He had been hired to kill another man's ex-wife, disabled son, and nurse to collect the insurance on their lives. At his trial, evidence was presented that showed he had read a book called *Hit Man: A Technical Manual for Independent Contractors*. Prosecutors proved more than 20 connections between advice in the book and steps the murderer had taken, including his using an AR–7 rifle, shooting the victims in the eyes, and his way of modifying and disposing of the weapon.

In 1995, also in Maryland, a 16-year-old stabbed a woman to death. He had dyed his hair orange and police said he was acting out a scene from the movie *A Clockwork Orange*. He told police he wanted to run away in a white Bronco like O. J. Simpson, and that he was planning a crime spree along the lines of the movie *Natural Born Killers*. Much was made of his "media-inspired" behavior, but it turned out he was also under psychiatric care at the time.

These are a few of many instances these days in which real life seems to imitate art, or at least imitates mass media, whether artistic or not. Such actions raise natural concerns about the effects of mass media, and for those who argue a direct cause-and-effect relationship between media and action, the next consideration is whether higher authorities should determine what can and cannot be communicated to the public through mass media, or even whether direct censorship should be used.

These issues have become particularly significant at a time when mass media seem so filled with violence and explicit sexuality.

It is important, then, that we try to understand precisely and to the best of our ability the effects of mass media. For much of the twentieth century, at least from the 1920s on, social scientists theorized and conducted research in an effort to provide answers to questions of media impact. This chapter summarizes the key theories and findings from nearly 8 decades of research. During that period, ideas about media effects have changed considerably.

RESEARCH DIFFICULTIES

At the outset of any such discussion, we must admit that proving a cause-and-effect relationship is extremely difficult. Any kind of research on human subjects always raises problems, because there seem to be an infinite number of variables; each human being is a separate individual; and messages and media can be almost as varied as humans themselves. Midway in the twentieth-century effort to study mass media effects scientifically, social scientists admitted these problems, and in 1948 sociologist Bernard Berelson (1949) concluded that all we can know is that "some kind of communication of some kinds of issues, brought to the attention of some kinds of people under some kinds of conditions, have some kinds of effects" (p. 500).

Berelson expanded on this somewhat a few years later when he and Morris Janowitz (1966) wrote:

> The effects of communication are many and diverse. They may be short-range or long-run. They may be manifest or latent. They may be strong or weak. They may derive from any number of aspects of the communication content. They may be considered as psychological or political or economic or sociological. They may operate upon opinions, values, information levels, skills, taste, or overt behavior. (p. 379)

This is still an appropriate caveat with which to begin any discussion of media effects, since all these variables still apply to all mass communication situations.

MASSIVE EFFECTS

Mass Society

The earliest thinking about effects suggested that media could have a powerful impact on human civilization, creating mass societies in response to mass media. These ideas first appeared in the late nineteenth century and were often proposed by those who felt that new sensationalist newspapers, with their lurid headlines, startling features, and crude comic strips, were attracting millions of readers and in the process degrading individual morality, lowering common dialogue, and bringing chaos to society. Such concern has often accompanied the rise of other new media as they have attracted new mass audiences—movies, radio, television, and even the Internet, in turn. Although it is easy to generalize about massive effects of the media, it has been far more difficult to achieve scientific cause-and-effect proof.

In 1938, Orson Welles unwittingly provided fuel for massive-effects theorists. For a Halloween CBS radio program, he produced a drama called "War of the Worlds." It used a news format, with bulletins interrupting a routine program of music, to tell 6 million radio listeners that Martians had landed in New Jersey and were about to invade the world. The program created one of the greatest Halloween scares of all time; streets crowded with families fleeing their homes in New Jersey and New York; bus terminals filled with people wanting to go anywhere to escape; police across the country reporting panic on a scale never seen before. It took days to restore normalcy, and as a result the Federal Communications Commission proclaimed that a news program should never again be used fictionally for dramatic productions without careful and constant disclaimers that the program isn't real news.

The "War of the Worlds" example has often been used to suggest that massive effects are always possible, given the appropriate combination of factors.

Magic Bullet, Hypodermic Needle

A variety of theories had developed by the 1920s which suggested that mass media could operate like magic bullets, or hypodermic needles, penetrating human minds and emotions to create specific responses, not dissimilar to the response to "The War of the Worlds." If one could create the right message with the right media mix, one could get the masses to follow heedlessly. These notions were used to justify enormous expenditures for huge national propaganda campaigns that dominated public communication in much of the world throughout most of the twentieth century.

In World War I, for example, communication and information were used for the first time in military history as essential weapons of warfare. When the American public resisted entry into the war, President Woodrow Wilson authorized an enormous national propaganda campaign, using every method of public communication—newspaper and magazine articles, books, motion pictures, billboards and posters, and public speakers—to persuade Americans that they should fight "the war to end all wars." The campaign was successful, but the promise to end all wars certainly wasn't.

The **campaign** has become a standard feature of advertising, marketing, public relations, and advocacy journalism. It is based on the strategy of using many different forms of media, or many different versions of the message, repeated over a period a time, to influence an audience or the public.

Propaganda

Both fascists and communists seized on propaganda techniques in the 1920s and 1930s to organize and control masses of society in Nazi Germany and the Soviet Union. In both cases, fascist and communist leaders took over their entire mass media systems to achieve total control of the message and the method of communicating it. The Nazi Joseph Goebbels felt he could make a science out of propaganda to obtain precisely the desired results from the masses. The Soviets were less concerned about science; they simply controlled the total communication of society—even including interpersonal—and silenced, imprisoned, exiled, or sometimes even annihilated those who resisted.

Theorists who study propaganda of all sides have attempted to differentiate various kinds. **Black propaganda**, of the sort used by communists and fascists, involves deliberate and strategic communication of lies. **White propaganda** involves intentional suppression of potentially harmful information and ideas while promoting positive information or ideas. **Gray propaganda** involves communicating ideas that may or may not be false. In the past, most Americans felt that the United States might be involved in white propaganda, or possibly in some strategic cases, in gray propaganda, but never in black propaganda. That certainly was the feeling of most Americans in World Wars I and II, and even during the Korean War. Now, however, with increasing revelations about American government lies about the Bay of Pigs invasion, the Vietnam War, the Watergate affair, the Irangate affair, and the Persian Gulf war, Americans are more skeptical of the propaganda efforts of their government.

Throughout the twentieth century national communication campaigns were conducted to affect social and human behavior. Many were successful, providing further support for massive effects arguments. During World War II, the American government's war campaign was even bigger and more sophisticated than it was in World War I, influencing Americans to enlist, to volunteer, to work hard, to save, to keep a "tight lip," all to beat the enemy and save the world for democracy. During the Vietnam War, America's information campaign was not so well organized or articulated, partly because the war was never officially declared by Congress and also perhaps because many Americans were ambivalent about that war. But in the Persian Gulf war in 1991, once again the government proved it could generate overwhelming support for war by thoroughly organizing and controlling public communication for the short duration of the war. Had the war lasted longer, that control might not have been possible.

Wars are not the only reasons why governments conduct nationwide campaigns. Using similar techniques, government has changed attitudes and behaviors about using seat belts in cars, reducing high blood pressure, volunteering for military service, reducing litter on the highways, and understanding the dangers of smoking. Governments are not alone in conducting such wide-reaching campaigns. Businesses are constantly using national advertising, much of it successful, to get us to buy, to eat, to diet, to smoke, to quit smoking, and many other exhortations.

NORMATIVE EFFECTS

Much research in the mid-twentieth century, however, suggested that mass media were not all that powerful. Many authorities argued that even in clever campaigns, mass media cannot make us do things against our will; they cannot force us to change our beliefs, our values, our customs, or traditions. Those who supported this view often suggested that media reflect normal values. They argued that media for the most part present a middle-of-the-road view of the world, rarely an extremist view, at least in a free market media system such as the United States'. They reasoned that, in a system in which the media can only survive when they make a profit, the natural inclination is to reflect views and values of the general public to attract a large enough audience to make a profit. Any attempt to express extremist ideas or information would alienate paying customers and put the medium out of business.

Normative ideas of media are somewhat related to a libertarian philosophy of the marketplace. If all citizens are free to speak, publish, or broadcast whatever they want in public, libertarians hold, people will select what is good and true. The market will ultimately drive out the false or defective. John Milton, in his 1644 essay *Areopagitica*, a document that influenced America's founding philosophers, wrote that in a fair debate, good and truthful arguments will always win out over lies and deceit.

In America a hundred years later, Benjamin Franklin echoed Milton by writing that truth will always win in a contest with lies. Thomas Jefferson built this idea into the Declaration of Independence by asserting that the individual right to express the truth was more important than government's right to control the individual and later into the First Amendment to the Constitution, saying that freedom of speech and press were absolutely essential to democracy, for only with such freedom would truth emerge in society.

In the late 1940s, as television was becoming a massive new medium, social scientist Joseph Klapper, who headed social research at CBS, wrote a book called *The Effects of Mass Media* (1960/1986) in which he argued that the free marketplace should be applied to the new mass medium—television—as well as to the printed word. Most studies, he wrote, show that mass media *"reinforce our old opinions more than they convert us to new ones* [italics added]" (pp. 8–9). Old opinions are the values, beliefs, customs, and traditions taught to us by our parents, teachers, and religious leaders. Once those values are set, Klapper suggested, it is unlikely that mass media can change them. In addition, he reasoned, because the media seek our attention, they are most apt to reflect merely what we already hold to be true.

Klapper held that mass media could affect the intensity with which we hold our opinions, or could *create new opinions on subjects for which we had no opinion, more easily than they could change existing ones*. In fact, some scholars argue that mass media lag behind the general public in taking stands on issues, waiting until strong opinions have taken hold of the public before joining the crowd, especially in controversial areas. For example, they say, it wasn't until after society had shown a general acceptance of gay and lesbian culture that television networks dared to have a prime-time sitcom ("Ellen") featuring a lesbian as the lead character.

OBSERVABLE AND DEMONSTRABLE EFFECTS

Mass media content may not affect all aspects of human behavior, nor affect all humans in the same way. But some effects have become clearly evident among parts of their audiences, if not a majority. These effects have been observed by many social scientists and can be easily confirmed by our own experiences, and we can label or categorize them.

First Exposure

Philosophers have usually held that the first exposure human beings have to an idea is apt to have the most powerful influence. Religious leaders have long felt that a person exposed to religious values at the earliest age would be unlikely to stray from that religion later in life. Psychologists stress that the formative years, from birth to kindergarten, are the most important in determining a person's values and behavior. After those values are formed, they are less likely to be changed, even by powerful mass media campaigns.

For example, young people whose early childhood was spent in a close family with strong convictions against cigarette smoking are less likely to be influenced by cigarette commercials in mass media than those whose childhood was spent in an atmosphere in which smoking was permissible. On issues in which other early childhood influences were minimal, the mass media can be more successful in promoting new behavior or creating new opinions. Gay and lesbian lifestyles shown on television probably would be more acceptable to those whose values on the subject were not formed in early life or those who had never held an opinion on that issue. But for those who already hold strong opinions, mass media exposure is much less likely to be influential.

Status Conferral

Mass media are likely to confer unusual social status on anyone or anything getting frequent exposure in the media. The bigger a name appears in headlines, and the more a person is depicted, and the more a name or depiction is repeated, the more status that person seems to acquire. This notion has led to the whole business of **celebrity**. Movie stars, rock stars, big-name politicians, as well as criminals and con artists can become celebrities without regard to their real social value. In wartime, generals whose names and pictures get repeated in the news media thereby seem to acquire special status. Almost all American wars have produced presidents who became popular leaders largely because they had acquired superstar status through their frequent mass media exposure during wartime.

Mass media repetition appears to confer status even on those who deserve it least. Charles Manson, a petty criminal, got wide media attention after he orchestrated the murder of Hollywood celebrities; the mass publicity made him well known, and for years while serving his life sentence in prison he was besieged by autograph seekers and offered contracts to publish his story. In the age of mass media, a person who commits a sensational crime might see his or her story made into a popular movie.

In the age of the Internet, status can be conferred on almost anyone who comes up with a new idea. Jennifer Ringley was an unknown 21-year-old college graduate when she went to Washington to work for the government. In her apartment on her Mac computer she positioned a small Connectix QuickCam camera set to snap the shutter once every minute, showing a view of her room and of Jenni when she was in it, doing all the normal things of living. She devised a Web site and offered those pictures to anyone who would send her $15 a year. She didn't do anything unusual for a 21-year-old living in a Washington apartment, although sometimes she could be seen naked making up her bed. Within months, she had 5,500 subscribers and was receiving more than a 100 million hits a week. Before long she was basking in celebrity, her pictures could be found everywhere, including in exhibitions; she was deluged with mail, couldn't go to the corner grocery store without being besieged, and had to delist her phone number and address

Bandwagon

Some research has shown that mass media, by exposing audiences to ideas, can influence people to "get on the bandwagon" and at least temporarily accept those ideas, so they will not feel left out of the crowd.

This phenomenon has been observed often by political scientists in election campaigns. People who haven't made up their minds about the candidates will often choose the name they recognize most, or the candidate who appears to be leading in the polls. In national presidential elections, this behavior has prompted television news officials to follow a policy of not announcing on the West Coast voting trends disclosed in the early evening news on the East Coast, since those results can influence western voters still casting their ballots to vote for the "leading" candidate, so they will be part of the winning side.

The theory has become part of much advertising strategy. "Everybody's doing it, so you should be doing it too." The rush of the masses not to be left out has become an important aspect of crowd psychology. In the first hours after the death of Princess Diana, television showed people in London putting flowers in front of Buckingham Palace; within a day or two tens of thousands of people were rushing to put out flowers to commemorate her death, and the route of her funeral procession was lined for many miles with crowds throwing flowers on her passing hearse.

Spiral of Silence

This theory is similar to the bandwagon idea. It suggests that people gradually perceive which opinions are gaining and which are losing ground, and then they publicly express only those views they feel are safe. Individuals who notice that their personal opinions are spreading and influencing others will voice their opinions self-confidently. But individuals who notice their opinions losing ground will be inclined to adopt a more reserved attitude.

For example, Dennis Rodman, a basketball player for the San Antonio Spurs, Chicago Bulls, and Los Angeles Lakers, had a large fan base of supporters who felt comfortable expressing their positive feelings about his athletic ability. But as he grew more nonconformist, his supporters became less vocal, and after he kicked a cameraman in a fit of temper during a game, his popularity dropped, and it became harder for people who admired his athletic prowess to express themselves. The death of Princess Diana provides yet another example. The news media were so effusive in their elegies and praise that a number of prominent critics remained silent and only much later confessed that they felt intimidated about expressing any critical sentiments about the dead princess.

This theory was given its most complete exposition by a German public opinion analyst, Elizabeth Noelle-Neumann (1993). She was searching for an explanation for why the German people did not speak out more forcefully against Hitler and fascism during the 1930s and World War II. She suggested that as the Nazis grew more vocal and more people seemed to be adopting Nazi ideas, those opposed fell into a growing *spiral of silence*. She has been accused of trying to use this notion to excuse Germans for not opposing the atrocities that were committed by the Nazis.

Information Overload

Mass media can so overwhelm us with information and with options that we turn off as if we were drugged. At the end of the twentieth century we became a society awash in information. Almost any fact we wanted was seemingly accessible and could be downloaded at 14,400 bits a second. Now, there is so much information available that we often forget or overlook the most basic facts, such as the name of our local member of Congress.

In *Data Smog*, author David Shenk (1997) suggests that we are overwhelmed with information coming at us from too many sources at too frequent intervals. In a sea of claims and counterclaims, we sometimes don't know what to believe. Journalists, especially, are bombarded with information by those who seek to influence the public through the news media. Shenk shows how the computer can be used to funnel particular information to specific journalists. An organization hoping to influence journalists can put names and addresses of all the journalists in the world into their systems, cross-referenced in a tier form—national media, regional media, trade press, foreign press, and so on—and then cross-referenced by interest codes. By fax or e-mail, information can be sent instantly to any target group, and journalists have to sort it all out, if they can.

Too much information may cause us to tune out. Some experts say consumers have seen so many government warnings that they are inured to them. Even the word *warning* is becoming ineffective and now must be replaced by scarier terms such as *lethal*, *fatal*, *toxic*, and *poison*. Warnings can backfire and encourage the opposite behavior. Studies show that stickers recommending parental guidance on rap albums, violent videos, and video games may attract the very children who are being warned away.

Perhaps most troubling, it seems that people can become so accustomed to violence that its portrayal by the media no longer has any impact. The news media are full of incidents in which people observing violent crimes stand by and do nothing to help, or stories about people engaged in or observing the most violent and gruesome behavior without concern or remorse.

Computers and the Internet also pose a problem. Stanford Medical Center psychiatrist Dr. Sara Stein suggests that computer addiction and overload can have serious consequences: depression, psychotic disorders, sleep disorders, and even drug abuse. And Stanford psychologist Philip Zimbardo suggests that computers are to blame for the increase in common and even chronic and debilitating shyness, reaching epidemic proportions. The growing use of e-mail, he says, is part of a large-scale deterioration of face-to-face communication.[1]

LIMITED EFFECTS

In the mid-twentieth century, social scientists began research that indicated mass media effects were personal, were different for each individual.

Individual Differences

Mass media affect people in different ways, because we each have our own selective perceptions of the world. We each see things with our own eyes, from our own background.

Selective exposure suggests that we only deal with those media that meet our individual needs, in our own language and culture, predisposed to present ideas and issues with which we already agree. An American business executive is much more likely to read *The Wall Street Journal* than the communist *Daily Worker*. A feminist is more likely to read *Ms.* magazine than *Playboy*.

Selective perception suggests that whatever we see or hear or read, we receive the messages that support our own frames of reference. Conservative readers will write letters to *Time* magazine criticizing its liberal bias in a story, while liberal readers see conservative bias in the same story. A radical feminist may read *Ms.* magazine and receive a much different message from it than a liberal feminist reading the same magazine.

Selective retention suggests that even after exposure, we selectively remember and use only those elements that fit comfortably with our preconceptions and reinforce opinions we already hold.

Agenda Setting

This theory suggests that mass media cannot guarantee public response, but they can at least create the agenda to which the public needs to respond. Gatekeepers can sometimes determine the agenda for much of society by deciding media's content. According to this idea, mass media decision makers decide what is newsworthy, what is entertaining, what is to be advertised and promoted. By doing so, they establish the topics that people think about. In his classic study on *The Press and Foreign Policy*, Bernard Cohen (1963) laid the foundation for agenda-setting studies by writing that the news media "may not be successful in telling people what to think, but [they are] stunningly successful in telling readers what to think about"(p. 13).

Agenda setting has been supported by a number of studies. For example, research on the number of drug stories in three newspapers, three news magazines, and network evening news shows was correlated with Gallup poll data which indicated that the public identified drugs as the most important problem in America at the time. Another study found a correlation between media coverage of environmental issues—air pollution, water pollution, and waste material disposal—with public attitudes about these issues. Television viewers who saw news stories about military weaknesses were later shown to be more concerned about military defense than viewers who had not seen those stories.

Agenda setting is particularly observable during political election campaigns. Candidates appear to be influenced in their platforms, policies, and points of view by the kinds of coverage issues receive. A candidate might float a trial balloon about a policy initiative, but if it isn't picked up by the media it will be dropped from the campaign. Voters appear to be similarly influenced by media coverage; the candidate who gets a lot of coverage is more likely to get a lot of votes. This theory has led to contemporary strategies of political advertising, as we see in the next section.

Agenda Building

An opposite idea suggests that it is possible for individuals, groups, organizations, and institutions to affect the media by managing information in such a way that it becomes news or otherwise gets into the stream of mass communication. Thus, the agenda-setting function of the media can actually be influenced by those outside the media.

For example, a political candidate who constructs the most clever campaign, manages it the best, with the most skillful use of media, will probably get the most coverage and thus have the most influence on the public agenda. A candidate who raises a lot of money can buy a lot of advertising and achieve dominant exposure by flooding the media with newspaper ads and television spots. That exposure can set the agenda. That is one reason why, at the end of the twentieth century, fund-raising became absolutely essential to political success, which depended on buying as much advertising as possible, especially television spots. Studies show that in the 1996 presidential campaign, reporters wrote more stories about the candidates' advertising messages than about their public speeches, an indication that the ads had actually built the agenda.

Uses and Gratifications

The effects of media are dependent on the way we use media and the satisfaction we receive from them. If we need information, seek it out, use it functionally, and take action on it, that information can have a powerful influence. If we turn to media passively, to be entertained or to have as background noise while we do other things, it will not have much impact.

In chapter 2, we discussed the functions of mass media, the reasons *why* we use them, the purposes they serve for us. Here we are concerned with *how* we use them. For example, if we deliberately look up the weather report in the morning newspaper to know what kind of clothes to wear, what we read will likely directly influence how we will dress for the weather of the day. On the other hand, if we watch the evening TV news and it just happens to have a story about the increasing incidence of storms in our region, it is less likely that the report will cause us to go out and get more insurance, put up storm windows, or take any other immediate and direct action. In the first instance, we are actively seeking information; in the second instance, we are passively exposed to information.

[Uses and gratification research is concerned with what people want from media. It provides a framework for understanding the consequences of increased or decreased involvement with mass media. The powerful effects model discussed earlier suggested that audiences were passive and could be manipulated by mass media. A uses and gratification model suggests that individuals are more in control of the process, that they use media to achieve the results they desire, either to be entertained or informed.)

Pornography and Violence

Much research has been done on the effects of pornography and violence in the media. Early research indicated limited effects, suggesting that the impact varied from individual to individual. Some persons reacted more than others. For example, one study showed that some youths who had watched a movie in which a victim was burned to death went out and committed exactly the same kind of crime. But the authors of the study hastened to point out that obviously not everyone who saw the movie committed the crime!

In a landmark study in the early 1960s, three Stanford scholars, Wilbur Schramm, Jack Lyle, and Edwin B. Parker (1961) reached the following conclusions:

> For some children under some conditions, some television is harmful. For other children under the same conditions, or for the same children under other conditions, it may be beneficial. For most children, under most conditions, most television is probably neither particularly harmful nor particularly beneficial. (p. 13)

A similar study published in 1958 concluded that television had little negative effect on children, except for those who were emotionally disturbed or predisposed to a particular stimulus. In other words, normal children would probably not commit a violent act as a result of watching violence on television (Himmelwaite, Oppenheim, & Vance, 1958).

This early thinking about limited effects applied to pornography as well as violence, and to adults as well as children. Later research began to show more direct effects to the general population, normal and abnormal alike, but especially to children and young people. By the end of the century, television had become the dominant mass media activity, especially for children, as we discussed in chapter 6. If preschool children, in their most formative years, have spent more time watching TV and less time with parents, teachers, and religious leaders, it is logical that their values, beliefs, customs, and traditions are going to come from television.

According to the American Psychological Association, the typical TV-watching American child will witness 8,000 murders and 100,000 acts of violence in his lifetime. Cartoons are among the most violent programs. In 1992, WGN's "Cookie's Cartoon Club," Fox's "Tom and Jerry Kids," and Nickelodeon's "Looney Tunes" averaged 100, 88, and 80 acts of violence per hour, respectively. All violence on TV is increasing. In 1980, for example, the most violent prime-time show registered 22 acts of violence per hour. In 1992 the most violent ("Young Indiana Jones") registered 60 acts of violence per hour.[2]

Increasingly, social scientists have found a link between media violence and behavior. In 1993, the *Christian Science Monitor* reported that more than 3,000 studies offered evidence that violent programming had a measurable effect on young minds. One such study, for example, a 1987 survey of 2,760 randomly selected 14- to 16-year-olds, determined that adolescents who engaged in risky behavior (sexual intercourse, drinking, cigarette and marijuana smoking, cheating, stealing, truancy, and driving a car without permission) were likely to spend more time listening to the radio and watching music videos and movies on television than were those who did not.[3] According to a 7-year statistical analysis by University of Washington professor Brandon Centerwall, half of the murders in North America can be attributed directly or indirectly to television viewing.[4]

Sexual explicitness has also increased in mass media. From 1977 to 1988, sexual behavior and sexual suggestiveness increased by 400 percent. A 1988 study found 27 instances per hour of sexual behavior on television. The study found that network TV transmits about 65,000 instances of sexual material per year during the afternoon and prime-time period alone. The average American child or teenager views nearly 14,000 sexual references, innuendoes, and behaviors each year, and less than 150 of those involve birth control, abstinence, sexually transmitted diseases, or personal responsibility. Perhaps the most popular TV channel for young people, MTV, tells stories that involve sexual imagery 75 percent of the time, violence more than 50 percent of the time, and when sexual imagery and violence are combined, the violence is directed against women 80 percent of the time (Brown & Steele, 1995).

In reviewing mass media's impact on sex in American society, Brown and Steele (1995) cited the following statistics: The United States has the highest rate of teenage pregnancy, teenage birth, and teenage abortion of any industrialized nation. Some studies show that more than a million teenagers become pregnant each year and that 80 percent of teenage pregnancies are unplanned. And one out of every six teenagers contracts a sexually transmitted disease. Such statistics do not prove that television caused this phenomenon, but they do verify that such behavior has become part of American culture.

CRITICAL AND POWERFUL EFFECTS

For the reasons cited in the previous paragraphs, by the last decades of the century new concerns were being raised about the powerful effects of mass media, particularly in the area of violence, especially on television. Theorists have become concerned with long-term effects more than short-term, even though long-term is harder to prove scientifically.

Accumulative and Cultivation Effects

Media images mold society by the long-term presentation of relatively uniform versions of social reality. This theory is based largely on 20 years of research by University of Pennsylvania scholar George Gerbner and his associates. Their research shows that mass media influence occurs because of continued and lengthy exposure, especially to television, not just exposure to individual programs or genres. Much of their research is based on differences among heavy, moderate, and light users of television. The "accumulated effects" of mass media exposure "cultivates" the way people think about things; the heavier the exposure, the greater the long-term impact.

For example, if most of the evening TV news every night focuses on violent crimes in our neighborhood, heavy viewers of those programs will be more likely to think of their neighborhood as much more violent than it might really be, or than light viewers think. Because of the heavy use of violence and promiscuity on television, people who watch the most television are most apt to be fearful of the world around them, and the most accepting of violence and promiscuity as a way of life. William J. Bennett, former U.S. Secretary of Education, states this theory in vivid terms:

> Television's real power is its capacity to alter moral sensibilities. It has become a modern template. A violence-filled movie does not by itself cause a viewer to arm up and kill. Nevertheless, lots of time spent before the television set must affect outlook. It does this in part through sheer saturation, through the constant panoply of vivid images—through "total immersion," if you will…. The philosophy being so powerfully promulgated [on much television] is basically this: The *summum bonum* of life is self-indulgence, self-aggrandizement, instant gratification; the good life is synonymous with freedom from all inhibitions; other people are to be used as a means to an end; and self-fulfillment is achieved by breaking rules.[5]

Cultural Effects

Culture is really a system of messages and images that regulate and reproduce social relations. If the mass media are the creators of society's messages and images, they are the creators of its culture. By defining what is normal or deviant, what is popular or unpopular, the mass media cultivate similar definitions in the public.

This theory can be demonstrated most clearly by looking at the impact of one culture's mass media on another culture. For example, because teenagers worldwide have spent more time watching American movies and television shows, they have dropped many of their local dress customs and patterns and have adopted the blue jeans of American teenagers. The process can be even more vividly demonstrated when primitive cultures are exposed for the first time to new media.

Cultural anthropologist Edmund Carpenter visited a remote mountain village, Sio, New Guinea, where the natives were still using stone axes and had never been exposed to the outside world. He made Polaroid pictures, movies, and audiotapes of the villagers and played them back. They had never seen themselves depicted, and their first fears turned to fascination, and then changed their lives. Carpenter (1973) later wrote:

When we returned to Sio, months later, I thought at first we had made a wrong turn in the river network. I didn't recognize the place. Several houses had been rebuilt in a new style. Men wore European clothing. They carried themselves differently. They acted differently. Some had disappeared down river toward a government settlement, "wandering between two worlds, one dead, the other powerless to be reborn." (qtd. in Jeffres, 1997, pp. 316–317)

As American mass media have become dominant in the world, growing concern has been expressed about **cultural imperialism**, the idea that American culture, spread by American mass media, overwhelms and changes other cultures. Those who value and want to preserve their own culture have often vehemently resented the intrusion of American mass media, and in a number of countries, attempts have been made to limit the import of American media to protect themselves from American media's cultural effects. Even America's next-door neighbor Canada has tried to restrict American media in order not to Americanize Canadians.

Critical Theories

One point of view is that mass media, especially those directed at the marketplace to reach the maximum number of people for maximum profit, will be so constrained in the production of market-driven content that they will inevitably reinforce the status quo and undermine useful efforts for constructive change. For example, critical theorists say, children's television is driven largely by the need to sell products through advertising, thus greatly reducing the use of television to educate and to make a meaningful contribution to the growth and development of the child.

These theories are usually put forward by neomarxists, who agree with Karl Marx that the hierarchical class system of capitalism is at the root of all social problems; the neomarxists assume that useful change can begin with peaceful ideological reform rather than with violent revolution, and they see the status quo reinforced by capitalist mass media as the major problem. These critics often suggest that the status quo is preserved by the way in which the media *frame* information, through selecting particular aspects of reality to highlight in a message and to make it salient—noticeable, meaningful, or memorable—to audiences. For example, advertising that uses the sex appeal of women to attract the attention of men inadvertently teaches social cues that can have long-term consequences, in this case dominant myths about women that are retold and reinforced.

Technological Determinism

In the long run, the lasting effects of media are not the contents or messages themselves but the medium that imposes its own logic on reality and thus affects the way the brain works. For example, as we indicated in chapter 1, each major change in the technology of society's dominant medium has been accompanied by sweeping and revolutionary changes in society. The Internet is currently changing the way we see ourselves and do business as much as the introduction of Polaroid pictures changed the inhabitants of the Sio village in New Guinea.

Marshall McLuhan in the 1950s and 1960s was the first widely quoted scholar to express this idea. He argued that each new medium, when it became dominant, disrupted tradition and reshaped social life. The rise of print media in the fifteenth century produced democracy and capitalism; the rise of electronic media in the twentieth was producing the new "global village."[6] Many scholars, however, regard the "medium is the message" as an oversimplification of the complexities of the communication process.

A more sophisticated but related version is the medium theory put forth by Joshua Meyrowitz in the early 1990s. He suggested that the nature of the medium itself is the key to its social impact. Media technologies can be powerful social forces in the ways they help organize and construct the cultural environment. This can best be seen in the new technological developments which by the late 1990s had extended the forms of electronic communication, erasing distinctions between media forms. For example, digital communication can link text, image, and sound. Everything can be contained in one personal computer to become the library, the movie theater, the stage, the classroom, the concert hall, or the disco club.

McLuhan wrote *The Gutenberg Galaxy* in the early 1960s about the technological revolution in communication. Sven Birkerts has written *The Gutenberg Elegies* (1994) in the mid-1990s to bring the medium theories up to date. He argues that new technologies of computers and the Internet are "reweaving" our social and cultural life and in the process changing our way of thinking. For example, he writes, we no longer value deliberation as much as decisiveness. We no longer need to know about the world; now we need to know how to access data that will tell us about the world. As we become more enmeshed in advanced computer technologies, he fears, we can lose any sense of unmediated experience. The social world of media will be the only world we know. Newer, faster, space-altering media will squeeze out older cultural forms, including reading and rigorous thinking.

FACTORS THAT INFLUENCE THE EFFECTIVENESS OF MASS MEDIA

Obviously, not all mass communication is equally effective. What makes the difference? We can identify at least three qualities that will influence how powerful a medium's message might be.

1. The Medium or Combination of Media Used.   Some media attract more attention than others. In general, a television program is apt to attract more viewers than a book can attract readers. However, some media require more intense concentration than others. For those who are willing to bring that concentration to their reading of a book, for instance, its message can be far more powerful than the message delivered from television in which the viewer is simply a passive participant. Most communication campaigns conducted to achieve a certain effect will orchestrate the campaign to use a variety of media in various modes to get the desired results.

2. The Presentation of the Message.   Skill and talent are still necessary to make media content attractive, powerful, and influential. A dramatic newspaper picture of a young Vietnamese girl running down the highway naked with burns from a napalm bomb probably did more to shock people about the Vietnam War than thousands of feet of film footage about the war or hundreds of thousands of words.

3. The Exposure Pattern. The way we use mass media is crucial to their impact. Watching a movie in a darkened theater is usually a much more powerful experience than watching that same movie on television. Why? In the darkened theater we are alone with the experience, the screen is large, the sound realistic; we can give ourselves over completely to the experience. When we watch that same movie on television, we usually do so at home, sometimes while doing other things, including eating, talking, even housework; the screen is small, the sound not as good, lights can be on, and we are not so apt to lose ourselves in the experience.

CONCLUSION

Most research on media effects suggests that messages in the mass media are not likely to affect our long-held ideas or to change our cultural values. For example, if we are raised to believe that smoking cigarettes is not healthy, advertisements for cigarettes, as alluring as they might be, are not apt to inspire us to start smoking. On the other hand, much research indicates that when exposure covers a long period of time—and especially when exposure occurs early in life before other factors such as parents, teachers, or religious leaders inculcate our values—then mass media can have a powerful impact. The mass media effects, in fact, can accumulate and thus come to influence the way we think about reality, the way in which our brain processes information, and the way in which we create the patterns of our culture. In such a case, mass media can indeed have a powerful impact.

This notion is especially crucial when we realize that more and more young, preschool children spend more and more time with mass media, especially television. Preschoolers who spend up to 9 hours a day watching television, and an average of only 7 minutes a day talking with their parents, will certainly be molded by the culture of television, not the culture of parents, teachers, or religious leaders.

Finally, the greater the exposure to mass media, the more powerful the influence. And the more effective the media mix and the presentation, the greater the effects.

Further Reading

Barker, Martin, and Petley, Julian. (Eds.). (1997). *Ill Effects: The Media/Violence Debate.* London: Routledge.

Berelson, Bernard. (1949). Communications and Public Opinion. In Wilbur Schramm (Ed.), *Mass Communications.* Urbana: University of Illinois Press.

Berelson, Bernard, and Janowitz, Morris. (Eds.). (1966). *Reader in Public Opinion and Communication.* New York: Free Press.

Birkerts, Sven. (1994). *The Gutenberg Elegies.* Boston: Faber & Faber.

Brown, Jane D., and Steele, Jeanne R. (1995). *Sex and the Mass Media.* Menlo Park, CA: The Henry J. Kaiser Family Foundation.

Bryant, Jennings, and Zillmann, Dolf. (Eds.). (1994). *Media Effects: Advances in Theory and Research.* Mahwah, NJ: Lawrence Erlbaum Associates.

Carpenter, Edmund. (1973). *Oh What a Blow That Phantom Gave Me.* New York: Holt, Rinehart & Winston.

Cavanaugh, John William. (1992). *Media Effects on Voters: A Panel Study of the 1992 Presidential Election.* Lanham, MD: University Press of America.

Cohen, Bernard. (1963). *The Press and Foreign Policy.* Princeton, NJ: Princeton University Press.

Fox, Roy F., and Gerbner, George. (1996). *Harvesting Minds: How TV Commercials Control Kids.* New York: Praeger.

Himmelwaite, Hilde, Oppenheim, A. N., and Vance, Pamela. (1958). *Television and the Child.* London: Oxford University Press.

Jeffres, Leo W., and Perloff, Richard M. (1997) *Mass Media Effects.* Prospect Heights, IL: Waveland.

Klapper, Joseph T. (1986). *Effects of Mass Communication.* Glencoe, IL: Free Press. (Originally published 1960)

Korzenny, Felipe, Ting-Toomey, Stella, and Schiff, Elizabeth. (Eds.). (1992). *Mass Media Effects Across Cultures.* Newbury Park, CA: Sage.

Lindlof, Thomas R. (Ed.). (1987). *Natural Audiences: Qualitative Research of Media Uses and Effects.* Greenwich, CT: Ablex.

Lowery, Shearon A. (1987). *Milestones in Mass Communication Research: Media Effects.* London: Longman.

McLuhan, Marshall. (1996). *The Medium Is the Message: An Inventory of Effects.* Santa Monica, CA: Hardwired.

Meyrowitz, Joshua. (1994). Medium Theory. In D. Crowley and D. Mitchell (Eds.), *Communication Theory Today* (pp. 50–77). Stanford, CA: Stanford University Press.

Noelle-Neumann, Elizabeth. (1993). *The Spiral of Silence: Public Opinion—Our Social Skin.* Chicago: University of Chicago Press.

Rosengren, Karl Erik. (Ed.). (1994). *Media Effects and Beyond: Culture, Socialization and Lifestyles.* London: Routledge.

Schramm, Wilbur. (Ed.). (1971). *The Process and Effects of Mass Communication.* Urbana: University of Illinois Press.

Schramm, Wilbur, Lyle, Jack, and Parker, Edwin B. (1961). *Television in the Lives of Our Children.* Stanford, CA: Stanford University Press.

Shenk, David. (1997). *Data Smog: Surviving the Information Glut.* San Francisco: Harper.

Signorielli, Nancy, and Morgan, Michael. (Eds.). (1990). *Cultivation Analysis: New Directions in Media Effects Research.* Newbury Park, CA: Sage.

Wanta, Wayne. (1997). *The Public and the National Agenda: How People Learn About Important Issues.* Mahwah, NJ: Lawrence Erlbaum Associates.

Notes

[1] Pope, Justin. (1997, September–October). Computers Make Our Lives Easier—and Pull Us Further Apart. *Stanford Today*, pp. 36–37.

[2] Statistics from the National Coalition on Television Violence.

[3] Klein, J. D., Brown, J. D., Childers, K. W., Oliveri, J., Porter, C., & Dykers, C. (1993). Adolescents' risky behavior and mass media use. *Pediatrics*, 92, 24–31.

[4] Link Found Between TV and Homocide Rates. (Fall, 1992). *The New Citizen*, 1(2), online edition: www.main.nc.us/cml/new_citizen.

[5] Television's Destructive Power, (1996, February 29). *The Washington Post*, p. A23.

[6] See especially *The Gutenberg Galaxy* (1962). Toronto: University of Toronto Press. And *Understanding Media: The Extensions of Man* (1964). New York: New American Library.

8

NEWSPAPERS

Newspapers have long been regarded as the *medium of record* in our society, reflecting social, commercial, and political events of a community. They have been considered a truthful account of important public events and reliable interpreter of their meaning. They have sometimes elevated ordinary events to levels of importance; if it was in the paper, then it had significance, not just for the persons involved—a family displaced by fire, a refugee receiving a scholarship, a proprietor closing a neighborhood business—but for the community at large.

Newspapers have served as an index to life. *News of record* includes listings of birth announcements, death notices, marriage licenses, bankruptcies, and legal notices. Community crime reports and community calendars often appear in the newspaper. So sometimes does the school lunch menu. Newspapers have also told us what has happened at city hall, the county court house, the state capital, the White House and Congress, the stock market, the United Nations, and the far-flung corners of the world. They have told us about the weather that is coming and the earthquakes and hurricanes that have struck elsewhere, about the dissensions in our own community and the conflicts anywhere in the world.

American newspapers have played many roles in more than 3 centuries of publication. They have been patriots, urging thoughtful citizens to the devotion to their country. They have been partisan voices, shouting down those with whom they disagreed. They have often stuck up for the little guy—immigrants, laborers, servants—who might not have a voice of their own. They have sometimes favored business and political leaders, and often they have been critical of those elites as well. They have often protected the public good, shining their spotlight of publicity on corruption, cruelty, and betrayal. They have often alerted us to our social and scientific achievements and have reminded us of our failings. They also have often been owned or controlled by powerful people, who sometimes have ruthlessly used the power of the press for their own purposes.

Newspapers reflect the complexity of American society. They serve a number of different functions, including expressing opinions in editorials and columns, selling through display and classified advertising, and entertaining through comic strips and features. However, most people think of news gathering as a newspaper's primary function. Local reporters are usually the backbone of a newspaper. These journalists are faced each day with the responsibility of making news judgments, weighing the importance of stories and the veracity of information on which they are based. Newspaper reporters must struggle daily with all the details of a community, to get all the facts, to tell the stories right, and to do it all quickly, under deadline pressure.

DEFINING NEWSPAPERS

Newspapers are regularly published periodicals produced for a particular town, city, or region, reporting on matters of current interest to those residents. Some newspapers serve a large region, sometimes with special *zoned* editions for local areas. A few serve a national audience, such as *The Wall Street Journal*, a newspaper about business and finance, and *USA TODAY*, a general-interest newspaper whose focus is news important to all U.S. residents.

Modern newspapers usually have many pages, printed on a type of paper known as **newsprint**. American newspapers are usually delivered to the homes of subscribers by carriers organized by the newspaper company; in many other countries of the world, they are delivered by the mail carrier. They are also sold from newsstands, from outdoor vending racks, and in some stores and restaurants.

Newspapers can be **broadsheets**, the large and more typical format, in which news appears above and below the paper's fold, or tabloids, the smaller size, which resemble magazines printed on newsprint. The broadsheet newspaper format is usually used by newspapers with large, stable home or office circulation and somewhat smaller street sales, such as *The New York Times, The Wall Street Journal*, and the *Los Angeles Times*. The front page generally contains a number of stories. American newspapers usually put no ads on the front page to underscore the importance of the news. (In many other countries, ads on page 1 are quite common.)

Tabloid style, on the other hand, is a format usually used by newspapers that depend more on street sales than home subscriptions. Tabloids such as the *New York Post* and *Daily News* generally put a compelling picture or one big news story on page 1. The purpose is to attract customers, often commuters hurrying to or from work, with "hot" news. Tabloids are also easier to read while commuting on a bus or subway. They have become associated with sensational revelations—hence the word *tabloid* often is associated with media sensationalism—but the physical format of the tabloid is also used by some community and specialty newspapers, such as *The Chronicle of Higher Education*, whose reporting would never be considered sensationalistic.

Newspaper layout and design provides a display of each day's essential information in a format that can be quickly digested by the reader. The page is divided into columns, usually five or six in a broadsheet paper, to enhance quick reading. Many stories can be displayed on one page, with headlines of larger type, again for quick comprehension. A **headline** usually contains a complete thought or idea, whereas **title** is usually just a word or phrase to attract attention. The lead paragraphs of each story usually contain the essential facts—the who, what, where, why, when, and how. Thus the newspaper is designed for quick reading. One can absorb much information at a glance.

DEVELOPMENT OF NEWSPAPERS

European Origins and Restrictions

It took about a hundred years after the development of Gutenberg's movable type and printing press in the mid-fifteenth century for publications to be started that printed periodical news. In the mid-sixteenth century, handwritten weekly news sheets called **gazettes**, were sold in the piazzas of Venice. Fifty years later, in 1609, *Zeitung*, a publication printed weekly with some rudimentary facts about local life appeared in Germany, and in 1650 the first daily, *Einkommende Zeitungen*, also was published in Germany. The first English daily, the *Daily Courant*, published in London, did not appear until 1702.

The kings of Europe maintained tight controls over printing presses in the sixteenth and seventeenth centuries. They made certain only the royal version of events was circulated, limiting their critics' and enemies' access to public expression. In most European countries, printers were required to be licensed and to submit their work to government authorities before publication. In the seventeenth century, the English Crown exerted its authority over printers with the Parliamentary Press Restriction Act, which forbade publishing anything that did not carry a licensed printer's signature and place of publication. Licensing requirements changed from time to time, but governments continued to control publishing by levying excessive taxes, imposing postpublication fines and jail sentences, and prohibiting publishing derogatory or inflammatory comments about ruling authorities.

First New World Efforts

The printing press came to Latin America as early as 1534 and was introduced in the North American colonies in 1638. That first press was owned by a Mistress Glover, of Surrey, England. She and her husband, a minister, sailed from England with the press; but he died at sea, so it was a woman who had the first press installed in the American colonies. She later married the president of Harvard College and moved the press there, and the college continued operating the press after her death. The printing craft in America passed down through families, through wives and daughters as well as through sons.

Those early printing presses were used primarily for publication of Bibles, hymnals, and other religious works, not for newspapers. Probably this was because newspapers required approval from the King of England, and there was at first little inclination to ask the King for special favors.

The first newspaper publisher–editor in the colonies emerged from the ranks of colonial entrepreneurs. Benjamin Harris had been a printer in London. Chafing under licensing requirements and the right of the Crown to censor publication, he emigrated to Boston and opened a bookstore. Later, he expanded the store to include a coffee shop, which became a popular place for gossip. On September 25, 1690, Harris probably used some of that gossip to produce the first newspaper in America, *Public Occurrences Both Foreign and Domestick*.

The paper on that Thursday consisted of three printed pages and a blank sheet. It reported a suicide (by hanging), the spread of smallpox, developments in the French and Indian wars, and adultery by the King of France, allegedly with his daughter-in-law. The Massachusetts authorities, infuriated by Harris's decision to publish the newspaper without a license and by his insults to Indian allies and the French monarch, threatened Harris with legal sanctions. His first issue was his last.

Colonial Newspapers

In the American colonies, royal restrictions on printers were enforced by local authorities, such as the colonial governor. Only a brave few resisted these press controls, which persisted into the eighteenth century. Sensitive topics were underplayed or ignored.

However, changes were in the air. In less than a hundred years, the American settlers had grown from scattered settlements to a network of colonies, each with its own local government. Most had come to the new world for religious freedom or for economic opportunity; they were not inclined to pay heed to the restrictions of some distant king. They were also becoming increasingly successful as landowners and merchants. By 1700, the colonists supplied much of Britain's raw materials and themselves constituted a large market for Britain. However, literacy was not widespread. There just were not enough readers to support newspapers, an obstacle as significant as government interference in slowing the development of colonial newspapers.

The communities able to make it worthwhile for a printer to publish a newspaper regularly were the larger town centers of Boston, Philadelphia, and New York. By 1704, Boston had a population of more than 7,000. And in that year, postmaster John Campbell attempted to pick up where Harris had left off. He started the *Boston News-Letter*, and it became the first continuously printed newspaper in the 13 colonies. He was able to obtain approval to publish because of his position as postmaster. His job also provided him with the built-in advantage of access to post riders, who delivered the mail and were good sources of news.

Making the newspaper interesting to readers was difficult for Campbell. He avoided comment on controversial matters (usually the most interesting). He was months late with news from abroad, which was often already known to Bostonians by the time Campbell published it. Perhaps because the *News-Letter* was too bland and too late with the news, it was never financially successful, and after 18 years, Campbell sold it.

Independent Newspapers

James Franklin had a better idea for a newspaper. He was the older brother of Benjamin, and he knew what would sell. He founded the *New England Courant* in 1721, the first newspaper to publish what would become traditional in American journalism: reporting on and critiquing government activity and exposing the agenda of special interests. His newspaper became a success, serving as a community forum, publishing shipping reports, information from neighboring towns, letters from Europe, and letters to the editor from Boston wits. These letters became a popular mainstay, poking fun at the city leaders' morals and manners. The paper irritated the Puritan-controlled government of Massachusetts, and when this kind of journalism ultimately landed James in jail, his younger brother took over the business. It was the beginning of Ben Franklin's illustrious career as printer, editor, author, scientist, philosopher, statesman, and newspaper magnate.

In 1735, in a defining moment for American journalism, another printer, John Peter Zenger, was tried for seditious libel for criticizing the colonial governor in his newspaper the *New-York Weekly Journal.* Even though under common law criticism was no less libelous if it was true, and no one disputed that Zenger had published the criticism, the jury acquitted him of the charge because of the truth of what he had written. For the first time, truth became a defense for publishing criticism. The Zenger case provided an important legal precedent for American newspapers, which have used this right to print the truth to expand the freedom to criticize. The Zenger decision demonstrated colonial Americans' developing consciousness regarding the importance of a free press, one that permitted journalists to be vigilant about matters affecting the public interest.

Revolutionary Newspapers

Colonial newspapers grew from 3 in 1720 to 22 by 1760, and they increasingly took the lead in challenging the authority of the English Crown. Many leaders in the fight for independence were printers, editors, and writers. Their newspapers had become influential in their communities, reporting on politics, economic pressure on the colonies by Britain, and local affairs. With passage of the Stamp Act in 1765, which taxed legal documents, business papers, and newspapers, the colonial press became defiant. Many printers printed without the stamps. Others closed their shops to avoid the tax and a confrontation with authorities, but these printers then faced the wrath of their neighbors, who pressured them to stand up to the Crown. The British Parliament finally repealed the Stamp Act, but the stage had been set for America's final break with England.

Although many British sympathizers lived in the colonies, many more colonists had come to think of themselves as Americans, not English subjects. With support from independent newspapers, which often contained essays about "Americans" and described the colonies as a single political entity, many colonists came to see that their interests and those of the mother country were diverging.

Printers grew more partisan in the 10 years before the Declaration of Independence in 1776. As the inevitable confrontation drew near, newspaper publisher Isaiah

Thomas (1970) published this passionate call in his newspaper, the *Massachusetts Spy*, on May 3, 1775:

> Americans! Forever bear in mind the Battle of Lexington!—where British troops, unmolested and unprovoked, wantonly and in a most inhuman manner, fired upon and killed a number of our countrymen, then robbed, ransacked and burnt their houses! Nor could the tears of defenseless women, some of whom were in the pains of childbirth, the cries of helpless babes, nor the prayers of old age, confined to beds of sickness, appease their thirst for blood—or divert them from their design of murder and robbery! (qtd. in Folkerts & Teeter, 1989, p. 74)

During the Revolution, American newspaper writers were usually patriots who were passionate advocates of the revolt; they were unpaid writers who submitted essays, sometimes using pen names, urging their fellow colonists to continue the fight for freedom. They were people such as Sam Adams, a fiery advocate for independence, and John Dickinson, a Philadelphia lawyer who wrote under the pseudonym of The Pennsylvania Farmer. Their anti-British sentiments and their championing of independence for the colonies were so fervent that they made no pretense of impartiality in what they wrote. For them, a newspaper was a means to one greater end: liberty.

Partisan Newspapers

After the Revolution, newspapers continued to grow in importance and in partisanship. In 1784, the first U.S. daily appeared, the Pennsylvania Packet and Daily Advertiser. This paper and others like it published essays urging citizens of the new nation to ratify the Constitution and adopt a democratic form of government. These essays, written by Alexander Hamilton, John Jay, and James Madison, later became known as "The Federalist Papers," one of the most significant acts in winning the acceptance of the Constitution and an American democracy.

Post-Revolution newspapers continued the custom of challenging authorities, but now they took political sides and attacked their opposite parties. They usually identified themselves with either the Federalist view (for a strong central government) or the Anti-Federalist, or Republican, view (for strong states' rights). Some were owned by political parties, but most others received some partisan financial support. All felt free to be highly subjective in their attacks on political enemies.

Even the revered father figure George Washington took his share of abuse in these political newspapers. Benjamin Franklin Bache, grandson of the famous patriot, published the *Aurora* newspaper, which printed the following on the conclusion of Washington's second term as President:

> The man, who is the source of all the misfortunes of our country, is this day reduced to a level with his fellow-citizens, and is no longer possessed of power to multiply evils upon the United States—If ever there was a period of rejoicing, this is the moment—every heart in unison with the freedom and happiness of the people ought to beat high with exultation, that the name of Washington from this day ceases to give currency to political iniquity and to legalized corruption. (qtd. in Stephens, 1988, p. 201)

Bache's newspaper office was trashed by a group of Revolutionary War veterans who were incensed by these kinds of remarks.

Indeed, the partisanship of newspapers was so vicious that Congress, in spite of the newly adopted Constitution's First Amendment guaranteeing freedom of the press, passed the Alien and Sedition Act, which made it treasonous to criticize public officials. But only Anti-Federalist editors were ever charged under this act by the Federalist-dominated government. And when Jefferson, an Anti-Federalist, became President, he allowed this act, which was clearly in violation of the First Amendment, to lapse. It has never been resurrected.

Newspapers continued to play a partisan role in politics until new printing technology allowed printers to speed up their presses and produce more copies for less money. At that point, they had to find new audiences who would go beyond the small number of readers committed to a political party.

Inexpensive Newspapers: The Penny Press

By 1825, the United States was said to have more newspapers circulating to more people than did any other nation. In addition to being a force for change and for government accountability, newspapering now assumed its place in commerce. Between 1835 and the end of the century, newspapers became successful business enterprises. They were freed of both governmental control and political parties. They were no less politically committed, but now the commitment came from private entrepreneurs who owed their power to large circulations, the force of their own personalities, and the work of journalists who reported news that people paid to read.

Population growth increased the need for newspapers, but fortunately improvements in technology allowed printers to meet that rising demand. New printing inventions, such as the rotary press, enabled printers to produce more copies more quickly and efficiently than ever before. This enabled the seller to reduce the price of the product and still make a profit.

Lowering the price of a newspaper copy to increase its sale started in 1833 when New York printer Benjamin Day began selling his *New York Sun* for 1 cent per copy rather than for the going rate of 6 cents. He hired vendors to hawk the paper on the streets, increasing sales, which in turn attracted advertisers to the larger audience attracted to such an inexpensive product. Within 4 months, Day was selling an unheard of 5,000 copies a day. The combination of revenues from the street sales, plus increasing revenues from advertisers looking for customers, became a model for newspaper economics for the next century and a half.

The success of penny papers ensured a shift from newspapering to benefit the political elite to newspapering for all classes. The development of the penny papers is regarded by many scholars as the beginning of American mass communication.

Rise of the Reporting Function

As newspapers sought to attract larger audiences, they recognized the need to have a reliable source of appealing content. Benjamin Day quickly realized he had to have something new in each issue of his newspaper to get more people to buy it every day. He turned to crime and human interest stories—even a hoax or two, such as one about life on the moon—to entice readers to spend a penny regularly for his paper. Others who followed him, such as James Gordon Bennett's *New York Herald*, and Horace Greeley's *New York Tribune*, imitated Day's sensational content and penny price.

The *Sun*'s motto became, "All the news of the day!" To get that new and interesting content, these editors sent their printers out to the streets, the police station, and the courthouse to get stories. Thus, modern journalism and the reporting function were born. Enterprising printers became reporters who filled the paper with news items that attracted customers. One of Day's young reporters was 21-year-old George Wisner, who specialized in reporting what was happening at the police station. One of his typical stories provides the flavor of the times:

> Mary Ann Coburn was found drunk in the street. She said she was not in the habit of getting intoxicated, but her husband, God Bless Him, had just returned from a five years' voyage—and although she had been married two or three times during his absence, yet she was so much rejoiced on seeing him again, that she went right down to Water Street and drank three glasses of rum.
>
> Magistrate: Why, I think your husband would have refused to live with you after such conduct on your part.
>
> Prisoner: I'll tell you what it is—he likes drink as well as I do.[1]

James Gordon Bennett sent his employees—amateur reporters—to varied locations to gather news. Some were deployed to the Atlantic in boats to meet ships coming into New York harbor so Bennett's paper would be the first with foreign news. This method of news gathering would eventually develop into the modern **beat** system. After the telegraph was invented in the 1840s and lines were stretched from New York to Washington, DC, Bennett was the first newspaper publisher to station a correspondent in Washington to telegraph news from the Capital. The telegraph quickly became indispensable in news gathering, especially as the nation expanded westward. In October 1861, the transcontinental telegraph was complete, speeding the delivery of news across the nation.

Throughout this period of growth in newspapering, publishers and editors steadily improved methods of news gathering, and the news business expanded. Many of today's metropolitan dailies got their start during this era. The *Chicago Tribune* opened in 1847, *The New York Times* was established by Henry Raymond in 1851, joining Bennett's *Herald* and Greeley's *Tribune* in the nation's largest city. The newcomer *Times* would outlast the other two. *The New York Times* and *Chicago Tribune* are now the third- and seventh-largest newspapers, respectively, in the United States.

In 1848, New York dailies formed the Harbor News Association to save money by sending just one boat to meet ships coming from Europe and then sharing the news. In 1856, this organization evolved into The Associated Press (AP), the news cooperative that continues to serve daily newspapers and broadcasters to this day. Figure 8.1 shows just how large this organization has grown.

Founded in 1848, the Associated Press was set up as a not-for-profit cooperative to cut costs of competition among six competing New York City newspapers. It eventually broadened its reach by offering reporting services to other news organizations that joined the cooperative and also allowed the cooperative's members to use their material. Today it provides news and feature reports to print, broadcast, and on-line media. By the end of 1997, the AP had:

144	domestic bureaus
93	international bureaus in 71 countries
3,500	employees
1,550	member newspapers
6,000	radio and television members
8,500	foreign subscribers
$473	million annual budget

FIG. 8.1. The Associated Press today.

War Sharpens News-Gathering Techniques

The Civil War stretched the boundaries of what had been amateur journalism. In a theater of war that ranged over hundreds of miles, under terrible conditions, American newspaper writers on both the Union and Confederate sides struggled to bring news to a population desperate for information. Newspapers were in much demand as readers sought information about battles and knowledge of victory or defeat. Who was injured, and who would never be returning? What did each battle's outcome portend? When would the war end? What would be left of the nation?

America's amateur journalists rose to the occasion, providing compelling eyewitness reporting that had never really been known before. Writers were sent directly to battlefields throughout the war. Raymond, publisher of *The New York Times*, even assigned himself to the war front. He was admired for his fast, accurate, and vivid reports.

War reporting brought about the **inverted pyramid** style of news writing. Writers compressed the most essential facts into short paragraphs to be sent by telegraph, transmitting the most important details first and the lesser details later. There were several reasons for using this *who, what, when, where, why,* and *how* approach. Telegraphed messages were not completely reliable during the war, so reporters sent the most important details first in case the remainder of their reports didn't get through. Also, wiring reports was expensive, so reporters strove for brevity. This style of news reporting remains in use today for most hard news stories in newspapers. Today, news stories are written this way for a different reason—because people are in a hurry for the important facts, not because the equipment might fail.

Photojournalism also got its start during the Civil War. A method had been developed for reproducing line drawings in print, so newspapers sent artists into combat to sketch realistic battle scenes. Cameras had been invented only a few years earlier, and photographer Matthew Brady and his assistants went to the battlefields to record photographic images of war, which had never been seen before yet are still haunting even today. Newspapers did not have the technology to reproduce actual photographs, but they became the basis for line drawings of war scenes that could be printed in the papers.

During the Civil War, questions were raised about the nation's rights to protect information during wartime as well as about journalistic loyalty. To what should the newspaper writer be faithful—to the North, to the South, or to the facts? Union general William Tecumseh Sherman called war correspondents spies and defamers who are the "direct cause of more bloodshed than fifty times their number of armed rebels."[2] Sherman believed the Confederate forces had received notice from journalists of the North's planned attack on Vicksburg and other targets. He had one correspondent tried by courts martial for spying, thus establishing the principle that the field commander would decide which correspondents would travel with his units. The government even imposed censorship in 1861—at first a voluntary plan that failed and then a more formal one in 1862—under which field provosts reviewed a writer's news copy and deleted military information.

Many of the journalistic techniques developed in the Civil War, and the questions they raised about the role of newspapers and journalism, are still with us at the beginning of the twenty-first century.

Newspaper as a Mass Medium

Inexpensive printing, improved journalistic techniques, and more new technology all helped to bring great advances to newspapering in the latter part of the nineteenth century, ushering in the newspaper as a mass medium. Newsprint became cheaper. The printing of photographs became possible. In 1873, the *New York Daily Graphic* was the first newspaper to reproduce a photograph, publishing a picture of Steinway Hall in New York City. The telephone appeared in 1876, giving reporters a tool they have relied on ever since. Three years later, Thomas Edison introduced the light bulb. In 1886, the Linotype machine was invented, greatly reducing production time and allowing for later deadlines. The Linotype automatically cast type from molten lead one line at a time; previously, type had been set by hand one letter at a time.

Technology wasn't the only factor altering the newspaper business. As the nineteenth century drew to a close, the *newspaper baron* emerged. One of the most prominent and innovative was Joseph Pulitzer, who helped develop a content formula that would appeal to mass audiences rather than an elite few. He developed the *St. Louis Post–Dispatch* and the *New York World* into popular papers. The World's circulation was 15,000 when he bought it in 1883; a scant 9 years later, he had increased it to 374,000.

Pulitzer targeted the working classes and championed reforms that assisted the city's immigrants and its poor. He filled his paper with stories that touched all emotions. He understood the circulation-building power of combining news with entertainment. He built a capable reporting staff that included Elizabeth Cochrane, who wrote under the pseudonym of Nellie Bly. Bly was admired for her undercover reporting on Mexican corruption, incarcerated women, and insane asylums. Her most famous assignment was to better the travel time set by the fictional Phileas Fogg in Jules Verne's novel, *Around the World in 80 Days*. She beat the record by a week, all the while filing front-page accounts to the *World* of her adventures.

Pulitzer innovated in other ways. In 1889, his *World* introduced the first regular comic section in a Sunday newspaper. Five years later, the comics began appearing in a primitive color—yellow. A character called the Yellow Kid was printed in yellow ink, giving rise to *yellow journalism*, a term applied to newspapers with sensational stories and comic strips. Yellow journalism was lurid reporting of crime, social scandals, sex, and sports, in which any fact could be embellished to make a story more exciting.

Pulitzer exploited his newspaper's popularity by using its burgeoning circulation to attract advertising. He standardized advertising space rates and made it easier for advertisers to custom-design ads with their own art. With increased revenues from ads (they accounted for more than 50 percent of the *World's* space by 1900), and with rising revenue from circulation, Pulitzer became extremely wealthy, and he dominated newspaper journalism in New York.

Newspapers as Power Centers

In 1895, another baron, William Randolph Hearst, moved in on Pulitzer's territory. Hearst's father had been a successful businessman in California who bought the financially troubled *San Francisco Examiner* and gave it to his son. William Randolph rescued that paper and made it successful using yellow journalism practices. He then purchased the *New York Journal*, with the same journalistic tactics in mind. His first order of business was to raid Pulitzer's *World* staff, hiring away many, including the artist who drew the Yellow Kid comic strip.

Hearst's father had used the *San Francisco Examiner* largely to support political ambitions. The younger Hearst did the same, and his newspapers served his political career. He ran twice for Congress, twice for mayor of New York City, and once for governor of New York. He won two terms in Congress and was a contender for the Democratic nomination for President in 1904.

Hearst's influence on U.S. policy was most powerful not as an elected official, however, but as a newspaper publisher. He used his newspaper's pages to push for U.S. involvement in the Spanish-American War, publishing articles—not all of them true, and Hearst knew it—about atrocities being endured by Cubans on an island only 90 miles from the U.S. mainland. Hearst believed a war could only be good for circulation. According to one account, an artist Hearst had sent to Cuba, Frederick Remington, cabled Hearst that the situation there seemed stable and that he wished to return to the United States. Hearst wouldn't hear of it. "Please remain," he cabled back. "You furnish the pictures and I'll furnish the war" (qtd. in Folkerts & Teeter, 1989, p. 276).

Hearst used his newspapers to hound President William McKinley, right into the grave, some would say. (McKinley was assassinated after a steady stream of vitriolic editorializing by Hearst publications.) Hearst was deeply critical of U.S. support for Britain during World War I. He opposed U.S. entry into World War II, changing his position only after the Japanese attack on Pearl Harbor. Hearst spent freely, even wildly, on editorial support of his various political causes, plunging his newspapers into the red. His wealth from other businesses helped to offset the losses.

Specialized Newspapers

Even while newspapers were evolving into mass-circulation periodicals, specialty newspapers had also been growing throughout the nineteenth century. *El Misisipí*, the earliest known newspaper for Spanish-speaking Americans, appeared in 1808. The *Cherokee Phoenix* and later the *Cherokee Advocate* were published for Native American readers.

The first newspaper for a black audience, *Freedom's Journal*, appeared in 1827. It lasted only 2 years, but before the Civil War, more than 40 newspapers were being published for black readers, most concerned with abolition of slavery. Among them was Frederick Douglass's influential *North Star*, launched in 1847 to crusade against slavery and for women's rights. By 1890, there were 575 black newspapers in America.

The foreign-language press also began to thrive, serving immigrants flocking to the United States. By 1880, approximately 800 newspapers served readers whose first language was German, French, Polish, Italian, Spanish, Yiddish, or one of the Scandinavian tongues.

Frontier Newspapers

Newspapers on the Western frontier had a character not unlike that of America's prerevolutionary newspapers. They exemplified a strong individualistic, feisty spirit. Some were unabashed boosters of particular advantages their towns offered in order to entice entrepreneurs and prospective settlers.

Others held highly charged political viewpoints. The racist, separatist *Frontier Index*, published in Nebraska and Wyoming in the 1850s and 1860s, preached white supremacy. The *Atchison Squatter-Sovereign*, whose first issue appeared in 1855, appealed to proslavery sentiments in Kansas, whereas the *Lawrence Herald of Freedom* preached against slavery. Many of these papers sought financial support from sympathizers as well as subscriptions and advertising. The *Lawrence Herald of Freedom* was almost completely dependent on the New England Emigrant Aid Society, an anti-slavery organization that helped those sympathetic to its cause settle in this region. These newspapers were caught up in, and fanned, the debate about slavery raging in Kansas and in the states that bordered it.

Responsible Newspapers

Adolph Ochs purchased *The New York Times* in 1896, just a year after Hearst had bought the *Journal*, but he had a completely different concept of "information." Unlike Pulitzer and Hearst, Ochs believed a newspaper did not have to resort to sensationalism to be successful. He believed it didn't have to entertain, so he published no comic strips or cartoons. He was convinced that a market also existed for a newspaper that emphasized news and information rather than entertainment and that a newspaper which published all the important information of the day would become a valuable and profitable social institution.

Under Ochs, *The Times* aligned itself with other New York papers such as the *Sun* and the *Press* to distinguish its brand of journalism from "the yellow press" of the *World* and *Journal*. In its promotional materials, the *Times* noted that its content "does not soil the breakfast cloth." It strove to be a newspaper of record, a clear and incisive account of the day's events told without the clutter of stunts, theatrics, or melodrama.

Ochs' circulation marketing schemes made it plain that he was targeting the educated middle and upper-middle classes. He solicited subscriptions by telephone. He offered a bicycle tour of France and England to the 100 persons who recruited the most new subscribers, gearing the campaign to teachers. It was very unlikely that either method would have brought him into contact with the laborers and shopkeepers who read the Pulitzer and Hearst newspapers.

TWENTIETH-CENTURY NEWSPAPERS

By the beginning of the twentieth century, newspapers had become as important a feature of American cities as their banks and courthouses, schools and theaters. They had become the arbiter of much social, political, and cultural matters. It was hard to imagine passing a day without them. At the beginning of the century, most aspects of today's newspaper business were in place. Across the country, newspapers were sensational tabloids, specialized publications for particular groups, or responsible institutions that assumed the role of being the official record of their communities. As the century progressed, all of these methods of newspapering continued to develop and thrive. The style and technique of newspapers in 1900 were pretty much the same in 2000, with only some changes brought about by the computerization of the writing, editing, and printing processes. The organization of a modern newspaper can become quite intricate depending on its size, as Fig. 8.2 shows.

Size and Reach

The United States has the second largest newspaper circulation in the world (56.7 million), behind Japan (72.7 million). It has more daily newspapers than any other country except India. However, circulation of individual newspapers did not grow as fast in the twentieth century as it did in the heady days of Pulitzer and Hearst; the circulations of their *World* and *Journal* grew by tens of thousands a year in the 1890s.

The combined total of morning and evening newspapers peaked in 1910, when 2,200 newspapers were being published. This number has declined since then, to 1,509 at the end of 1997. Of course, the aggregate circulation of those newspapers greatly exceeds what it was in 1910, when it was about 20 million. Nationwide, after peaking at 62.8 million in 1987, the combined average daily paid circulation of U.S. dailies settled down to 56.7 million in 1997. Sunday newspaper circulation was higher at 60.5 million.

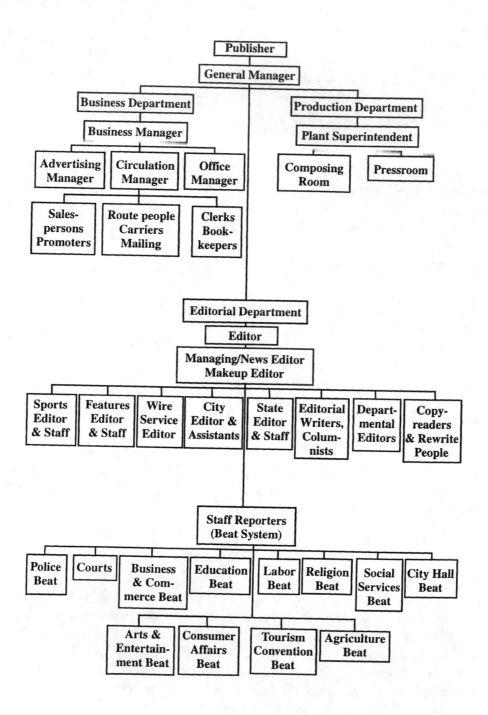

FIG. 8.2. Example of newspaper organizational chart.

In the 1990s, *The New York Times* had a circulation of slightly more than 1 million, the largest newspaper in a city with fewer competing newspapers than Pulitzer and Hearst faced. Of the 1,509 daily newspapers currently publishing in the United States, the vast majority have fairly modest numbers of readers; 1,289 have circulations under 50,000.

Newspapers' High Costs

The economics of newspapers has changed dramatically since newspapers began to search for a mass audience. James Gordon Bennett launched the *New York Herald* in 1835 with an investment of $500. By 1900, it would have taken $1 million to start a daily newspaper. But certain costly investment didn't deter the Gannett Company, the largest newspaper chain in the United States, from starting a national daily newspaper in 1982.

USA TODAY was launched using a model not dissimilar to that of the colonial printer's, who used his other business to support the news sheet he published. Gannett, borrowing reporters and editors from other newspapers it owned and using the marketing, circulation, and business expertise available throughout the company, plus some of the printing and production capacity of Gannett's own daily newspapers, was able to start *USA TODAY* and carry it through the lean years in which it lost money. Gannett spent hundreds of millions on *USA TODAY* before the national newspaper began turning a profit.[3] Gannett has been rewarded for its investment with gratifying profits at *USA TODAY*, thanks to its popularity with readers and advertisers.

It is less costly to purchase a newspaper than to start one, although prospective purchasers still need a lot of money in today's market. Newspapers are bought and sold for tens of millions or even hundreds of millions of dollars. Media General in 1997 paid $48 million to acquire the *Potomac News*, a weekly in Woodbridge, Va. Knight Ridder purchased four daily newspapers in 1997, the *Kansas City Star*, *Fort Worth and Arlington* (Texas) *Star-Telegrams*, *Belleville* (Ill.) *News-Democrat*, and the *Times Leader* in Wilkes-Barre, Pa., for $1.65 billion.

Newspaper Consolidation

These acquisitions are typical of how newspapers changed hands at the end of the twentieth century. Metropolitan dailies have, for the most part, passed out of the hands of families that controlled them and into the hands of large corporations. At the end of 1997, the 25 largest newspaper companies owned newspapers whose combined circulation was approximately 37.8 million—more than 60 percent of the total daily newspaper circulation in the United States.

In 1900, newspapers competed with one another for readers and for advertising, but consolidation through the century changed that. Washington, DC, for example, had five daily newspapers in mid-century. The *Times* merged with the *Herald* in the 1920s, and then the *Times-Herald* merged with the *Post* in the 1950s. The *Evening Star* merged with the *Daily News* in 1972, and the combined newspaper went out of business in 1981, leaving *The Washington Post* the only major daily newspaper in that city. City after city found itself without competing newspapers. Typically, once one newspaper had gained dominant share of readership and advertising, others lost their viability and closed.

Newspaper Competition

Dailies that survive the shakeout among competing newspapers still have to compete for audience and advertising with many other media: broadcast television, cable television, radio, free-standing newspaper inserts, direct mail, shopping newspapers, outdoor advertising, online computer services, and, in many locations, increasingly popular weekly and semiweekly newspapers.

CURRENT ISSUES

Growth

In the twenty-first century, newspapers are regarded as a mature industry, one in which growth is slowing because the product has reached its capacity in many markets. Supply and demand, as measured by circulation patterns, tells us there seem to be enough newspapers to meet the needs of those who want to read them. There are not many new frontiers left, at least not for the newspaper as we have known it.

Newspapers are a mass medium on the local level, and to survive and grow in the twenty-first century most experts and newspaper executives agree they will need to expand their definitions of content and audiences, build their circulations, and compete for advertising.

Expanding Content and Audience

Newspapers are experimenting with new content to make them more relevant and interesting to casual readers, in hopes of making them regular readers. Many are already supplementing the printed product with online journalism, using a mix of information from the print version and features designed expressly for the newspaper's Web site.

Newspapers are reexamining their relationship with the community and making changes to firm up that relationship. And as the demographics of communities change, newspapers are changing as well. Many are adding special editions to serve the needs of particular communities within their markets. For example, the *Miami Herald* has added a Spanish-language edition, *El Nuevo Herald*, to serve its Hispanic community.

Special newspapers serving minority readers and recent immigrants are growing. Most are nondailies, but several cities have minority readerships large enough to sustain dailies. Hispanic readers can enjoy *La Opinión* in Los Angeles and in New York, *El Diario-La Prensa,* the oldest Spanish-language daily in the United States. Newspapers such as the *Atlanta Daily World* and the *Chicago Defender* provide daily journalism for African Americans. In greater San Jose, CA, a swiftly growing population from Southeast Asia can read 4 dailies and 10 weeklies, including *Viet Mercury*, a Vietnamese-language weekly introduced by the *San Jose Mercury News* in 1999.

Building Circulation

Since the mid-1980s, newspapers have been challenged to grow their readership. They have been unsuccessful in selling many more newspapers each day, but they have been successful in attracting more readers per copy. So although the number of copies sold has been declining, readership is growing because of "pass-along" readership, which accounts for about 14 percent of all newspaper readers. Table 8.1 lists the 25 most widely circulated daily newspapers in the United States.

TABLE 8.1

Top 25 U.S. Daily Newspapers By Circulation

		Average Daily Circulation
1.	*The Wall Street Journal*	1,820,186
2.	*USA TODAY*	1,715,245
3.	*The New York Times*	1,110,143
4.	*Los Angeles Times*	1,095,007
5.	*The Washington Post*	808,884
6.	*New York Daily News*	730,761
7.	*Chicago Tribune*	655,522
8.	*Newsday*	571,283
9.	*Houston Chronicle*	553,387
10.	*Chicago Sun-Times*	494,146
11.	*San Francisco Chronicle*	490,003
12.	*Phoenix Arizona Republic*	484,630
13.	*Dallas Morning News*	484,597
14.	*Boston Globe*	472,668
15.	*Philadelphia Inquirer*	433,489
16.	*New York Post*	432,707
17.	*Newark Star-Ledger*	405,333
18.	*Cleveland Plain Dealer*	400,421
19.	*Minneapolis/St. Paul Star Tribune*	386,807
20.	*San Diego Union-Tribune*	385,995
21.	*Detroit Free Press*	381,599
22.	*Miami Herald*	367,029
23.	*St. Petersburg Times*	366,212
24.	*Orange County Register*	364,404
25.	*Portland Oregonian*	357,333

Source: Based on *Audit Bureau of Circulations*, ABC *FAS–FAX*, average daily circulation for 6 months ended March 31, 1998. Used with permission.

Newspaper circulation declines for a variety of reasons. For example, it usually falls somewhat when newspapers raise their subscription or single-copy prices. Newspapers try to save money by reducing distribution in areas that are expensive to deliver to, such as outlying communities some distance from the paper's core market. When they do this, naturally, circulation falls. Competition from other media, particularly television, cuts into reader loyalty as well. Today, the local daily newspaper reaches 59 percent of adults each day. Local television news reaches 71 percent. No time to read or *time poverty* is also often given as a reason for declining circulation.

Geodemographic mapping techniques are being used in building circulation. *Geodemographics* consists of profiles of neighborhoods and the people who live in them, and they can supply information on household income, personal and professional interests, leisure activities, and product preferences.

For example, Knight Ridder's Philadelphia newspapers the *Inquirer* and the *Daily News* use database software to identify *core subscribers*, those who have paid full price for the paper for at least one year without any stops in service, and develop individual profiles for them. That information is used to acquire and retain subscribers. They have found, for example, that individuals who share many traits with core subscribers but are not yet subscribers themselves are more likely to buy and to maintain their subscriptions than other individuals might be.

Circulation directors are developing new ways to sell more copies and court prospective readers. For example, in 1997 the *Chicago Tribune* used a TV and radio campaign to sell the Sunday newspaper to time-pressed young marrieds with children. *The New York Times* searches for readers outside New York City and the New York, Connecticut, Pennsylvania, and New Jersey counties it considers to be its home market. The *Times'* research indicates there are untapped readers farther away. One way it plans to reach them is to print its Boston and Washington editions in those cities to permit later deadlines, allowing fresher news in the paper that lands on subscribers' doorsteps.

Special events, especially sporting events, can present opportunities for spikes in circulation sales. The *Courier-Journal* in Louisville, Ky., prints special editions each year on Kentucky Derby Day and sells them at the race track. And when baseball great Mark McGwire of the St. Louis Cardinals broke Roger Maris' home-run record in 1998, demand for the *St. Louis Post-Dispatch* was so great that the paper (with a circulation of 318,997) sold more than 1.5 million copies and extras. Overzealous baseball fans followed *Post-Dispatch* carriers on their routes, stealing papers off lawns as soon as they were delivered. Police had to be called when crowds surrounded a delivery van and broke its windows in an attempt to get papers. The newspaper's production department ran out of ink; the phone system crashed. Examples such as this show the newspaper's enduring power as the medium of record.

Newspapers are also trying to attract younger readers—teens and young adults who haven't yet developed the newspaper reading habit. They are also trying to find ways to retain female readers, whose newspaper readership is falling slightly faster than that of males, and to attract minority readers. "There is no greater challenge confronting newspapers," said Albert E. Gollin, senior vice president of research and marketing services director of the Newspaper Association of America.[4]

Competing for Advertising

Advertisers continue to rely on newspapers when they want to saturate a mass market with a message. But as other media alternatives present themselves, advertisers are demanding more flexibility from newspapers. Although they like the "massness" of newspapers, they also feel newspapers compare unfavorably with media targeted to narrower categories of specific consumer audiences.

For example, grocery stores may want to reach everyone in a given radius, but car dealers may want to reach only certain households that meet their specific criteria. Newspapers respond to challenges like this by relying on market research to find out more about their market and audience. They invest in database programs to help them determine with greater precision who their readers are, what their readers' media usage habits are, and what their purchasing patterns are like. Newspaper advertising sales staffs are becoming more proficient at *consultative selling*—identifying key reader segments for their advertisers and developing advertising space buys on specific days, and in particular sections of the paper most likely to reach the advertiser's intended market. They also help advertisers determine what other advertising options will work for them in combination with advertising in the newspaper.

To help the car dealer advertise most effectively, and to ensure that the newspaper gets a slice of the dealer's ad budget, the newspaper often offers *value-added services* to the dealer. For example, the newspaper might offer to match the dealer's customer list with its subscriber list. Using geodemographics, the newspaper ad staff can come back to the auto dealer with data telling him whom he will reach and whom he might miss with newspaper ads. The newspaper ad rep can then suggest the dealer complement his ads in the newspaper with direct mail aimed precisely at those non-newspaper households that meet the dealer's consumer profiles. Value-added service preserves the newspaper's share of the client's advertising budget and solves a problem for the client.

NONDAILY COMMUNITY NEWSPAPERS

Weekly and semiweekly newspapers represent a strong segment of American publishing. By the end of 1997, there were approximately 8,000 paid and free-circulation newspapers publishing on a nondaily basis, with a combined circulation of about 80 million. These nondailies fall into three types: traditional community newspapers, special-market newspapers, and alternative newspapers.

Traditional Nondailies

Traditional nondailies operate much as dailies do, albeit with smaller staffs and fewer pages. They are the newspapers of record for their communities, providing their readers with strictly local items concerning people and events in their community—politics, zoning matters, obituaries, weddings and engagements, school and sponsored team sports scores, community calendar, editorials, and letters to the editor. They usually don't carry wire-service news.

Weekly and semiweekly newspapers have circulated in rural areas and small towns for many years. Generally, their readers know one another or know of one another. Robert Karolevitz (1985), in his history of community newspapers, aptly described their special character:

> The intimacy of the local paper has always presented editors with pressures less often faced by their metropolitan counterparts who are well insulated by the veil of anonymity. It is a special reward for the community publisher to report the happy news about the people with whom he or she shares a morning-coffee relationship, but the reverse is also true when the story has a theme of tragedy, ill-fortune or shocking revelation.

> Sometimes tearful, even desperate appeals are made to keep the details of a suicide or a drunk-driving charge out of the paper. It also takes an extra measure of courage for an editor to challenge a questionable decision of the county commissioners or dig into closed-door actions of the school board when the chairman is a neighbor or even a relative. This mixed blessing will continue to be a part of small-town journalism in the future as it has been in the past, with some editors responding fearlessly to difficult responsibilities and others taking the easy way out. (p. 198)

Suburban newspapers have emerged as a potent force in nondaily publishing. As Americans began to build "bedroom communities" around urban centers in the 1950s, and as businesses began establishing themselves in these suburbs, the groundwork was laid for a medium that would meet the needs of these new communities and the advertisers located there. The suburban newspaper, appearing weekly, semi-weekly, or, in some suburbs, as many as three times a week, is now an important part of the American newspaper publishing mix. Unlike readers of small-town, rural newspapers, readers of suburban newspapers tend to be affluent, with incomes about 43 percent above the U.S. average, making them attractive targets for advertisers.

Special-Market Newspapers

Also contributing to the rich texture of the nondaily newspaper segment are newspapers serving minority and special-interest readers. The nation's capital has a number of examples. The *Washington Afro-American*, founded in 1892, each week offers its black readership a mix of local, national, religious, and social reporting. *Washington Jewish Week*, founded in 1930, provides coverage of local, national, and international Jewish interests. The *Washington Blade* provides coverage of news and legislation of interest to the gay and lesbian community.

Dozens of communities have weekly or biweekly newspapers reaching African Americans, including the *Birmingham* (Ala.) *World, Long Beach* (Calif.) *Times, Tri-City Journal* in Chicago, the *Amsterdam News* in New York City, *The Skanner* in Portland, Oreg., and the *Philadelphia Tribune*. The nation's Hispanic and Asian communities also have many nondailies serving their readers.

Alternative Newspapers

Contemporary alternative newspapers originated with the social movements of the 1960s and 1970s. Politically liberal, the first alternative newspapers opposed the Vietnam war, supported expanded civil rights, and devoted themselves to unmasking the agenda of "establishment" politicians, university leaders, and corporate executives. *The Village Voice*, started in New York in 1955 by Dan Wolf, Ed Fancher, and Norman Mailer, claims to be the founding father of alternative weeklies. *The Voice* was known for its free-form, high-spirited, provocative journalism. Other papers followed the example. Bruce Brugmann, who founded the *San Francisco Bay Guardian* in 1966, said he did so "to provide an alternative to the big monopoly dailies—to print the news and raise hell."[5]

The Association of Alternative Newsweeklies' 110 North American member newspapers have a combined circulation of 6.8 million, and it is growing. Although theirs is only a fraction of daily or traditional weekly newspaper circulation, the alternatives play an important role in contemporary journalism. Their "outsider" approach to politics, culture, and the arts, in sharp contrast to that of mainstream periodicals, produces material that is provocative and hard-hitting. In spirit, they are much like the early colonial periodicals that challenged the royal establishment of the British sovereign. In content, they are often ribald, raw, and radical in language and subject.

CONTENT AND RELATIONSHIP WITH READERS

Newspapers have a distinct advantage over broadcast media when it comes to detail and depth. For example, TV has a finite amount of airtime in which to get information across. It relies heavily on visual images to sustain viewer interest. TV is superior in covering breaking news, but newspapers outshine television when it is time to explain what it all means.

Unlike television, newspapers can expand or shrink their *newshole*—the space in the paper not occupied by advertising—as the need arises. A newspaper can increase pages, add a special section or even an extra edition if events require it. And if it invests in a Web site, it can update material that appeared in the printed paper, or even break a story online, as the *Dallas Morning News* did in 1997, when its online edition announced that Oklahoma City bombing suspect Timothy McVeigh had confessed to his attorneys. (Nearly all the nation's top 100 newspapers by circulation have online products.)

In spite of the daily newspaper's special qualities, journalists and the readers they serve are not always of the same mind about what makes for interesting reading. In every newspaper readership study carried out in the 1990s, news and information about the local community dominated the list of readers' interests. In a survey conducted in 1996 by the Gannett Company's Newspaper Division, local themes were of greatest interest to readers, but readers were not completely satisfied with the coverage they were receiving. Interest and satisfaction didn't align for other key categories, as Table 8.2 shows.

Newspaper journalists are struggling to make their papers more compelling not only to meet the expectations of their readers but because they themselves feel newspapers need to improve. In 1997, the American Society of Newspaper Editors polled more than 1,000 editors, reporters, photographers, copy editors, and editorial writers at 61 newspapers, asking them what they thought of the newspapers they worked for. Sixty-four percent replied that they only occasionally or rarely considered their papers

TABLE 8.2

Reader Interest Versus Reader Satisfaction With Newspaper Reporting

Interest Ranking	Topic	Satisfaction Ranking
1st	Good things happening in the area	15th
2nd	Local news	13th
3rd	World and national news	9th
4th	Local growth and development	12th
5th	The environment	20th
6th	Places to go and things to do	8th
7th	Education and local schools	10th

Source: Gannett Co. Inc., survey. *Gannetteer*, September–October 1996. Reproduced with permission.

"a good read." Equally sobering, 55 percent said they believe newspapers will play a less important part in American life in 10 years than they do now. In 1989, 33 percent felt that way.[6]

The reasons for the disconnect between journalists and their readers and for the pessimism among newspaper journalists are complex. Some of it can be attributed to some journalists' reluctance to change traditional ways of doing things. For example, the suburbs represent the fastest-growing areas in a newspaper's market, but in many markets, newsrooms have been slow to reallocate resources to provide better coverage of the suburbs.

Some of it can be explained by Americans' attitudes toward media, which have grown more negative. Many Americans believe the news media have their own agendas, resort to sensationalism all too often, and fail to understand their increasingly diverse audiences. These people are more critical of newspapers and less forgiving of their shortcomings.

Some of it can be blamed on tight newsroom resources, which make it more difficult to do the in-depth stories that make a newspaper a pleasure to read. Modest salaries, especially for entry-level journalists, make recruiting talented people more challenging. Of course, newsroom resources and employee compensation vary widely by newspaper, with the smaller circulation dailies, where most young journalists get their start, able to offer the fewest incentives (although they do provide the greatest range of opportunities for a young journalist to acquire broad experience). There is no doubt that these matters affect newspapers' ability to attract and keep good journalists and, therefore, have an impact on newspapers' ability to produce good journalism.

LOOKING AHEAD

All these circumstances have stirred the nation's newspaper editors and their staffs to better understand their readers' wants, needs, and expectations. They are establishing more points of contact and designing newspaper projects such as newspaper-sponsored public forums, where newspaper staff and citizens discuss important community issues; reader advisory boards with rotating membership, which give individual readers an opportunity to interact in small groups, on a regular basis, with reporters and editors; and the creation of *public editor*, *public life reporter*, and *listening post* positions. Journalists with these assignments are expected to anticipate reader concerns and to alert the newsroom to them.

The Civic Journalism Argument

These initiatives, and some others, are often associated with *civic journalism* or *public journalism*. Jan Schaffer, executive director of the Pew Center for Civic Journalism, explained the concept when she decried "the tendency to write stories as though only the most obvious players have a stake—either professional, political or economic—in the outcome. The rest of us are just spectators in the particular cat fight, legislative battle, or election campaign being reported."

Civic journalism attempts to treat readers and viewers as participants in an election, a budget debate, welfare or health reform, the governance of our democracy.

Such treatment is forcing journalists into an entirely different master narrative. For instance, where does the reporter gather information? Through interviews with the major players? Or through a conversation or dialogue that tries to tap into a broader base of participants? One civic journalism technique is to change the nature of the interaction with sources from a standard interview model, from asking to a conversational model.

Schaffer says this means that journalists move from a "sterile environment that has no interest in the outcome of a public issue," to an "objective attachment that reflects a belief that the news media, if we do our jobs well, have a role to play helping citizens do their jobs as citizens." This kind of journalism still "involves being independent, objective, and accurate in purveying information, but it also involves delivering information in ways that readers and viewers can find their connection to the story—why they should care and what they could do about it."[7]

The Larger Challenge

Civic journalism is but one approach to embedding the reader's interests in the newspaper's way of doing things. Not all journalists agree with it. Many are cautious about exchanging the newspaper's traditional role of noninvolved community watchdog for a more activist role of civic involvement. Regardless of one's philosophy, however, the challenge for newspapers is quite specific.

"Newspapers must concentrate more on providing meaning rather than just information," says Mark Silverman, editor and publisher of *The Detroit News*. "People get information from many sources: radio, television, conversations with friends. It is meaning that will differentiate us and make us indispensable."[8]

The Newspaper Association of America says that, in terms of editorial content and experience, in the future newspapers must be more intensely local, covering community news better. They must report on solutions as well as problems, be relentlessly useful, promote depth and understanding, be relevant, and create more emotional response. If they can do these things, newspapers will continue to be a mass medium of force throughout the twenty-first century.

Further Reading

American Society of Newspaper Editors Ethics and Values Committee. (1996). *Journalism Values Handbook*. Reston, VA: ASNE.

Baldasty, Gerald J. (1992). *The Commercialization of News in the Nineteenth Century*. Madison, WI: University of Wisconsin Press.

Beasley, Maurine, and Gibbons, Sheila. (1993) *Taking Their Place: a Documentary History of Women and Journalism*. Washington, DC: The American University Press/University Press of America.

Berger, Meyer. (1951). *The Story of the New York Times*, 1851–1951. New York: Simon & Schuster, 1951.

Bradlee, Benjamin C. (1995). *A Good Life: Newspapering and Other Adventures*. New York: Simon & Schuster.

Coleridge, Nicholas. (1994). *Paper Tigers: The Latest, Greatest Newspaper Tycoons*. New York: Birch Lane Press.

Crouthamel, James L. (1989). *Bennett's New York Herald and the Rise of the Popular Press*. Syracuse, NY: Syracuse University Press.

Danky, James P., and Wiegand, Wayne A. (1998). *Print Culture in a Diverse America*. Urbana, IL: University of Illinois Press.

Emery, Michael, and Emery, Edwin. (1992). *The Press and America* (7th ed.). Englewood Cliffs, NJ: Prentice Hall.

Folkerts, Jean, and Teeter, Dwight. (1989). *Voices of a Nation: a History of the Media in the United States*. New York: Macmillan.

Ghiglione, Loren. (1990). *The American Journalist: Paradox of the Press*. Washington, DC: The Library of Congress in cooperation with the American Society of Newspaper Editors.

Hiebert, Ray Eldon, Ungurait, Donald F., and Bohn, Thomas W. (1991). *Mass Media VI: An Introduction to Modern Communication*. New York: Longman.

Hutton, Frankie, and Reed, Barbara Straus. (1995). *Outsiders in 19th-Century Press History: Multicultural Perspectives*. Bowling Green, OH: Bowling Green University Press.

Karolevitz, Robert F. (1985). *From Quill to Computer: The Story of America's Community Newspapers*. Arlington, VA: National Newspaper Foundation.

Marzolf, Marion Tuttle. (1977). *Up From the Footnote: A History of Women Journalists*. New York: Hastings House.

Mills, Kay. (1988). *A Place in the News: From the Women's Pages to the Front Page*. New York: Dodd, Mead.

Sim, John C. (1969). *The Grass Roots Press*. Ames: Iowa State University Press.

Stephens, Mitchell. (1988). *A History of News*. New York: Penguin Books.

Thomas, Isaiah. (1970). *The History of Printing in America* (reissue). New York: Weathervane Books.

Weisberger, Bernard A. (1961). *The American Newspaperman*. Chicago: University of Chicago Press.

Notes

[1] Wisner, George. (1834, August 1). *New York Sun*, p. 2. Cited in Ghiglione, *The American Journalist*, p. 19.

[2] General Sherman as quoted in Ewing, Joseph H. (1987, July–August). The New Sherman Letters. *American Heritage*, p. 24. Cited in Ghiglione, *The American Journalist*, p. 76.

[3] For more on *USA TODAY's* development, see McCartney, James (1997, September). USA TODAY Grows Up. *American Journalism Review*, pp. 19–25; Farhi, Paul (1997, August 11). Good News for "McPaper." *The Washington Post*, Washington Business, p. 13; and Prichard, Peter (1987). *The Making of McPaper*. Kansas City, MO: Andrews, McMeel, & Parker.

[4]Gollin, Albert E. (1994, January 25). *Targeting Women and Minority Readers: The Challenge of Diversity*. Speech to the Newspaper Association of America Research/Promotion and Market Development Conference, p. 15. Vienna, VA: Newspaper Association of America.

[5]Smith, Larry. (1995, July–August). High Noon in 'Frisco. *Columbia Journalism Review*, p. 39.

[6]Survey Says Newspapers Are Alive, Well and No. 1 Ad Source. (1996, September–October). *Gannetteer*, p. 4. This study, directed by Gannett Co., Inc., was conducted in March and April 1996 and included telephone interviews with 2,645 adults ages 18 and older.

[7]Schaffer, Jan. (1996, December 9). *Civic Journalism Washington-Style: Reporting Beyond the Beltway*. Speech to the Regional Reporters Association, Rosslyn, VA, pp. 3, 4. Washington, DC: Pew Center for Civic Journalism.

[8]Silverman, Mark. (1991, October 13). Democracy, Demography and New Directions for News. *News Watch*, a newsletter of the Gannett Newspaper Division, p. 1.

9

BOOKS, MAGAZINES, AND NEWSLETTERS

Newspapers have traditionally been considered the most important medium for current news, but they are by no means the only mass medium in the world of print. Books, magazines, and newsletters are also vital to the whole range of human communication in contemporary society, and they have reached mass audiences. In fact, books were the first form of printed material, and newsletters even preceded newspapers in historical development.

BOOKS

Books are still the most intimate, most permanent, and probably most respected medium in the whole galaxy of media. They are the most intimate, because they require the most intense personal relationship with their users. Unlike newspapers and magazines, books draw their readers in for a longer period of time, with fewer disruptions. Each page generally contains one or at most two columns of text, with no headlines, only titles and subtitles, which unlike headlines, do not contain a full thought, so one must read the text to get the meaning. Books do not generally have lead paragraphs that summarize all the essential information; one must read a book in its entirety to fully understand the author's purpose.

To get the message of a book, the reader must be immersed in the process of reading. The lines are longer, requiring more intense concentration than the short lines of newspapers and magazines. The content of a book is rarely disrupted with varied messages, with advertising, or promotions between the pages, or with sound effects. The author and reader are connected in an intimate, one-on-one dialogue.

Books are also the most permanent medium, for several reasons. First, unlike most other media (exceptions are video and sound recordings), books can be shelved, so they can be easily retrieved simply by looking at the title on the spine. That enables books to be organized in some methodical way, alphabetically or numerically or by category. The messages of newspapers, magazines, newsletters, over-the air broadcasts, and film cannot be so easily organized and retrieved. Most books (fiction and poetry can be exceptions) are organized internally with linear and verbal logic, with a table of contents at the beginning and an index at the end, so the contents can be easily accessed at any point. Until the computer came along, books were the only medium with their own built-in search engine.

In short, a book is the handiest package of information that has ever been devised. A CD-ROM, of course, can retrieve far more information far faster than any book. In fact, a project is under way to scan all the great books of all time into computers that can be accessed over the Internet by anyone, in any language, with color, pictures, charts, graphs, and even sound if needed, with linkages that allow them to be searched for any specific content. But you won't be able to put those CD-ROM books in your pocket and take them out to the hammock to read at your leisure. You will need access to computers, telephone lines, modems, and electricity, all much more expensive than any modest collection of books. The simple book requires none of that—just a reader and a volume to read.

Because the book has been the handiest way to store and retrieve both knowledge and literary expression, in many ways it has become the most highly regarded medium. We often save books in our homes, whereas we generally throw away newspapers, magazines, and newsletters. We have bookcases for this purpose and we create home libraries. Libraries of books have become essential to education at all levels. Today, we might keep our videotapes and sound recordings organized on our shelves at home, as well, but we cannot take them off the shelf and casually leaf through them to find a specific passage or item of information. It is much harder to search a tape or recording than a book.

Books also depend exclusively on the support of their purchaser. In general they contain no advertising and thus are freer of pressures that any outsider might bring to their content. This has given books greater credibility than most other media, which has made books the most useful medium for objective analysis and learning. Because they have formed the backbone of human education, books have gained a dignity and respect far beyond any other mass medium.

Early Book Publishing

Books seem to have been important throughout recorded human history, even when they were handwritten as scrolls or bound volumes in limited quantities. When Johannes Gutenberg invented movable type around 1454, multiple copies of books could be produced for the first time. The printing craft grew rapidly, and so did the number of printed books. More than 30,000 different titles were produced within 50 years after Gutenberg printed a Bible, his first book. Until the nineteenth century, however, book production was tedious work, in which typesetting, papermaking, and press operation were all accomplished by hand.

In 1640, a Cambridge, Mass., printer, Stephen Daye, published the first book in the colonies, *The Whole Booke of Psalms*. As it had been in Europe, early book publishing in the colonies was devoted mainly to religious content. Even though only a few thousand families lived in the colonies at the time, Daye sold all 1,750 copies he printed. It may have been the first and only book these families ever purchased, except of course the Bible. For many American families, having a book was important, even though they may not have been able to read it.

Ben Franklin, who influenced other forms of publishing (and so many features of American life), in 1744 imported the first book to be reprinted and sold in colonial America, and perhaps the first nonreligious book. It was called *Pamela; or, Virtue Rewarded.* Books about politics began to appear and, like newspapers, were used to persuade colonists to break with England.

A few early American settlers who could read and afford books sometimes brought them along when they emigrated from Europe. Most colonists were too poor and illiterate to be book owners or readers. If they became financially successful in the colonies, they might import books and display them proudly in their homes, whether, as mentioned, they could read them or not. Literacy grew slowly in America, taking almost 300 years for the United States to achieve 90 percent, from the time of the first settlement in Virginia in 1607 to the end of the nineteenth century.

Books as a Mass Medium

By the last third of the nineteenth century, the nation had stretched from coast to coast, and public and private education had been established in most communities. Industrial methods had replaced old-fashioned, labor-intensive printing operations. Books, which had been the possessions mostly of clergy and academics in the fifteenth and sixteenth centuries, and of the aristocracy in the seventeenth and eighteenth, were now enjoyed by a much larger reading public.

But books did not reach a mass audience until they became affordable and marketable to the masses. In the late 1800s, print technology and book content came together to make mass marketing possible. With the new technology, book publishing became much more efficient and the cost of production greatly reduced. At the same time, writers were turning to forms and subjects, primarily entertaining stories, that would be popular with mass audiences. Exciting and dramatic tales, cheaply produced, were put on the market at the lowest possible price to entice a mass market. What the penny press did for mass consumption of newspapers in the 1830s, the dime novel did for mass book readership in the 1860s and 1870s.

By 1885, one-third of all the books printed in the United States were cheap editions, designed primarily to bring popular fiction to a mass audience. Publishing houses replaced small business printers to produce books in volume. Cheaply bound popular books, hardcover classics, and educational textbooks were produced by these new publishing houses, which not only sought talented authors but also established models of marketing and distribution as well. Some of the best-known houses—Rand McNally, Macmillan, Harper & Brothers, Scribner's, Dodd, Mead, and Doubleday— began their businesses in the early to mid-nineteenth century.

Modern Books

About 40,000 titles were published annually in the United States at the beginning of the twenty-first century, and this number seems unlikely to increase in the near future. At the beginning of the twentieth century, the majority of publishing firms were independent, family-owned businesses, but this arrangement changed during the course of the century. Through most of that period, however, publishers tended to specialize in one of four categories of books, segregated within the industry largely because of the differences each requires in marketing.

Trade books are usually fiction and nonfiction for a general readership and include both hardcover and paperback books. This category is further divided into adult, young adult, and juvenile lines. Trade books account for the largest share of sales in the United States and are usually marketed through bookstores and book clubs. These are often the least expensive of cloth-bound books because they can be mass marketed.

Professional books are published for business, law, medicine, engineering, computer science, and other scientific and professional fields. They are usually marketed through direct mail to professionals, experts, and specialists who constantly need to update their knowledge and keep abreast of all changes and developments in their special areas. These books are often the most expensive because they usually deal with complex treatments of complicated technical material; because they are costly to produce, often for a small market; and because they are aimed at a market that can afford higher prices.

Textbooks are usually divided into elementary and secondary school and college markets. The combined sale of all textbooks nearly equals that of trade books. Textbooks at the college and university level are usually marketed directly to instructors, who "adopt" them for their courses and require their students to purchase them, usually through campus bookstores. Elementary and high school books are usually selected by committees of educators, administrators, or school boards who choose books for their classes and libraries after evaluating the materials and sales proposals of various educational publishers.

Mass-market paperbacks, unlike trade paperbacks sold mainly in bookstores, are sold in grocery stores, drugstores, department stores, airports, and similar outlets, sometimes even in automatic vending machines. Sales figures for this category are less than one-third of trade books, but that is caused by their low price, not their popularity. Because they are priced well below trade hardcovers and paperbacks, mass-market paperbacks usually sell well, accounting for two of every three books sold in the United States. Romance fiction represents nearly half the mass-market paperback category.

Current Issues

Competition.   The book industry faces more competition than ever before. Not only do Americans have a wider array of leisure activities, they also have more magazines, movies, recorded music, and especially television to consume their time. Books are still a part of the mix, but audiences no longer spend as much time on them as they used to. On the other hand, specialized knowledge is becoming more important for all Americans, and specialized books are increasingly crucial for individuals who need to stay current in their fields.

Conditions within the book industry itself have conspired to weaken book publishing and to limit its offerings, suggesting a number of key issues, beyond competition, that the industry will have to confront in the years ahead.

Lack of Periodicity. This trait accounts for why the book industry has lost some readers to other media, or has had difficulty attracting readers who use other media. Books usually do not have the periodicity of other media. Mass media audiences use media habitually; one gets into the habit of periodically reading the same newspaper; subscribing to the same magazines week to week, month to month, year after year; watching the same television program every day or every week. Only one sale is needed to get a customer to subscribe to a year's worth of newspapers and magazines, and once sold, the customer is likely to stay for many years. But each book is usually a brand new product, to be sold individually, and requiring its own marketing campaign to get customers to purchase it. That greatly increases the cost and lowers the profit margin of each title.

Some efforts have been made to build periodicity or habitual buying behavior into the book business. Book clubs are one way to get readers to buy on a regular, habitual basis. Books published serially, sometimes all editions using the same format, or the same characters, are another way. A growing number of romance novels and other pulp fiction products dealing with lurid or sensational subjects are using this technique of marketing. But the general lack of periodicity or habitual book-buying behavior continues to plague the industry.

Rising Production Costs. Books are expensive to produce. A book's retail price must cover printing, binding, and promotion; distribution, marketing, and advertising; overhead (rent, salaries, and other costs of doing business); the author's royalty; and the discount to the bookseller and returns of unsold books from bookstores. Large advances paid to authors are lost if their books don't reach sales targets. Several publishers, including Simon & Schuster, Random House, and Penguin Putnam, wrote off tens of millions of dollars in unearned advances in 1996.

Returns of books that don't sell also represent another big cost, the shipping charges in two directions—to and from the bookseller—and the cost of storing unsold copies. In 1996, for instance, 35 percent of all published adult hardcover trade books were returned unsold. Returns are eventually destroyed, recycled into paper, or sold as discounts at a fraction of their cost.

Changes in Retailing. The superstore concept has begun to dominate the book industry, which now has chain superstores such as Borders Group, Inc.; Barnes & Noble; Crown Books; and Books-a-Million, Inc. These chains sell a quarter of all books in the

United States. Their large sales volume allows them to cut favorable deals with publishers, but they have squeezed out many independent bookstores, the small entrepreneurs who develop an inventory suited to their local clientele. In contrast, the far-away corporate owners of superstores tend to emphasize national mass marketing campaigns for selected "blockbuster" books. The superstores may vary somewhat in size, but their inventories pretty much follow a single retailing plan.

The tension between the two types of retailing may eventually affect the types of books published. Book fans and authors fear that quality trade books selling a few thousand copies slowly to a small but devoted audience will be eliminated by the pressure to find titles that sell tens of thousands of copies quickly in superstores.

Independent booksellers also face intensifying competition from nonbookstore outlets, such as discount department stores (Wal-Mart and K-mart), membership warehouses (Price Club, Sam's Club), supermarkets and drugstores. These outlets sell about a quarter of all books. Together with bookstore superchains, they sold nearly half of all books in 1996.

Perhaps the biggest development is the use of the Internet for buying and selling books. Amazon.com and BarnesandNoble.com at the beginning of the twenty-first century still constituted only a fraction of total book sales, but their volume was growing as rapidly as their stock market prices. (Amazon.com grew from about $25 a share to about $400 a share in 2 years.) This certainly poses an increasing competitive threat to and further loss of business for traditional booksellers, but it may be an enormous boon to book publishers.

Consolidating Ownership. Small publishing houses that produce specialized books in limited content are increasing, but their volume is still small compared to publishing giants. The big book publishers are shrinking in number but growing in size as one company swallows another. For an illustration of how this occurs, see Fig. 9.1. Consolidation also allows publishers to acquire valuable backlists—previously published works—as well as to increase their market share and reduce their costs. They can also use all forms of marketing to publish in any and all book industry categories.

The combination of megapublishing houses selling to megabookstores is radically altering the economics of the business. Less competition among publishers and retailers has profound implications for the marketability of books yet to be written. By the beginning of the twenty-first century, the top 20 North American book publishers already produced about 86 percent of the books published on the continent as Table 9.1 illustrates.

Sales Instability. Publishers more interested in making quick profits than in producing quality books are affecting all aspects of the book market. Large print runs of heavily promoted celebrity books often do not meet expectations, resulting in costly returns. One example was "Tonight Show" host Jay Leno's book, *Leading With My Chin*. HarperCollins paid Leno an advance of $4 million and printed 600,000 copies of which 400,000 were returned unsold. With these kinds of results, publishers often have less money to spend on quality trade books or less inclination to gamble on small-market books.

Random House, the world's largest English-language general trade book publisher, was founded in 1925. It publishes hardcover, trade paperback, mass-market paperback, and reference books, plus works in electronic, multimedia, and other formats.

Beginning in the 1930s, the company moved into publishing for children, and entered the reference publishing field in 1947.

In 1960, Random House acquired the publishing house of Alfred A. Knopf Inc, and a year later, Pantheon Books, a company that had been established in New York by European editors to publish works from abroad.

Random House, Inc., was itself acquired in 1965 by the major electronics corporation, RCA. Random House continued to expand with the acquisition of Ballantine Books, whose mass-market paperback publishing program enabled Random House to reach a much broader and diverse readership.

In 1980, Random House was acquired by Advance Publications, Inc., a privately held corporation. A number of acquisitions followed: Fawcett Books, in 1982; the creation of Villard Books in 1983; the purchase of Times books from The New York Times Co., in 1984; and Fodor's Travel Guides, acquired in 1986.

Random House had set up Canadian operations in 1944. The 1980s saw international expansion with the acquisition of British publisher Chatto, Virago, Bodley Head, & Jonathan Cape, Ltd., and then Century Hutchinson, Ltd. The group is known as Random House UK, with subsidiaries in Australia, New Zealand, and South Africa.

In 1988, Random House grew again with the acquisition of Crown Publishing, whose imprints include Crown, Clarkson Potter, Inc., Harmony Books, and the Outlet Book Co., a publisher of low-priced books now known as Random House Value Publishing.

In 1998, Random House was acquired by media giant Bertelsmann. Bertelsmann organizationally united all the English-language publishing divisions worldwide of its long-held Bantam Doubleday Dell Publishing Group, which includes Bantam Books, the 102-year-old Doubleday, and Transworld UK, with those of Random House. The newly combined Random House maintains the strong traditions of editorial autonomy and publishing diversity held by the former companies it now comprises.

FIG. 9.1. Growth of a giant: Random House, Inc. Reproduced with permission of Random House, Inc.

No doubt sales instability caused by blockbuster economics has hurt trade books, and they declined in 1990s sales, especially books for adults. Although the juvenile and book club categories have remained relatively strong, negative signs in the industry's dominant trade book category is usually bad for the book business as a whole.

Looking Ahead

What books retain is their importance as a method of introducing ideas and analyzing events. Nonfiction can provide in-depth analysis and perspective on any subject. Fiction and poetry offer the possibility of gripping drama and compelling art. These traits continue to make books a vital part of culture and important to the advancement of society. At this stage of civilization, books will certainly continue to be the most efficient and most often chosen medium through which we teach our young, continue to educate our adults, create our fantasies, recreate our feelings, and record and interpret anything and everything we humans regard as important.

TABLE 9.1

Top 20 Book Publishers in North America, Ranked by 1997 Sales
and 1998 Projections (Estimated in Millions of Dollars)

	1997			1998	
Rank	Company	Sales	Rank	Company	Sales
1	Simon & Schuster	2,470	1	Pearson (1)	3,716
2	Pearson	1,796	2	Random House (1)	2,220
3	Thomson Corp.*	1,580	3	Harcourt Brace	1,800
4	McGraw-Hill	1,570	4	Thomson Corp.	1,580
5	Harcourt Brace	1,376	5	McGraw-Hill	1,570
6	Random House	1,250	6	Wolters Kluwer (2)	1,200
7	Reader's Digest*	1,203	7	Time Warner	1,120
8	Time Warner	1,120	8	Reader's Digest	1,100
9	Bertelsmann Grp*	970	9	Reed Elsevier	950
10	Wolters Kluwer	930	10	Houghton Mifflin	797
11	Houghton Mifflin	797	11	Scholastic	790
12	Scholastic (3)	737	12	HarperCollins	700
13	HarperCollins (3)	737	13	Simon & Schuster / trade	550
14	Reed Elsevier*	700	14	Torstar	530
15	Times Mirror*	650	15	John Wiley & Sons	480
16	Torstar	508	16	Encyclopaedia Britannica	390
17	John Wiley & Sons	467	17	Grolier	370
18	Encyclopaedia Britannica	390	18	Holtzbrinck	320
19	Grolier	370	19	Tribune	310
20	Holtzbrinck*	320	20	Golden Books	244
Total		**$19,994**			**$20,737**

Source: *Subtext*. (1998, July 8, p. 3). Darien, CT: Open Book Publishing, Inc. Reprinted with permission.

(1) After Pearson acquired Simon & Schuster and Bertelsmann acquired Random House.

(2) 1998 sales projection included the Waverly and Plenum acquisitions made in early 1998.

(3) Latest fiscal year results unavailable when chart was composed.

* *Subtext* estimates.

MAGAZINES

At almost any newsstand or bookstore in America, racks are bursting with consumer magazines covering hundreds of different special interests. More than 12,000 *consumer magazines*—those available to the general public—are published in the United States. Many other printed publications, especially specialized magazines and newsletters, although not readily available at newsstands or stores, are circulated by organizations of every type as a means of keeping their members informed or persuaded. If one counted every membership periodical, including local churches, schools, clubs, and organizations, the number would range into the hundreds of thousands.

Magazines are portable, colorful, and relatively inexpensive, providing readers with a blend of information and entertainment. Using a mixture of photographs, art work, briefs, short articles, and longer-form reporting, magazines can provide variety in makeup and content.

Most magazines get most of their support from advertisers. Some, in fact, are totally dependent on advertising and can give copies free to readers. Others carry no advertising and are completely dependent on support from their readers. Scholarly journals, for example, are high priced. Why? Because they usually have a fairly small readership, and they contain little or no advertising, which means the publisher must depend wholly on subscriptions to cover cost. However, by forgoing advertising, the publishers also are free from the perception that advertisers can influence the editorial content. This makes it possible for these publications to offer objective information with more credibility, thus making them more useful in education.

Early History

Magazines got their name from the word *magazin*, French for department store or storehouse. Magazines were originally thought of as storehouses or a department store of information, offering a variety of products for readers. Daniel Defoe launched the first English magazine, *Review*, in England in 1704 as a forum for an elite class interested in politics, literature, and social decorum. Imitators quickly followed, publishing a varied collection of essays, poetry, and stories.

Two great colonial American media entrepreneurs, both in Philadelphia, competed to be the first to publish a magazine in the colonies in 1741. Andrew Bradford won the competition by three days. His magazine was called *American Magazine, or A Monthly View of the Political State of the British Colonies*. His competitor was none other than that media giant of colonial America, Benjamin Franklin. His magazine was called *The General Magazine, and Historical Chronicle, for All the British Plantations in America*. Neither lasted long. The magazine medium was competitive from the beginning in America, and developed in fits and starts for the remainder of the eighteenth century.

At the beginning of the nineteenth century, despite numerous start-ups and nearly as many failures, only a dozen magazines were being published in the new nation. Like newspapers, magazines needed a literate audience and a cost-effective printing and distribution system. Neither was readily available in the thirteen colonies in the first years of the new nation. But improvements in printing technology in the early 1800s, particularly the invention of the cylinder press, and broader use of the postal system for periodical distribution, made possible the rise of general-interest magazines. As a young nation began building its future, its citizens' appetite for uniquely American literature and information grew steadily. By 1825, about 100 magazines were being published in the United States.

One of the most enduring titles to come out of the early nineteenth century was the *Saturday Evening Post*, which first appeared in 1821. It published short stories, essays, humor, and political and social commentary. Other long-running periodicals were *Harper's* (founded in 1850) and *The Atlantic Monthly* (founded in 1857). Known since their earliest days for the high quality of their literary content and social commentary, both are still being published. These magazines were high priced and were aimed at an elite, not a mass, audience.

Magazines Become a Mass Medium

The Civil War created opportunities for magazines to produce content that might have a larger appeal. Magazines could do things that neither newspapers nor books could do so well: They could better debate current issues, provide more in-depth background on events, explain personalities in the news, and reveal larger meanings than day-to-day journalism of newspapers or the slow process of book publishing. Slavery, the war, and the viability of the Union were topics of enormous concern for magazine editors and their readers.

All this helped create a greater public interest in magazines that continued after the war. By 1885, 3,300 magazines were being published in America. The same dynamic that had made newspapers and books into mass media—technology, cost, and marketing—was also applied to the magazine medium. Magazines of high quality remained relatively high priced and aimed at an elite market. *Harper's Monthly* and the *Century Magazine*, for example, sold for 35 cents a copy in the 1880s (which also was the price of a full meal or a night's lodging). But inexpensive magazines began to appear, and they quickly found a mass audience. The *Ladies' Home Journal* was started in 1883 by Cyrus H. K. Curtis as a cheap eight-page magazine that sold for 50 cents a year, later raised to $1.

The *Ladies' Home Journal* quickly reached a circulation of half a million, and Curtis became a magazine baron with a group of mass appeal magazines that included the *Saturday Evening Post*. He put more popular articles in the *Post* and lowered its price. A monthly magazine called *Comfort*, published in Maine, also lowered its price to 50 cents a year and in 1895 was the first to reach a circulation of 1 million. The *Saturday Evening Post* in 1903 became the first weekly magazine to reach 1 million subscribers. The penny newspaper and the dime novel had been joined by the nickel magazine, and another mass medium was born. By 1940, 23 magazines in America had circulations of more than 1 million.

One way of building magazines into mass media was by having content that would attract mass audiences. One group of magazines attracted wide readership by publishing articles exposing the ills of society. The writers and editors of these magazines became known as *muckrakers*, journalists who stirred up the filth and dirt of the nation. The muckrakers were crusading journalists who used their magazine articles to expose business fraud, corporate monopolies, political bribery, abuse of laborers, slum conditions—all stories with implications for the nation's health and prosperity. Chief among the muckraking magazines were *McClure's, Cosmopolitan, Collier's, Every-*

body's, and *Arena*. Many reached mass audiences at the height of their appeal in the late 1890s.

Special Magazines for Women

Women's magazines have been popular since the earliest days of magazine publishing in the United States. They, too, experienced the start-ups and failures of general-interest magazines. They provided an outlet for women writers of fiction and non-fiction and gave women readers a forum for discussion of matters important to them. *Godey's Lady's Book*, published by Louis Godey and edited by the remarkable Sarah Josepha Hale, offered advice, fashion, consumer tips, romantic fiction, and advice on self-improvement, household management, and relationships. Hale signed on as Godey's editor in 1837 and kept the job for 40 years. Her formula set the standard and established the framework followed by most women's consumer magazines for more than a century. Many other magazines, such as *Peterson's* and *Graham's,* copied *Godey's* formula and achieved similar success.

Magazines also grew out of the women's rights movement in the 1840s. Amelia Bloomer started *The Lily, A Ladies Journal Devoted to Temperance and Literature,* in 1848. *The Lily* promoted dress reform and full participation of women in the political process, including the right to vote. Susan B. Anthony published *The Revolution,* which promoted women's suffrage. Magazines launched and operated by women in this era had fragile finances. Most of those focused on social issues, such as abolition of slavery and promotion of women's rights, were dependent on financial resources of wealthy benefactors or on small women's organizations and rarely attracted the readership or advertising revenue to become self-sufficient.

In the last third of the nineteenth century, even more women's magazines were started, some with names that still appear on newsstands today: Joining *Ladies' Home Journal* were *McCall's, Good Housekeeping,* and *Harper's Bazaar.* Competition for the same readers and advertisers kept intensifying, and both *Godey's* and *Peterson's,* which had been the top-circulation women's magazines before the Civil War, declined by the century's end, perhaps because they were not inexpensive enough for a mass market that by then had more choices in magazines.

Other Magazine Specialization

Such specialization came to other magazines as well. Westward expansion and industrialization reshaped the nation in the last third of the nineteenth and first third of the twentieth century. The rapid pace of change stimulated specialization among magazines, which were now reaching national audiences. By 1885, magazines were being published for nearly every occupation, activity, and interest.

In the last decades of the nineteenth century, as the magazine medium became more horizontal, more *mass* in reach, it also became more vertical, more *specialized* in scope. Specialization of subject matter and the corresponding segmentation of audiences increased opportunities for advertisers to focus their messages for specific readers. With advertisers more eager to use magazines for efficient targeting of their markets, the magazine industry prospered. Such specialization continued until it became the prime characteristic of the entire magazine field in the twentieth century. See Table 9.2 for a list of the 25 largest circulation magazines as of 1998.

Modern Magazines

General-interest magazines such as the *Saturday Evening Post* and *Collier's* continued to enjoy success well into the mid-twentieth century. These were family publications, containing something for every reader, and each issue was often read by all family members—mothers, fathers, brothers, and sisters of all ages. But they faced formida-

TABLE 9.2

Top 25 Consumer Magazines by Paid Circulation (First Half 1998)

Rank	Publication	Circulation
1	*Modern Maturity*	20,402,096
2	*TV Guide*	13,085,971
3	*National Geographic*	8,783,752
4	*Better Homes & Gardens*	7,616,114
5	*Family Circle*	5,005,084
6	*Ladies' Home Journal*	4,521,970
7	*Good Housekeeping*	4,517,713
8	*McCall's*	4,239,622
9	*The Cable Guide*	4,169,103
10	*Time*	4,124,451
11	*Woman's Day*	4,079,707
12	*People*	3,719,925
13	*Sports Illustrated*	3,269,917
14	*Newsweek*	3,227,729
15	*Prevention*	3,152,814
16	*Playboy*	3,151,495
17	*Redbook*	2,854,448
18	*The American Legion Magazine*	2,691,252
19	*Cosmopolitan*	2,581,985
20	*Via Magazine*	2,489,605
21	*Southern Living*	2,470,202
22	*Seventeen*	2,437,194
23	*Martha Stewart Living*	2,235,723
24	*Glamour*	2,208,926
25	*National Enquirer*	2,206,747

Source: Audit Bureau of Circulations FAS–FAX for 6 months ended June 30, 1998; BPA International. Used with permission.

LIVERPOOL JOHN MOORES UNIVERSITY
LEARNING SERVICES

ble competition from special-interest magazines and then from new media, including radio and movies at first, and finally television, and slowly died. The *Saturday Evening Post*, for example, went out of business in 1969, not for lack of subscribers but for lack of advertising. For reasons that have to do primarily with the cost of marketing and the rates of advertising, specialized magazines targeted at specialized audiences have grown, whereas general interest magazines have withered.

Magazines Distinguished by Content

Many magazines are still aimed at a fairly broad range of readers, almost broad enough to be considered general interest, but the contents of the magazines themselves are specialized. For example, their emphasis may be news content, photography, or material digested from other magazines. Following are some of the dominant categories.

News magazines in America owe their origins to founders with strong political views and broad interests in news and public affairs. Their beginnings in the 1920s and 1930s played a key role in the rise of modern magazine publishing. *Time,* started in 1923 by Henry Luce and Briton Hadden, was a digest of national and international news, and contained reports on medicine, culture, economics, and politics, all departmentalized for quick reference by the reader and written with an economy of words. *Time* interpreted the news it covered, reporting the facts but also offering its view on the significance and rightness or wrongness of ideas and policies.

A decade later, in 1933, *Time*'s foreign editor, Thomas S. Martyn, raised money from a group of wealthy investors and launched *Newsweek.* Martyn said his magazine would be more straightforward and less cavalier in style, but in actuality, *Newsweek* essentially imitated its older rival. Both were similar in style and reflected the politics of their Republican founders and editors. *Newsweek* magazine was later purchased by the Washington Post Company.

Syndicated columnist David Lawrence, a political conservative, started *United States News*, a successor to *The United States Daily,* a newspaper he had founded in 1926. It was recast as a magazine in 1940. Its content was heavy with political analysis, Lawrence's forte. In 1946, he founded *World Report* magazine to capitalize on the increased post-World War II interest in international affairs. He merged the two magazines in 1948 to form *U.S. News & World Report.*

Photo magazines captured national interest from the start. In 1936, Luce launched *Life* as a newsweekly with a photo essay format. An oversized magazine packed with dramatic images of war, personal triumph and tragedy, everyday life as well as glamour, *Life* was an instant success in those pretelevision years. *Look* appeared in 1937 first as a monthly, and then as a biweekly. Whereas *Life* had a hard-news emphasis, *Look* was more feature oriented.

Both magazines had imitators, a number of which departed from *Life*'s and *Look*'s wholesomeness by emphasizing sexual content. But television competition took a heavy toll on all these magazines. Both *Life* and *Look* went out of business in the early 1970s, although *Life* was revived in 1978 as a monthly, concentrating on heavily illustrated features rather than on photo essays.

Digests use previously published articles and condense them, producing a compact publication for readers short on time. DeWitt and Lila Wallace introduced the *Reader's Digest* in 1922 and they captured a large market of readers in a hurry and on a budget. The digest format provided access to articles from numerous periodicals large and small that a single reader probably would never subscribe to. *Reader's Digest* was so popular that for many years it was the largest circulating magazine in America, and editions published in local languages with local content worldwide made it into the largest circulation magazine on earth. In many other countries, *Reader's Digest* is the most widely read magazine.

Other digests, some devoted to specialized subjects, also were introduced over the years. A widely successful digest launched in the last decades of the twentieth century was the *Utne Reader*, a magazine that digested material from sources that were not always mainstream.

Television magazines, not surprisingly, emerged as television grew into the most massive medium of all and the activity on which most Americans spend most of their time. TV is the subject of 2 of the top 25 magazines, *TV Guide* and *The Cable Guide,* both with impressive circulations that are testimony to the vast influence of television on our culture.

Tabloid magazines are a genre of sensational news weeklies usually sold at newsstands and grocery store checkouts, including the *National Enquirer, The Globe,* and *The Star.* They serve up tales of the fantastic ("B–52 Found on Moon"; "Woman Has Elvis's Love Child") and of celebrity gossip ("Neil Diamond Fights Cancer Nightmare"; "JFK Jr. Walks Out—Ex-Lover Jets in as Wife Battles to Win Him Back").

Circulation of the tabloids has slipped since mainstream media have become more sensational in their selection and treatment of news stories. Celebrity-oriented tabloid television programs such as "Hard Copy" and "Access Hollywood" also have dimmed the popularity of their print counterparts. Circulation of supermarket tabloids is about half what it was in the late 1980s; for example, the *National Enquirer*'s circulation for the first half of 1998 had fallen to 2.2 million, down from 4.3 million in 1989.

Pulp magazines are another category with widely varied readership of specialized content. They are similar to tabloid magazines in their concentrations on sensational topics and lurid detail and usually printed on cheap paper with lots of startling pictures. But they deal with subjects less timely than news, and with fiction. They are often called "true" detective, or "true" confessions, or "true" westerns.

Magazines Distinguished by Demographics

A growing number of magazines are aimed at specific customers rather than being tailored by specific content. These magazines target various niches in the general population, often by demographic groupings, including the demographics of occupation or interest. Following are some of the dominant types.

Contemporary women's magazines as a group remain a substantial component of the mass-circulation category, including 10 of the top 25 highest-circulation periodicals, perhaps because women dominate the purchase of magazine subscriptions and single copies, accounting for three of every four single-copy sales and two of every three subscriptions. A number of these magazines represent durable titles with origins in the late nineteenth or early twentieth century. (See Table 9.2).

Within the women's genre are service magazines emphasizing home and family, such as *Ladies' Home Journal, McCall's, Good Housekeeping, Family Circle,* and *Woman's Day.* Another category is fashion, with titles such as *Vogue* and *Elle.* Another is fitness and health, such as *Shape, Self,* and *Women's Sports & Fitness.* A teen category includes *YM* and *Seventeen.* In a class by itself is *Ms.,* the independent feminist monthly founded during the modern feminist movement of the 1960s and 1970s.

Shelter magazines are a variation on women's magazines; they have a mixed female and male readership, but the majority of readers are women. The category includes *Better Homes & Gardens, House Beautiful,* and *Southern Living.* E. T. Meredith began publishing *Better Homes and Gardens,* the first of the genre, in 1922. *BH&G* told its target audience of men and women it would help them become knowledgeable about their properties and ways to maintain them and make them more attractive.

Contemporary men's magazines have emphases on sex (*Playboy, Penthouse, Hustler*), sports (*Sports Illustrated, Field & Stream*), or lifestyle (*Esquire, GQ, Details*). *Playboy* and *Sports Illustrated* are in the top 25 in circulation. *Sports Illustrated* is gradually making room for material about women athletes in hopes of drawing more female readers.

Ethnic and race-based magazines serve specialized groups within the diverse American readership. Magazines for blacks started publishing as early as the 1830s, but slavery and adverse social and economic conditions even for free blacks undercut their chances for long-term success. In contrast, the black community at the beginning of the twenty-first century has a range of magazine choices: *Ebony* and *Jet,* in the more general-interest category; *Black Enterprise,* for entrepreneurs and professionals; *Emerge,* an upscale lifestyle magazine; *Essence* and *Black Elegance,* for women; and *Vibe,* a lifestyle, music, and entertainment magazine. The nation's fast-growing Hispanic population has *Hispanic, Hispanic Business,* and *Latina.*

Membership magazines are aimed at members of particular organizations, and some are among the top 25, illustrating the power of membership organizations to generate far-reaching communication. *Modern Maturity* (published by the American Association of Retired Persons) and *The American Legion Magazine* reflect the shared interests of millions of readers who are members of these influential groups. *National Geographic,* published by the National Geographic Society, calls itself a membership magazine primarily for tax purposes, but since anyone can "join," it is really a special interest magazine.

Niche magazines have really become the salient characteristic of the industry. They are magazines that concentrate on special audiences within larger specialties. They have smaller circulations, but their readers are more desirable to advertisers, because the message can be more carefully targeted and thus more effective, even while the cost of the advertising can be more efficient.

An example of niche publishing is *Working Mother*. Women's magazines such as *Ladies' Home Journal* and *Good Housekeeping* reach homemakers with an emphasis on home and family. By contrast, *Working Mother* represents a clearly defined niche within the women's publishing category.

Many niche magazines attract substantial readerships. Regional and city magazines are flourishing. Computer enthusiasts can purchase *Wired, Byte,* and *PC World.* The corporate world is served by *Business Week, Fortune, Forbes,* and *Inc.* Interest in an epicurean lifestyle is no longer the province of the French; in America, a new wave of concern about living the good life has produced magazines such as *Gourmet, Food & Wine, Saveur, Cooking Light,* and *Martha Stewart Living.*

Current Issues

Response to Competition. This is changing many magazines. The news weeklies, for example, after suffering circulation slumps in the 1980s, revamped their content to better distinguish themselves from their print and electronic competition. Like newspapers, news weeklies have been affected by the advantage of immediacy that television, radio, and online information can offer. Instead of trying to compete with these faster media on breaking news as they once did, the news weeklies have developed more in-depth analyses on a wider variety of current issues and have reduced their political and public-affairs coverage in favor of trend-type stories on such subjects as health, education, economics, science, technology, and personal growth.

Advertising's Encroachment. Advertisers have become more aggressive in determining editorial environment, which is causing tension within the magazine industry. Some have kept their ads from placement near articles dealing with content the advertiser thinks could be offensive to readers. It is no longer unusual for advertisers to ask for advance summaries of a magazine's content, or even insist on reviewing articles before publication.

Advertiser demands have gone well beyond the traditional courtesy magazines have extended to them of separating competing ads or keeping ads apart from incompatible content, such as placing a tobacco ad opposite an article on cancer. In 1997, for example, *Esquire* killed a short story about a gay man who wrote college term papers in exchange for sex after Chrysler threatened to withdraw all four of its ads from that issue.

Distributor Demands. Some retailers who sell magazines, such as Wal-Mart and Winn-Dixie supermarkets, have refused to display copies they find objectionable, also increasing tensions between the publishers and their outlets. In 1997, Winn-Dixie rejected an issue of *Cosmopolitan*, Wal-Mart an issue of *Vibe.* Mounting pressures on magazine editors by advertisers and distributors may bring significant change to magazine content, especially in periods when the national economy is weak and advertising declines. During such periods, magazine executives may have little choice but to accommodate advertiser and distributor demands to survive.

Looking Ahead

Magazines will continue to be an important medium for new ventures. To start a new magazine is still less expensive than to start any other mass medium, with the exception of newsletters and some online media. Young people with new ideas but without money can still get into the magazine business relatively easily. In 1997 alone, 852 new magazines were launched in the United States—110 of them sex titles, the perpetual top category for new magazines. This does not mean, however, that large media conglomerates will not continue to dominate the field, for new magazines as well as those long established.

The rapid development of computerized communication has prompted magazines to establish an online presence and to become interactive periodicals. Online subscriptions to magazines are likely to become common in the years ahead, although all indications are that readers loyal to the print versions will continue to prefer the portability and intimacy of the hard-copy version.

NEWSLETTERS

As a mass medium, newsletters are a twentieth century phenomenon, although they were probably the first form of printed communication to be distributed periodically. An early form first appeared in the fifteenth century containing financial information and distributed by banking houses in German mercantile centers. And early colonial American newspapers were somewhat similar to today's newsletters in format and content.

Newsletters are the most narrowly targeted of print media. They may deliver information on a precisely defined subject or report about an organization to individuals interested in that organization. Newsletters can be *for profit* or they can be distributed free, depending on their purpose and target audience. More than 20,000 subscription newsletters were regularly produced in America at the beginning of the twenty-first century, and countless others were available privately to members of organizations and institutions.

Subscription newsletters are generally one of two types. **Consumer newsletters** are usually priced below $100—more often in the $25 to $45 range—and are aimed at the general public. The subject matter is usually relatively general in nature, although it is often more specialized than niche magazines. *Retire With Money*, for example, is a 12-page newsletter aimed at any senior citizen who invests in the stock market. The subscriber is generally an individual.

The second type is the **business-to-business newsletter**, which usually contains very specific niche information for an extremely small audience. The subscription is most often paid for by a business subscriber. Almost every profession and industry has them, and as the world grows more complex and high-tech, more of these newsletters appear. They can also be very expensive, ranging in subscription rates up to thousands of dollars per year. They are generally published on a weekly basis, and delivered by mail, fax, or e-mail. An example is *The Browning Report*, a highly specialized newsletter for a select few financial analysts who need information about world weather patterns to make financial predictions.

Nonsubscription or institutional newsletters are produced by thousands of religious, educational, nonprofit community organizations and other social and civic groups. They come in all shapes, sizes, and levels of professional quality.

History

The modern newsletter does not have a long history. The individual credited with launching the newsletter as a successful media enterprise was Willard M. Kiplinger. A former journalist who covered the U.S. Treasury and Commerce Departments as an Associated Press reporter after World War I, he realized that banks had a special need for information about government financial matters. He started writing a weekly newsletter with inside information about government financial activities in 1923 and offered his four-page *Kiplinger Washington Letter* to banks.

Kiplinger saw that a larger market existed for his newsletter than banking and business executives, so he set a low price—about 50 cents an issue for an annual subscription. For many years he lost money on his newsletter, but when World War II began and more people wanted inside information on what was happening in Washington, subscriptions began to rise, ultimately bringing success to his business. In 1997, the *Kiplinger Washington Letter*'s circulation was 267,000, and it was part of a family of other Kiplinger newsletters on agriculture, tax, retirement, Florida, and California, in addition to *Kiplinger's Personal Finance Magazine*.

Characteristics

Other publishers came into the business in the 1920s, 1930s, and 1940s, but the first boom started after World War II, and the second after the development of computers made possible desktop publishing in the 1970s and 1980s. Newsletters often have the following characteristics in common.

Personal style is one of the newsletter's hallmarks. It is often a very personal medium. Kiplinger maintained that newsletters should be written with an intimate style, not the formal style of newspapers. He thought the reader should feel as if the writer were a personal friend or family member. Even after it became popular, each edition of his newsletter contained his signature printed in blue ink, as if he had signed it with his own pen. And it was sent by first class mail like a personal letter, not the second-class mail of newspapers and magazines. Because it was a personal message, Kiplinger mixed factual reporting with his strong opinions. "That violated all the rules of newswriting," he said in 1960. "But I felt a reporter couldn't tell everything if he were restricted to the facts, and I still think so."[1]

Inside expertise is another byword in newsletter publishing. By subscribing to a newsletter, the reader pays for a sophisticated level of analysis about a subject important to that person. Newsletter reporting must, of course, be timely and accurate, but it must also contain a specialized technical depth that mainstream media cannot provide.

Credibility of newsletters tends to be higher than magazines and newspapers, not only because of the technical expertise displayed but also because of the lack of external influences that might color the information. Newsletters generally don't carry advertising but depend entirely on subscriptions for the bulk of their revenues. However, some newsletter publishers offer other products and services, such as books, speakers, seminars, and conferences from which they obtain revenues.

Accessibility also marks this medium because of the relatively low cost of entry into the field. Desktop publishing capabilities brought about by computers have made it possible for almost anyone with a small budget to produce a newsletter that might compete with top-of-the-line consumer or even business-to-business newsletters. Desktop publishing technology has been responsible for rapid growth in the newsletter industry: About two-thirds of the for-profit newsletters publishing in 1995 were launched after 1980, when computer technology made typesetting and design accessible to individual users, including writers and editors.

Newsletters are easier to start than magazines, and as a result they offer a unique opportunity to young entrepreneurs who want to produce media. Perhaps the best example of success in the field is Phillips Publishing International in Potomac, Md. It was founded by Tom Phillips in 1974, when he was a young man recently out of the army and graduate school. He began with an investment of $1,000 and two newsletters, using a garage as his editorial office. Today, Phillips publishes dozens of magazines and newsletters and in 1997 earned $300 million in sales. His publishing company has grown into the largest independent newsletter company in America. Figure 9.2 illustrates the scope of this company.

Multiple-title publishers are also increasingly characteristic of this medium. Like many other newsletter publishers with many titles, Phillips grew largely by acquiring individual newsletters from independent publishers. Today, newsletter publishers often group related newsletters into specialty groups for editorial and marketing efficiency. For example, McGraw-Hill in New York specializes in energy newsletters, publishing 20 of them, supplemented with online and fax versions. Capitol Publications, Inc., in Alexandria, Va., has seven newsletter specialties—economic and financial forecasting, education, energy, grants, health, management, and telecommunications. It publishes multiple newsletters within each group.

Looking Ahead

The fragmentation of the information market, with more individuals seeking expert information tailored to highly specialized interests, bodes well for the newsletter industry. However, the increased empowerment the Internet affords individuals seeking specialized information could undercut the influence of newsletters. Consequently, many newsletter publishers are establishing Web sites and guiding online information seekers to their sites in hopes of turning them into subscribers. The newsletter industry's advantage is a reputation for expertise, which their publishers believe gives them an edge over more general print media and online offerings of varying quality. That should keep them operating as viable mass media well into the twenty-first century.

Phillips Publishing International operates Phillips Business Information, Inc., and Phillips Publishing, Inc. Both produce dozens of magazines and newsletters for narrowly targeted audiences. Phillips Business Information concentrates on industry-specific titles, Phillips Publishing on more consumer-oriented periodicals.

Phillips Business Information, Inc.

Communications/Media Group
Advanced Intelligent Network News
Broadband Networking News
CableFax Daily
Communications Today
Document Imaging Report
EDI News
Electronic Messaging News
Fiber Optics News
Global Positioning & Navigation News
Healthcare PR & Marketing News
Interactive PR & Marketing News
ISDN News
Land Mobile Radio News
min—Media Industry Newsletter
Mobile Phone News
Mobile Satellite News
Multimedia Week
Optical Memory News
PCS Week
PR News
Satellite News
Video Technology News
Wireless Data News

Defense/Aviation/Banking Group
Air Cargo Report
Air Safety Week
Aircraft Value News
Airline Financial News
Bank Automation News
Card News
C4I News

Commuter/Regional Airline News
Commuter/Regional Airline News
   International
Corporate EFT Report
Helicopter News
Item Processing Report
Space Business News
Voice Technology & Services News
World Airline News

Phillips Publishing, Inc.

Adamo's Inside Track
Dr. David Williams' Alternatives
Fabian Fax Hotline
Fabian Market Watch
Fabian Premium Investment Resource
Forecasts & Strategies
The Garzarelli Outlook
Health & Healing
Health Wisdom for Women
Heart Sense
Independent Adviser for Vanguard
   Investors
Intelligence Report
Invest With The Masters
Investor's World
Louis Navellier's Blue Chip Growth
   Letter
Mutual Fund Investing
Profitable Investing
The Retirement Letter
Dr. Sherry Roger's Total Health
   in Today's World
Straight Talk on Your Money

FIG. 9.2. Portrait of a specialized newsletter publisher: Phillips Publishing International.

Further Reading

Books

Clement, Richard W. (1996). *The Book in America*. Golden, CO: Fulcrum.
Coser, Lewis A., Kadushin, Charles, and Powell, Walter W. (1982). *Books: The Culture and Commerce of Publishing*. New York: Basic Books.

Geiser, Elizabeth A. (Ed.). (1985). *The Business of Book Publishing.* Boulder, CO: Westview Press.

The Subtext 1997 Perspective on Book Publishing: Numbers, Issues & Trends. (1997). Darien, CT: Open Book Publishing.

Schreuders, Piet. (1981). *Paperbacks USA: A Graphic History, 1939-1959.* San Diego, CA: Blue Dolphin Enterprises.

Smith, Datus C., Jr. (1989). *A Guide to Book Publishing* (rev. ed.). Seattle: University of Washington Press.

Tebbel, John. (1987). *Between Covers: The Rise and Transformation of Book Publishing in America.* New York: Oxford University Press.

Magazines

Baughman, James L. (1987). *Henry R. Luce and the Rise of the American News Media.* Boston: Twayne.

Garvey, Ellen Gruber. (1996). *The Adman in the Parlor: Magazines and the Gendering of Consumer Culture, 1880s to 1910.* New York: Oxford University Press.

Humphreys, Nancy K. (1989). *American Women's Magazines: An Annotated Historical Guide.* New York: Garland.

Husni, Samir. (1998). *Guide to New Consumer Magazines.* New York: Oxbridge Communications.

McCracken, Ellen. (1992). *Decoding Women's Magazines: From* Mademoiselle *to* Ms. New York: St. Martin's Press.

Mott, Frank Luther. (1957). *History of American Magazines 1850-1905* (5 vols.). Cambridge, MA: Harvard University Press. (Originally published in 1938)

Scanlon, Jennifer. (1995). *Inarticulate Longings: The* Ladies' Home Journal, *Gender, and the Promises of Consumer Culture.* New York: Routledge.

Wood, James Playsted. (1967). *Of Lasting Interest: The Story of the* Reader's Digest (rev. ed.). New York: Doubleday.

Woodward, Helen. (1960). *The Lady Persuaders.* New York: Ivan Obolensky.

Newsletters

Fanson, Barbara A. (1996). *Producing a First-Class Newsletter: A Guide to Planning, Writing, Editing, Designing, Photography, Production and Printing.* North Vancouver, BC: Self-Counsel Press.

Hudson, Howard Penn. (1988). *Publishing Newsletters* (3rd. ed.). New York: Scribner's.

Note

[1]Temple, Truman R. (1960, September 30). Kiplinger's Daring Reporting Style Marks Top Journalistic Enterprise. *Washington Star.*

CHAPTER

10

Motion Pictures

"You despise me, don't you, Rick?"

"I probably would if I gave any thought to it."

And with that reply, tough-guy Humphrey Bogart, playing a World War II nightclub owner in Morocco, informs the character played by Peter Lorre of his utter contempt for him. The movie was the 1942 film classic, *Casablanca.*

Based on a play, *Everybody Goes to Rick's*, *Casablanca* tells the story of European refugees fleeing the Nazis and of Casablanca residents who either help or hinder their escape. It is a fictional story based on the gritty reality of the time. Fortunately for the movie, as well as for the real town in which the story was set, American forces captured German-occupied Casablanca just as the film opened in the United States. While the film was still showing in theaters, President Franklin Roosevelt and British Prime Minister Winston Churchill chose Casablanca for a summit meeting. These events involving the real Casablanca boosted publicity for the film of the same name and assured its box-office success. Casablanca's liberation by U.S. troops provided the real-life ending moviegoers likely wanted for the fictional Rick and his friends.

And therein lies the ingredient that makes motion pictures so compelling: their ability to combine fantasy and realism in a seamless fashion so that fiction seems authentic, believable, and on some very important level, true. The believability of movies has generated intense debate about the effects they have on their audiences. And those audiences are vast: The power of motion pictures to satisfy the illiterate as well as the literate, foreign audiences as well as domestic, children as well as adults, has made movies universally popular. American movies are among the nation's most successful exports. Their domination of world film production gives them a stunning amount of exposure and influence.

FIRST YEARS

Motion studies in the United States and abroad provided the basis for the eventual development of movies. An early experiment in California, in about 1867, captured the movement of a galloping horse by using a row of simple cameras whose shutters were tripped by wires. Because of the physiological phenomenon called *persistence of vision*, the horses appeared to the eye to be moving when the pictures were flashed rapidly in sequence.

Credit for the first motion pictures made with a *single* camera goes to Frenchman Etienne-Jules Marey in 1882. Marey was able take pictures in quick succession, but he had to rely on individual photographic plates.

The challenge of speeding up film's ability to record motion was met in 1889 when Hannibal Goodwin developed celluloid, a flexible film that could pass through a camera and capture a series of images on one piece of film. George Eastman, founder of Eastman Kodak, built on Goodwin's work and manufactured the first motion-picture film.

The lab of inventor Thomas Edison played an important role in the development of motion-picture technology, and later, because of the patents he held on equipment, Edison was able to assert considerable control over motion-picture production. William Dickson, Edison's assistant, developed a motion-picture camera called the *kinetograph*. In 1893 the Edison labs also developed a viewing system, called a *kinetoscope*. The kinetoscope allowed one person at a time to peer into a box in which images moved by on film strips. These were the *peep shows* that made their way into fairs and arcades; their usual presentations were fan dancers and sparring boxers.

In France, the Lumière brothers, Louis and Auguste, built the first projection device, the *cinematographe*, in 1895. This enabled them to project images not just to an individual, as the peep shows did, but to a small audience. The Lumières showed the shortest of short subjects, mostly quick views of everyday life, some quite comical, such as a child trying to grab a fish out of a bowl. Shortly thereafter, Edison improved the kinetoscope and in 1896 introduced the *vitascope*, which allowed for projection to large audiences films of longer length.

The inventors had done their part. Motion pictures could now be seen by more than one person at the time. Now artists had to play their role, creating films that audiences would pay to see.

SILENT ERA: 1896–1926

Early experimental films made to demonstrate film equipment simply recorded sights for later projection—such as fire wagons dashing to an emergency, or the endless cascade of Niagara Falls—to show the capability of the technology. In these early demonstration films, the camera usually stayed in a fixed position and recorded the action directly in front of it.

Narrative Films

Films that actually told a story, *narrative films*, originated in 1896 in France with George Méliès. His films, though fantasies (*Cinderella* and *A Trip to the Moon*), had a linear story organization and boasted some of the industry's earliest special effects: the dissolve, the split screen, the jump cut, and superimposition. In America, Edwin S. Porter also employed the narrative style, though he based his movies on realism. In *The Great Train Robbery*, released in 1903, Porter broke away from theater-style staging by shifting the camera's point of view within scenes and by deftly editing together sequences shot in different places, to generate the story's suspense and excitement.

Film Exhibitors and a New Mass Medium

At the same time, the motion picture exhibition industry began to evolve in the United States. Entrepreneurs opened small, makeshift theaters in converted shops (called *nickelodeons*, because they charged 5 cents' admission) and showed whatever they could get. Usually these were filmed news events, comedy that relied heavily on sight gags and practical jokes, and dramatic shorts. Few ran more than 10 minutes.

The public warmed to the new motion-picture medium, and nickelodeons began to multiply. Entrepreneurs began to build more comfortable and more lavishly appointed motion-picture theaters. By 1908, nickelodeons were attracting 80 million admissions per week when the U.S. population was only about 100 million. The penny newspaper, dime novel, and nickel magazine were joined by the 5-cent movie, and motion pictures became mass media.

Film Companies and the Struggle for Control

Demand was there, but supply had to be beefed up to keep an eager public constantly entertained. Moviemaking began on a much larger scale after an interesting assortment of individuals walked away from other careers to start their own movie companies. The earliest film corporations were organized by former bookmakers, druggists, glove salesmen, and real estate agents. They ran the business side and hired the creative talent they needed to make the films.

Their progress was hampered by the Motion Picture Patents Co. (MPPC), a consortium of firms that pooled the patents they held on filmmaking equipment in an attempt to consolidate control of the fledgling movie industry. The MPPC, formed in 1908, intended to freeze out nonmember producers at the production stage by denying them use of MPPC-patented equipment, and at the distribution and exhibition stages as well by refusing to sell or lease its members' films to any distributor that acquired a film produced by a non-MPPC company.

Thomas Edison, the MPPC founder who had patented much of the equipment then in use, had been tenacious in tracking down and prosecuting producers who were operating without an Edison license or using stolen or copied equipment. The creation of the MPPC forced independent and foreign producers to find ways to make movies and to distribute them without the MPPC's knowing of their projects until their films were already in the hands of the few independent movie exhibitors willing to show them.

To evade detection by the MPPC, these independent producers began to look at production locales other than metropolitan New York, where the young industry had been producing most of its films. Cuba and Florida offered the advantage of distance from, and better weather than, New York and New Jersey. Southern California beckoned as well, for its climate and its stunning and varied scenery. Ultimately, a little suburb of Los Angeles, an area called Hollywood, became the center of the entire movie industry.

The MPPC was not broken until 1915, when a successful lawsuit by William Fox (founder of what would become Twentieth Century Fox) proved the organization had violated restraint-of-trade laws by trying to keep nonmember companies from producing films and exhibiting them.

Evolution of the Studio System

The split between MPPC film companies and maverick organizations that operated outside its jurisdiction led to fundamental differences in how the two camps of filmmaking organizations operated. The MPPC member studios did not identify the actors who appeared in their films. By keeping their performers relatively anonymous, they were able to retard development of individual actors' reputations and therefore keep their salaries low. Yet even these studio heads knew that moviegoers were developing interests in the actors they saw on screen regularly.

To better compete against the MPPC, independent producers such as Adolph Zukor began developing individual performers as celebrities and placing them in films designed to boost their popularity, all while under exclusive contract. In this system, the studio groomed actors for "stardom" and then benefitted from the stars' exposure in picture after picture. Moviegoers soon became fans, devoted to favorite actors, determined to see their every film.

The studio heads put directors, writers, cinematographers, and other artists under exclusive contracts. In this way, they were able to control enough talent for movie production to be nearly constant. This organizational approach came to be known as the *studio system*.

Feature Films

The years between 1915 and 1926 saw the development of movie technique and form, the growth of local censorship, and many productions that demonstrated the new medium's powerful impact on culture and society. Film techniques had developed rapidly but were in a formative stage in 1915. Movies were, of course, black and white, somewhat grainy, and silent. Dialogue was expressed with subtitles on the screen; the only sound was occasional musical accompaniment, usually performed by a piano player in the theater, or later in the 1920s by sound recordings played on a phonograph. Until 1915, movies were usually about 20 minutes long; only about 20 percent were feature length, 2 hours or more.

The lengthier feature began to take shape in the work of David Wark Griffith, whose sophisticated yet sensitive shooting of scenes and editing marked the final break with stage conventions that had characterized early moviemaking. Griffith used mobile cameras, variations in shots (particularly close-up and tracking shots), and inventive camera angles to make his work more dynamic and less stilted, greatly improving film's ability not only to tell a story but to communicate emotion.

These techniques were used effectively in *The Birth of a Nation*, released in 1915, Griffith's interpretation of the Civil War, an unheard of 3 hours in length. That movie was the blockbuster of its time, considered the first modern film in which all technical and stylistic advances of cinema's early years were combined, and because of its innovations it is still often listed among the great movies of all time.

Controversy and Censorship

Also in 1915, controversy and censorship came to the fledgling industry. Searching for popular content, the new movie makers often turned to sex and realistic portrayals of adult situations. But films such as *Damaged Goods*, which dealt with venereal disease, and *Traffic in Souls*, about prostitution, provoked public protests and led to confrontation in the courts.

In a 1915 decision, the U.S. Supreme Court effectively denied motion pictures the First Amendment protection accorded to the press, literature, and the theater. Motion pictures, said the court in ruling against the Mutual Film Corporation, were amusements, "a business, pure and simple," not artistic works entitled to the protection of free speech.

This made movies liable to censorship. Citizen censorship boards were established by some cities and states (a few had already come into existence as early as 1907) to assure that film content met local standards of morality. These boards continued to exercise control over local exhibition for decades. In 1952, the Supreme Court, in an about-face, ruled that motion pictures were entitled to the freedom guaranteed by the First Amendment, but it took until 1981 before the last state censorship board (in Maryland) was abolished.

Movie Genres

More important in the long run, however, the 1915 to 1926 period saw the emergence of film forms that captured great audiences. Comedy quickly became a popular movie genre, taken to new heights by the slapstick antics of the bumbling Keystone Cops and by the unique expressive talents of actors and directors such as Charlie Chaplin. Lighthearted romances became popular fare. The Western, using all the myths of the wild West's cowboys and Indians and cattle rustlers and train robbers to dramatize the struggle of goodness over evil, became an essential part of American culture.

In spite of the growing popularity and impact of movies in the mid-1920s, continued technical improvements had to be made to enable the medium to keep up with the competition from other media, especially the new medium of radio. Live broadcasts heard on a radio set in the living room were becoming the new rage.

TALKIES ARRIVE: 1926–1930

Experimentation with matching sound to film had been under way since the late 1890s, with the Lumière brothers and the Edison laboratories, among others, trying different methods. The efforts didn't start paying off until the mid-1920s, with the advent of sound systems with commercial potential. As with every new technology, several different types of systems became available.

Some executives who ran the Hollywood film studios hesitated. They recognized that moving from silent to sound films would require enormous change and investment. When they made their move, they wanted to be sure they were making the right choice. The cost of installing sound equipment in a theater then could be as much as $20,000, or more than $100,000 in today's dollars. Since studios owned many of the theaters in which their movies were exhibited, they had to absorb the cost of the conversion to sound at the exhibition end as well as at the production stage. Studio heads also had to persuade operators of theaters they didn't own to modify their facilities for sound.

Warner Brothers took the plunge. Using equipment manufactured by the Western Electric Co., in 1926 the Warner studio selected *Vitaphone*, a sound-on-disc process, for movie theaters they owned. Their first program was a film of the opera Don Juan, with vocalists and musicians of the New York Philharmonic synchronized with the action in the film.

The Fox Film Corporation invested in a rival sound system called *Movietone*, in which recorded sound was imprinted onto a strip of the film. Using this technology, William Fox began adding voice narration to *newsreels,* which had been widely popular as shorts between feature films almost since the beginning of the industry. Fox newsreels had a coup in May 1927, when they featured a segment, with narration, of Charles Lindbergh taking off in The Spirit of St. Louis in his bid to become the first person to fly solo across the Atlantic Ocean. That newsreel segment was greeted with amazement. The Movietone method eventually became the standard for the industry.

The first feature film in which a character actually spoke was *The Jazz Singer*, released in October 1927. The movie had four talking segments in which the star Al Jolson also sang, but other than that there was no other dialogue. The opening-night audience loved it. The following year, the first all-talking picture, *Lights of New York*, was produced.

Talkies were good for studios, but they ended the careers of many veterans of silent films. Audiences reacted with dismay if the actual voice of an actor didn't match the sound they had imagined during years of watching the soundless actor. One of the greatest movie stars of the era, handsome Rudolph Valentino, saw his career shattered when audiences heard, for the first time, his squeaky voice. The transition from silent films to talkies was delightfully spoofed many years later by the movie, *Singin' in the Rain* (1952). A romantic comedy, it shows how studios had struggled with the new sound technology of the 1920s and tried to make intelligent-sounding speakers out of their sometimes less-than-brilliant silent stars who had weak voices and never had had to memorize a script.

Rise of Self-Censorship

The threat of censorship by state and local film boards was never far away. In the mid-1920s, Hollywood executives, anxious to appear sensitive to concerns about the rectitude of their stars and the sexual situations in their movies, and hoping to avoid being forced to answer to hundreds of regional boards on every film they made, appointed their own ombudsman, Will Hays, a former member of President Warren Harding's administration.

Hays developed the *morality clause* to be used in employee contracts, which required studio talent to conduct their personal as well as their professional lives in an ethical manner. He also composed a list of "do's and don'ts" for film content, which in 1930 was formalized as the *Production Code*. The code required Hollywood films to uphold the sanctity of marriage, demonstrate that crime doesn't pay, and avoid portraying explicit sexual situations, among other points. It also imposed some ridiculous prohibitions, such as portraying on the screen the udders of cows, the profiles of women, and the insides of bathrooms.

Whether the Hays Office was instituted to be window dressing for the studios or to address genuine concerns of the public is in dispute, according to film industry author Barry Norman (1988), who observed that "the stronger producers in particular could circumvent any or all of these rules if 85 minutes of screentime sin were followed by five minutes of redemption" (p. 111). The Hays Office previewed films and ordered the excision of offensive content before giving the film its seal of approval. Later, the Production Code was administered by the Motion Picture Association of America (MPAA) and eventually led in 1968 to the development of the ratings system in use today.

GOLDEN AGE: 1930–1946

The Jazz Singer and other talking movies had an enormous impact on movie attendance; by 1929, more than 110 million Americans were attending movies each week. The advent of sound allowed moviegoing to grow as a national pastime and reduced the competitive threat posed by radio.

During the 1930s, seven major studios dominated movie production: Metro-Goldwyn-Mayer (MGM), Paramount, Warner Brothers, RKO, Universal, Columbia, and Twentieth Century Fox. The studios were all located in the Los Angeles and Hollywood area. Each had its own stable of stars and a distinct style. The studios also owned companies that distributed films and movie theaters that exhibited them, ensuring that their productions always had excellent placement.

Movies in the Great Depression

As the nation struggled through the crippling economic depression of the early 1930s, movie studios produced lighthearted, escapist fare, comedies, song-and-dance productions, and musicals light on plot but heavy on costumes and singing. But Hollywood also produced films that matched the seriousness of the times. *The Public Enemy, I Was A Fugitive From A Chain Gang,* and *Scarface* pull no punches about brutality, violence, and gangsters. *Faithless* and *Blonde Venus* portray prostitution as a means of survival, the Production Code notwithstanding. The light content gave movie audiences a few hours of escape from their troubles; the dark side reflected bleak times and their impact on individuals.

Movies in Color

Until the mid-1930s, all movies were still produced with black and white pictures. Walt Disney's *Snow White and the Seven Dwarfs*, released in 1937, was the first feature-length animated film in color, using a trademarked process called *Technicolor*. *The Wizard of Oz* and *Gone With the Wind*, both released in 1939, were among the first full-color feature films with real characters. These movies contain memorable scenes in rich and vivid colors—Snow White's magical forest setting, Oz's field of poppies where Dorothy falls asleep, the burning of Atlanta in the Civil War— showing the use of color in film at its finest. Scenes in full color of the ravaged South in *Gone With the Wind* brought home the horrors of war to a moviegoing public. Perhaps the movie attracted such large and responsive audiences because so many feared the war that loomed ahead, which had already started in Europe.

World War II

Hollywood closed ranks in support of the war after the 1941 bombing of Pearl Harbor, adapting to the inevitable business changes required by wartime emergency. A number of top male stars left for active duty in the military. Those who stayed behind helped the studios produce a spate of military adventure films, such as *Devil Dogs of the Air, Here Comes the Navy,* and *Rear Gunner.* These no doubt helped the government stir patriotism and recruit young people to serve in the war.

The immorality of Nazism was laid bare in such movies as *Confessions of a Nazi Spy.* Charlie Chaplin produced *The Great Dictator*, a parody of the Axis leaders who were given the names of Adenoid Hynkel and Benzini Napolini. *Escape* shows a man's daring rescue of his mother from a Nazi concentration camp. *The Mortal Storm* depicts how Nazism split a German family. Many movies provided sarcastic treatment of Japanese war lords, Italian fascists, and German storm troopers.

Among the most memorable is *Mrs. Miniver*, a moving film about the bravery of working-class Britons determined to withstand assault by the Nazis. The rousing sermon of the vicar in the film so touched Franklin Roosevelt that he had copies printed and dropped by air in European countries where citizens might not be sure of the side they were on. Winston Churchill called it propaganda worth 100 battleships. The film's "importance as a morale-booster and winner of support for Britain is almost impossible to overstate," writes Norman (1988, p. 111).

Hollywood's involvement went much deeper than making movies with war plots. Its stars traversed the country, selling war bonds to raise funds to finance the war and visiting military trainees and servicemen on leave to boost morale. Bob Hope's legendary shows sponsored by the United Service Organization (USO) used a bevy of actors, singers, dancers, and comedians. They went into actual combat areas to perform for those on active duty. (Hope's wartime shows continued in all of America's subsequent military involvements, including Korea, Vietnam, and even the Persian Gulf war in 1991.)

The war years saw an extraordinary amount of collaboration between Hollywood and the government. Some of Hollywood's leaders put their creative genius to work directly for the U.S. government to produce motion pictures that promoted the government's war efforts as well as training films for troops. Between 1942 and 1945, director Frank Capra made the immensely influential seven-part documentary series, *Why We Fight*. Director John Ford, working for the government's Office of Strategic Services (OSS), made *The Battle of Midway* to extol the government's superiority at sea in the war with Japan.

Some films were made to stress the importance of the democratic system in contrast with the fascist political doctrines of the enemy. Still others were made for exhibition in European communities that had pushed back the Axis forces. These films included news reviews to bring the people up to date on world events—news they had not received while their towns and cities had been occupied by the Nazis. Americans also produced positive feature films about these countries to lift their sagging spirits and to help cement friendship with their American liberators.

DECLINE: 1946–1969

Hollywood's work had changed during the war, and it was to change even more when the war was over. For the studios, the differences were nearly overwhelming. Movie attendance went into a free fall at war's end. In 1946, more than 90 million Americans attended the movies each week. That number began a precipitous slide that year and declined each year thereafter before bottoming out at 17.5 million weekly admissions in 1969. Weekly attendance hovered in the 20-million range for most of the last 30 years of the century.

New Competition

Perhaps the main reason for the decline was new competition for people's time. With war's end, American manufacturers retooled their factories to produce consumer products not widely available during the war, including home appliances and automobiles. Americans began using their leisure time differently, spending it in their new homes in new suburbs sprouting all over the country. Their new cars offered them access to travel opportunities and social activities that the war had interrupted. Going to the movies every week became just one of a number of leisure-time choices, no longer the main one.

The greatest competition, probably, came from television. By 1948, as we will describe more fully in chapter 12, television sets were being sold to the public. When radio had threatened to divert audiences from movies, motion picture studios introduced sound and later color. But television already combined visuals and sound and soon would add color, and its pictures could be delivered directly to one's living room. TV had the advantage of convenience and, of course, novelty. It represented a much more direct and compelling competitor for motion pictures than radio had been.

By the mid-1950s, movie studios became convinced they had to work with rather than against the new medium. They began producing material especially for television as well as selling networks the broadcast rights to their film libraries.

Antimonopoly Measures

Other events were shaking the motion picture industry as well. In 1948, the Supreme Court ordered the studios to end their system of *vertical integration*, under which each studio produced, distributed, and exhibited its own films, giving them a virtual monopoly. The court ordered studios to divest themselves of one of the three operations. Most chose to sell their theater chains, loosening the monopolistic grip the studios had long held on the U.S. film exhibition business.

Foreign Films

Overseas film companies that had been inactive during the war were vigorously renewed afterward. Americans welcomed motion pictures from Britain, France, Italy, Sweden, India, and Japan, intrigued by the different styles, story lines, and philosophies of foreign filmmakers. These imports represented yet another source of competition for the Hollywood studios at a time when overall movie attendance was declining.

Communist Scare

The threat of communism in the 1950s posed a curious threat to Hollywood. As Stalin consolidated and increased his power in postwar Europe, anticommunist sentiment grew in America. Many movie actors and crafts artists were union members, and political conservatives were suspicious that organized labor was sympathetic to communism. These conservatives feared that Hollywood would treat communism and socialism sympathetically while being critical of democracy and capitalism in its films. Fearful of the propaganda power of motion pictures, they sought to purge the industry of "communist sympathizers" and urged the House Un-American Activities Committee to investigate communist activities in Hollywood.

In 1947, the committee held brief hearings and then resumed its investigation of Hollywood in 1951, meeting periodically thereafter until 1954. During that time, the committee subpoenaed movie writers, actors, directors, engineers, cinematographers, and others thought to be sympathetic to leftist causes. Those who refused to testify or cooperate were *blacklisted*, or boycotted, by the industry, and some were sent to jail for contempt of Congress. Those who did testify and were found to have communist sympathies or associations were barred by the industry from working on Hollywood productions.

It was the studio owners, not the government, that barred and blacklisted these movie people, probably because the owners were sensitive to government threats, or perhaps because they themselves were anticommunist. At any rate, the result of this witch hunt was that hundreds of talented, experienced professionals were unable to work in their field, went abroad to work, or worked under pseudonyms until the effects of the blacklist began to fade in the early 1970s. Many of them didn't live long enough to reestablish their reputations. The movie industry staggered with the loss of this talent and did not fully recover for years.

Transformation of the Studio System

Buffeted by economic reverses caused by shrinking audiences and loss of talent in the mid-1950s, the studios began restructuring. In 1956, Warner Brothers sold control to Boston bankers. The same year, United Artists went public and diversified into television, records, and music publishing.

A new company, American-International, was formed and began producing horror movies, science fiction, and musicals capitalizing on the popularity of rock 'n' roll, all aimed at teenagers. The agents' powerhouse, Management Corporation of America (MCA) bought Universal and, later, Decca Records. MCA's ascent demonstrated how power was passing from the studio bosses to the artists and their representatives.

Studios began acting less as producers and more as investors in independent productions and distributors of films. Studio heads rented out their space to independent production companies, which used them to make independent films and shows for television. The old studio system became less important as studios declined to renew expensive contracts for actors, directors, and other employees and sought new talent to work for lower wages. In 1961, distributors developed a new after-market for feature films: the in-flight movie, sold to airlines. Still, the studios' financial situation remained precarious throughout the 1960s.

B Movies and Unexpected Classics

The dire straits of the movie industry were reflected in the uneven quality of the movies made during the 1960s. *B movies*, generally featuring acting newcomers and undistinguished scripts, kept the supply of films constant, as did thrillers produced for the teenage set.

Even so, a few gems were produced in the 1960s that are regarded as classics even today. Dramatic movies of the period were characterized by increased realism and probing character studies. *The Magnificent Seven* (1960), a brooding Western about the brutal lives of hired gunmen, revitalized the Western genre. The movie spawned the *spaghetti westerns*—so named for their Italian directors, Sergio Leone and Duccio Tessari—that starred a young TV actor named Clint Eastwood. *The Hustler* (1962), starring Paul Newman, Jackie Gleason, and George C. Scott, is a masterful, perceptive film about characters whose lives revolve around a pool hall. *The Pawnbroker* (1964) explores the emotional wreckage, left by the Holocaust, in one man's life.

Big, lush film productions had become rare, but those that were made during this time are true classics. David Lean's *Lawrence of Arabia* (1962) was a stunning epic that has lost none of its luster over the years. *My Fair Lady* (1964) and *The Sound of Music* (1965) showed that the musical could still be magical.

As the decade ended, rebellion by young people against the Vietnam War and the political establishment became the subject of movies reflecting that disenchantment, including such films as *The Graduate* (1967), *Easy Rider* (1969) and *Alice's Restaurant* (1970).

REFOCUSING: 1970–PRESENT

In the 1970s and 1980s, movie producers began casting their lot with the youth market, which had grown up with television and was inclined toward visual excitement. By the mid-1980s, 75 percent of box-office revenues represented ticket purchases by moviegoers under 30. The movie industry launched into productions that would appeal to this group, especially to young males.

Adventure and action prevailed. Story line and narrative became far less important. Location shooting, special effects, heavy advance promotion, and escalating compensation for big-name stars drove up costs and meant less profit per picture. Fewer movies were made, and more movies followed similar content formulas.

The dominant blockbuster films often involved an ingenious hero, who triumphed over evil forces and insurmountable odds. *Rocky* (1977) and all its sequels are variations on this theme, as is the *Rambo* series. So are *Raiders of the Lost Ark* (1981) and *Indiana Jones and the Temple of Doom (1984); Superman* (1978) and *Superman II* (1980); and later, *The Terminator* (1984) and *Terminator II: Judgment Day* (1991).

This theme was brought to perhaps its most advanced level in the *Star Wars* trilogy, a sci-fi morality play that pits good against evil. *Star Wars* (1977) demolished all previous box-office records, and its sequels, *The Empire Strikes Back* (1980) and *Return of the Jedi* (1983), helped establish sequels as a model for movie moneymaking in the 1970s and 1980s.

The Walt Disney Company, long associated with entertainment for children and families, continued that focus with movies such as *The Little Mermaid* (1989), *Beauty and the Beast* (1991), and *The Lion King* (1994). Disney also produced some movies with mature themes, but the company made more profit from its animated films, whose characters could be spun off as toys, dolls, jewelry, clothing, and even home textiles for the family market.

The motion-picture industry's emphasis on the youth market hasn't eliminated dramatic films with more adult themes, but there have been fewer distinguished efforts in this category. *Diner* (1982), *Mask* (1985), *Driving Miss Daisy* (1989), *Do the Right Thing* (1989), *The Piano* (1993), *Schindler's List* (1993), and *Forrest Gump* (1994) represent high-water marks in motion-picture excellence.

Movies that appeal to a broad audience—male, female, young, old, white and minority—are produced less often than films targeting a specific sector of the moviegoing audience. One notable exception is *Titanic* (1997), the most expensive motion picture made to that date. *Titanic* was a commercial and critical success. The movie cost $200 million to make; just 4 months after its release, it became the first film to earn $1 billion dollars in global receipts, proving that a well-made movie with a good story, appealing characters, and professional execution can draw broad audiences and achieve an excellent financial return. The list of the all-time biggest money makers (Table 10.1) provides an interesting insight into movie appeals and audience interests.

CURRENT ISSUES

Cross-Marketing

At the beginning of the twenty-first century, major film studios generally are owned by large diversified entertainment conglomerates. Unlike the early days of the Hollywood studios that devoted themselves exclusively to film production, distribution, and exhibition, today's movie studios are part of larger entities with other media holdings. These larger entities can promote a movie in a number of ways.

Companies such as Viacom, consisting of a movie studio, a book publishing unit, a television network, broadcasting stations, cable systems, and production companies, can, if they choose, release a movie, publish a book based on the movie, arrange for the movie's creators and stars to be interviewed on its broadcasting stations, and produce a program on how the movie was made for distribution on cable TV. These corporate combinations can provide powerful cross-media exposure for a single media product.

Exhibition

Motion picture studios have reentered the exhibition business after most had withdrawn from it following the 1948 Supreme Court ruling against monopolistic practices by the film industry. Antitrust regulations were relaxed during President Ronald Reagan's administration, so companies have begun once again to invest in motion picture theater chains to be able to control the exposure their films receive and to capture more of the profits from attendance.

The studios or their parent companies generally are investment partners in exhibition chains, not sole owners. For example, Loews Cineplex Entertainment is 51 percent owned by Sony, the parent company of Columbia Pictures. Universal Studios, a division of Seagram Inc., has a 26-percent stake in Loews Cineplex. The exhibition industry has been consolidating since the early 1980s, with various exhibitors merging with or being acquired by others. At the beginning of the new millennium, a handful of chains dominated the movie exhibition business; it was estimated that the top 3 percent of the nation's theater owners controlled about 61 percent of the nation's 34,000 screens.

These chains have invested heavily to build *multiplexes*, or multiscreen theater complexes with as many as 1 or 2 dozen separate theaters and screens. The multiplex concept has created huge demand for films, but that demand favors blockbuster films rather than artistic movies that may attract smaller audiences. Venues for the latter are disappearing, as the independent theaters and art theaters are being crushed by the high-volume business moving through multiplexes. Small theaters simply cannot strike cost-effective deals with distributors as high-volume multiplexes can.

TABLE 10.1

Top 30 All-Time Highest Grossing Movies, Based on Domestic Gross Theater Ticket Receipts, as of 1998, in Millions of Dollars[1]

	Movie	Year Released	Total Gross
1.	*Titanic*	1997	$601
2.	*Star Wars*	1977	461
3.	*E.T.*	1982	400
4.	*Jurassic Park*	1993	357
5.	*Forrest Gump*	1994	330
6.	*The Lion King*	1994	313
7.	*Return of the Jedi*	1983	307
8.	*Independence Day*	1996	306
9.	*The Empire Strikes Back*	1980	290
10.	*Home Alone*	1990	285
11.	*Jaws*	1975	260
12.	*Batman*	1989	251
13.	*Men in Black*	1997	250
14.	*Raiders of the Lost Ark*	1981	242
15.	*Twister*	1996	242
16.	*Beverly Hills Cop*	1984	235
17.	*The Lost World: Jurassic Park*	1997	229
18.	*Ghostbusters*	1984	221
19.	*Mrs. Doubtfire*	1993	219
20.	*Ghost*	1990	218
21.	*Aladdin*	1992	217
22.	*Back to the Future*	1985	211
23.	*Saving Private Ryan*[2]	1998	207
24.	*Terminator 2: Judgment Day*	1991	204
25.	*Armageddon*	1998	202
26.	*Gone With the Wind*	1939	200
27.	*Indiana Jones & the Last Crusade*	1989	197
28.	*Toy Story*	1995	192
29.	*Snow White and the Seven Dwarfs*	1937	189
30.	*Dances With Wolves*	1990	184

Copyright © 1995–1999 Millennium Internet Corporation/Movieweb.™ Reprinted with permission. Sources include Exhibitor Relations Company. Updated March 9, 1999.

[1]Not based on theater attendance. Thus the list is skewed to recent movies because of inflation and higher admission costs. *Gone With the Wind* is probably still the all-time most attended movie.

[2]Still in theater circulation, as of this publication.

Financial Health

The 1990s saw the movie industry greatly improve its profitability. U.S. box office gross reached $6.2 billion in 1997, the motion-picture industry's best year to that point. Table 10.2 lists the top 13 studios' gross receipts for 1997. Attendance rates have risen gradually since 1980, when there were slightly fewer than 20 million admissions per week. By 1997, there were almost 27 million. The most valuable audience assets the motion-picture industry has are *frequent moviegoers*, who attend a movie theater about once a month. They constitute 81 percent of total admissions. By ethnic grouping, whites are 66 percent of admissions; Hispanics, 15 percent (the fastest-growing admissions group); blacks, 13 percent; and all other audience segments, 6 percent.

Ticket prices have risen at a more rapid rate than the increase in admissions, bringing increased box-office revenue for studios and theaters to share. In 1980, the average admission price was $2.69. In 1997, it was $4.57.

Typically, the studio keeps 70 percent to 80 percent of a film's ticket income in the first 2 weeks it is showing, declining to 60 percent later and then 50 percent after some time. After 4 or 5 weeks, exhibitors begin keeping the larger part of each dollar. If films do well in the first 2 weeks, but die afterward, theaters won't turn a profit unless they were packed during the first 2 weeks of the run. Movies that don't become blockbusters are quickly removed from exhibition.

TABLE 10.2

Top Motion Picture Studios in 1997

Distributor (Releases)	Grosses (Millions)	Market Share
Sony (38)	$1,271.1	20.4%
Buena Vista (34)	890.7	14.3
Paramount (27)	734.9	11.8
Warner Bros. (27)	680.3	10.9
Fox (20)	651.3	10.4
Universal (13)	613.3	9.9
Miramax (33)	421.0	6.7
New Line (31)	389.6	6.2
MGM (13)	158.5	2.5
DreamWorks (3)	89.4	1.4
Gramercy (13)	76.0	1.2
Fox Searchlight (9)	49.4	0.8
Polygram (1)	48.3	0.8
Other (137)*	166.6	2.7
TOTAL: (399)	6,240.4	100.0

Source: How the Studios Stack Up in '97, *Daily Variety*, January 5–11, 1998, p. 96. Used with permission.

*No film in "Other" attained a market share greater than 0.5 percent.

But box-office gross isn't the only source of revenue for a movie. There is also income from ancillary markets, venues that show movies after they have had a first run. These include in-flight and in-hotel movies, home video sales and rentals, television, cable, and pay per view. Moviemakers worried about the impact of the videocassette when it debuted, fearing it would keep people out of theaters, but the videocassette has simply enlarged the movie-viewing experience and has been a lucrative supplement to box-office income.

American moviemakers are earning a larger share of their income from exhibition abroad. American movies have done well as exports, although some foreign countries, particularly members of the European Union, have taken steps to limit the number of American films shown in their countries. Nations obviously need to protect the livelihood of their own filmmakers from American competition, but they also fear the influence of an avalanche of American films that might depict different cultural values.

Ratings

In 1968, the Motion Picture Association of America adopted a rating system to guide parents as to the appropriateness of movie content for their families. The ratings, established by a board of parents, are **G**, suitable for all audiences; **PG**, parental guidance suggested; **PG-13**, parental guidance plus a suggested minimum age; **R**, restricted—no one under 17 admitted without a parent; and **NC-17**, no one under 17 admitted. See Table 10.3 for the number and percentage of films in different rating categories.

The ratings are somewhat vague; they do not indicate what elements of the film would be suitable for one age group but not another. The vast majority of films produced receive the R rating, which signals that the film can include explicit sex, graphic language, and extreme violence. A common belief is that the R-rated films are the big moneymakers for Hollywood, but that hasn't been borne out by box office receipts. In an analysis of the top 10 box-office hits of the 1980s, only one—*Beverly Hills Cop*—was rated R, even though R films accounted for more than 60 percent of the titles released during the decade.

TABLE 10.3

Ratings of the Classification and Rating Administration
(a Division of the Motion Picture Association)

Rating	1997 Films	1997 Percentage of Rated Films
G	23	3.4
PG	97	14.4
PG-13	117	17.4
R	432	64.2
NC-17/X	4	0.6
TOTAL	673	100.0

Source: Motion Picture Association, 1997 U.S. Economic Review, Theatrical Data. Used with permission.

At the same time, PG films represented fewer than 25 percent of all releases, but they occupied 6 of the top 10 spots on the list of the leading film moneymakers. Hollywood's preference for producing R-rated movie fare persists, as Table 10.2 shows for 1997 films.

The value of the ratings is debatable. Enforcement of age-based ratings is up to the judgment of movie exhibitor or video-store employees. Some are strict; many more are lenient about admitting young people to films or renting them films rated above their age level. Such films are also available on cable, so if an older person in the home is watching an R-rated movie, chances are a child is, too.

Violence

The motion-picture industry continues to receive criticism for the amount of gratuitous violence present in many, if not most, movies. No one can argue with the fact that violent action in movies escalated in the last decades of the twentieth century. Film scholar Peter Brunette observed in *The Washington Post* in 1995 that acts of violence in one movie raise the bar for acts of violence in the next. "Movies are based on giving people thrills that they don't get in real life," he writes. "So there's a built-in worsening process—if the violence is based on reality, it's not good enough. It has to be edgier and edgier."[1]

Periodically, alarm is raised over *copycat crimes* that seem to imitate violence in motion pictures, as we showed in chapter 7. Those who defend violence in movies say that, obviously, millions of people go to movies that depict horrifying acts of violence and don't act them out in their own lives. They say there is no proof that a movie "makes" a person take a specific kind of violent action, or any kind of action at all. They argue that so many factors contribute to the commission of a violent act that it isn't possible to blame movies or television alone for that type of behavior.

Others suggest that violence in the movies merely reflects violence in society, as writer Richard Leiby noted in 1995 in *The Washington Post*. "More mayhem in the streets, more mayhem on the screen: a mirror reflecting a mirror," he wrote. "The debate over which comes first—real violence or screen violence—has been going on since the 1903 release of *The Great Train Robbery*, which ends with a character inexplicably firing his pistol directly at the audience. By now, all sides are entitled to say they're right."[2]

However, the public seems to be dismayed, not inspired, by escalating movie violence. In a 1995 *Los Angeles Times* poll, the public indicated its disapproval of the amount of sex and violence in movies, television, and popular music. The poll was conducted after then-Senate Majority Leader Robert Dole rebuked Hollywood for the entertainment content it was producing. Nearly three quarters, 71 percent of those polled, said they agreed with Dole that the industry produces too much sex and violence. Nearly as many, 61 percent, said they thought the content was getting worse, not better.

Though young people had more favorable views of entertainment than older respondents, a substantial majority of every demographic group surveyed expressed concern with entertainment content. Movies drew the least favorable responses, with only 37 percent of survey participants saying they had a favorable impression of the movies made by America's film industry (contrasted with 46 percent for television and 44 percent for popular music). Nevertheless, those polled preferred self-restraint by the entertainment industry to restrictions imposed by government to address the sex and violence content of entertainment.

Stereotyping

The motion-picture industry has also received criticism for its dearth of roles for women and minority actors, and for stereotyping female and minority characters in many of the roles it does offer. In particular, roles for older female characters are rare. Female characters are often highly sexualized. Non-white characters of either sex usually are not the central or lead characters of a film.

By the beginning of the twenty-first century, this was beginning to change, as more women and minority directors were moving into the profession and obtaining the backing to make movies with broader interpretations of women, girls, and minority characters.

Copyright

Currently, a key movie-industry issue is that of copyright protection for motion pictures. American-made films are enormously popular at home and abroad; demand for them has given rise to bootleg operations that copy and distribute movies for their own profit. Such illegal copying of films deprives the artists and investors who made the film from receiving their fair share of remuneration for their effort. The Motion Picture Association of America has been vigilant in pressing for better enforcement of copyright laws that protect the originators of feature films. In 1998, the U.S. Congress assisted in this effort by ratifying two international treaties that lift the level of copyright protection around the world for all types of intellectual property, including motion pictures.

LOOKING AHEAD

The motion-picture industry enters the new century in relatively good health. Demand for feature films is likely to continue at a steady level, driven in part by the many viewing options and increasing flexibility in viewing time and location that movie lovers have.

The Motion Picture Association of America predicts that by the year 2010, the increase in the U.S. population will lift movie admissions by 12 percent—not blockbuster growth by any means, but enough of an increase to assure motion pictures' place as a substantial part of the mass media mix and an important cultural influence. The over-40 age group is expected to lead the growth in admissions.

The industry still faces skyrocketing costs in the making of movies, including the cost of marketing and advertising feature films. This economic factor poses no small threat to the financial viability of motion picture studios. Risk is high and profits by no means assured, even for the largest studios.

An important issue for the future is the survival of independent and foreign producers, whose films generally depart from big-studio content formulas and usually attract smaller audiences. Will they have a fair chance in a movie climate that favors teens and young adults as the most frequent moviegoers? The answer is not certain.

Further Reading

Baughman, James L. (1997). *The Republic of Mass Culture: Journalism, Filmmaking and Broadcasting in America Since 1941* (2nd ed.). Baltimore: Johns Hopkins University Press.

Baxter, John. (1973). *Sixty Years of Hollywood.* Cranbury, NJ: A. S. Barnes.

Cameron, Kenneth. (1997). *America on Film.* New York: Continuum.

Dick, Bernard F. (1997). *City of Dreams: The Making and Remaking of Universal Pictures.* Lexington: University Press of Kentucky.

Ellis, Jack C. (1979). *A History of Film.* Englewood Cliffs, NJ: Prentice-Hall.

Gomery, Douglas. (1986). *The Hollywood Studio System.* New York: St. Martin's Press.

_____ (1991). *Movie History: A Survey.* Wadsworth.

_____ (1992). *Shared Pleasures: A History of Movie Presentation in the United States.* Madison: University of Wisconsin Press.

Hanson, Steve, and Hanson, Patricia King. (1990). *Lights, Camera, Action! A History of Movies in the Twentieth Century.* Los Angeles, CA: Los Angeles Times.

Hellman, Lillian. (1976). *Scoundrel Time.* Boston: Little, Brown.

Katz, Ephraim. (1994). *The Film Encyclopedia.* New York: HarperCollins.

Mast, Gerald. (1986). *A Short History of the Movies* (4th ed.). New York: Macmillan.

McMurtry, Larry. (1987). *Film Flam: Essays on Hollywood.* New York: Simon & Schuster.

Medved, Michael. (1992). *Hollywood vs. America: Popular Culture and the War on Traditional Values.* New York: HarperCollins.

Norman, Barry. (1988). *The Story of Hollywood.* New York: New American Library Books/Penguin.

Phillips, Julia. (1991). *You'll Never Eat Lunch in This Town Again.* New York: Signet/Penguin Group.

Shipman, David. (1982). *The Story of Cinema: A Complete Narrative History, From the Beginnings to the Present.* New York: St. Martin Press.

Sklar, Robert. (1975). *Movie Made America: A Cultural History of the Movies.* New York: Vintage.

Notes

[1] Quoted in Leiby, Richard. (1995, December 3). Movie madness: Does screen violence trigger copycat crimes? *The Washington Post*, p. G2.

[2] Leiby, op. cit.

11

RADIO AND SOUND RECORDINGS

Imagine what life would be like today without radio or sound recordings. The world would suddenly be a much quieter place. Because of radio and records, our lives are filled with sound, mostly the sound of music. Our homes have radios in many rooms, and most homes have complex, multi-speaker stereo systems that can give us radio transmissions or recordings from long-playing records, audio cassettes, or CDs at the flick of a remote control.

A growing number of homes have CD players in their sound systems, storing hundreds of CDs programmed to play precisely the tunes wanted in the order needed for hours on end. Our automobiles come equipped with stereo radio, audio cassettes, and CD decks that create an aural experience as good as the finest concert halls, cathedrals, or acoustically engineered auditoriums.

Even outside our homes and automobiles, we can carry radio receivers and cassette or CD players with us wherever we go, in a package small enough to fit in the palm of our hand. They have lightweight earphones or earplugs that can give us stereo sound of the highest quality. This portable equipment costs no more than a good hardbound book or a meal for two at a good restaurant. As we walk across campus or stroll through the park, we can hear our favorite musicians playing our favorite music on recordings, or we can get over-the-air broadcasts of music aimed at our tastes, with periodic reports about what is happening in our community, our nation, or the world.

Radio and sound recordings that developed in the twentieth century changed the entire aural environment in which we live. They have made sound into aural furniture or decoration, whether in our homes or cars, on elevators, in airports, or at the dentist's office. Before the twentieth century, sound was ethereal, never repeated. You heard it once and it was gone forever. Music was only known to those who were in the place where it was performed, and once performed it was gone. The sounds people heard were the singing of birds, the rustle of wind, soft human voices and only those within earshot, the quiet movement of bodies, the shuffle of feet, a door opening and closing, and the rare live presentation of a singer, a choir, or musical instruments.

Radio and sound recording changed all that. They are interdependent industries that account for a large portion of media use in the United States today. Radio is the principal way sound recordings get public exposure, and sound recordings are the core of nearly all radio broadcasting.

RADIO

Radio is used in a passive way, primarily as an adjunct to other activity such as driving, socializing, working around the house or the yard. Few sit and listen to radio with undivided concentration. However, at one time, it attracted full attention. In its golden era before television, radio was like the nation's fireplace, around which millions gathered to listen intently to concerts, plays, dramatic readings, and the news.

Origins: 1844–1920

All electronic media had their origins in nineteenth-century science and invention. In 1844, Samuel Morse transmitted the first electromagnetic message over wire, leading to wiring the nation for telegraph service. In 1876, Alexander Graham Bell used electromagnetic current to carry voice communications over wire, creating the telephone. In 1864, James Maxwell theorized that electromagnetic waves could be sent through the air without wires, and in 1887, Heinrich Hertz demonstrated that it could be done. In 1897, Guglielmo Marconi received a patent for wireless telegraphy, the beginning of radio.

Marconi established Marconi's Wireless Telegraph Company Ltd. to send business letters through the air. His communications were electronic signals, not voices or music, but merely the Morse code of dots and dashes. It took another twenty years before radio advanced beyond radiotelegraphy.

First Voice Broadcasts.   In 1906, Reginald Fessenden gave the first public demonstration of a radio voice transmission. His employer, General Electric (GE), was anxious to test radio's potential, especially ship-to-ship and ship-to-shore communication for one of its contractors, the U.S. Navy. GE built a transmitter for Fessenden at Brant Rock, Mass., from which he sent out his first broadcast on Christmas Eve. Fessenden read the Christmas story from the Bible and played "O Holy Night" on his violin.

Previous experimentation had sent wireless signals from one point to another. Fessenden's transmission was different because it was *broadcast* to any receiver within listening range tuned to his frequency. Ships at sea near the Massachusetts coast that had been equipped with receivers for wireless telegraph messages suddenly heard the crackling sound of the Christmas story and Christmas music coming through the night. The era of broadcasting was born.

Also in 1906, Lee DeForest, a competitor of Marconi's, pushed the technology to the next step when he developed a vacuum tube called the *audion* to amplify radio signals. After further experimentation, in 1910 he was able to broadcast live music from the Metropolitan Opera in New York City. Although only a few fellow technicians heard the operas, he had established a starting point for popular application of radio technology.

GE and American Telephone and Telegraph (AT&T) experimented with variations on radio technology, but they still regarded radio as the telegraph business without wires, for commercial, strategic, and military uses. The U.S. government began to regulate the use of radio with the Wireless Ship Act of 1910, requiring passenger ships to have radio transmission equipment. The Radio Act of 1912 made licensing of radio operators mandatory and established the government's authority as regulator of the airwaves.

On April 4, 1912, the world's largest ship, the SS *Titanic*, hit an iceberg in the North Atlantic on its maiden voyage with 2,200 passengers on board. The *Titanic* was equipped with the latest in radio transmitters and receivers, and its crew sent out distress signals as it sank into the ocean. Ships at sea that heard the message came to the rescue. They were able to save nearly a third of *Titanic's* passengers.

Visions of Popular Broadcasting.   In New York City on that April night in 1912, a young telegrapher, who had learned the Morse code to get his first job, was sitting at work in the Marconi Telegraph office. Suddenly he received the distress signal from the *Titanic* and frantically relayed the message to other ships. It was a moment he never forgot, and it convinced him that radio could be a powerful new force in human life. That young man was David Sarnoff, and he ultimately helped radio achieve the power he had envisioned. Four years later, in 1916, young Sarnoff wrote a memo to his boss at American Marconi:

> I have in mind a plan of development which would make radio a "household utility" in the same sense as the piano or the phonograph. The idea is to bring music into the house by wireless .... The receiver can be designed in the form of a simple "Radio Music Box" and arranged for several different wave lengths.

The company, responding to that vision, promoted Sarnoff and gave him more authority over its radio business. When Marconi sold its American subsidiary to General Electric in 1919, GE formed the Radio Corporation of America (RCA) and gave Sarnoff the green light to pursue his dream. Ultimately, he became one of broadcasting's most powerful and influential pioneers as RCA's president and chairman of the board.

Other companies were also experimenting with radio. Westinghouse in Pittsburgh employed an engineer, Frank Conrad, who worked on radio transmission signals. He wanted to learn how different kinds of transmissions would affect the signals. In 1916, he set up a small transmitter in his garage and began broadcasting recorded music and readings on a frequency licensed as 8XK. He urged local newspapers to list the schedule of his music. He asked listeners to send him postcards if they received his transmissions. By looking at the origins of the cards, he could tell where the signals were good and could figure out why.

Becoming a Commercial Mass Medium: 1920–1929

What surprised Conrad and Westinghouse was that so many people were responding. They had built crystal sets and other rudimentary radio receiving devices and were eagerly listening for programs. Conrad and Westinghouse realized they had stumbled onto something important. Soon Westinghouse made 8XK into a *radio station* licensed as KDKA, the first station to broadcast regular popular fare to a public audience. In 1920, it made the first formal scheduled broadcast when it aired the Harding–Cox presidential election results. But KDKA was certainly not the only radio operation. Between 1912 and 1920, several hundred licenses had been granted across the country, primarily to amateurs and hobbyists.

One problem with the developing medium was the cost and availability of radio receivers. Amateur crystal sets, which anyone could make at home, produced only crude sound. Better receivers, with the kinds of vacuum tubes DeForest had invented, were expensive. Yet industry, prodded by Sarnoff, pursued the market. AT&T manufactured transmitting equipment, while RCA and Westinghouse produced radio receivers.

In 1922, Sarnoff's RCA introduced the Radiola console, with a price reduced to $75, still expensive for many but affordable to enough people for RCA to sell $11 million worth of Radiolas in that first year. Within 3 years, they were selling $60 million worth of radio sets each year. The growth of radio broadcasting exploded after that, with stations opening in every major city; by 1927, there were more than 700. The crowds were buying receivers and listening to radio, which was on the way to becoming a new mass medium.

Arguments for a Commercial System.

Some of the stations then operating were owned by AT&T, GE, and Westinghouse, who up to the mid-1920s had been making money in radio mostly by building and selling radio equipment. Other stations were owned by businesses, such as newspapers and department stores, or by universities. These owners subsidized their radio station operations to enhance their reputations, not to make money. Corporations and business owners argued that for broadcasting to grow, to obtain quality content, and to reach larger audiences, they had to find a way to make radio profitable.

Great Britain formed the British Broadcasting Company (BBC) in 1923 and used public taxes on radio receivers to pay for broadcasting and its growth. American radio entrepreneurs rejected that model. They were not keen to have government involved with radio, fearing that restrictions and heavy taxation would limit growth.

Growth of Advertising.

The solution to financing was found in the sale of radio air time to advertisers. AT&T station WEAF in New York City is credited with launching *toll broadcasting*, the forerunner of the advertising model used in today's broadcasting. WEAF's first advertisement aired in August 1922, a 10-minute spot for $50 sold to the Queensboro Corporation, which promoted co-op apartment sales in Jackson Heights, N.Y.

Advertising sales were slow at first, but the concept spread. Other stations began selling air time, and radio broadcasting become a revenue-producing business. In addition to selling individual spots, stations also sold sponsorship opportunities, allowing ad messages to be worked into skits by a program's performers. Sponsors such as battery maker National Carbon Company, whose "Eveready Hour" aired on WEAF, took pride in the quality and originality of their sponsored programs.

Many sponsors elected to produce the shows themselves, hiring actors, musicians, and scriptwriters, and paying radio stations to air their performances, It was argued that this approach provided continuity in theme or story line and helped build listener loyalty, guaranteeing high audience levels.

Noncommercial and Educational Radio Loses.   Noncommercial broadcasters didn't share in commercial radio's early success. In the 1920s, the Harding, Coolidge, and Hoover administrations were all sympathetic to corporate business interests in America. When Herbert Hoover was Secretary of Commerce in 1924, he began working on the problems of radio spectrum crowding. He sided with the larger radio operators, such as AT&T, who contended that noncommercial stations represented special interests whereas the commercial stations represented the broader public interest.

Hoover decided that educational stations, religious stations, and other noncommercial stations operated by farmers, labor unions, boards of education, and citizen groups should be purely local in ownership and appeal, so he assigned them lower power, typically 100 watts, and they were usually relegated to a poor dial position. Commercial stations were often given high-powered channel assignments, some as high as 50,000 watts, receivable within a radius of hundreds of miles.

With the development of this pecking order for radio stations, Hoover managed to accommodate the rising demand for radio licenses within the limits of the broadcast spectrum. But he also doomed noncommercial radio, particularly educational radio, to the role of bottom fisher in the radio ocean, a position from which it struggled vainly to rise.

Government's Role.   Corporate executives prevailed in arguing that radio could not grow if government played too strong a hand. They strenuously argued against any legislation that would have given the U.S. government or its military a role in manufacturing radio equipment. They vigorously opposed government's developing broadcasting content or owning and operating broadcasting facilities.

Even though commercial radio content was attracting larger audiences and more eager advertisers, technical difficulties persisted. Finite space in the broadcast spectrum and rapid growth of broadcast stations caused a good deal of channel interference. Signals of broadcasters on adjacent frequencies would occasionally drown out one another. Reception was poor or unreliable in many locations. Commercial broadcasters felt the U.S. government should help rectify these problems and continue to license users of the airwaves to protect those who had received licenses.

In response, Congress passed the Radio Act of 1927, which created a Federal Radio Commission to better organize the licensing and allocation of frequencies on the radio spectrum. In 1934, as mentioned in chapter 2, the FRC became the Federal Communications Commission (FCC), and its regulatory powers were extended to telephone, telegraph, and later, television communications.

Radio Networks.   To increase their profitability, groups of stations began banding together in networks to share broadcasting transmissions. These groups were a combination of stations owned by a single entity, called *O and Os* for owned and operated, and other stations, called *affiliates*, that subscribed to the network's programming.

The National Broadcasting Company (NBC) was formed in 1926 as the first comprehensive network. On New Year's Day 1927, the first coast-to-coast network program, the Rose Bowl football game, was broadcast play-by-play from Pasadena, Calif. When AT&T decided to bow out of radio, it sold WEAF to NBC, and it became WNBC, the flagship station of the new network.

Another network, United Independent Broadcasters, Inc., was formed the same year. In 1928, it was acquired by William Paley, who changed its name to the Columbia Broadcasting System (CBS).

Golden Age: 1929–1950

By the late 1920s, radio receiver sets were available in a wide range of prices. Their availability even to families of modest means ensured radio's rise as an important medium. The Great Depression in the 1930s brought a big boost for radio. When people could no longer afford to keep up their payments on their new vacuum cleaners, washing machines, or even the Model A Fords, they still scraped together enough money to make their monthly payments on their radio receivers. After all, radio provided free entertainment and a connection to the world without even having to leave home. Most families had one radio set, usually a large console that was placed in the living room where everyone could sit around it and listen to programs together.

Programs.   Programs that would keep people listening now became radio's most urgent need, and the industry recruited talent of all sorts—actors, actresses, writers, announcers, singers, and musicians. The late 1920s and 1930s saw the debut of many long-running programs that, because of the networks, reached national audiences. These programs were often recorded on 78-rpm discs and sent across the country for simultaneous broadcast by network O & Os or affiliates in several time zones.

In 1929, "Amos 'n Andy" debuted, a sort of radio comic strip about the misadventures of two black male characters, voiced by two white actors. Most listeners thought the characters were black because radio provided only the sound of their voices. When the program shifted to television in the 1950s and the characters could be seen, the roles were given to black actors. In later years, the program was criticized for stereotyping blacks, but in the early days of radio, when good programs were scarce, it was accepted as good fun.

In 1931, "Clara, Lu, and Em," the first soap opera, debuted on WGN. That station was owned by the *Chicago Tribune,* and its call letters stood for "world's greatest newspaper." A year later the program moved to the NBC network. The daytime radio soap opera format (so named because of its sponsorship by soap manufacturers) became widely popular, with programs such as "Our Gal Sunday," "Road of Life," and "The Guiding Light," the last of which continued on television.

"The Rise of the Goldbergs," a serial about a Jewish family from the Bronx and forerunner of many ethnic family radio programs, first aired in 1929. It was still going 20 years later when its creator and star, Gertrude Berg, took it to television.

Children around the nation were captivated by a variety of after-school serials, including "Captain Midnight"; "Jack Armstrong, the All-American Boy"; and "The Aldrich Family," featuring the mishaps of the son, Henry Aldrich. "The Lone Ranger" was popular on radio and later enjoyed a successful run on television. Sunday afternoons were packed with mystery dramas, such as "Ellery Queen" and "The Shadow."

A variety of other programs came to radio. Quiz shows were introduced, including "Information Please," "Double or Nothing," and the "Sixty-Four Dollar Question" (later, on television, it became the $64,000 Question). The popular big bands of the period were heard regularly, as were individual artists ranging from popular crooners such as Bing Crosby to sopranos and tenors from the Metropolitan Opera. NBC even had its own symphony orchestra, formed in 1937.

Radio and Politics.   Networks began broadcasting the major political parties' national conventions in the 1920s, ultimately transforming American politics to the electronic age. Radio led to the election of Franklin D. Roosevelt, who had been disabled in midlife by a crippling attack of polio. He could not stand on his feet unaided and spent most of his time in a wheelchair. If he had been depicted in his wheelchair on television, he might well have been perceived as too weak for the presidency. But television didn't exist then, so he was "seen" on radio. His illness had caused him to work hard to build his upper body strength, and in the process he developed a resonant, commanding voice. He was perceived on radio as a very powerful man, because his voice projected such authority. Journalists of that era also protected his disability, never discussing it in print or using photographs of the President in his wheelchair.

Roosevelt was America's first (and only) radio President, and he knew how to use the new medium to his advantage. His inaugural address in 1933, famous for its line, "We have nothing to fear but fear itself," set the tone for a new administration that passed radical measures of the New Deal to solve problems of the Depression. Roosevelt used radio addresses to urge Congress and the voters to accept his new proposals. He broadcast national speeches 20 times during his first and most crucial 9 months in office. He then adopted a weekly radio format he called his "Fireside Chats" to talk to Americans about his plans for recovery through the 1930s, and as war loomed at the end of the decade, he used his radio chats to urge Americans to save, to work hard, to enlist, to accept a role in another world war, and to win.

Radio and Power.   By 1935, more than 22 million American homes had radio receivers. Automobile manufacturers began offering radios as options for purchasers of new cars.

And then on Halloween eve in 1938, on the "Mercury Theater of the Air," actor–director Orson Welles broadcast an adaptation of *War of the Worlds*, H. G. Wells' novel about an invasion of Earth by Martians. As we mentioned earlier in this book, Welles's adaptation of the novel into an extended news report, complete with "eyewitness accounts" of Martians attacking communities, panicked listeners across the country and jammed police switchboards. Some people even armed and barricaded themselves in their homes.

The FCC adopted regulations that limited radio's use of the news format in dramatic presentations. But more important, the Orson Welles drama proved in the 1930s that radio was indeed a powerful new medium that could sway the masses.

Radio News.   World War II provided the opportunity for radio to demonstrate its capacity as a unifying force and as a means of receiving instant information worldwide. From the moment Roosevelt's address to Congress went out over the airwaves to the American people after the Japanese assault on U.S. forces in Pearl Harbor, radio became the conduit to a nation's consciousness. December 7, 1941, Roosevelt thundered, would be "a date which will live in infamy."

News had not played a very important role in radio until that point. News bulletins were aired as necessary, but regular newscasts were not a standard part of the radio broadcast day until the late 1930s. The war that enveloped the world gave radio news a new importance, with CBS taking a particularly strong role in providing bulletins and commentary from the front. Much of it was produced by Edward R. Murrow, CBS's chief European correspondent at the beginning of the war in Europe. Murrow's stirring radio broadcasts during the war became legendary.

Radio correspondents broadcast from close to the battlefront and their live dispatches sent over thousands of miles made for compelling reports in living rooms across the United States. Their newscasts from Europe, or North Africa, or the South Pacific reduced the psychological distance between the men at the front and the people back home who cared about them and about the progress of the war.

Repositioning: 1950–1990

At the war's conclusion, television suddenly became a new threat to radio. Programs that had been the staple of radio broadcasting abruptly migrated to the new medium. With them went much of radio's talent, its advertisers, and ultimately its audiences. Radio would have to reinvent itself to succeed. During the 1950s and 1960s, several important events occurred that changed radio and enabled it to survive.

Transistors.   Radio sets had been heavy, wood-encased assemblies of bulky vacuum tubes and wires. In 1947, Bell Telephone Laboratories announced a new invention, *transistors*, small electronic semiconductor devices a fraction of the size of the old vacuum tubes they replaced. Not only were they much smaller, but they were also much more durable. Transistors allowed the miniaturization of receivers, making radio cheaper and more portable.

By 1954, transistor radios were on the market. Operated by batteries, they were lightweight and portable, some models so small they could fit in a pocket. Now radio could go anywhere its listener wanted to go, with major implications for the industry. Families began to acquire multiple sets, which allowed family members to listen to separate programs when and where they chose. People began listening to more radio away from home.

FM.   FM (*frequency modulation*) had been developed in the early 1930s, after AM (*amplitude modulation*) already dominated the radio business. FM offered higher-quality, no-static reception, but for years because of its late start, it remained a supplemental service to mainstream AM stations. Many AM station owners set up FM stations to repeat their signals. Educational and classical stations reaching small audiences usually used the FM band.

In 1964, the FCC issued a ruling that duplicate programming for AM and FM by a single owner could not exceed 50 percent in cities with populations over 100,000. Stations in larger communities that had been using FM to repeat their signals were forced to develop those stations as independent entities. FM stations began to proliferate, and listenership grew as FM's superior sound became popular.

By the late 1970s, FM audiences reached parity with AM listeners. Today, FM outpulls AM for audience share and is far more profitable. AM has its following, however, and counts among its audience many listeners loyal to talk radio, found most often on the AM band.

Music Replaces Live Performance.   By the early 1950s, having lost much of its dramatic and comedy programming to television, radio returned to its roots. It broadcast recorded music, interrupted with a few features, a little regular news, and commercials. The only live performers were the *disc jockeys* who announced the music and the *newscasters* who read the news.

Stations paid an annual fee for the rights to play recorded music. The fees were collected by Broadcast Music, Inc. (BMI), and the American Society of Composers, Authors and Publishers (ASCAP), which in turn paid royalties to record companies, recording artists, and song writers. That practice continues.

Specialized Radio.   With individual transistorized radios in the place of the bulky old family consoles, and with many more stations on the air with the expansion of the FM band, radio was set to become specialized. Before its specialization, the most common radio format was called *middle of the road*. That is, programming providing a little bit for everybody—some comedy, some drama, some news, some public affairs, some classical music, some popular music, some jazz or swing or country or western.

When radio specialized, it targeted program content to specific groups. Advertisers were more interested in sending commercial messages to the market most likely to buy their product, so they supported specialized radio. Demographic studies were done showing that different groupings within the general population had different tastes in music and news. Young people, the middle aged, and seniors all had different musical interests. Blacks, whites, Hispanics, Asians, urban, suburban, rural, male, female—all could be given programs that had special appeal. Stations chose different music formats based on their understanding of their markets.

Formats deliver a specific type of program content designed to attract a group of listeners similar in age, income, race, ethnicity, or gender, thereby making it easier for advertisers to reach their target audiences. The first radio format was "Top 40," the most popular recordings according to weekly record sales. This format was soon overtaken by the rock 'n' roll phenomenon, which changed radio and sound recordings dramatically, as we see later in this chapter.

Public Radio.   The Public Broadcasting Act of 1967 at last gave noncommercial radio a better chance for success in a marketplace dominated by commercial interests. The act created the Corporation for Public Broadcasting (CPB), the largest single source of funding for public television and radio programming. National Public Radio was created in 1970 to produce and distribute news and cultural programs to its 560 member radio stations (the total number of noncommercial radio stations receiving CPB assistance is nearly 700). NPR operates a national satellite program distribution system, with uplinks for public radio stations and other producers. NPR has assumed the only heavy news responsibility among all radio stations. Its two daily programs, "Morning Edition," and "All Things Considered" in the evening, provide the best example of what radio can really do to present news vividly and effectively.

Public radio stations depend on government funding, foundation and corporate donations, and listener support to stay on the air. The level of government funding for public broadcasting is erratic, depending on political sentiments in Congress, which makes annual appropriations for public broadcasting. Ironically, with the decrease of government funding in the 1980s and 1990s, noncommercial stations had to become more commercial just to stay on the air.

Current Issues

By the 1990s, radio had again become a profitable medium generally, with stations delivering demographically distinct audiences to advertisers in search of demographically distinct customers. By the beginning of the twenty-first century, radio had achieved a fair level of stability. Approximately 12,000 radio stations were on the air throughout the United States, with AM stations numbering about 4,800 and the balance on the FM band. The average greater metropolitan listening area had about 70 stations that could be heard, about 40 FM and 30 AM. Table 11.1 illustrates the continued growth in number of radio stations in the last years of the twentieth century.

Formats and Fragmentation.   Radio formats have settled into more than a dozen different types. Country radio has been dominant, claiming nearly one-quarter of commercial stations in 1997. Its ratings began to dip in 1994, partly because country singing stars began recording music that crosses over into other formats, such as soft rock.

TABLE 11.1

The Growth of Radio Stations in America, 1985–1997

	AM	FM	Noncommercial	Total
1985	4,754	3,716	1,172	9,642
1992	4,988	4,539	1,497	11,024
1997	4,812	5,488	1,899	12,199

Source: National Association of Broadcasters. Reprinted with permission.

Although country still dominates as a *station format*, *news/talk* radio attracts the greatest share of listeners. (See Table 11.2 for the rankings of all formats.)

Criticism has been rising about the narrow range of radio programming, and radio that has been reduced to stereotypical formulas. Some charge that the decline of radio's middle-of-the-road and family programming is spurring the fragmentation of society. Radio listening is now such a personal activity that it is no longer a unifying force, in the community or the family. All of us go off in our own direction, listening to our own favorite stations and formats, weakening the glue that holds people together.

Consolidation and Limited Choices.   Consolidation of radio ownership that occurred after the passage of the Telecommunications Act of 1996 has greatly reduced the number of companies now controlling most radio stations. As chapter 4 showed, by 1998 four corporations had gained control of nearly one-third of America's radio stations. When CBS purchased the American Radio Systems Corporation in 1997, for example, it added 98 stations and raised its total number of stations to 175. Only 15 years earlier, it would have been limited to 14 (7 AM and 7 FM). That trend will continue.

More crucial, perhaps, is the declining range of choices in radio listening available as a result of these consolidations. Since the limits on the number of stations controlled by a single owner in any one listening area have been reduced by the 1996 law, corporations that own more than one station in an area can change formats to those that are most popular. They can give all their stations country formats or rock 'n' roll formats. Already some forms of music are being played less on radio, especially classical and jazz.

This can happen even to public broadcasting stations. WDCU, the educational station of the University of the District of Columbia, had the fourth largest black audience of any public radio station in the country. It specialized in a jazz format. When the university ran out of money, the station was sold to C-Span, which changed the format to simulcast C-Span's television public affairs broadcasts. The result was that the Washington, DC, area lost its only radio station that had devoted a majority of its programming to jazz.

Mobile Audiences and Fragmented Attention.   Radio stations program their broadcast day around audience interests. The most common time and place for radio listening has become *drive time,* when people are in their cars going to and from work. Gen-

TABLE 11.2

Share of Listeners By Radio Format (Persons Age 12 and up) in Fall 1998

Format	Share
News/talk	14.2
Urban	10.6
Country	8.3
Adult contemporary	8.3
Contemporary hits radio	7.1
Spanish	6.0
Oldies	4.8
Album-oriented rock	4.8
Classic rock	4.2
New rock	3.4
Adult standards	2.8
New adult contemporary/jazz	2.6
Hot adult contemporary	2.5
Classical	1.5
Adult alternative	1.1
Black gospel	1.0
Religious	0.5
Contemporary Christian	0.4
Easy listening	0.3
Ethnic	0.2
Christian country	0.1
Other/unassigned listening*	15.3

Source: Interep Research analysis of Arbitron audience estimates, Monday through Sunday, 6 A.M. to 12 midnight. Share represents the percentage of total radio listeners in the average quarter hour for the specified time period. Used with permission.
*Radio listening that cannot be assigned to a particular format.

erally, the weekday *morning drive* (6 to 10 A.M.) and *afternoon drive* (3 to 7 P.M.) draw the largest audiences, so stations put their best talent into those time slots.

Most radio listening is done away from home and nearly all of it done while the listener is doing something else, usually driving, besides listening. Listeners' locations have changed and attentiveness has lagged dramatically since radio broadcasting began, causing concern especially for advertisers.

Automation.   An increasing number of stations have automated some or all of their broadcast programming. Program services prerecord a daily program of music in the client station's format. This *canned* programming allows for the insertion of commercials and local announcements. Even news and weather reports can be automated and delivered from a central news service. Automation allows stations to reduce staff to a few ad sales representatives, an engineer, and administrative staff, saving a great deal of money by doing without live talent and a music library. But it has also limited such stations' personal relationships and interaction with their communities. They have become mere music services with commercials.

Declining News.   Few radio stations any longer have substantial local news staffs. Some all-news stations exist, but they are in a tiny minority. Most stations use news and commentary from networks and services such as ABC Radio Networks, Associated Press Broadcast Services, Bloomberg Business Information, and traffic, weather, and sports feeds. Disney–ABC's ESPN Radio Network offers daily sports coverage, live game coverage, and sports talk shows. Accu-Weather, Inc., provides taped or live national weather forecasts. Westwood One distributes news-talk, sports, and entertainment programming. Except for NPR and all-news radio, few stations broadcast more than 5 minutes of news at a time, usually on the hour.

Commercialized Public Broadcasting.   With the reduction in government subsidy for PBS and NPR, public broadcasting has had to turn increasingly to corporate funding. Deregulation has allowed stations more latitude in their pursuit of contributions from businesses, even as the lines between underwriting credits and advertisements have gotten increasingly blurry. One example of this latter tendency was Public Radio International's daily business program, "Marketplace," whose theme music concluded with the familiar tune from General Electric's corporate jingle, "We bring good things to life." Some critics have called this subliminal advertising and creeping commercialism.

Looking Ahead

By the beginning of the twenty-first century, many questions about the effects of ownership consolidation on radio's future remain unanswered. Will diverse viewpoints be expressed in the future? Will there be much local news? Will public service programming, educational programming, hard-hitting documentaries that examine business tactics, and public service announcements be reduced or even eliminated? Will automated stations and canned programming further crowd out local identity?

In the future, if all goes well, radio will grow as a specialized medium, as formats continue to be designed around ever more precise groupings of audience characteristics. This will serve both advertisers and audiences. Advertisers will be able to reach the particular markets most interested in their products, and audiences will be able to have their individual needs met.

The Internet will also pose new challenges and opportunities. Several thousand radio stations already have Internet Web sites, which are used to promote the station's format, its on-air personalities, its contests, and other forms of listener interaction. All-news stations post headlines and news summaries on their sites. Many of the radio station Web sites also offer *bitcasting*, their station's audio carried over the Internet for play through a site visitor's computer speakers.

The Internet also presents an opportunity for individuals to have more control over the content of broadcasts and choice over what they want to hear. Approximately 1,550 stations from more than 100 countries already broadcast music, news, and other programs over the Internet, available to anyone who can access the Internet worldwide. At the beginning of the twenty-first century, radio's emerging availability on the Internet is extending the medium's reach in new, interesting ways and suggests that radio's role as primarily a local and a personal medium could change dramatically in the years ahead.

SOUND RECORDING

The invention of recorded sound proved to be essential to motion pictures and radio. Without it, motion pictures probably would not have survived the competitive threat of radio, nor would radio have survived the inroads later made by television. Movies became more lifelike and more sophisticated. Radio, which lost many of its live performers to television, was able to modify its programming by expanding its use of recorded music. But more than being just an adjunct to other media, sound recording gradually became a mass medium of its own.

Sound recording went through an evolution somewhat similar to other mass media. It was first conceived as a business tool and emerged as a fairly expensive medium produced primarily for an elite audience. Not until the second half of the twentieth century, after considerable technological advancements and the development of popular content, did sound recording become a mass medium.

Early History: 1877–1899

Thomas Edison first reproduced the sound of his own voice in 1877. His apparatus included a telephone transmitter and a membrane diaphragm, which vibrated when sound waves from the transmitter reached it. Edison attached a stylus to the diaphragm, and it responded by making marks on paraffin-coated paper run beneath it. Then the etched paper was run beneath the stylus again. If all went as planned, the diaphragm relayed the sound that had been "recorded" by the stylus.

As Edison shouted into the transmitter, the stylus cut irregular grooves onto the waxed paper. When the paper strip was pulled back under the stylus, Edison's assistants heard, very faintly, the sound of their employer's shouted message. The first *talking machine* had been born.

Business Devices.   That same year, the Edison laboratories refined this device into a cylinder, which was turned by a crank. This time the stylus etched sound waves into tin foil rather than paraffin on the turning cylinder. By 1887, Edison had replaced the hand-crank with a motor and the tin foil with a more durable wax.

Edison had a narrow vision for his invention. He thought of it as a dictating device, a way to record a letter by voice, so a secretary could type it on his or her own time and thus become more efficient. To produce dictating machines with his device, Edison formed a company called Dictaphone, which continues in business today.

Discs That Could Sell.   Other inventors of the time continued to improve on Edison's cylinder, but Emile Berliner went in an entirely different direction. In 1888, he introduced a talking machine that employed a disc rather than a cylinder, and he developed a method of copying discs so they could be more easily marketed. By 1893, he was selling records to the public. Edison's cylinder recordings produced clearer sound, but Berliner had developed a superior system for copying and marketing recordings.

In 1896, Berliner's Gramophone Company contracted with New Jersey machinist and inventor Eldridge Johnson to work on the sound quality problem. Johnson's records were made of a combination of wax and metal dust, and later shellac, eliminating the surface noise in Berliner's discs and producing louder sound than Edison's cylinders. His system was a breakthrough that allowed the *talking machines* and the records they played to have commercial potential. By 1897, about 500,000 records were sold in the United States. Only 2 years later, in 1899, Americans had purchased 2.8 million records and a new industry was under way.

Recordings Seek Content: 1900–1940

At the turn of the century, there was no music industry to scout talent, write contracts, record artists, and distribute their records. The technicians who had developed the medium now had to search for content. Johnson formed a company called Victor Red Seal Records. But he had to find something to record that would sell.

Phonographs that played records were large apparatuses, almost as big as a modern refrigerator. They were expensive items, far too costly for the average household. Discs were expensive, too, far more costly than the mass-produced books, magazines, and newspapers of the day. In order to be marketable to the elite, upper income audience that could afford phonographs and records, the fledgling industry had to produce elite content.

Classical Music.   Victor Red Seal Records turned to operatic and classical music talent, such as the great Italian tenor Enrico Caruso. In 1902, still early in his career, Caruso recorded 10 songs for Victor Red Seal records. Surprisingly, enthusiasm was so great that vendors had trouble keeping the Caruso records in stock. The strategy of recording classical artists enabled the record companies to share in the high status of the performing arts and completed the transition of the phonograph from a mere novelty to an enhancement to American life, a status item for the home.

Until the end of the Depression years of the 1930s, however, the record business was aimed primarily at this elite audience. Some popular music was recorded, but few popular singers or music groups became best sellers or made much money. Classical and semiclassical music dominated the industry.

Joining Radio.   Owners of the sound recording industry feared radio, with good reason. When radio appeared, sales of records began to fall. Why pay for music if you could hear it in live performances, with more clarity and volume, *at no cost*, on your radio? The advent of radio at first kept the sound-recording medium from reaching the masses.

Record manufacturers gradually came to realize that radio could actually help them promote their recordings to the general public and stimulate sales. Radio needed recorded music to help fill the broadcast day. A symbiotic relationship began to flourish in the late 1930s, so that by the 1940s, 75 percent of all programming on American radio came from records.

Becoming a Mass Medium: 1940–1990

If you have the means to promote a product to the masses, that product must have content with mass appeal. Thus the record industry turned from "high-brow" content to popular music. Dance bands began recording the tunes they had been playing at hotel and restaurant dinner dances. Big bands and their leaders of the 1930s and 1940s began to emerge as popular names everyone knew.

For the first time in history popular, musicians became nationally famous, including band leaders such as Benny Goodman, Glenn Miller, and Duke Ellington and singers such as Frank Sinatra, Ella Fitzgerald, and Nat King Cole. They recorded romantic ballads, country songs, jazz, and swing. Radio broadcast their performances and touted their records, and people bought phonographs and rushed to the stores to get recordings by their favorite artists, whose work they were able to save permanently.

Mainstream Music.   A number of musical forces converged in the early 1950s. Radio faced up to its increased dependence on recorded music to replace the live programming it lost to television. At the same time, record-industry executives recognized that radio was the way to promote new recordings. This eagerness to showcase new music and track its popularity among record-buyers brought about the creation of the *top 40*, a list of the best-selling records in any given week. In the 1960s, this evolved into a radio format that attracted audiences eager to listen as individual songs climbed the charts in the all-important drive to the number 1 spot.

As the top-40 radio format became more popular with listeners and more stations adopted it, record companies felt increased pressure to get their artists' singles on the playlists of radio stations. Their theory was that more airplay equals more sales equals a spot on the top 40, which leads to more airplay and more sales and a higher spot on the top 40, and so on.

In the 1950s and 1960s, lush orchestral arrangements of popular ballads and classical music selections were popularized by musicians such as Percy Faith and Mantovani. Motion pictures, which borrowed heavily from the classical repertoire in making movie soundtracks, also drew on the talents of popular music composers such as Cole Porter, Johnny Mercer, and Henry Mancini. They helped make movie scores into sought-after albums in the 1960s and 1970s.

Technological Advances.   After World War II new technology not only improved the quality of sound recording but also lowered the cost of buying records. Researchers experimented with many new recording materials, including wire, magnetic tape, and vinyl discs to replace the standard shellac platters.

Long play records (LPs) in the late 1940s and early 1950s probably made the biggest difference in the market. The old 78-revolutions-per-minute (RPM) records, which had about 5 minutes of playing time per side, gave way to the long-playing 33⅓ vinyl album and plastic 45-RPM disc, the latter favored by disc jockeys and jukebox owners. These reproduced clearer and cleaner sound than the old 78-RPMs and expanded the record repertoire dramatically. They were the first wave of changes in recording media that altered the business.

Stereophonic equipment, using multichannel systems, did much to solidify the record market, because it improved and enhanced sound quality to a level that even the most discriminating could appreciate. Such equipment began to be marketed in 1958 and lent increasing sophistication to home and commercial playback systems. This technical enhancement was a breakthrough for both artists and listeners.

Audiotape cartridges and **cassettes** began to replace records and reel-to-reel tape in the 1960s. Tape cartridges reproduced sound even better than LP discs and are still used by disc jockeys in many radio studios. The next development was the cassette, even smaller than cartridges, with two great advantages. They were small enough to be used in hand-held players, and they could be used by anyone to record any sound.

Compact discs, which came on the market in the early 1980s, completed the evolution of recording media in the twentieth century. The sound they could reproduce was the best of any medium yet. And by the end of the century, CDs had become the overwhelmingly favored recording medium.

Rock Music Develops.   Well into the 1950s, the record industry marketed most of its products to a mainstream white audience. Not wanting to miss an important market, companies recorded black artists and distributed their records to retailers who served black listeners. Sales to whites and blacks were tracked separately: *pop* charts meant white and *race* charts meant black. Race charts were designated *rhythm and blues* in 1949, and later *soul* and then *urban contemporary*.

Independent companies such as Chess and King specialized in recording black talent. Bigger labels, such as Columbia Records, also had enormous success recording black artists, especially vocalists such as Bessie Smith and Ethel Waters, even in the late 1930s and 1940s. But a dividing line ran through every element of the business, often resulting in ruthless exploitation of black artists.

Musicians had long been influenced by the blues and jazz of the black musical community. In the 1950s, young white artists began to adapt rhythm and blues motifs to create a new sound for a largely white teenage audience. "Rock Around the Clock," performed by Bill Haley and the Comets, reached number 1 on the pop charts in 1955, a year after black listeners had given the tune a spot on the rhythm and blues charts.

Elvis Presley recorded rhythm and blues songs, and in the process changed mainstream popular music dramatically. Presley helped to make black music forms popular with white consumers in a still-segregated United States. His interpretation of the hillbilly, gospel, and blues sounds of his Mississippi youth was repackaged as the 1950s musical phenomenon of rock 'n' roll. Presley's success elevated interest in the original performers of rhythm and blues songs, and black artists' recordings began crossing over from the rhythm and blues charts to the pop charts, blurring the racial boundaries those charts had represented.

The rockers began to own the top of the pop charts, and the rhythm and blues artists began appearing there as well. In 1959, a former lightweight boxer and autoworker from Detroit named Berry Gordy founded the Tamla label, later to become Motown, to meet the demand for music by black artists.

The Rock Revolution. Music is often a reflection of the times during which it is made, and this was particularly true of rock 'n' roll, which reflected the cultural changes under way in the United States from the 1950s into the 1970s, changes involving race relations, sexual freedom, and trust in government and business.

Rock 'n' roll represented a youthful working out of young people's emerging sexuality and antiestablishment sentiments. It was exuberant, throbbing, danceable music. Rock stars sang of teenage angst, sexual longing, and desire for personal freedom. It thrilled teenagers and panicked their parents, their teachers, and the clergy. Rock music has seen many variations in the years since Presley swiveled his hips on "The Ed Sullivan Show." Especially important were the British invasion (such as the Beatles and Rolling Stones), folk rock (such as Bob Dylan and the Byrds), and hard rock (such as Led Zeppelin and Jimi Hendrix). Rock is still by far the biggest selling type of recorded music, as indicated in Table 11.3.

Without question, rock 'n' roll music, more than any other idiom or mass media content, has changed sound recording, radio, television, motion pictures, American culture, and perhaps world culture as well.

Current Issues

The main consumers of sound recordings at the end of the twentieth century were completely different from those few who bought records at the beginning of the century. Today's consumer is part of the masses, as likely to be female as male, and between the ages of 25 and 49. Half of recorded-music buyers make their purchases in record stores, now dominated by CDs rather than records or cassettes. About 14 percent buy

TABLE 11.3

Types of Recordings Sold in America, in Percentages, 1998

Rock	25.7
Country	14.1
Rhythm and Blues	12.8
Pop	10.0
Rap	9.7
Gospel	6.3
Classical	3.3
Jazz	1.9
Other	11.3
	100.0

Source: Recording Industry Association of America. Reproduced with permission.

music recordings through clubs. Online recording purchases are becoming popular and will certainly increase.

Recording Companies and Consolidation.   In the 1950s, the three largest record companies were RCA Victor, Decca, and Columbia. These were regarded as the *majors*, because they handled their own nationwide distribution. Along with these were scores of smaller companies, known as *independents*, including Chess Records in Chicago, which recorded Chuck Berry; King Records in Cincinnati, which recorded James Brown; and Sun Records in Memphis, which had recorded Elvis Presley.

The independents were excellent at finding new talent. The major companies monitored public sales of an artist recorded by one of these minor labels, and if sales were good they would buy the artist's contract from the independent company. RCA Victor acquired Presley from Sun Records for $35,000 plus a $5,000 signing bonus. Sometimes the majors simply bought an entire independent label in order to get the performer they were after.

The need to have a constant flow of new talent into the recording pipeline and a sufficient market share to support the costs of contracts, recording, and distribution led in the late 1970s to a flurry of acquisitions that resulted in today's consolidation of ownership within the record industry. Bertelsmann Music Group (BMG), a division of the German media conglomerate, acquired the Arista, RCA Victor, RCA Records, Iguana, and Paradise labels in addition to a 50 percent interest in Windham Hill and Reunion. Warner Music, a division of Time Warner, Inc., acquired control of more than a dozen record labels including Asylum, Atlantic, Elektra, Reprise, Sire, Slash, and Tommy

Boy. Sony Music Entertainment bought Columbia Records, long a jewel in the crown of CBS, whose research department developed the original LP.

Financial Trends.   Demand for recorded music slowed somewhat during the 1990s, although the recording industry remained relatively robust. The number of cassettes sold has been declining since 1988, whereas sales of CDs have increased. In 1997, sales of CDs accounted for more than three-quarters of total music recording sales ($9.9 billion of total recording sales of $12.2 billion). Cassettes were a distant second with $1.5 billion in sales.

The company owning the label receives the largest share of a record's income, from a quarter to a third of the selling price. The rest is distributed among wholesale distributors and retail stores, promotion and advertising costs, recording and studio charges, design and packaging, miscellaneous expenses such as shipping and other talent fees, and artist's royalties. The artist's share is typically the smallest, depending on the performer's track record and clout. Bigger names obviously command greater compensation.

Attacks on Content.   Disapproval of popular music and worry about its ability to influence the socialization of young people has existed since Elvis burst on the scene in the 1950s, and since the Rolling Stones had to change the words of "Let's Spend the Night Together" to "Let's Spend Some Time Together" for an Ed Sullivan Show appearance in the 1960s. Anxious parents were increasingly concerned about the music their children were listening to. That concern reached a peak in 1985, resulting in the formation of the Parents Music Resource Center, a group spearheaded by Tipper Gore, wife of then Senator, later Vice President Al Gore. This center succeeded in pressuring the record industry to formulate its own voluntary system of placing parental-advisory labels on all recordings containing sexually explicit or violent lyrics.

A decade later, controversy flared over *gangsta rap*. A number of songs from this music genre described and seemed to urge sexual abuse of women, violence, and murder. Police in Broward County, Fla., arrested members of 2 Live Crew in 1990, saying their album "As Nasty as They Wanna Be" was obscene. A federal appeals court ruled that it was not obscene after a psychologist, two music critics, and a former Rhodes scholar turned professor attested to the music's artistic value and authentic expression of societal realities.

Promotion and Payola.   Competition is fierce in the recording business. In any given week, hundreds of new songs compete for airplay, trying for a place on the top 40 or on the music charts of different formats, such as country or urban contemporary. For several decades the industry used a form of bribery to persuade radio disc jockeys and program directors to give special attention to certain songs and occasionally to have them deny airplay to a competitor's records. This custom became known as *payola*.

Money, drugs, merchandise, and prostitutes were offered to radio personnel for pushing or withholding certain records. Congress in 1959 and the U.S. Justice Department in 1973 investigated the relationship of record companies and "independent promoters" they hired to advance the airplay of their releases. Some individuals paid fines and went to jail. In 1989, several more independent promoters were indicted, but the problem persists. Radio stations and record companies need each other too much for payola to vanish.

Music Television.   Promotion has always been an enormously important factor in the creation of a hit. Since 1981, another vehicle has been added to record promotion. Music Television (MTV) targets viewers and record buyers in the 12 to 34 age group. Television has become a much more powerful influence on popular music than motion pictures or radio. In the 1980s, MTV reached an audience of more than 40 million young adults, the most sought-after record buyers. Rock video became essential for record promotion, far more important than radio.

A video in "heavy rotation" on MTV would be replayed three to five times a day, 7 days a week, for up to 2 months. That could sell millions of records. By 1990, the MTV music video reach was up to 56 million homes, and by 1997, the reach was 66 million homes, only a portion of its worldwide reach. The cable channel could also be received in 289 million households in 81 other countries. Other cable networks also showcased music video, including The Nashville Network (TNN), Black Entertainment Television (BET), and Video Hits One (VH1).

Copyright Infringement.   A thorny problem for the industry has been unauthorized use or manufacture of recordings. Music pirates account for almost $300 million in lost record sales annually in the United States, trading illegally on the investment and creativity of others. Foreign counterfeiting in countries where antipiracy laws are weak, unenforced or nonexistent, compounds the economic loss.

The owner of a song's copyright is entitled to a royalty whenever that song is played on radio, on television, or for a special event or production such as a commercial or a convention, or in commercial establishments such as hotels, restaurants and stores. The American Society of Composers, Authors and Publishers (ASCAP) and Broadcast Music, Inc. (BMI), are the largest of the groups that collect royalties on behalf of songwriters and music publishers and other owners of copyrighted music. Federally licensed entities such as radio and television stations pay annual fees for the right to play recorded music, but other organizations, who are either ignorant of copyright restrictions or just plain ignore them, frequently use music they have not paid to use as part of their events. They risk prosecution when they do this, but copyright infringement of recorded music is hard to track, and most offenders are not caught.

Piracy is the term used to describe all forms of illegal duplication and distribution of sound recordings. The Recording Industry Association of America lobbies aggressively for enforcement of state and federal laws prohibiting illegal duplication of recordings to protect the economic interests of its members because:

Pirate recordings are unauthorized duplications of only the sound of one or more legitimate recordings, including unauthorized digital recordings on the Internet. *Counterfeit recordings* are unauthorized duplications of the prerecorded sounds as well as the unauthorized duplication of the original artwork, label, trademark, and packaging of prerecorded music. *Bootleg recordings* are the unauthorized recording of a musical broadcast on radio or television or of a live concert.

Cultural Influence.   Perhaps the most important issue of sound recording is its cultural influence. Recorded sound, in some ways, has done for aural expression what the book did for verbal logic. Records can be stored, retrieved, and replayed almost as efficiently as books. And when we add videotapes to recordings, the recording industry has also made visual imagery as important as aural expression and verbal logic.

As record historian Andre Millard (1995) wrote, recorded sound has been a "great educator," a "means of diffusing styles and bringing ethnic or regional music to a large audience." Music that went unrecorded would fade from history without a trace, and recorded music could survive from generation to generation. Recordings of new music link us to younger generations and their concerns. In this way, sound recordings facilitate cultural linkages between individuals and groups (Millard, 1995, p. 12).

Looking Ahead

In the future, recorded music will be more accessible in more different ways to more different people than ever before. Protecting the rights of recording artists and companies to which they are under contract will be problematic as emerging media spawn new forms of listening and copying opportunities. The battle to protect this intellectual property won't be won easily, especially when the product sold may be nothing more tangible than a series of electronic pulses downloaded onto a computer hard drive or diskette.

But just as technology is creating digital products, bought and sold in potentially untraceable electronic transactions, technology also holds the promise of providing the mechanisms that can regulate such commerce. However, along with promising technical intervention in acts of copyright infringement, there must also be a corresponding legal framework under which violations can be enforced. A giant step toward bolstering that legal framework was taken in 1998 when the U.S. Congress ratified two international treaties negotiated by more than 100 nations that will secure copyright protections online and help strengthen copyright laws around the world.

Artistic freedom will likely continue to be a point of controversy. Music and other recorded entertainment will continue to challenge mainstream cultural values as diverse artists bring their unique vision to recordings. U.S. law protects freedom of expression, and recent tests of this have upheld the rights of the artists and the companies that back them. Nevertheless, disagreement with artists' inclusion of explicit sexual themes and pointed hostility toward specific groups in their work will continue to draw criticism and pressure on corporate owners to modify creative content.

And, as with other media described in this book, the computer and the Internet pose new challenges and opportunities for recordings. A potentially important new product category is the enhanced CD, which is compatible with both standard audio CD players and computers with multimedia ROM capability. In addition to the recorded music, enhanced CDs can include video clips, still pictures, artist interviews, discographies, lyrics, and other information.

By the beginning of the twenty-first century, the Internet was providing not only a new way of searching for and buying tapes and records; it was also allowing users to download recordings of all kinds, and to mix sound almost as if individuals were operating their own personal sound or video studios. The opportunities may be unlimited.

Further Reading

Radio

Archer, Gleason L. (1938). *History of Radio to 1926*. New York: American Historical Society.

Barfield, Ray E., and Inge, M. Thomas. (1997). *Listening to Radio, 1920–1950*. New York: Praeger.

Barlow, William. (1998). *Voice Over: The Making of Black Radio*. Philadelphia: Temple University Press.

Barnouw, Erik. (1967). *A Tower in Babel: History of Broadcasting in the United States*. New York: Oxford University Press.

Douglas, Susan. (1997). *Inventing American Broadcasting, 1899–1922*. Baltimore: Johns Hopkins University Press.

Engelman, Ralph. (1996). *Public Radio and Television in America: A Political History*. Thousand Oaks, CA: Sage.

Hilmes, Michele. (1997). *Radio Voices: American Broadcasting, 1922–1952*. Minneapolis: University of Minnesota Press.

Lasar, Matthew. (1999). *Pacifica Radio: The Rise of an Alternative Network*. Philadelphia: Temple University Press.

Lewis, Tom. (1991). *Empire of the Air: The Men Who Made Radio*. New York: HarperCollins.

Looker, Thomas. (1995). *The Sound and the Story: NPR and the Art of Radio*. New York: Houghton Mifflin.

MacDonald, J. Fred. (1979). *Don't Touch That Dial! Radio Programming in American Life From 1920 to 1960*. Chicago: Nelson-Hall.

McChesney, Robert W. (1993). *Telecommunications, Mass Media, and Democracy: The Battle for Control of U.S. Broadcasting, 1928–1935*. New York: Oxford University Press.

Maltin, Leonard. (1997). *The Great American Broadcast*. New York: Dutton/Penguin Putnam.

Smulyan, Susan. (1994). *Selling Radio: The Commercialization of American Broadcasting, 1920–1934*. Washington: Smithsonian Institution.

Yoder, Andrew. (1995). *Pirate Radio: The Incredible Saga of America's Underground, Illegal Broadcasters*. New York: Hightext.

Sound recordings

Chanan, Michael. (1997). *Repeated Takes: A Short History of Recording and Its Effects on Music*. New York: Verso Books.

Dannen, Fredric. (1990). *Hit Men: Power Brokers and Fast Money Inside the Music Business*. New York: Random House/Times Books.

Dickerson, James L. (1998). *Women on Top: The Quiet Revolution That's Rocking the American Music Industry*. New York: Watson-Guptill.

Eisenberg, Evan. (1987). *Recording Angel: Music, Records and Culture From Aristotle to Zappa*. London: Picador.

Gelatt, Roland. (1977). *The Fabulous Phonograph: 1877–1977*. New York: Macmillan.

Haring, Bruce. (1996). *Off the Charts: Ruthless Days and Reckless Nights Inside the Music Industry*. New York: Birch Lane.

Heylin, Clinton. (1996). *Bootleg: The Secret History of the Other Recording Industry*. New York: St. Martin's.

Hull, Geoffrey P. (1998). *The Recording Industry*. New York: Allyn & Bacon.

Millard, Andre. (1995). *America on Record: A History of Recorded Sound*. New York: Cambridge University Press.

Sanjek, Russell. (1988). *American Popular Music and its Business*. New York: Oxford University Press.

Scheurer, Tim. (Ed.). (1989). *American Popular Music*. Bowling Green, OH: The Popular Press.

Steane, J. B. (1993). *The Grand Tradition: Seventy Years of Singing on Record*. New York: Timber Press.

Welch, Walter, Broadbeck, Leah, and Stenzel, Burt. (1994). *From Tinfoil to Stereo: The Acoustic Years of the Recording Industry, 1877–1929*. Gainesville: University Press of Florida.

Note

[1]Quoted in Archer, Gleason L. (1938). *History of Radio to 1926*. New York: American Historical Society, p. 85.

12

TELEVISION

The hearse rolled quietly through the English countryside, accompanied by a motorcycle escort, on the 75-mile trip from London to the Althorp estate. Along the way, tearful women, men, and children tossed bouquets at the vehicle. Thousands had gathered along the English roads to watch the last journey of Diana, Princess of Wales, as her coffin was taken to its resting place at her family home. But they represented a scant fraction of the mourners that August 1997 day. Because of television, they were joined for some part of the way by an estimated 2.5 billion people in one of the most widely viewed telecasts of all time.

Television can bring an audience to an event in a way that creates powerful meaning for viewers. It enabled the world to see astronaut Neil Armstrong's boot touch the lunar surface; watch Nelson Mandela walk out of his South African jail after years of imprisonment; see missiles rain down on Middle Eastern cities during the Persian Gulf war. TV can let us see every play in the World Series and the Super Bowl and tornadoes and hurricanes that look as though they might explode in our living rooms. It takes us into the Oval Office to watch a speech by the President, into the Capitol to watch a congressional debate, and to battle sites on the other side of the planet.

Television is far more than a box of electronic circuitry that delivers news updates and dramatic programming. More than any other device, except possibly the automobile, television has altered American life. In many households, television is the center of attention, rather than the people living in the house. It has been suggested that television can interfere with personal development by impeding conversation between family members and friends, diminishing time spent in meaningful human contact, reducing learning through reading and play—in short, substituting electronic touch for the human one. Critics blame television for perpetuating violence and antisocial behavior among hard-core viewers. It would be fair to say that television is our most controversial medium (although the Internet may in the future give it some competition for that title).

"Television has gradually *become* our culture," wrote Neil Postman (1985, p. 79) in his widely respected book, *Amusing Ourselves to Death*. Postman says that although we rarely talk about television, we are involved with what is *on* television, and this involvement directs our understanding of the world around us and cues us to ways we engage in social and civic activities. "Today, like it or not, TV is our literature," said television writer Donna McCrohan (1990, p. 15).

Television is an interpretive medium. Its news programs assign value and urgency to the news it covers. It uses pulsing music to open the evening news, signaling portentous announcements to get viewer attention. Carefully coiffed announcers sit before a bank of monitors tuned into world capitals. Some argue that television news exaggerates the amount of disaster, travail, conflict, and danger present in the world and that it "hypes" events beyond their actual importance. Television news directors respond that they simply report what happens in the world and that their experience indicates people are genuinely curious about bad news.

Similar criticism is made of other TV programming as well. Executives who purchase nonnews content for television say they attract bigger audiences with action-oriented, suspenseful shows in which danger and desire are main elements. They and the news directors agree on this point: People are interested in, perhaps even fascinated by, programs featuring crime, mayhem, and sex. Many studies have confirmed that the relatively small screen of a television set requires movement to capture and maintain attention; some indicate that the more aggressive, violent, vivid, and colorful the movement, the greater the viewer's attention.

What are the effects of this kind of programming? As we saw in our discussion of media effects in chapter 7, there is no simple answer, although we know that television is powerful. It is difficult to generalize about television's effects on all people, since viewers represent a range of media usage habits, from light to heavy viewing, and from using few other media to using many. The enormous expansion of television channels accessible to the average American home certainly emphasizes the vast array of programming constantly available. See Table 12.1.

TABLE 12.1

Growth in the Number of Television Channels Available in the Average American Home

1950	2.9
1960	5.7
1970	7.1
1980	10.2
1990	27.2
1999	50.8

Source: *TV Dimensions '99*, published by Media Dynamics, Inc. www.MediaDynamics.com, (212) 683-7895. Used with permission.

We can say with confidence that television reaches a mass audience, the largest of any mass medium, and thus it plays an enormous role in the culture, with great potential to inform, entertain, educate, and influence. In fact, television has changed our understanding of all media, because it forced us to see that technology made a difference in how and what we communicate, giving us a much better grasp of the languages and codes of all mass media.

TV'S EARLY DAYS: 1925–1945

Television proved to be a technical possibility in 1923 with the transmission by wire of silhouette pictures and in 1925 with the rudimentary transmission of moving images over the airwaves. Many scientists worked on its development, and many nations claim that their scientists invented it. In the United States, Charles Jenkins, Philo T. Farnsworth, and Vladimir K. Zworykin usually get most credit for important technical innovations that led to early television, but many people have been involved in the experimentation that made today's television possible.

Perfecting the emerging technology continued throughout the 1920s and 1930s. In 1928 in the United States, telecasting began on an experimental basis, without commercials or an audience, when General Electric Company in Schenectady, N.Y., launched what is today WRGB. Television receivers were in the early stage of development and far beyond the reach of the average citizen, but those who saw a future in the medium pushed for its continued development. In 1931, CBS introduced the first regularly scheduled TV news program, during which host William Schudt, Jr., interviewed reporters. However, few people were able to watch the program. By 1936, Germany was able to televise the Olympics experimentally, and that same year, Great Britain began regularly scheduled programming for a few hours a day, although few Germans or Britons could receive those telecasts.

In April 1939, television took a leap forward in America when RCA's network, NBC, televised President Franklin Roosevelt's speech from the World's Fair in New York, the first presidential address on television. In May, it broadcast the Columbia–Princeton baseball game, the first U.S. sports telecast. On July 1, 1941, CBS launched a television schedule with 15 hours of service weekly, including two 15-minute news programs Monday through Friday.

On the same day, on the NBC station then using the call letters WNBT, the first television commercial was aired. The program was a Dodgers–Phillies baseball game, and the advertiser was Bulova Watch Company. The camera focused on a Bulova watch with the second hand ticking as the announcer read the correct time. The spot was adapted from radio, where Bulova time checks ("It's 3 o'clock, Bulova watch time") had been a staple of radio advertising.

By the end of 1941, 10 commercial stations were telecasting in the United States but the audience was still infinitesimal by today's standards. A television receiver cost many thousands of dollars. Receivers were large, bulky pieces of furniture, the size of a piano, with dozens of vacuum tubes, any one of which could blow out easily. Homes with television receivers were estimated at 5,000 to 10,000, or less than .001 percent of the population. By comparison, radio, with its four networks, was reaching nearly all American homes by the beginning of World War II. World War II slowed development of the fledgling television medium as the nation turned its scientific and technological efforts to supporting the war effort. Radio and motion picture newsreels, not television, delivered news of the war.

BECOMING A MASS MEDIUM: 1945–1952

The period of the late 1940s through the 1950s saw television succeed on four fundamentals: supplying a mass audience with receivers; encouraging that audience to watch; selling that mass audience to advertisers; and developing variety in broadcast content.

Technical Challenges

In the flush of confidence and prosperity that followed World War II, Americans rode a wave of progress and modernization. The massive manufacturing infrastructure that had geared up to support the war effort now turned its attention to the consumer market. Restyled automobiles and time-saving home appliances were at the top of everyone's wish list.

Increased sophistication in electronics was a by-product of U.S. involvement in the war, and television became the chief beneficiary. Assembly lines that had been used for military hardware such as radar, field transmitters, and walkie-talkies were turned over to the mass production of television sets. That enabled the industry to lower prices for individual sets. By 1948, the average cost was reduced to $400, still a considerable sum at that time. But Americans were curious about this new product, and they bought more than 1 million sets that year. One of the most popular sets was RCA's black-and-white model with a 7-inch screen.

AT&T began installing intercity coaxial cable in 1948, linking the East and West coasts by 1951, which made national network television possible. Beyond major metropolitan areas, however, small towns and rural areas had to wait until the mid-1950s and in some cases even later for a TV signal to reach them.

Financial Challenges

Viewers had to work hard to get $400 to buy a TV set, but investors had to invest considerably more money developing an infrastructure, building stations, purchasing equipment, hiring staff, finding audiences large enough to attract advertisers, and acquiring enough programming to keep audiences tuned in. It cost a fortune to compete in television, but visionaries such as RCA's David Sarnoff, CBS's William Paley, and Allen DuMont, founder of the DuMont network, knew there was a fortune to be made if one invested early and wisely. They sold their vision to other investors, and by 1952 almost every major population area was reached by at least one television station.

The major financial breakthrough came from the marketplace. By 1950, mass production had reached a stage in which television sets could be rolled off the assembly line at a greatly reduced cost. When the price finally reached $99 a set, it was considered affordable to the average American household. And when that happened, Americans by the millions bought their first television set. By 1952, a third of all American households had one. The penny newspaper, nickel magazine, and dime novel had been joined by the $99 TV set, and television had become a new mass medium.

Government Challenges

Unlike print media, radio and television were regulated by the federal government because they used public property, the airwaves, to communicate. The Federal Communications Commission involved itself in television on many fronts. It was concerned with technical issues such as preventing stations' signals from interfering with one another, standardizing equipment so that improvements in transmission and reception could be introduced, and setting up an orderly process of granting broadcast licenses to qualified applicants. In order to evaluate all these issues, the FCC froze allocations for new television stations from September 30, 1948, to July 1, 1952. Even with the freeze, audience growth mushroomed, as previously licensed stations went on the air and consumers continued to buy sets.

The FCC regulation concerning ownership of radio stations—allowing an individual or company to own a maximum of seven stations—applied also to the television. The purpose was to encourage broadcast media to be broadly owned, to prevent this powerful instrument from falling into the hands of a few people and to promote local ownership to serve local community needs. This limitation on ownership might have limited the growth of television had it not been for the development of networks.

Network Challenges

Networks of radio stations had already established themselves in the late 1920s, the 1930s, and the early 1940s. These networks were loose affiliations of separately owned stations that joined together to share programming, thus increasing the efficiency and profitability of individual stations. RCA/NBC, CBS, and DuMont were among the first radio networks. In 1943, the FCC obtained a government ruling that NBC's ownership of two radio networks was monopolistic, forcing the company to sell one of its networks, which eventually became ABC Radio. These radio networks were the basis of the television networks.

Television networking began during the 1948–1949 season. The networks owned their limit of seven stations, but they also had agreements with other stations to carry their programming. By combining stations carrying the same programs, they created an audience large enough to attract enough program sponsors to cover production costs and overhead and to make a profit. Individual stations, in turn, received programs to fill their schedules. They also generated their own programming to fill any gaps in network programming. And they also bought programs from syndicates, third parties who distributed movies and other filmed productions. Today syndicates sell reruns of network hits, talk shows, and other made-for-TV fare.

Programming Challenges

In the early 1950s, television program content mirrored radio's: game shows, mysteries, variety shows, soap operas, situation comedies, and news. Early television was live, because videotape did not exist and film was clumsy and slow. Even many commercials were live. Food companies hired actors to demonstrate cooking recipes in a live TV studio kitchen. Appliance manufacturers used actors to extoll the virtues of refrigerators, freezers, and stoves. Soap makers dipped grease-stained clothes in detergent on camera, then displayed them with the stain gone. Because it was live, disasters were inevitable: burnt recipes, refrigerators that refused to open, spilled detergent, stubborn grease stains. But these live commercials laid the foundation for the extremely sophisticated—and relentless—marketing associated with contemporary television.

Television programming was much more expensive to produce than radio had been. Radio listeners could use their imaginations to picture the scenery, the appearances and expressions of characters, and the changes from day to night and winter to summer. Television required visual realism: a set, scene changes, and actors who looked the part. TV also required lighting and sound technicians, camera operators, makeup and wardrobe staffers, and set designers. It was a far more complex undertaking than a radio production.

In the early 1950s, TV was on the air just a few hours a day, often without enough programming to fill a broadcast day. To get more mileage (and more profit) from each show, sponsors began filming performances for repeat use. It made sense to have copies of programs and to expand broadcasting of prerecorded programming. Many advertisers continued to be loyal to radio, since they were unsure of television audiences, even though the audiences were growing rapidly. But as television found its footing, the loyalty to radio, for both the consumer and the advertiser, began to ebb.

TELEVISION'S GOLDEN AGE: 1952–1960

With the end of the FCC's freeze on station licensing in 1952, television's growth became explosive. By 1960, more than 500 stations were in operation, and more than 45 million homes (almost 90 percent of American households) had television sets. One result was a period of great creativity in every aspect of television, but especially in programming. By the end of the period there was something on television for every age group, and everyone seemed to be hooked.

In the mid-1950s, the DuMont network folded, leaving three commercial networks in place: NBC, CBS and the still-developing ABC. The three began competing in earnest, filling their programming schedules with Westerns, situation comedies, and quiz shows. Hollywood, skeptical about the new medium's durability but at the same time apprehensive that it might prove to be formidable competition for feature films, began producing programming for television.

Sponsored Programs

Television copied radio's economic model, continuing the policy of advertising support for programming, while giving it free to the consumer. TV broadcasters at first often sold entire programs to advertisers, as radio often had. Procter & Gamble, the giant manufacturer of household products, started its own TV production company in 1949. It introduced the "Fireside Theater" in 1951, a series of individual dramas designed to appeal to adults, particularly women who might buy Procter & Gamble products for their households. The dramas were a hit, and reruns were often broadcast.

Other corporations followed the successful format, such as the "Kraft Television Theater" and the "U.S. Steel Hour." It may be difficult for today's student to imagine a company such as Coca-Cola getting into the made-for-TV movie business now. But it made sense in the era of sponsored programming, when one company controlled all the advertising time connected with a single production.

Much criticism was leveled at sponsored programs, because they were seen by some to be simply extended commercials for a product. The networks ultimately wanted more control over programming, so they became producers and allowed advertisers to purchase participation in their programs. *Participation* involved buying advertising for a specific time slot instead of sponsoring an entire program. This also brought in revenue from companies unable to afford sole sponsorships. Advertiser participation is standard today; a few exclusively sponsored telecasts, such as the "Hallmark Hall of Fame," still appear, but they are a rarity.

Comedy and Variety

Entertainer Milton Berle made a successful transition from vaudeville, radio, and nightclubs to television with his "Texaco Star Theater," which had started on radio and debuted on television in 1949. The versatile Berle, puffing on a cigar and often dressed in drag, hosted a program of slapstick, acrobats, animal acts, and skits with celebrity guests. Berle fathered the modern variety show, a format successfully used by Jackie Gleason, Ed Sullivan, and Red Skelton through the late 1950s. Years later, Johnny Carson, Jay Leno, and David Letterman adapted the variety-show format for late-night television.

Soaps and Sitcoms

By 1955, viewers initially mesmerized by anything on television wanted more choices in programming. Advertisers looked for other ways to reach audiences and ensure their loyalty. The result was the series: programs in which the same characters appeared in each episode in a story line that was advanced with each telecast.

Daytime soap operas appeared, nicknamed, as we pointed out earlier, for the soap companies that were their original sponsors. The remarkably durable *soaps* are still a staple of television, captivating perhaps because of the way relationships are intertwined over a long period. They are morality plays whose characters and situations are black or white, good or evil. Series such as "As The World Turns" and "The Guiding Light" have been broadcast for 4 decades, drawing fans from multiple generations of family members worldwide.

Serial comedies were also developed, including perhaps the most successful and enduring television comedy series of all time, "I Love Lucy." It was launched in 1951 by its stars, Lucille Ball and Desi Arnaz. Arnaz pioneered many of television's early production innovations. He rejected NBC's suggestion that the show be shot in inexpensive kinescope format in favor of more costly filming of each episode. *Kinescopes* were motion pictures made of televised images; they were of poor quality and deteriorated quickly. Had Arnaz not insisted on film, "I Love Lucy" episodes would have vanished shortly after they were performed. Instead, they continue to be telecast in syndication long after the deaths of both stars and are still on the air on cable channels at the beginning of the twenty-first century.

Arnaz also insisted on studio space ample enough to accommodate a large studio audience so the cast could do the show in front of live audiences to heighten the energy of their performances. Arnaz was a production perfectionist. He had a special floor installed so that cameras could move smoothly across the set. He suspended lights from the ceiling instead of mounted on stands, permitting uniform lighting with no shadows or obstructions to the audience's view. The multi-talented couple made television history on and off the screen. They founded Desilu Productions, which went on to become an entertainment production powerhouse.

Children's Programs

Children's television genre took shape during this time with hits such as "Howdy Doody," a little-boy puppet in Western dress whose partner was real-life Buffalo Bob Smith, from Buffalo, N.Y. Howdy and Buffalo Bob, with Clarabelle the Clown, played to a live audience of boys and girls. "The Mickey Mouse Club" was a musical variety show. It mixed singing, dancing, and skits by the *Mousketeers*, young children and teens whose performances appeared between animated shorts starring Disney characters. Cartoons proliferated in the after-school and Saturday morning time slots.

News

Monday-through-Friday network newscasts were a staple of television almost from the outset, although they played a minor role. In 1949, "The Camel News Caravan" sponsored by Camel cigarettes, debuted on NBC, airing nightly at 7:45 P.M. It was narrated by John Cameron Swayze, who early on recognized the limitations of using the newsreel-narration format designed for movie theaters on television; he wanted news writing and filming designed especially for TV audiences. Camel's contract with NBC required that a Camel cigarette be burning in a prominently placed ashtray on Swayze's set. Competitor CBS also aired a 15-minute newscast, anchored by Douglas Edwards, at 7:30 P.M.

Television newscasts were short, usually 15 minutes, with a single narrator reading news items from the wire services, occasionally with some supporting film footage and interviews. Within a few years, newscasts evolved from this format to lengthier, more comprehensive reports of the day's headlines and then to the more complex formula of live and prerecorded stories reported from remote locations, accompanied by compelling visual images.

In 1956, the anchor team of Chet Huntley and David Brinkley replaced the Swayze program with "The Huntley–Brinkley Report." By 1960, this popular news duo was far out in front of CBS in newscast ratings. ABC was a distant third in news, still struggling to compete with the longer established networks. Competition in news became a hallmark of network television.

TV COMES OF AGE: 1960–1976

It is important to note that only three network stations and a few independent stations were on the air in any viewing area at this time. Cable television existed only as a service enhancing reception for households in mountainous or geographically remote areas where the over-the-air broadcast signal was poor. It was not yet distributing programming. Thus networks loomed large as a cultural influence.

Public Affairs Programming

As one of the responsibilities of broadcasting "in the public interest," licensees are required to devote some airtime to *public affairs programming*. This is a broadly defined category, generally including programs on civic, social, and political matters. After the quiz-show scandals of the 1950s, when it was discovered that a number of the shows were rigged, television came under increasing pressure to add more responsible public affairs programming. The time was right for news to expand, and the big events of the 1960s gave television an opportunity to grow.

Technology also helped news and public affairs programming offer more images to viewers in less time. The development of videotape in 1956 reduced the time involved in bringing prerecorded images to the air. Unlike film, videotape did not have to go through a developing process. One could shoot it, then show it. In 1962, the launch of satellites made timely live reports possible from distant locations.

TV as Political Power

Politics was a prime public affairs area, and its coverage made TV into a political power. Television coverage of national elections began in 1952, but the medium's political power wasn't widely apparent until 1960. In that year, the first televised debate between candidates for U.S. President occurred. John F. Kennedy, junior senator from Massachusetts, and Richard M. Nixon, vice president, met on stage in front of TV cameras to take questions from a panel and to respond to each other's comments in their campaign for the nation's highest office.

The debate marked the beginning of the ascendancy of the *telegenic* political leader. Kennedy seemed at ease with the format and television technology; Nixon seemed nervous. Kennedy used makeup, which Nixon refused. Kennedy looked cool and remained focused on the camera and the questioners. Nixon perspired heavily and glanced frequently around the set. He looked haggard and distracted. It is interesting to note that radio audiences thought Nixon had won the debate, whereas the television audience gave the edge to Kennedy. Many analysts credited the television debates with Kennedy's eventual ballot victory and in the process inferred that television had become a major force in American politics. From that day forward, television has been an essential tool of political victory, influence, and power.

TV News Becomes Influential

In the 1960s and 1970s, television news became a dominant force in America. This period saw the establishment of TV news at the local level and the expansion of the broadcast news schedule. News grew from 15 minutes of news briefs to a 30-minute program at the national network level.

No one symbolized the new influence of TV news better than CBS anchor Walter Cronkite. In September 1963, CBS replaced Douglas Edwards on the evening news with Cronkite, and expanded the newscast to 30 minutes. Cronkite was familiar to viewers, having reported from political conventions and hosted CBS documentary programs such as "You Are There" and "The Twentieth Century." He projected a middle-of-the-road objectivity that viewers warmed to. He was a calm, professional personality on the air, although not cool. He could weep, as he did announcing President Kennedy's assassination in 1963, and he could be speechless with amazement and delight, as he was when astronaut Neil Armstrong stepped from his spacecraft onto the moon's surface in 1969. He was called *avuncular*, the good uncle in whom everyone could believe, television news' human face, the man with whom millions connected.

In 1966, *Time* magazine put Cronkite on its cover, praising him as "the single most convincing and authoritative figure in TV news." Media writer Edwin Diamond (1991) wrote, "When the Kennedys [John and Robert] and King [Martin Luther Jr.] were killed, when the body bags came home from Vietnam, when the Chicago police rioted [at the 1968 Democratic convention], and when the astronauts got stuck in orbit, it was Cronkite who anchored the nation's emotions" (p. 41).

Development of local news paralleled the rise of network news. Community news, sports, weather, and light features were the formula then and remain the formula today. Strong local newscasts made money for their stations, because they were inexpensive to produce relative to the advertising revenue they could attract. A popular local newscast also provided a strong *lead-in* benefit to the network news that aired after it, meaning that a loyal local audience was likely to stay with that channel when the local newscasters handed off to national anchors. The one-two punch of local and national newscasts helped to develop the evening news-watching habit, establishing television as an important arbiter of community, national, and international matters—and leading to the demise of the evening newspaper.

TV Coverage of Social and Civic News

The years from 1960 to 1976 illustrated the theory that television content echoes rather than leads social change. Television's programming, except for news, did not give much emphasis to the 1960s protest movements seeking gender equality and racial justice. Only after attitude shifts were under way in the early 1970s did broadcasting's program content begin to reflect these concerns. However, those social movements were reported on the news. Domestic disquiet dominated not only Cronkite's reporting but that of other local and national anchors as well. Thus televison news became an increasingly important facilitator for helping Americans to sort out their emotions in those years of social turbulence.

As a nation, the United States was in turmoil over a war in Vietnam and civil unrest at home through the 1960s and into the 1970s. The nation was forced to confront years of discrimination against minorities, especially blacks, and women. An extremely unpopular war in Southeast Asia was extinguishing young lives, and young people were rioting in protest. President Nixon was elected to office in 1968, in the middle of the year of greatest civic unrest in America since the Civil War. And he was returned to office in 1972, only to be dogged by the Watergate scandal that eventually forced his resignation, the first for a U.S. President. These dramas were played out nightly as viewers watched television reports in anguish. The Vietnam War came to be known as *the living room war.*

Social Values in Entertainment Programming

While television news was maturing, television entertainment was undergoing dramatic changes as well. The darker themes of the 1960s and 1970s—racial and generational conflict, betrayal of trust by persons in authority, drug use, sexual experimentation—slowly found their way into prime-time programs. "All in the Family," through the interplay among bigoted but sometimes lovable Archie Bunker and his family, explored racism, sexism, morals, and values with a remarkable blend of humor and pathos.

"M*A*S*H," a series set in a U.S. combat surgical unit during the Korean War, performed a similar function for a TV audience bleary-eyed and depressed by the Vietnam War. Its characters—Hawkeye, Colonel Blake, Hot Lips, Klinger, and Radar—became fixtures in American culture.

Like Archie Bunker, they were cynical but not too cynical; they were eccentric but not crazy; they were basically good people, although they made mistakes, sometimes costly ones; they lived as best they could under the circumstances. The characters were not unlike the viewers watching them. That was the magic. Television provided a way for American audiences to view difficult, even painful, matters through a kaleidoscope that changed from sadness to laughter with the twists and turns of a series plot.

Programs in which family members helped each other learn life's lessons also were popular, perhaps reflecting the concern in the 1970s with the *generation gap.* Among the most successful programs was "Sanford and Son," a comedy whose story lines re-volved around the loving but contentious relationship between a black junk dealer and his son. "The Waltons" were a farm family in which three generations lived in harmony under one roof. Later, "The Cosby Show" attracted a loyal audience interested in a family in which both parents were working professionals (a physician and a lawyer) raising children who threw at them all the challenges so familiar to most parents watch-ing at home: teenage rebellion, adult struggle to instill values, keeping lines of commu-nication open when kids clam up.

Courtship of female audiences continued in daytime as well as prime time. The 1960s had produced the second wave of the women's movement, in which women pushed society to accept them in more roles. They asked for respect for what they ac-complished in the home as well as the opportunity to compete in the world outside. Television producers picked up on the new theme of *liberation* and worked it into sit-com and soap opera plots. The soap opera schedule expanded in the early 1970s to in-clude favorites such as "All My Children" and "The Young and the Restless." Prime time had "The Mary Tyler Moore Show" and other programs that showed independent women with careers. Later shows such as "Murphy Brown" and "Friends" continued to explore the life of the single, working woman.

Fantasy mixed with realism also had its place. Programs such as "Dallas" and "Dy-nasty," featuring the super-rich and the super-sneaky, become the soap operas of the night. Like their daytime counterparts, these series consisted of variations on the battle between good and evil. The plot lines seesawed between revenge and reconciliation. These were morality plays in which the good guys didn't always win, as they had in the 1950s in the Westerns popular at the time. "Dallas" and "Dynasty" reflected some of the disillusionment and conflict, as well as fascination, with sex and wealth that surged around Americans in the 1970s and 1980s.

NEW ALTERNATIVES EMERGE: 1976–1984

Between 1951 and 1976, television had been through a dizzying transformation. So had society. By 1976, one entire generation of American children had grown up with television as part of their lives. The three commercial networks set the tone for most of the news and entertainment experienced in the home. Inevitably, that changed. Talent and technology in the hands of people with new visions began to generate an assort-ment of viewing alternatives.

Over-the-air broadcast television in this period began to face serious competition from cable television, direct broadcast satellite, pay-per-view broadcasting, and vid-eocassette recorders that enabled audiences to *time-shift* their television watching by taping programs for later viewing. Broadcast TV audiences began to decline as view-ers spread their TV viewing across the broader range of options. Advertisers moved their spending around accordingly, dealing a financial blow to the broadcast networks which had monopolized television until the 1980s.

Cable Television

Television broadcasting first got into business by sending electronic signals over the airwaves to receiver sets. In some areas, reception was blocked or diminished by topography. When that occurred, antennas were erected on mountaintops or other high points, and homes were wired and connected to these towers to receive the broadcast signals. In this fashion, viewers in isolated locations were able to see over-the-air television through an intermediary. This was Community Antenna Television (CATV), which evolved into *cable TV.*

In the late 1950s, when cable operators began to take advantage of their ability to pick up broadcast signals from hundreds of miles away, the fledgling cable television industry realized that it need not only retransmit broadcast signals, but could in fact offer additional programming choices. Not surprisingly, the broadcast industry was alarmed at this potential competition. In response to broadcasters' concerns, the FCC placed restrictions on the ability of cable systems to import distant television signals and offer them as programming alternatives.

The restrictive policies on cable-delivered programming began to be relaxed in 1972. That year, the nation's first pay-TV network, Home Box Office (HBO), was launched. This venture led to the creation of a national satellite distribution system. HBO beamed its signal to a domestic satellite, which beamed HBO back down to backyard dishes. The next user of this delivery system was Atlanta, Ga., station WTBS. Broadcasting primarily sports and classic movies, WTBS became known as the first *superstation*, using satellite transmission to reach well beyond its metro-Atlanta market.

By 1998, cable had become the top source of programs that people watched on their TV. See Table 12.2.

CNN Redefines News

WTBS's owner, R. E. "Ted" Turner, did not stop with his superstation. He went on to found Cable News Network (CNN) in 1980, broadcasting news 24 hours a day. The three commercial networks, CBS, NBC, and ABC, previously had dominated national TV news. They mocked Turner's upstart network, calling it the "Chicken Noodle Network." It took Turner just 5 years before CNN turned its first profit, an achievement his network competitors had to admire, however grudgingly. Their news divisions had rarely proved to be profitable.

CNN's 24-hour format also made it better prepared to provide near-instant response to new events than the networks were. In January 1986, CNN was the lone TV newscaster broadcasting live from Cape Canaveral when the space shuttle Challenger exploded. On Friday, October 16, 1987, the Dow Jones Industrial Average plummeted. All weekend, investors fretted about what would happen Monday morning went the stock market reopened. CNN was live at the opening in New York as the market plunged even further, losing 22 percent of its value. CNN's business correspondents reported the story from nervous markets in Tokyo, Frankfurt, and London.

TABLE 12.2

Top Television Program Source, Winter 1998
(By Average Hours of Weekly Set Usage per U.S. TV Home)

Program Source	Hours	Share
Ad-Supported Basic Cable	19.27	31.4
ABC/CBS/NBC Programs	15.18	24.8
Barter Syndication	6.40	10.4
Independent Stations[1]	4.81	7.8
ABC/CBS/NBC Affiliates	4.77	7.8
Pay Cable	3.30	5.4
Fox, UPN, and WB Networks	2.72	4.4
VCR Play[2]	2.41	3.9
PBS Stations	1.76	2.9
Video Games	.72	1.2
TOTAL[3]	61.34	100.0

Source: *TV Dimensions '99*, published by Media Dynamics, Inc. www.MediaDynamics.com, (212) 683-7895. Used with permission.

[1]Locally produced and all-cash syndicated shows only.
[2]Rented or bought tapes only.
[3]Includes simultaneous set usage to more than one program source

CNN's reciprocal arrangements with TV stations and networks around the world enabled it to partner with journalists to provide swift, broad, deep coverage of news events. By the beginning of the twenty-first century, CNN was the most widely available source of daily news in the world, watched by heads of state, travelers in hotels and airports, and ordinary viewers at home.

Direct Broadcasting Satellite

Direct Broadcasting Satellite (DBS) represents a return to the backyard dish, but with some distinct differences. Dish owners of the 1980s had steerable dishes. Users turned the dish to scan the skies, pointing the dish at satellite after satellite in search of the programs being bounced off different satellites. The DBS dish is much smaller, and it is not steerable. It is pointed directly at one satellite that a program packager is using to transmit programming to a DBS subscriber. DBS technology is popular in communities that are not yet wired for cable or where wiring the community simply isn't practical. However, most DBS systems don't include access to local over-the-air stations or basic cable.

Videocassette Recorders

Videocassette recorders (VCRs) debuted in 1975, when Sony introduced its *Betamax* line. Competitors brought out the more economical *Video Home System* (VHS) version of VCRs, the version that dominates today's market. By 1996, VCRs were in 88 percent of U.S. households.

The expansion of television's offerings through cable, direct broadcast satellite, and VCRs has resulted in the growing democratization of television (Stark, 1997, p. 267). From 1980 to the mid-1990s, control of television viewing gradually shifted from the original three network broadcasters to viewers themselves. Viewers now have many more choices about what to watch and when to watch it. VCRs enable users to time-shift by recording television programs for later use and to augment their entertainment viewing by renting movies and other videos. They have effectively turned the television set into a movie projector, and have allowed television to be used as a reviewable resource, much as books are, with many homes acquiring a library of videotapes to be shown on demand.

Electronic news gathering (ENG) equipment was also developed to capitalize on videotape and satellite technology, allowing the use of hand-held cameras to videotape or transmit television pictures easily and inexpensively from almost any location on the globe. Once television crews began using it, the speed of television news delivery accelerated rapidly.

The Creation of Public Television

On September 29, 1948, when the FCC suspended the granting of licenses for TV stations, it had reserved no channels for educational, or public, stations. American educators organized the Joint Committee on Educational Television, through which they persuaded the FCC in 1951 to set aside 209 noncommercial educational channels whose signals would cover most of the nation.

Colleges and universities had decades of experience in radio broadcasting, with the earliest license having been granted beginning in 1922. Later, many of these stations were put on the FM band, but for decades, radios that could receive FM signals were manufactured at a much slower pace than those with AM capability. Educational stations on the AM band had been nudged off by commercial stations, or relegated to low-power frequencies. Their unfavorable dial positions and signal strength predicted that educational radio stations would be relatively marginal operations, with small audiences.

Educational broadcasters were determined not to repeat this unfortunate history with the new television medium. To avoid losing out on shares of the precious television broadcast spectrum, the educators mounted an aggressive effort to secure reserved spots, which succeeded. Funds from private foundations, especially the Ford Foundation, helped get the earliest educational television (ETV) stations on the air. The first was KUHT, Channel 8, in Houston, Tex., which went on the air May 25, 1953. Initially, the license was given jointly to the University of Houston and the Houston public schools and later was held exclusively by the university.

In 1967, the Public Broadcasting Act created the Corporation for Public Broadcasting (CPB), a nonprofit agency separate from the federal government whose purpose was to facilitate program production and distribution and to protect broadcasters from interference with, or control of, program content. From this point on, public television would be funded by a combination of government subsidies, foundation and corporate support, and later, viewer contributions. CPB established the Public Broadcasting Service in 1970 to coordinate program procurement and distribution for public television.

It wasn't until the mid-1970s, however, that public television began to be a forceful alternative to commercial telecasting. It made its reputation with public affairs documentaries, dramatic programming (much of it historical), and educational programming for children. These program categories typically drew small audiences, which is why commercial networks avoid doing them. But public broadcasting can supply an important, high-quality, often provocative stream of such programming. PBS was able to do this partly because it did not have to worry about offending advertisers or cable systems dependent on advertising revenues.

However, public television programs have occasionally offended members of Congress, and this can have repercussions. Congress can put pressure on public television by cutting the federal subsidy, forcing stations to become more dependent on viewer contributions and corporate sponsors. Because of these tensions, the independence of public television has been uncertain. It may succumb to advertising pressures, if it is forced to become dependent on corporate funds, as well as to political pressures. By the beginning of the twenty-first century, it was more dependent on corporate sponsorship, but most critics felt it remained a more enriching part of American culture than did most commercial television.

CRITICAL ISSUES INTENSIFY: 1984–1999

Television clearly became the single most dominant cultural element in American life in the last 2 decades of the twentieth century. As a result, crucial aspects of television were magnified and became a matter of national, perhaps even international, concern. Following were the key critical issues.

Deregulation

During the presidency of Ronald Reagan, government deregulation of industry was a key element of that administration's public policy initiatives, particularly in the field of broadcasting. Deregulation in the 1980s increased the number of stations one could own while restricting any single company or network to ownership of stations that reached no more than 25 percent of the total nation's households. Deregulation also relaxed the procedures for license renewal and completely removed the old Fairness Doctrine from the rule books.

In February 1996, after much political wrangling, Congress passed and President Clinton signed into law the Telecommunications Act of 1996. This was the first comprehensive rewriting of the Communications Act of 1934, changing the ground rules for competition and regulation in nearly all sectors of the communications industry. This new law further deregulated aspects of television. It increased television ownership limits to 35 percent of the nation's households, and allowed networks to own cable TV systems but prohibited them from acquiring other networks.

Those who advocated the changes argued that deregulation would encourage newer and more technologically sophisticated players to enter broadcast markets. They stressed that the new law helped free the market to develop new methods of delivery and that increasing competition would further accelerate the rate of growth in what was referred to as the *information superhighway*. Those who were opposed worried that deregulation would lead to further concentration of ownership in a few hands and that customers would ultimately pay higher rates for television services.

Deregulated Cable

Earlier, the 1984 Cable Act had effectively deregulated the cable television industry. Investment in cable distribution systems and in programming for cable then skyrocketed. From 1984 through 1992, the industry spent more than $15 billion wiring American homes and businesses to receive cable television and billions more in program production. Backyard satellite dish owners were able to pick up cable programming in areas too remote to be wired, but cable programmers quickly scrambled their signals so only paying subscribers could receive programming. Dish owners had to pay for descrambling codes for their equipment to be able to receive cable programming. In the 1980s, backyard dishes boosted cable's audiences, much as cable's forerunner, CATV, had expanded over-the-air broadcasters' audiences in the late 1940s.

As of 1997, more than 6 in 10 televison households (more than 64 million) subscribed to cable television, with many channels available. The average cable TV subscriber could choose from more than 40 channels, and 45 percent of all subscribers received 54 channels or more. By 1997, the number of national cable video networks had grown to 162. The 1996 Telecommunications Act further relaxed the rules governing cable systems and allowed the cable industry more freedom to set rates it charged subscribers.

Television News

A significant portion of TV viewing is of news, and it has become a very important part of our information system, but its critics have become more vocal. News has expanded at the local level, especially in late afternoon and early evening. Local news now consumes the 4 to 7 P.M. period in many markets, in addition to sunrise and midday reports. Network news has expanded into evening *news magazines* such as "20/20," "Dateline NBC," and "48 Hours."

In the 1980s and 1990s, the line between news and entertainment blurred, as television news adopted more entertainment traits in the race for viewers: News became less formal, faster paced, more titillating. Because of the compressed nature of television news, even though the who, what, when, where, and how are reported, the why of a story is often omitted. Thus Americans were obtaining news about the world they live in from the medium least able to provide detail and interpretation. More than half of those polled in a 1997 survey (54 percent) said they tune in more regularly to TV news than to any other source of news and information, and 53 percent said they trusted all or most of what local TV news anchors say.

Such dependency on television news is troubling, says critic Neil Postman. He feels that television news does not deliberately aim to deprive Americans of a coherent, contextual understanding of their world, but by packaging news as entertainment, the inevitable result is that "we are losing our sense of what it means to be informed" (Postman, 1985, p. 107).

Crime and Violence

Violent and criminal activity have become staples of much of television programming, perhaps because the small screen needs aggressive movement to attract viewers' attention. In drama, violence can be seen as cathartic entertainment. But in news, which is supposed to represent reality, the exaggeration of violence has important consequences.

Crime, violence, and tragedy have become staples of local newscasts, leading to the catchphrase, "If it bleeds, it leads." Stations routinely feature sensational stories at the start of their newscasts, after promoting the newscast in the hours preceding it: "A raging apartment fire kills five children in Fairfax County. Fire officials suspect arson. Details at 11." During the newscast, the anchors deliver the horrifying details, look solemn for a moment, and then swing into "happy talk" with one another. They address the camera earnestly in an attempt to establish contact with the home viewer. It is a curious mix of camaraderie and concern, all delivered somewhat breathlessly and with almost no context provided for the viewer.

The emphasis on crime is mirrored at the network level as well. Since 1990, 1 out of every 10 stories on the network evening news has dealt with crime, according to the Center for Media and Public Affairs. Even as the actual rate of serious violent crime has fallen, network news coverage of crime has soared. Homicides declined by 13 percent between 1990 and 1995. Yet on the ABC, NBC, and CBS evening newscasts for the same period, coverage of murders increased by 336 percent even after excluding the O. J. Simpson double-murder case.[1] See Table 12.3 for an indication of the extent of crime coverage on network news, 1990–1996.

Rocky Mountain Media Watch, a television monitoring organization, calculates the percentage of the news that deals with violent topics—crime, war, terrorism, and disaster—as the *Mayhem Index*. In 1997, the Mayhem Index for all 100 newscasts in its sample averaged 42.6 percent—almost half the news. The percentage of mayhem in local news items on newscasts is even higher, averaging 50 percent.[2]

Also featured heavily in the network evening news were stories about political and international conflict, many of which contained acts of violence and death. A good illustration of conflict-driven news is election coverage, in which political contests are most often depicted as horse races; the stories focus on which candidate has the edge on any given day, not what his or her positions are on campaign issues.

The result is that the tone of local and national news is more disturbing than ever. The world, as seen through the prism of TV news, seems to be deeply troubled and unable to find solutions to its problems. Its leaders seem to be competitive, not coopera-

TABLE 12.3

Top 10 News Topics, 1990–1996, Based on the ABC, CBS and NBC Evening Newscasts

Category	Number of Stories
Crime	9,391
Economy/business	6,673
Health issues	6,047
USSR/Russia	4,962
Persian Gulf War	4,867
Yugoslavia/Bosnia	3,780
Israel/Palestinians	2,674
Campaign 1992	2,427
Campaign 1996	1,865
Iraq	1,547
TOTAL STORIES	95,765

Source: Center for Media and Public Affairs, analysis of "ABC World News Tonight," "CBS Evening News" and "NBC Nightly News." Cited in *Media Monitor II* (see endnote 1). Used with permission.

tive. To some degree, the world may really be the way television depicts it. But to what degree? And to what extent do distortions of the world's difficulties foster attitudes of cynicism and hopelessness?

Cultural commentator Steven Stark (1997) contrasted 1997 newscasts with those of the 1960s, when news became established as an important feature of television. He wrote that in 1968, nearly half of all sound bites in stories lasted for 40 seconds or longer. In 1997, fewer than 1 percent did. He found that the pictures were far less sophisticated and more "instantaneous." News in 1968 revolved around words; in 1997, it was more theatrical (pp. 126–127).

Viewer Discontent

The sheer size of television's audience and the length of the average viewing day—now 6 hours, 57 minutes—indicates that television clearly pleases a lot of people. But there is deep dissatisfaction among viewers, too, even among loyal TV watchers. A 1997 Gallup Organization Survey conducted for *The Wall Street Journal* found 59 percent of those polled said television had changed for the worse over the preceding decade, with 30 percent saying the shows were improving. This was almost a perfect flip-flop of the results when the question was asked in 1965, when 50 percent said television was changing for the better and 23 percent said it was changing for the worse.[3] Table 12.4 indicates the type of programs most watched by American TV audiences.

In 1995, Washington Post television critic Tom Shales wrote that he believed the quality of television's first days was superior to television in 1995, because virtually all 1995 content dealt with crime and punishment or trauma of some kind. In the 1950s, he wrote, television was perhaps less controversial, less issue oriented, less volatile, but it was more universal in theme and appeal, trying to enhance American culture, enlightening the culture and improving the quality of life.[4]

One explanation for current viewer discontent is that the vastly expanded programming choices now available haven't made for better television. "It's getting more and more difficult to be unique," said Garth Ancier, former president of entertainment at Warner Brothers. "At some point, there's just a saturation of how many things you can make and still make them distinctive."[5]

Daytime talk shows in the late 1990s certainly tried to be unique, with the result that they became more and more outrageous, and in that respect, more alike, running completely counter to their intentions. The programs were orchestrated by a host who played the part of psychologist–counselor, drawing guests into explicit disclosures about their lives. Sex, family dysfunction, addictions, body image—these topics were explored over and over again, from every angle. The most extreme of the programs represented a kind of institutionalized voyeurism. During a taping of "Jenny Jones" in 1995, a guest was told he would meet a secret admirer on the show. He expected a woman, but his admirer turned out to be a young man. Furious, several days later the

TABLE 12.4

Top Television Program Genres, Winter 1998
(By Average Hours of Weekly Set Usage per U.S. TV Home)

Program Genre	Hours	Percentage
Feature films	9.99	16.3
Sitcoms	8.38	13.7
Newscasts	7.69	12.5
Drama series[1]	5.88	9.6
Talk/information	5.35	8.7
Children's	4.77	7.8
Sports	3.30	5.4
Serials	1.95	3.2
Varieties	1.79	2.9
Talk/variety	.89	1.5
Primetime newsmagazines	.77	1.3
Quiz/game	.75	1.2
Other newsmagazines	.55	.9
All others[2]	9.28	15.0
	61.34	100.0

Source: *TV Dimensions '99*, published by Media Dynamics, Inc. www.MediaDynamics.com, (212) 683-7895. Used with permission.
[1]Excluding daytime serials.
[2]Pay-per-view, local cable access, home shopping, etc., as well as one-shot specials of all types.

guest shot the "admirer," killing him. The manipulation of the guests that talk-show hosts practice led to tragedy in this case.

Daytime talk shows and early-evening reality-based programming exemplify the *tabloidization* of television programming. In an effort to halt the decline of network audiences, who had more viewing choices than ever, production houses developed ever-more sensational formats with which to titillate audiences. "Rescue 911," "Hard Copy," "America's Most Wanted," and others of this genre dramatized real-life events, using reenactments of crimes, fires, natural disasters, and scams. They tapped into a basic human response: fear.

Stereotyping

Stereotypical depictions in the late 1990s persisted on television, despite years of pleas by activists for more realistic portrayals, especially of women and minorities. But there has been some improvement. More female characters have been introduced on prime-time television since the early 1970s, and they have been given more versatile life experiences to portray. But women continued to be underrepresented (55 percent men to 45 percent women). Most characters were in the under-45 age group, and the few older-woman characters, those 65 or older, tended to be portrayed as dependent and ineffective. Their male counterparts, on the other hand, were portrayed as wise men and survivors.

In a 1997 study of gender roles on television shows, male characters were more likely to be shown on the job (41 percent) than female characters (28 percent). Men were also more likely to talk about work (52 percent) than women (40 percent). Women were more likely to talk about romantic relationships (63 percent) than men (49 percent).

Nevertheless, by the beginning of the twenty-first century, the prime-time schedule was beginning to mirror more of women's interests. Series built around a male adventure theme, featuring lawyers, physicians, cowboys, military men, and spies have been in gradual decline on ABC, CBS, and NBC. In their place have come programs such as "Dr. Quinn, Medicine Woman," "Grace Under Fire," and "Ally McBeal."

Television roles also expanded for minority characters. Programming in the 1990s saw minority characters become the central figures in prime-time shows. African American characters constitute the majority of TV's minority faces.

Children and Television

Perhaps the most crucial issue of all is the relationship between children and television. In a society in which both parents are likely to work outside the home, preschool children are apt to spend a good part of the day watching television, either at home with little supervision or in day-care centers where proper supervision may not be assured. Some studies show that some preschool children spend as many as 9 hours a day watching television. Most important, they are watching television in their formative years, a time in their lives when they are most impressionable and most vulnerable, when their values and morals and worldviews are being formed. In the past, these values came from parents, teachers, religious leaders, and books. Now they are apt to come from television.

Since television became widely available in the 1950s, there has been heated debate over how big a part of children's lives television should be. Different groups have contended that the issue is not how much the child watches but what the child watches; that the issue is not what the child watches but the act of watching itself; that adult-oriented content (complex dramas, explicit sexuality, conflict) is ubiquitous and children are being exposed to it before they are ready, in spite of parents' best efforts; that television has failed in its duty as a publicly licensed entity to provide more educational programming for children; that exposure to televised violence causes some children and teens to resort to violence; that high amounts of television viewing decreases children's verbal development and lowers their prospects for academic achievement.

For each of these theories, there are conflicting research studies and rebuttals by the television industry, whose representatives insist that television, when watched in reasonable amounts and with parental guidance, affords families an opportunity to broaden a child's world while entertaining the child. As highly charged as the debate about TV's influence on children continues to be, there are things we do know about children's involvement with this medium.

Most studies agree that there is a positive, though weak, relationship between exposure to television violence and aggressive behavior. Although television violence cannot be pinpointed as the sole factor causing aggressive tendencies and antisocial behavior, it is among the risk factors involved. Of considerable concern is the fact that consequences of violence all too often go unpunished in the fantasy world of television. For example, a 1996 analysis of 2,600 programs for 20 weeks of the 1994–1995 season found that violence occurred on 57 percent of the programs viewed. But perpetrators went unpunished in 73 percent of all violent scenes. Children's programs were least likely to show the long-term effects of violence, and they frequently mix violence with humor. This research concluded that when violence is presented without punishment, viewers are more likely to conclude that violence is a successful method for achieving one's goals.[6]

Parents are more concerned about television's influence on their children than they are about the influence of music lyrics, movies, video games, news, or magazines. Of all these media, 58.6 percent of parents in a study by the Annenberg Public Policy Center named television as the number 1 concern. Music lyrics was a distant second at 21 percent.[7]

Young viewers have acknowledged that television suggests behavior to them. Whether the idea of imitating television actually translates into action is another matter. However, a nationwide survey of 10- to 16-year-olds, conducted in 1995, found that one-third of young people often want to try things they see on television, and two-thirds said they believe their peers are influenced by what they see on TV. Nearly two-thirds—62 percent—said that sex on television (and in the movies) influences young people to become sexually active when they are too young. The survey also confirmed that young people frequently watch programs designed for an older viewership.[8]

It is extremely difficult to establish a cause-and-effect relationship between sexual actions in fictional TV programs and copying behavior by young viewers. "Nevertheless," said media scholar Jane Brown (1995), "the few existing studies consistently point to a relationship between exposure to sexual content and sexual beliefs, attitudes and behaviors. Ultimately, which comes first may not be the important question. Of greater significance is the cumulative effect of media saturated with the sounds, images and politics of sex" (p. 3).

REMEDIAL EFFORTS

Of course, much is being done to make television better. Many activist groups have formed to pressure the industry and the government for improvements. And the industry itself has taken steps to address criticism.

For example, in 1996 an Austin, Tex., television station decided to change course on sensational coverage. KVUE-TV's viewers had told the news department, via e-mail, telephone, letters, and community meetings that they were weary of sensational crime reporting. They said they had an exaggerated sense that they might become a victim of such crimes. They asked for more responsible, balanced reporting on crime. As a result, KVUE established new guidelines for its news in broadcasting a crime story. Stories that didn't meet at least one of these guidelines would not appear in newscasts:

- Is there an immediate threat to public safety?
- Is there a threat to children?
- Do viewers need to take action?
- Is there significant community impact?
- Is it a crime prevention effort?

KVUE's efforts received national and international attention. By bucking the trend, the station was rewarded with its highest ratings in a decade. But it remained largely alone in taking a systematic approach to crime reporting.

Children's television has also been the subject of much remedial activity. Milton Chen (1997), director of the Center for Education and Lifelong Learning at PBS station KQED in San Francisco, offered the following advice to TV audiences:

> Think of TV as a stranger in your house. Would you allow a stranger to entertain your kids by joking about sex, demonstrating gunplay and offering candy bars and salty snacks? Parents would never permit this stranger in the house. So be wary of letting the TV speak to your children in these ways day after day.

Chen doesn't suggest parents get rid of the television. He advises families how to live with television and get the most out of it. Among his suggestions: Understand that all TV is educational—kids are always learning from TV, so parents have to make sure the lessons are appropriate. Talk with kids about what they are watching. Be selective.

Don't just turn the TV on. Mix pure entertainment with more educational programming. Be prepared to talk with children about breaking bad news—plane crashes, murders, devastating events such as the Oklahoma City bombing.[9]

Chen and other children's advocates who want to see youngsters have a healthy connection to television have some government regulations on their side. Broadcast licensees are required to air at least 3 hours of *educational* children's programming weekly. It may not sound like much, and what educational programming consists of is largely up to the broadcaster's discretion, but the regulation does require television stations to make room on their schedule for an audience segment not able to speak up for itself.

The concerns raised by monitoring studies and parent and educator activists have resulted in two significant measures aimed at managing the viewing of violent content by youngsters: the V-chip and ratings of television content.

The V-Chip

The *V-chip* (for *violence*) was invented by a Canadian, Tim Collings. The Telecommunications Act of 1996 required television manufacturers to install V-chips in all television sets with screens larger than 13 inches. It is an electronic device that allows each TV program to be encoded with a rating. Parents can set their television V-chip at the most advanced rating they wish their children to experience. The V-chip blocks signals from any programs that exceed that rating.

Development of Program Content Ratings

The introduction of this technology also required development of a *ratings system*. Television executives at first were apprehensive about assigning content ratings about explicit sex, profanity, or violence to programming, believing advertisers would avoid buying time in programs that carried such warnings. But Congress made it clear it expected the industry to develop and implement the ratings systems on its own, suggesting that resistance would invite congressional action.

So the industry essentially came up with a ratings system that mimicked that of the Motion Picture Association of America: *TV-Y, TV-Y7, TV-G, TV-PG, TV-14,* and *TV-MA*. As the system was implemented, most programs were assigned TV-PG and TV-14 ratings, but viewers did not know what factors accounted for the difference in ratings. Parents' organizations, educators, and legislators protested vehemently, complaining that the vagueness of the system was designed to camouflage objectionable content. A revised system was implemented in September 1997, which added the letters S (sexual situations), V (violence), L (coarse language), D (suggestive dialogue), and FV (fantasy violence) to the original six ratings.

However, it is important to note that television news and on-air promotions for rated shows are not rated for the V-chip.

THE BUSINESS OF TELEVISION

Except for public broadcasting, American television is a profit-making industry more than a service operating in the public interest. Television is, first and foremost, a business that must make a profit to survive, and entertainment is the most profitable aspect of its business. It is important to be acquainted with the business operations of television to fully understand the influential role it plays in American culture and commerce. See Fig. 12.1, which shows the typical organization of a television station. Different broadcasting entities make their profits in somewhat different ways.

Television networks make money from selling airtime to advertisers. They sell airtime in the *upfront* market, during the summer, before the new fall program lineup debuts, and in the *scatter* market, after the shows are on and their performance in the ratings is better known. Typically, advertisers purchase the majority of available slots in the upfront market. Buying in the scatter market is a gamble; prices for commercial spots may be lower if a program performs below expectations, but they can be much higher if the show is a ratings winner. To secure what they expect to be the most desirable advertising slots in the most promising programs, the majority of national advertisers lock in their advertising slots for the season in the upfront market. If the audience

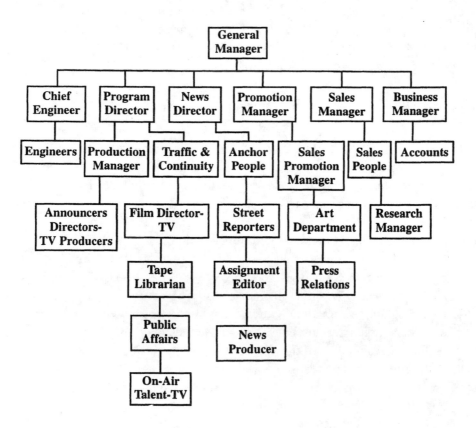

FIG. 12.1. Example of TV station organizational chart.

levels turn out to be below what the networks have predicted, the networks have to provide *make-goods* to advertisers who overpaid. Make-goods are free ads in shows with audiences comparable to what the advertiser paid for in the upfront market. See Table 12.5 for a list of U.S. broadcast networks.

Cable TV operators charge viewers for access to cable programming. The operators, in turn, pay a fee to cable program suppliers. For example, in Montgomery County, Md., Cable TV Montgomery charges its customers a monthly subscription fee. Cable TV Montgomery then pays CNN, HBO, MTV, and other programming providers a fee based on the number of subscribers signed up to receive programming from Cable TV Montgomery.

In addition to receiving a share of cable subscriber fees, cable programming providers also make money from selling commercial spots within their programs to advertisers. Program providers leave some space in their shows for national and local spots. Generally, a program provider, such as ESPN, will sell national advertisers time in its own program while leaving some space available for local advertisers. The local cable system sells time to local advertisers and places it on cable channels the advertiser has asked for.

Local broadcast television stations make money from selling advertising time. They sell time on the programs they originate, such as news, and they also are given a small amount of time in network-provided programs to sell to local advertisers (the networks sell the rest of the ad spots to national advertisers). They also receive compensation from networks with which they are affiliated. Paying individual stations to carry network programming makes it possible for the networks to assemble a large national audience and to charge high rates for airing commercials that reach this audience.

The individual station benefits because it can use programming provided by the network to secure its own audience. The station is also free to preempt network programs it doesn't wish to use and to substitute a syndicated show or a program produced by the station itself. With the substitutions, the station is able to control all the ad spots within the show and thus keep all the advertising income for itself. If a network program is doing poorly in the ratings, individual stations may find it more productive to substitute a show that will attract a larger audience and, therefore, provide more advertising income.

Television stations command high prices in today's market. Their value lies in their possession of a broadcast license and their ability to command an audience. The number 1-ranked station in a market will be worth more than the number 2, and so on. But even number 2 will be worth quite a lot. Stations trade for tens and even hundreds of millions of dollars. , the Warner Brothers network affiliate in San Francisco—and not the market leader —brought a bid of $174 million when Granite Broadcasting made an offer to buy it in 1997. West Palm Beach stations WPBF-TV and WTVX-TV were sold the same year, WPBF for $85 million (to the Hearst Corporation) and WTVX for $34 million (to Paramount Stations Group, Inc.). The size of the market, the station's ratings success, and its financial performance all influence the sale price.

Individual program ratings determine the amount of money that can be made from advertising on that program. Having a show that is a winner not only brings in advertising revenue for that program; it helps draw advertisers to the shows adjacent to

TABLE 12.5

U.S. Television Broadcast Networks (Alphabetical Listing)

ABC Television Network
CBS Television Network
Ethnic-American Broadcasting Company
Fox Broadcasting Company
Fox Children's Network
NBC Television Network
PAX NET
Telemundo
United Paramount Network
Univision Network
The WB (Warner Bros.)

Source: Standard Rate and Data Service *TV & Cable Source*, First Quarter, 1999. Reproduced with permission.

that program, and it confers status on the network that airs it and the stations that carry it. That reflected glory can be converted into higher asking prices for advertising on those programs.

"Seinfeld" was the first TV series to command more than $1 million a minute for advertising. It was estimated to cost NBC more than $120 million to bring it back for the 1997–1998 season, its ninth and last. "That's more than 10 percent of NBC's entire prime-time budget for 26 shows, but it's probably worth every penny, even before you start counting the $180 million or so the network will get from advertising alone," said *Business Week* magazine in 1997.[10]

"Seinfeld" was the rarest commodity in the entertainment business—a sure thing. The show's strategic importance to NBC reached far beyond the network's profit on the show. NBC had leveraged "Seinfeld" and its prime-time strength in such a way as to put considerable distance between it and other broadcast and cable networks. Indeed, by delivering the key demographics advertisers seek, NBC in 1997 was nearly seven times as profitable as ABC, the only other network to make a profit in 1996.[11]

Cable TV viewing, VCRs, and programming alternatives such as DBS have steadily eroded the three main broadcast networks' audience share. So have upstart broadcast networks such as Fox, UPN, and WB. The Big Three (ABC, CBS, and NBC) still deliver the largest audiences but no longer the only audiences. To continue to compete, they must be able to secure market share. Consider NBC's example: It has moved into cable with its CNBC and MSNBC channels and partial ownership of more than a dozen others, including Arts & Entertainment, Court TV, and American Movie Classics. NBC's diversification is a strategic business application of the old adage, "If you can't beat 'em, join em." To review the multiplicity of cable choices, see Table 12.6.

LOOKING AHEAD

Enhanced technology has pushed television capacity beyond what television's inventors probably ever envisioned. Since television began to reach a mass market in the 1950s, viewers have seen their channel choices move from two or three to dozens.

TABLE 12.6

Cable Network Distribution

Network	Household Universe (in Millions)
TBS	74.8
ESPN	74.1
Discovery	74.0
CNN	74.0
USA	73.8
TNT	73.6
Nickelodeon/Nick at Night	72.9
FAM	72.2
A&E	72.0
TNN	71.8
Lifetime	71.8
TWC	70.6
MTV	69.7
Headline News	68.9
CNBC	66.1
TLC	65.9
VH1	62.8
ESPN2	59.5
BET	54.2
Prevue	51.7
Cartoon	51.9
Comedy	51.9
E!	50.9
History	50.4
Sci-Fi	50.2
WGN	44.8
HGTV	43.4
CMT	42.0
MSNBC	42.4
Animal Planet	41.6
FX	36.0
Court TV	34.6
Food	33.6
Fox NC	33.0

continued on next page

TV Land	30.0
Odyssey	28.8
Golf Channel	19.1
Travel	18.4
Game Show	13.5
Knowledge TV	13.0
America's Health Network	8.5
Good TV	5.0

Source: *Cable Avails*, October 1998. Reproduced with permission of Intertec Publishing

High-definition television (HDTV), a digital technology that will eventually replace the current analog system by which television audio and video are transmitted, became available in 1998. HDTV can provide a television picture of exceptional quality and allow broadcasters to provide more than one program at a time, using the same channel capacity that has previously sent a single service to television sets. The conversion to HDTV requires a staggering investment in equipment for the broadcaster and homeowner. It is estimated that about three-quarters of all TV towers in the United States will have to be replaced and then disposed of. Viewers will have to buy new television sets and new VCRs. There will be a phase-in period during which analog and digital television will coexist. After that, the analog channels will be returned to the government.

The advent of HDTV and related applications will open up a new era in the evolution of television. There will be many more channels, but there may not be quality programming to fill them. How interactive they will be remains a question. Broadcasters and cable companies may not be able to deliver meaningful audiences to advertisers if viewership becomes more fragmented. Television could cease to be a mass medium. If that happens, what kind of medium will television be? Following are some possible answers:

Most analysts think television will be most successful if it raises, not lowers, content quality standards. For example, Austin, Tex., news viewers signaled their approval of KVUE-TV's careful consideration of crime reporting by making it the ratings winner in its market. Talk show host Rosie O'Donnell attracted large audiences by adhering to a witty and fun talk-show format rather than one lurid and exploitative. Viewers can reward good productions with their time and attention.

Interactivity is likely to become a more important feature of television. Innovations that increase the viewer's options will be popular. Interactivity is available through a touch-tone phone, through e-mail and the Internet on the home and office computer, and through cellular communications. Work to broaden the interactive capabilities of television is already underway and is likely to increase. For example, cable television operators are working to develop a new generation of cable boxes that would allow viewers to access the World Wide Web and watch digital video. These new cable boxes would also provide e-mail, electronic TV program guides, home shopping, download-able movies, interactive games, and online chat based on TV shows the user has watched. With this technology, interactive communication wouldn't be limited to the PC on the desk in the den or bedroom.

For the time being, however, television will continue as a mass medium. Even with declining viewership, broadcast television networks deliver an enormous audience to advertisers seeking national exposure, and cable and public television offer attractive advertising niches. Television viewing remains the number 1 at-home leisure activity. It is likely to keep this distinction for a long time to come.

Further Reading

Auletta, Ken. (1991). *Three Blind Mice: How the TV Networks Lost Their Way.* New York: Random House.

Blakely, Robert J. (1979). *To Serve the Public Interest: Educational Broadcasting in the United States.* Syracuse, NY: Syracuse University Press.

Bliss, Edward, Jr. (1991). *Now the News: The Story of Broadcast Journalism.* New York: Columbia University Press.

Brown, Jane D., and Steel, Jeanne R. (1995). *Sex and the Media.* Menlo Park, CA: Kaiser Family Foundation.

Diamond, Edwin. (1991). *The Changing Face of the News: 1985–1990.* Cambridge, MA: Massachusetts Institute of Technology Press.

Engelman, Ralph. (1997). *Public Radio and Television in America: A Political History.* Thousand Oaks, CA: Sage.

Federman, Joel. (1996). *Media Ratings: Design, Use and Consequences.* Studio City, CA: Mediascope.

Friendly, Fred W. (1967). *Due to Circumstances Beyond Our Control.* New York: Random House.

Jankowski, Gene F., and Fuchs, David C. (1995). *Television Today and Tomorrow.* New York: Oxford University Press.

Joyce, Ed. (1988). *Prime Times, Bad Times.* New York: Doubleday.

Klite, Paul, Bardwell, Robert A., and Slazman, Jason. (1997, February 26). Baaad News: Local TV News in America. *Rocky Mountain Media Watch.*

Koppel, Ted, with Gibson, Kyle. (1996). *Nightline: History in the Making and the Making of Television.* New York: Times Books/Random House.

Lowe, Carl. (Ed.). (1981). *Television and American Culture.* New York: H. W. Wilson.

McCrohan, Donna. (1990). *Prime Time, Our Time: America's Life and Times Through the Prism of Television.* Rocklin, CA: Prima Publishing & Communications.

Media Studies Journal. (Fall 1994). Children and the Media (special issue). New York: Freedom Forum Media Studies Center.

Moeller, Susan D. (1998). *Compassion Fatigue: How the Media Sell Disease, Famine, War and Death.* New York: Routledge.

Postman, Neil. (1985). *Amusing Ourselves to Death: Public Discourse in the Age of Show Business.* New York: Penguin Group.

Prisuta, Robert H. (1996). *Virtually Invisible: A Content Analysis of How Midlife and Older Women Are Portrayed in Prime Time TV.* Washington, DC: American Association of Retired Persons.

Stark, Steven D. (1997). *Glued to the Set: The 60 Television Shows and Events That Made Us Who We Are Today.* New York: The Free Press/Simon & Schuster.

Whittemore, Hank. (1990). *CNN, The Inside Story: How a Band of Mavericks Changed the Face of Television News.* Boston: Little, Brown.

Winn, Marie. (1985). *The Plug-In Drug: Television, Children and the Family.* New York: Viking Penguin.

Notes

[1] In 1990s TV News Turns to Violence and Show Biz. (July–August 1997). *Media Monitor 11.*

[2] Klite, Paul, Bardwell, Robert A., and Slazman, Jason. (1997, February 26). Baaad News: Local TV News in America. *Rocky Mountain Media Watch, 1*, p. 7.

[3] Pope, Kyle. (1997, June 27). Many Shows, Little to Watch: Viewers Pan the Lowbrow, Hanker for How-To Advice. *The Wall Street Journal*, p. R4.

[4] Shales, Tom. (1995, Nov. 5). Some Say That Network Television Has Never Been Better. They're Wrong. *The Washington Post*, p. G8.

[5] Pope, Kyle. p. R4.

[6] Robichaux, Mark. (1996, February 6). Television Shows Too Many Violent Acts That Go Unpunished, New Study Finds. *The Wall Street Journal* (article about the "National Television Violence Study" conducted by Mediascope, Inc., and researchers at the University of California, Santa Barbara; the University of North Carolina, Chapel Hill; the University of Texas, Austin; and the University of Wisconsin, Madison), p. B1.

[7] Television in the Home: The 1997 Survey of Parents and Children. (1997, June 9). National survey by Chilton Research Services, Inc., conducted for the Annenberg Public Policy Center of the University of Pennsylvania, p. 6.

[8] Stepp, Laura Sessions. (1995, February 27). Youth Say TV Shapes Values. *The Washington Post*, p. B1 (about survey conducted for Children Now, by Fairbank, Maslin, Maulin & Associates, Los Angeles, Calif.).

[9] Chen, Milton. (1997, March–April). Taming the Tube: 10 Tips for Parents. *Stanford*, p. 83.

[10] Lesley, Elizabeth, with Grover, Ronald, and Dugan, I. Jeanne. (1997, June 2). Seinfeld: The Economics of a TV Supershow and What it Means for NBC and the Industry. *Business Week*, p. 116.

[11] Ibid.

13

ADVERTISING

Most people think advertising does not affect them. We rarely pay attention to it, they say. "Our eyes glaze over when the commercials come on. In one ear, out the other." But that is not the whole story. As we saw in chapter 7 on effects of mass media, the content of media has become so pervasive that our minds absorb the messages without our even being aware of it. The communication has become our culture, our vocabulary, the fabric of our lives. And that includes advertising. Repeated many times in a variety of media, the calls to action of ads and slogans have acquired lives of their own, images and messages that are now nearly inseparable from our culture, our social exchanges, our dialogue, and our self-image.

> You deserve a break today
> So get up and get away
> To McDonald's.

That advertising jingle (used with permission from McDonald's Corporation) is probably remembered by more adults than the words to the "Star Spangled Banner" or "Jingle Bells." A survey in the mid-1990s, before Joe Camel was removed from tobacco industry ads, showed that more children could recognize him and knew what he stood for than could recognize the President of the United States or Mickey Mouse.

Think of the slogans that have become part of our mind-set. "Don't leave home without it." "Just do it." "It's the real thing." "Plop, plop, fizz, fizz, oh what a relief it is!" "The heartbeat of America." Most readers of this book will know automatically what products they sell.

Advertising images are the wallpaper of America. At the beginning of the twenty-first century, the average American adult is being exposed to about 3,000 advertising messages each day, or more than a million a year. We are surrounded and bombarded by messages trying to get us to buy or believe or do or feel something. Ads dominate the pages of newspapers and magazines and are beamed at us many times an hour by radio and television. They pop up when we surf the Net.

Even if we turn off television and radio, log off the Internet, and close our magazines and newspapers, we will still be exposed to advertising messages—on billboards, on the outsides and insides of buses and commuter trains, on walls and floors of sports arenas, at gasoline pumps, on elevators, in restroom stalls—everywhere we turn. Open the mailbox and out tumbles an avalanche of direct-mail advertising. Even individuals have become walking advertisements, with commercial messages on their T-shirts, sweatshirts, hats, and jackets.

Tennis star Andre Agassi, in a television commercial selling camera equipment, proclaimed the basic mantra of the age of mass media when he said, "Image is everything." Images are not only everything; they are everywhere.

ADVERTISING AND MASS MEDIA

Advertising is essential to many mass media, especially radio, television, newspapers, and magazines, the media that reach the largest audiences. Advertising is not a mass medium itself, given the way we've defined mass media in chapter 2. It is a separate industry that depends on mass media for most of its purposes, while most of mass media require it for their financial support. (See Table 13.1.) Advertising's reach has increased as mass media have proliferated. As mass media have become more sophisticated and ubiquitous, so has advertising.

TABLE 13.1

Influence of Advertising, Based on Percentage of Dependence on Advertising
Versus Percentage of Dependence on Consumer

	Advertising Support/ Dependence	Consumer Support/ Dependence
Broadcast television	100	0
Broadcast radio	100	0
Newspapers	80	20
Magazines	63	37
Cable/subscription video	18	82
Film	5	95
Internet	1[1]	99
Recorded music	0	100
Book publishing	0	100

[1]This figure is increasing rapidly.

ADVERTISING'S ORIGINS

Before Mass Media

Spoken advertising existed before the printing press, from Greek and Roman times through the Middle Ages, when literacy was limited to the elite few. As early as the first century B.C., *barkers* called out attributes of a merchant's wares, much as town criers and fleet-footed messengers announced the news in later centuries.

Barkers became more common as the centuries passed and settlements spread north into Europe, followed by the expansion of commerce and trade. Ad agencies had a rudimentary start in 1141 A.D., when 12 criers in Berry, France, organized a company and obtained a charter from the king giving them exclusive domain over town crying in the province. Five were assigned to *crying wines* for taverns. They went about the region praising the local vintage and offering samples. They used horns to get a crowd's attention before launching into their spiel. For their efforts, they received a fee from the taverns, most likely a few coins and a flask of wine.

Signs and symbols had long been in use to identify the specialty of a place of business. Taverns and inns were among the earliest establishments to use signboards. Merchants and craftsmen also used them to illustrate the principal products or services of their shops. Bottles, grapes, and food would be depicted, as would animals and angels. Many signboards were whimsical. Their variety showed how innkeepers attempted to differentiate their businesses from competitors.

Written announcements were used as well. Archeologists have confirmed that written advertising was in use as early as the first century. Excavations of Pompeii, buried in lava from Mount Vesuvius in 79 A.D., revealed advertising messages posted on walls, the earliest known examples of outdoor advertising. But few societies had enough literate inhabitants to make this a widely used advertising technique until many centuries later.

Handwritten announcements prepared by scribes and posted in public places came into use in England near the end of the 15th century. The printing press made multiple printings of these ads possible. By the seventeenth century, printed handbills, distributed on the streets, were popular with merchants eager to spread the word about their wares.

Early Newspaper Advertisements

The first newspaper advertisement published in the English language appeared in 1625 in a *newsbook*, a weekly digest of news. It heralded the publication of a book about the engagement of Charles, Prince of Wales, to Henrietta Maria, sister of the King of France. However, periodical advertising such as this remained sparse until the middle of that century, when more newspapers came to be published, and merchants began to realize their potential to reach an elite group of customers.

Advertising was common in American media from the very beginning. The first paid advertisement appeared in 1704 in *The Boston News-Letter*, the first regularly published periodical that succeeded in the colonies. The ad was for property on Long Island, available for sale or rent.

When Benjamin Franklin and a partner assumed control of the *Pennsylvania Gazette* in Philadelphia in 1728, they enthusiastically encouraged advertising. Franklin said it was good for the newspaper and good for local commerce. He paid close attention to an advertisement's ability to catch the reader's eye, introducing design standards, imaginative choice of typefaces, and graphic elements in ads, all innovations at the time and a modest beginning for newspaper display advertising in the United States.

In the nineteenth century, many events contributed to the increased use of newspapers to reach customers. The Industrial Revolution brought workers to the cities, developing a concentrated audience. The penny press brought newspapers to that market. Westward expansion spawned new communities hungry for goods and services. The Civil War increased the appetite for news, drove up newspaper circulations, and saw the introduction of newspapers on Sunday, which quickly became and still is the biggest day of the week for newspaper advertising.

Early Magazine Advertising

Advertisements appeared in colonial magazines from the very first, too. Some publishers shunned advertising at first, thinking it cheapened the content of their publications. Economic realities eventually forced them to reconsider. After the Civil War, with the steady increase in magazine titles and readers, the medium became attractive to advertisers seeking a national audience.

Magazines in the latter half of the nineteenth century increasingly offered a way to reach specialized as well as mass audiences. Newspaper ads usually announced goods and services to fill immediate needs of a general audience, but magazines began to offer an environment through which to sell *image* keyed to the character of the magazine's content, as well as *product*. In this way, magazines also began to change the nature of advertising.

TYPES OF ADVERTISING

Product Advertising

The most common advertisement in the United States sells commodities, both to consumers and to the trade. A *consumer ad* for a line of cosmetics might be placed in newspapers and consumer magazines and on radio and television to persuade individuals to buy that line of lipsticks and perfume. A *trade ad*, on the other hand, would be placed in retail trade periodicals to persuade stores to carry the cosmetics. For products to be successful, they must usually be advertised effectively to the trade first, then to the consumer, and then, as consumer acceptance builds, readvertised to the trade. See Table 13.2 for a list of the largest advertisers.

Promotional considerations are a subtle form of product advertising. For example, an airline that provides trips as prizes for a television game show receives a men-

TABLE 13.2

Top 25 Leading National Advertisers

1997 Rank	1996 Rank	Advertiser	Total U.S. Spending (Millions of Dollars)
1	2	General Motors Corp.	$ 3,087.4
2	1	Procter & Gamble Co.	2,743.2
3	3	Philip Morris Cos.	2,137.8
4	4	Chrysler Corp.	1,532.4
5	8	Ford Motor Co.	1,281.8
6	7	Sears, Roebuck & Co.	1,262.0
7	5	Walt Disney Co.	1,249.7
8	6	PepsiCo	1,244.7
9	12	Diageo	1,206.6
10	9	McDonald's	1,041.7
11	11	Time Warner	1,013.2
12	17	IBM Corp.	924.9
13	14	Johnson & Johnson	920.2
14	13	Unilever	908.9
15	16	J. C. Penney Co.	906.2
16	19	Bristol-Myers Squibb Co.	885.2
17	18	Toyota Motor Corp.	851.9
18	15	Tricon Global Restaurants	851.2
19	10	AT&T Corp.	781.1
20	23	Sony Corp.	777.5
21	28	Federated Department Stores	750.1
22	20	Viacom	744.8
23	25	Coca-Cola Co.	710.8
24	24	Dayton Hudson Corp.	685.8
25	32	L'Oreal	650.7

Source: *Advertising Age's Agency Report*, Sept. 28, 1998. Reproduced with permission.

tion on that program—a free ad, as it were. The station announces that it has received promotional consideration (the airline tickets) in return for that mention.

Not as straightforward, however, are the promotional considerations that are not announced as such. Some companies pay to have their products featured in motion pictures or TV shows, but the viewer does not know the movie or TV program has been paid to give public exposure to that product. If a scene takes place in a restaurant or kitchen, a beverage company might pay to have its product featured exclusively. When the handsome hero picks up his soft drink, the company that paid to put it there is receiving an advertisement, but the public is usually unaware that it has been exposed to a paid-for ad.

Cause-related ads combine product promotion with support for a charitable cause. An example is an annual campaign by credit card companies during the Thanksgiving-to-Christmas season. The company advertises that it will donate money to a charitable organization each time a customer uses the credit card during the season. Customers increase their use of the credit card to support a good cause, the charity gets support, and the company not only increases its revenue but also reaps good will and probably some tax benefits.

Institutional Advertising

Institutional advertising helps build reputations and differentiates an organization from its competitors. For example, a military aircraft manufacturer might announce that it has won a government contract to build a new generation of fighter jets. The ad copy would likely extol the company's role in protecting the nation rather than the specifications of the planes to be built.

Institutional ads often promote a company's social responsibility. In 1997, General Motors (GM) took out an ad in national publications to announce that it had received *Self* magazine's Pink Ribbon award for its contribution to the fight against breast cancer. The ad did not necessarily sell cars but, it suggested that GM cares about women. This not only enhanced GM's reputation as a socially responsible corporation; it was also good business strategy since women influence most car-purchasing decisions in U.S. households.

Institutional advertising is sometimes used to offset bad news as well. Companies that find themselves the subject of negative publicity often develop ad campaigns to take their messages directly to readers, viewers, and listeners, bypassing journalists who write the news that creates the negative public opinion in the first place. AT&T, roundly criticized in 1995 for announcing tens of thousands of layoffs, took out ads in national publications to explain why the firings were necessary, to announce the formation of a job bank, and to invite other organizations to consider hiring the talented AT&T employees who were going to lose their jobs.

When Nike was criticized by editorial writers, labor activists, and "Doonesbury" creator Garry Trudeau for using foreign contractors who exploited workers, the company used institutional ads to counteract the criticism. In their ad copy, Nike accepted the rebukes and vowed to make amends. The ads said that "Nike is doing a good job ... but can and should do better."

Advocacy Advertising

Advocacy advertisements set forth a point of view. Issues such as health care reform, global warming, international trade tariffs, underage smoking and drinking, and, of course, political agendas are debated in print advertisements and broadcast commercials.

These ads are used by a variety of special-interest groups, including trade associations, membership organizations, political parties, and political activist groups. Sometimes single-issue organizations are formed to rally support for one specific item of legislation or policy. Advocacy ads usually appear in mainstream media, and their placement tends to correlate with the presence of key policymakers, especially legislators. *The Washington Post*, for example, is often used for such ads, because so many legislators and policymakers work in the national capital. *The New York Times* and *Wall Street Journal* are often used, as well, because they are supposed to have an elite and influential readership.

Advocacy ads usually depict a serious problem and the consequences if corrective action isn't taken. Here is an example of an ad that ran in 1994 as Congress debated the pros and cons of national health insurance. It was sponsored by the American Association of Retired Persons (used with permission):

On the Screen: The ad opens with a black screen with the words "One Family's Story," then shows a kitchen scene where a husband and wife are sitting at a table with an older woman while a teen-ager walks in the background.

Husband: I've been trying to get a better job for years, but I have a heart condition. Other companies' health plans won't touch me.

Wife: Well, yeah, I feel lucky, in a way. Compared to Phil and Amy. He's been laid off for seven months now. She's pregnant. They don't have any insurance.

Words appear on screen: Every Family Is At Risk.

Announcer: This is so messed up. Every family is at risk of losing health benefits. Tell your members of Congress, keep universal coverage in health care reform. Our families need it.

Political Advertising

Political ads have become the single most powerful method of political persuasion in America. In fact, in the 1996 and 1998 election campaigns, candidates engaged in fewer debates and gave fewer interviews to journalists, using advertising instead, particularly on television, to make the case for their election. More news stories were written about the content of the ads than about the speeches and interviews of the candidates.

Political advertising has changed the nature of politics and elections, because advertising costs money, and effective advertising often requires extensive research, enormous creative effort, and expensive production. Television is especially costly and yet has become indispensable to winning an election campaign. Thus in America at the beginning of the new millennium, to be successful in politics one has to be very wealthy or have the backing of wealthy interests or the ability to raise a lot of money.

In the heat of political battle, where there can be only one winner, political advertising tends to concern itself less with issues and more with the credibility, judgment, and character of the candidates. Political advertising is perhaps the most personal of all advocacy advertising. Most political ads have become negative, no doubt because research has shown that negative ads are better remembered than positive ones. Negative advertising has come to characterize political campaigns.

A classic example is the 1988 presidential campaign between Vice President George Bush and Massachusetts Governor Michael Dukakis, which produced one of the most notorious ads in presidential campaign history. Since Americans were increasingly worried about rising crime and diminished personal safety, Bush strategists set out to show that Dukakis was a northern liberal soft on crime.

They created an ad showing an African American man in a mug shot. A voiceover revealed that the man, a convicted murderer, had committed rape while he was out of prison under a furlough program operated by the state of Massachusetts. A head shot of Dukakis was pictured, then the convict again, with the pictures continuing to flip-flop as the announcer asked if being soft on crime was what Americans wanted during the next presidency. Most experts felt the ad pandered to racial prejudices and seriously damaged the Dukakis candidacy. It was regarded then as a low point in negative advertising, but the level went down even further in subsequent elections in the 1990s.

If the Bush ad represents one end of the political advertising spectrum, Ronald Reagan's "Morning in America" campaign ads represent the opposite. Reagan's ads were as upbeat, sentimental, unabashedly optimistic, and patriotic as the candidate himself. Against wholesome images of good neighbors, healthy, happy children at play, and fluttering flags, the narration urged voters to look with pride on their future. "It's morning in America" was designed to make people feel good about Reagan, not to help them understand his policies.

Both types, typical of the genre, attempt to influence voters by appealing to their emotions rather than their intellectual grasp of ideas, party platforms, or campaign issues, promoting electioneering that is driven by personality rather than policies or ideas.

Public Service Advertising

Public service announcements (PSAs) are produced in the public interest by businesses, ad agencies, and mass media, usually donating their time and talents to help a worthy charitable organization, a nonprofit institution, or a government agency pushing a good cause. The mass media generally publish or air these ads free of charge.

PSAs exist mainly because the original mandate for broadcasting required radio and television to operate in the public interest, since they use public property, the airwaves. The law specified that they were supposed to devote some of their airtime to public service. The free ad for a good cause is one of the results, and other media have followed suit to a lesser extent. It should be pointed out, however, that PSAs are likely to be relegated to the back of a magazine or to a broadcast slot where the audience is small. PSAs are usually used only when media have unsold advertising time or space. Radio and television stations usually air them late at night or on Sunday morning.

The Advertising Council was organized by the ad industry to help coordinate, produce, and place PSAs. The council receives proposals for its services and accepts a few each year for its campaigns. It gets leading creative talents from ad agencies to donate their time in producing the ads, which it then sends in a variety of forms to mass media, with the request that they be used without charge.

The Ad Council has produced campaigns for the U.S. Social Security Administration, the Urban League, and the United Negro College Fund, to name a few. It has developed advertising for child abuse prevention, crime prevention, gender equity in education, seatbelt use, high blood pressure prevention, infant immunization, and many more. Among its many famous creations was Smokey the Bear, whose admonition became part of the culture and probably saved a lot of trees and lives: "Only YOU can prevent forest fires."

ADVERTISING TECHNIQUES

Market Research

Advertisers have increasingly turned to the social sciences to help make their messages more effective, an effort that started seriously in the 1920s and 1930s. They turned to psychology, including the work of Sigmund Freud, to help them learn what would motivate people to buy or believe or accept an advertising proposition. To persuade their audiences, they sought to understand people's conscious and subconscious feelings, sensations, and attitudes.

Increasingly they turned to sociological research in their work in the late 1940s and early 1950s, using survey research techniques to define the demographics of their markets and to devise strategies to target their messages to different demographic groupings. They used focus-group research to probe more deeply into attitudes and feelings. For example, they would probe a focus group of homemakers for their reactions to cake-baking, and the results would help the advertiser decide the best arguments to sell cake mix, to devise more sophisticated appeals to consumers, and even to design the package, so it would have the strongest appeal on the grocery store shelf.

More sophisticated research tools that produce information useful in shaping advertising messages include *psychographics* and *geodemographics*. The pioneering psychographic methodology known as *VALS* (values and lifestyles) was developed during the 1960s and 1970s. It assumes that consumer choices are influenced by values and lifestyles and that identifying a consumer's VALS profile can help companies develop the most effective advertising. VALS research established eight types of consumers: *actualizers, achievers, believers, makers, fulfilleds, experiencers, strivers*, and *strugglers*. Each type requires a different approach for the message to be effective.

A variant of this type of consumer analysis is geodemographics, which interprets the consumer in terms of age, education, household income, residential location, and known buying behavior. By merging this data, researchers can break communities down into population segments from which probable consumer purchasing decisions can be predicted. This, too, enables advertisers to anticipate marketing opportunities for their products.

Emotional Appeals

Modern American advertising is also based on the work of economists who have demonstrated that mass production has created supply far greater than demand. Rational arguments are not very effective in getting people to buy products pouring off the assembly lines if they really don't need them. American advertising has turned to emotional appeals instead.

Vance Packard (1965) was one of the first analysts who produced a popular book describing how advertising was trying to persuade Americans. His classic work, *The Hidden Persuaders*, described the eight hidden or emotional needs marketers had identified: *emotional security, reassurance of worth, ego gratification, creative outlets, love and tenderness, a sense of power, a sense of roots*, and *immortality*. Packard showed how advertising was created to assure that their products—ranging from beauty cream to garden tools, from tricycles to automobiles, from ice cream to life insurance—would help fulfill those needs.

Packard and other analysts have also suggested that American culture is largely based on the notion of upward mobility, that getting richer and smarter and thinner and younger is essential to our well-being. Advertising has turned to emotional appeals to stimulate buying behavior so consumers can demonstrate that they are living the American dream. The product in the advertisement or commercial is positioned to assist the consumer realize the American dream, whether the consumer actually needs it or not.

Differentiating Consumer Appeals

Developing the creative aspect of advertising—theme, visual design, and message—is a marriage of science and art. Ad copywriters first review the scientific research on the product or cause, the target consumer, and the environment in which the product or cause is to be positioned. They then decide on the best method and medium to ensure the ad's effectiveness with the target audience. By using research results on the one hand, and instincts and experience on the other, the ad copywriter's message can be developed and then fleshed out visually. Some standard categories of advertising appeals have been accepted by the industry.

- **Superior efficacy** claims that the product performs better than its competitors ("our pickup truck outperforms all the others") whereas **superior value** addresses cost considerations ("our motor oil costs less per mile").
- **Product enhancement** plays to loyalty of current customers while touting the product's improved potency to prospective customers ("our new flavor is tastier and less filling").
- **Market domination** confers special status on the product ("more people use our toothpaste than any other").
- **Celebrity endorsement** assumes that the celebrity's popularity and other positive personal qualities will be transferred to the product ("Sammy Sosa eats our burgers").
- **Social success** suggests that fulfilling social outcomes depicted in ads will occur when the product in the ad is purchased or consumed ("the guy who's got our convertible/beverage/apparel is going to get the girl").

The Unique Selling Proposition

Before any of these appeals to the consumer can be chosen, the advertiser needs to have a *unique selling proposition*. The concept, developed by advertising pioneer Rosser

Reeves, was described by Martin Mayer (1991) in *Whatever Happened to Madison Avenue?* Reeves came up with it after a client came into his office with two half-dollars, threw them on Reeves' desk and said, "Mine is the one on the left. You prove it's better" (p. 223). Reeves took this as a challenge to find some attribute of a client's product, or something about its manufacturing process, that was not being advertised by anyone else and that was of some value to consumers.

The power of the unique selling proposition lies in its ability to help differentiate a product from its competition and to solidify its power as a brand. The various types of appeals listed previously all help to support a unique selling proposition.

Advertisers generally agree that as product choices have expanded, consumers have become more sophisticated about their purchasing decisions. They remain interested in a product's unique selling proposition, but they also respond favorably to ads that take into account consumers' needs and desires and acknowledge their discriminating tastes.

Contemporary advertising thus frequently depicts an item as a resource for the consumer's lifestyle, not just a good product. This subtle shift can be attributed to the relative affluence of the American consumer and the expectations of those living in a society of consumption. Images and messages that portray consumption as an essential component of self-fulfillment have become embedded in our culture. Barton White (1993) called them "images that stay with us longer than even the names of friends and relatives, images that are indelible and are stored in our long-term memory as a permanent part of our knowledge base" (p. 34). Advertising appeals have permanently linked the consumption of products with our sense of well-being.

ADVERTISING'S PLACE AND ROLE IN DIFFERENT MEDIA

As we showed earlier in the book, each medium has its own language and encodes reality in its own way. Advertisers must understand those differences, sometimes subtle ones, in order to maximize the effectiveness of a persuasive message.

Almost from the start, advertisements in newspapers differed from those in magazines. Even before scientific analysis, advertisers instinctively understood some of these differences. Newspapers which carried fresh news bulletins and business and sports reports were compatible with ads that offered ready solutions to practical, day-to-day concerns. Weekly or monthly magazines, characterized more by literary content and lifestyle matters, were better for ads that spoke more to the reader's personal development and aspirations.

This differentiation was echoed in broadcast media. Radio advertising tends to offer information listeners can act on right away. Television advertising works more on a viewer's attitudes and desires and interprets those to define the viewer in relationship to the image projected by the commercial. Different criteria determine the appropriate medium.

The audience of the medium must include the customers the advertiser wants to reach. Media decisions are based not only on research about the product, but also on its likely users and the media's ability to reach those users.

The cost-effectiveness of the medium can be a crucial concern. A medium that reaches the largest audience may not be the most cost-effective. Advertising costs are measured by *cost per thousand*, or CPM, a figure that shows how much an advertiser has to spend to reach 1,000 users of each medium. CPM enables advertisers to compare the cost of running an ad in a newspaper against running an ad on a local television station, or in a magazine, or any other medium. Table 13.3 shows the financial support of advertising to various mediums.

Newspapers

Until the mid-1990s, newspapers traditionally attracted the largest share of advertising dollars spent in the United States. That changed in 1996 when television edged newspapers as the number 1 medium for advertising expenditures. Television advertising had been gaining steadily for nearly a decade, reflecting gradual declines in newspaper circulation.

However, newspapers remain the principal medium for local advertising in all markets, regardless of size. *Zoned newspapers*, in which sections or parts of sections are dedicated to news of a single community and delivered only in that community, have made targeted newspaper advertising more precise and affordable by reducing the CPM.

Newspapers carry three kinds of advertising: classified, retail, and national. Revenues from advertising constitute the largest single stream of income for daily newspapers, exceeding that of circulation revenues. Newspapers get about four-fifths of their income from ads and devote about two-thirds of their pages to them. Table 13.3 shows the financial support of advertising for various media.

TABLE 13.3

Advertising Revenue by Type of Medium

Medium	1997 (Millions)	Percentage of Total
Daily newspapers	$41,341	22.1
Broadcast television	37,145	19.9
Direct mail	36,925	19.8
Radio	13,180	7.1
Yellow pages	11,470	6.1
Magazines	9,975	5.3
Cable television	5,275	2.8
Miscellaneous*	31,575	16.9
Total/national	110,432	59.1
Total/local	76,454	40.9
TOTAL/ALL MEDIA	186,886	100.0

Source: Newspaper Association of America, McCann-Erickson, Inc., in NAA's "Facts About Newspapers 1998," p. 9. Reproduced with permission.

*Includes weeklies, shoppers, pennysavers, bus, and cinema advertising. Estimates include all costs: time and talent, space and production.

Magazines

Most magazines no longer offer a general national audience to advertisers. From *Country Living* to *Road and Track* to *The New Yorker*, most magazines offer a special demographic slice of readers to advertisers seeking only those types of readers. Even nationally distributed magazines can have zoned editions that allow local advertisers to use that magazine to reach a local audience, again greatly reducing the CPM. Today's magazine readers tend to have above-average incomes, are better educated, more sophisticated, and likely to read periodicals that address their special interests.

Advertising revenues make up more than half of total magazine revenues, with the rest coming from subscriptions and newsstand sales. In terms of the makeup of the magazine, advertising represents about 45 percent of magazine pages, with the rest devoted to editorial content. Some magazines, of course, carry no advertising and get all their support from subscribers, whereas others offer their publications free to customers and get all their support from advertising.

Radio

Advertising on radio is somewhat similar to magazines. Readers select magazines because of their editorial content, whereas listeners choose radio stations because of their programming. Both media have what is called *audience franchises*.

An advertiser can buy radio time in four ways: *local radio; national spot*, national advertising placed on a market-by-market basis; *wired network*, formal networks, such as ABC's and CBS's; and *unwired network,* custom groupings of unaffiliated stations for the purpose of promoting a specific ad campaign. Radio stations make the most money from local and national spot advertising.

In radio's early days, performers such as Jack Benny, George Burns, and Gracie Allen personally promoted their sponsor's products as part of their nationally broadcast programs. Talent on locally broadcast programs did the same. Prerecorded radio commercials started in the late 1930s, when announcers began playing records over the air and ad time began to be sold between musical selections.

Television

Television's popularity as an entertainment medium has made it a natural partner for commercial messages. Television time can be purchased as *network, spot, local*, and *national syndication.*

Advertising has become a growing part of the broadcast hour: On the Big Four networks (ABC, CBS, NBC, and Fox), the number of minutes per hour that TV devotes to commercials, promotions for other programs, credits, and other nonprogram content accounted for a significant portion of what viewers saw. For example, during prime time on the Big Four, nonprogram minutes rose from 12 minutes and 26 seconds per hour in November 1989 to 15 minutes and 22 seconds in November 1997.

Local broadcast stations and, to a lesser extent, local cable stations, generate millions of dollars through sales of airtime during program hours they produce themselves.

Cable Television

Cable has also come into its own as an advertising medium, offering advertisers lower prices because of its smaller audiences and thus making at least some television exposure affordable to advertisers who can't afford broadcast network rates. Cable channels with the larger audiences, such as ESPN, get most of cable's national advertising revenue.

Cable TV, videocassettes, and the Internet have given consumers many more choices, and this has reduced the number of broadcast television viewers. Still, broadcast television remains the only way a national advertiser can reach a national audience quickly. Costs range from network broadcasting at the high end, to spot buys on groups of local stations in the medium range, to cable or low-power TV on the lower end.

Out-of-Home Advertising

This category is also called *outdoor advertising*, but *out-of-home* better describes the variety of nontraditional media now used for advertising messages. Out-of-home advertising communicates to an audience that is on the go, usually in transit. An industry that was 90 percent billboards in 1970 now encompasses advertising venues such as bus shelters, transit (exteriors of buses and lighted panels on subway platforms) kiosks, indoor settings such as airports and malls, and street furniture such as newsstands or benches.

By its very nature, the larger-than-life out-of-home medium attracts advertising that is big and bold. The top categories have been entertainment and amusements; tobacco, not carried on television and radio since 1971; and retail. The industry has sought replacements for tobacco advertising dollars because of government initiatives to further restrict advertising of tobacco products. Much of the new growth has found its way to the bus shelter, which allows public transit systems to protect their patrons from the weather and at the same time gives advertisers unusual access to college students and young urban workers.

The out-of-home industry has faced pressure from environmentalists and beautification advocates who dislike what they regard as roadside clutter presented by billboards. The 1965 Highway Beautification Act created a procedure for removing billboards from scenic roadsides and restricting them to commercial and industrial areas. The act requires that billboard owners be compensated for the removal of their property.

Direct Marketing

As everyone who has received unwanted telephone solicitations and opened mail boxes full of junk knows, advertisers have increasingly sought to narrow the target of their prospective customers through direct marketing. Computer databases have helped identify consumers most likely to become customers, and many direct-marketing techniques have been designed to reach and woo them. They include *direct mail, telephone marketing, catalogs, online marketing, and direct-response ads* in newspapers, magazines, television, and radio. In 1997, telephone marketing constituted the largest category of direct marketing media spending, followed by direct mail and direct-response television.

Online Advertising

The newest advertising medium is the World Wide Web. As the popularity of Internet access began to grow, there was some initial resistance to the idea of turning what had been a free network into a commercial medium with advertising. But by the mid-1990s, as consumers increasingly paid monthly fees for Internet access and e-mail services, and as they began to participate in online commerce, advertisers began venturing onto the Internet in search of these customers. Online service providers such as America Online and search engines such as Yahoo!, InfoSeek, and Excite have realized a promising revenue stream from companies placing advertising with them.

It is still difficult to measure the audience and evaluate the effectiveness of online ads. The solution should become clearer as more households acquire computers and interactive capability, and online services better document their users' exposure to ads.

THE BUSINESS OF ADVERTISING

Four key players participate in the advertising process: *advertiser, advertising agency, media* chosen to carry the advertiser's message, and the *consumer* who is the target of the advertising message. Some advertisers prefer to bypass the agency and develop their advertising campaigns *in-house*. But by and large, most national advertisers employ agencies to create ad campaigns and place advertising in different media.

Role of the Advertising Agency

The shift from hand production to mass production in the Industrial Revolution of the nineteenth century made a new type of media specialist necessary, the *advertising agent*. The first advertising agents bought newspaper space, marked up the price they paid for it, resold it to advertisers, and kept the difference as their commission. Agents then began designing and writing ad copy for their customers. Today, agencies typically receive a 15 percent commission for these services, and agencies have grown enormous and powerful worldwide. See Table 13.4 for a list of the largest agencies.

Advertising agencies vary tremendously in size, from shops of half a dozen to those with hundreds of employees. The largest agencies have offices in multiple locations, the better to serve key clients in those locations. All agencies, regardless of size, staff the following functions. *Account executives* are responsible for managing existing client relationships and bringing in new business. *Media buyers* choose the media best suited to delivering the desired audience for a product, and purchase the time (on radio and television) or the space (in print media) needed to give an ad campaign proper exposure. The *creative department* is made up of artists, graphics designers, and copy writers who give an ad campaign its identity. A *research department* analyzes audiences and studies the impact of advertising messages. *Operations staffers* manage the agency's billing, payroll, overhead, and other administrative matters.

TABLE 13.4

Top 25 Global Ad Organizations, Ranked by Gross Income

1997 Rank	1996 Rank	Ad Organization	Headquarters
1	1	Omnicom Group	New York
2	2	WPP Group	London
3	3	Interpublic Group of Cos.	New York
4	4	Dentsu	Tokyo
5	5	Young & Rubicam	New York
6	7	True North Communications	Chicago
7	6	Grey Advertising	New York
8	8	Havas Advertising	Paris
9	10	Leo Burnett Co.	Chicago
10	9	Hakuhodo	Tokyo
11	11	MacManus Group	New York
12	13	Saatchi & Saatchi	London
13	12	Publicis Communication	Paris
14	14	Cordiant Communications Group	London
15	17	Carlson Marketing Group	Minneapolis
16	18	TMP Worldwide	New York
17	15	Asatsu	Tokyo
18	19	Tokyu Agency	Tokyo
19	16	Daiko Advertising	Tokyo
20	23	Abbott Mead Vickers	London
21	21	Dai-Ichi Kikaku Co.	Tokyo
22	20	Dentsu, Young & Rubicam Partnerships	New York
23	22	Cheil Communications	Seoul
24	30	CKS Group	Cupertino, Calif.
25	26	Gage Marketing Group	Minneapolis

Source: Reprinted with permission from the April 27, 1998, issue of *Advertising Age*. Copyright © 1998 Crain Communications, Inc.

REGULATION OF ADVERTISING

Role of the Federal Government

As we showed in chapter 5, the federal government can regulate advertising to a small degree. *Truth in advertising* is part of the Federal Trade Commission's (FTC) consumer protection mission. The FTC can evaluate complaints about advertising in terms of fairness, deception, and substantiation of claims made by an advertiser. For example, if an ad says "tests prove," "doctor recommended," or "studies show," the FTC can ask the advertiser to show data for tests, affidavits from physicians, and results of studies. The FTC considers complaints "from the perspective of a consumer acting reasonably in the circumstances."

Advertisers that have, in the view of the FTC, violated truth-in-advertising standards can be directed to cease running an ad or to revise the ad to bring it up to standard. They can also be prosecuted if the FTC believes the public interest has been put at risk because of advertiser claims.

For example, in 1994 Eggland's Best Inc., a Pennsylvania producer of specialty eggs, was accused of using advertising to make false claims about the cholesterol content of its eggs, claiming its eggs wouldn't raise consumers' cholesterol levels. The company signed a consent decree with the FTC promising to cease making these claims but continued advertising with the same theme. Because each individual use of an ad can be fined, in 1996, Eggland's Best was fined $100,000. The FTC also cited N. W. Ayer, Eggland's advertising agency, for creating the deceptive ads. The company hired a new ad agency and revised its advertisements.

One of the largest fines ever levied for fraudulent advertising was assessed against The Reader's Digest Association in 1971 for failing to adhere to an FTC order to cease and desist using simulated money and bonds in its direct mail campaigns; the fine was $1,750,000.

Congress can also regulate advertising to some extent on radio and television, because that body writes the laws which establish the FCC's regulation of broadcasting. In 1971, Congress passed a law banning the advertisement of cigarettes, cigars, and pipe tobacco on radio and television. It could not have banned such ads in the print media.

Self-Regulation

A number of advertising organizations espouse voluntary codes of behavior to accommodate public sentiment and to avoid government regulation. For example, members of the Outdoor Advertising Association of America have long observed a custom of placing billboards with ads for alcoholic beverages and cigarettes no closer than 500 feet from a church or school. Manufacturers of hard liquor voluntarily withdrew advertising from radio and television in the 1940s for all alcoholic beverages except beer and wine. But in 1996, with liquor consumption declining while beer and wine consumption was rising, the industry ended its voluntary ban. However, broadcasters, including major networks, were reluctant to accept hard-liquor ads, and as of 1998, the ads were appearing only infrequently on cable channels.

Cigarette manufacturers refrain from advertising in media directed expressly at teens. To do otherwise would likely trigger a public backlash and government intervention. However, that is not to say that they haven't created advertising images in general media designed to catch the eye of a young person. As already mentioned, increasing government concern about the Joe Camel character's bold appeal to youngsters caused Camel maker R. J. Reynolds to discontinue use of the character in advertising of the brand.

CRITICAL ISSUES

Advertising triggers strong reactions. In some societies, such as communist countries, it is regarded as evil. In societies motivated by efforts to conserve resources and preserve the natural world, advertising is regarded with suspicion as a potential destroyer. In almost every society, there are those who regard advertising as manipulative and exploitative. Ongoing debates are increasing about advertising's power over individuals and the world around them. What follows is an overview of the most persistent concerns about advertising content.

Pushing Values of Consumption. Advertising has led to "a fellowship of goods," said writer Randall Rothenberg (1995), which assumes that "we are united not by what we believe but by what we buy, that our lives are circumscribed not by where we live, but by the advertising media to which we attend" (p. 181). Rothenberg isn't suggesting that the United States is a nation without values, but rather that buying things has become our core societal value.

Producing Waste and Destruction. The rampant buying of things, whether needed or not, some critics charge, produces waste that pollutes air and water, robs the earth of trees, forests, oil, minerals, wildlife, and naturalness. American advertising fosters overconsumption, with the nation using far more than its share of the world's resources, according to these critics.

Replacing Verbal Logic With Visual Images. Other critics claim that advertising has degraded language and thought. Advertising no longer informs and explains with verbal logic. Instead, it uses visual imagery to evoke feelings. One cannot argue the merits of a product promoted with images. One can only feel something about it. We are shown images of a grandmother's tearful reunion with a grandson over the telephone to sell us a mobile phone. We are shown pictures of a joyful family holding hands as they run through a meadow to sell us hamburgers. The commercial doesn't tell us why the telephone works well or the hamburger tastes good, why the product is affordable or nutritious. It says we will feel good if we buy these things.

Setting Unreachable Goals. Idealized standards of physical perfection predominate in the images of men and women in print and broadcast ads, but they are particularly pervasive in depictions of women and girls. Impossibly thin, with a distant gaze that indicates the self-consciousness of being on display, models strut through fashion spreads and across television screen for us to admire their clothes but, most important, their bodies.

Women's magazines are dense with advertising images that promote a certain look, weight, height, and body type. Whether that physique is right for a woman is another matter altogether. The lucrative weight-loss industry is proof that many women will try to achieve that body type, even risking their health to do so. But so pervasive are the ads, so consistent are the images, that the anxiety they produce is taken for granted.

The unattainable perfection of advertising models reduces women's feelings of self-worth. Many feel bad about themselves because they are not as thin, as young, as rich, or as beautiful as the models they see thousands of times a day. But advertising also proposes the solution: Take this pill, eat this food, buy this dress, go on this diet, buy this new car, drink this diet beverage. If you do these things, the ads promise, you will get what you want. You will be like those perfect models in the ads.

Exploiting Sex.   Advertising has long accepted that using sex is one of the best ways to sell. Writing in *Channels of Desire*, Stuart and Elizabeth Ewen (1982) described an ad that has become fairly typical:

> On Broadway, at Seventy-second, a bus rattles to its stop …. Looking up we see a poster ad that, running along the entire roof of the bus, offers an outrageous display: an assembly line of female backsides, pressed emphatically into their designer jeans …. We see the figures from waist to mid-thigh, yet we know they are women. We have seen it before. These buttocks greet us from a rakish angle, a posture widely cultivated in women from time to time, in place to place …. The bus moves along. Pinned to its rear, we see its final reminder: "The Ends Justify the Jeans … Gloria Vanderbilt for Murjani." (p. 109)

This image of the fashionable woman, the Ewens wrote, was of "an animal in perpetual heat" (p. 109). It would have been impossible for any normal person not to have noticed the ad. But the sexual exploitation involved not only sold jeans but sent a message about women's bodies. It certainly conveyed the strong suggestion that for women to get attention, they'd better be able to fit into those jeans. The ad reinforced thousands of other advertising messages women have received during their lifetimes that make women wonder if their bodies are good enough. The message: Buy these jeans and they will be.

Critics of the sexual sell complain that appropriation of female sexuality and children for sales purposes diminishes a precious human quality and opens women and children to further exploitation. Nevertheless, it is a widely used technique. Women's bodies are used to sell almost everything from beer, fast food, shaving cream, and power tools to automobiles, boats, and trucks.

Objectifying Bodies.   The jeans ad essentially was a display of women's body parts in seductive poses. This objectification, in which a sexual area of the body is magnified, denies any sense of the total person. The objectification and eroticization of children and teen-agers by some advertisers, such as in some Calvin Klein ads, also has aroused intense criticism.

Influencing Risky Behavior.   As we've indicated earlier, television, with its small screen, needs vivid action to command our attention. Automotive ads often portray cars and trucks as high-performance, acrobatic vehicles, speeding around hairpin turns, jumping creeks, rarely observing speed limits or the laws of gravity. Small disclaimers on the screen that say "closed course/professional driver/do not attempt" are the ad's way of saying don't try this at home. Yet they clearly suggest that the thrills of driving in this manner are available to you if you purchase the vehicle. Perhaps it is not surprising that automobile accidents have become one of the leading causes of death for young adults and that road rage has become a national disease.

Advertising often sends mixed messages. Most beer ads urge consumption, mixing footage of the product with images of attractive young women enjoying themselves with young men. A few urge moderation in drinking, with no women in sight and no one having any fun. Commercials that show a whole crowd of people having a good time together, each with a beer in hand, appear far more often than those that urge patrons to use designated drivers and drink responsibly.

Blurring Advertising With Editorial and Program Content.

We expect to know when one is trying to inform us about something, and when another is trying to persuade us or sell us something. Journalists claim that their credibility is based on their presentation of objective fact, untainted by an effort to influence or sell. Yet advertisers would like to exploit the credibility of journalists and factual news reporting, or the excitement of good entertainment, to sell their products. Blurring the distinction between reporting and advertising, between entertainment and influence, has always been a concern. But that blurring is increasing.

The *infomercial* is a growing genre and further blurs the difference between advertising and reporting or entertaining. Infomercials are television programs in which the entire program is simply an extended commercial for an advertiser. They have mushroomed since the proliferation of program-hungry channels made possible by cable and satellite delivery. Many infomercials have high production values and look like regular television programming, which is the problem. Infomercials try to make viewers forget that they are watching a commercial. Most infomercials provide only cursory notice of their true nature, and it is easy to miss their disclaimers.

Widely respected newspapers and news magazines are also selling entire sections to advertisers. Foreign countries have been using this technique, buying a whole section of a newspaper or magazine to sell their countries to tourists. These pages are known as *advertorials*. The pages are laid out with stories and photographs as if they were objective news, but in fact they are trying to influence the newspaper's readers.

Furthermore, as we showed earlier, advertisers increasingly try to control the placement of their ads. For example, tobacco companies do not like their ads placed next to an article about lung cancer, and an airline likes to have its ads appear next to a happy story about travel. Media that accommodate their advertisers' wishes on placement and allow the advertiser some say in editorial or program content are subtly influencing their audiences.

IN DEFENSE OF ADVERTISING

The purveyors of advertising have a very different view of the messages contained in their campaigns than the critics. Advertising's defenders say that people who see evil in ads miss the importance of advertising to the economy, and fail to appreciate the whimsy, fantasy, and playful quality of advertising. Consumer advertising is meant to be attention getting and entertaining, they say, not a literal interpretation but an escape from the world or a new interpretation of it.

The Calvin Klein company said its ad campaign featuring teenagers who appeared to be runaways had been misunderstood, that the images sent a "positive message" about the "spirit, independence and inner worth of today's young people."[1] A Wonderbra marketing executive, defending the suggestive slogans and revealing photos used in its bra ads, said they were "about taking control and empowerment."[2]

Newspaper columnist James K. Glassman defended liquor companies when they decided to end their self-imposed ban on broadcast advertising after nearly a half-century off the air. He wrote that the power of advertising to get people to do destructive things was overrated. Without ads, he said, "Russia still managed to become a widely intoxicated nation." With the end of communism and the return to advertising, Russia was adopting more temperate drinking behavior and lighter, healthier Western tastes. "The truth," wrote Glassman, "is that advertising—especially if government keeps its hands off—leads to wiser, not dumber, decisions by consumers, who have learned to respond to information at least as much as to emotional appeals."[3]

Advertising's defenders also say that advertising is a logical and necessary component of a free-market system. It promotes the movement of goods and services, strengthening the economy to the benefit of all. Many also feel that taste is subjective and too personal to be regulated by industry codification or government review. What some might find offensive, others might regard as clever parody.

Consumers themselves indicate ambivalence about advertising. In a study published in 1997 by the Cummings Center for Advertising Studies at the University of Illinois, a majority of adults in a national telephone sample (52 percent) said they like to look at most of the ads they are exposed to (versus 37 percent who did not). They generally agree (61 percent to 30 percent) that most advertising is informative. However, a majority (52 percent) also say they do not generally feel they can trust advertising, and more agree (47 percent) than disagree (40 percent) that advertising insults their intelligence. Nearly half the respondents (47 percent) reported feeling offended by advertising at least sometimes and more than two-thirds (69 percent) reported feeling misled by advertising sometimes.

Its controversial aspects notwithstanding, advertising makes possible inexpensive media use by paying for nearly all radio and television's financial needs, and most of the needs of newspapers and magazines.

LOOKING AHEAD

In the future, effective advertising will depend on the ability of media planners to identify opportunities in new media while adapting older media strategies to a rapidly changing marketplace. The advertising industry must be prepared to respond to the continual creative reinvention of the craft.

New media are changing the relationship between advertisers and customers. As one-way delivery systems of broadcast and print media give way to newer, interactive, computer-driven media, individuals will increasingly be able to find information that serves their interests and filter out messages they do not wish to see or hear. Although this is a benefit for individuals, the fragmentation of what had been a large, relatively cohesive mass audience into smaller, more diverse, more sophisticated subgroups poses new challenges for advertisers.

Among these challenges are: developing *one-on-one marketing* strategies, as contrasted with mass marketing; measuring the effectiveness of *online advertising*; and answering *concerns about privacy*.

Privacy will become a heightened concern in the twenty-first century. Interactive media are able to capture enormous amounts of information about users, including children, for sale to advertisers. A step in the right direction was taken when voluntary guidelines for proper use of information gathered about online users were drawn up by the American Association of Advertising Agencies with the Association of National Advertisers, and by the Electronic Frontier Foundation with CommerceNet.

Clutter in advertising will grow in cyberspace. Hundreds of millions of Web pages are already accessible. Advertisers will have to be strategically linked to reach potential customers and be creative and clever in making images and messages stand out. To make that happen, cyber advertising in the future will be enriched with interactive graphics, audio, and video.

The new independence of online advertising will be a challenge. With the Internet, advertisers are able to bypass traditional media and send a message directly to the consumer the advertiser wants to reach. The advertiser can do so with *push technology*, such as sending advertising messages via e-mail, or by finding ways to attract the user directly to its site for exposure to advertising messages. Advertisers have invested much more in creating and maintaining their own sites than they have spent on purchasing advertising on independent editorial Web sites.

Most advertisers see these challenges as opportunities, and we can expect the ad industry to make the most of these possibilities as they have with the development of each new mass medium in the past.

Further Reading

Adler, Richard. (December 1997). *The Future of Advertising: New Approaches to the Attention Economy.* Washington, DC: Aspen Institute.

Albion, Mark S. (1983). *Advertising's Hidden Effects: Manufacturer's Advertising and Retail Pricing.* Boston: Auburn House.

Ewen, Stuart. (1988). *All Consuming Images: The Politics of Style in Contemporary Culture.* New York: Basic Books.

Ewen, Stuart, and Ewen, Elizabeth. (1982). *Channels of Desire: Mass Images and the Shaping of American Consciousness.* New York: McGraw-Hill.

Fowles, Jib. (1996). *Advertising and Popular Culture.* Thousand Oaks, CA: Sage Publications.

Frith, Katherine Toland. (Ed.). (1997). *Undressing the Ad: Reading Culture in Advertising.* New York: Peter Lang.

Hiebert, Ray, Jones, Robert, Lorenz, John, and Lotito, Ernest. (Eds.). (1976). *The Political Image Merchants: Strategies in the New Politics.* Washington, DC: Acropolis Books.

Jacobson, Michael F., and Mazur, Laurie Ann. (1995). *Marketing Madness: A Survival Guide for a Consumer Society.* Boulder, CO: Westview Press.

Kirkpatrick, Jerry. (1994). *In Defense of Advertising: Arguments from Reason, Ethical Egoism, and Laissez-Faire Capitalism*. Westport, CT: Quorum.

Krugman, D. M., Reid, L. M., Dunn, S. W., and Barban, A. M. (1994). *Advertising: Its Role in Modern Marketing*. Orlando, FL: Dryden.

Lears, Jackson. (1994). *Fables of Abundance: A Cultural History of Advertising in America*. New York: Basic Books.

Mayer, Martin. (1991). *Whatever Happened to Madison Avenue? Advertising in the '90s*. Boston: Little, Brown.

Packard, Vance. (1965). *The Hidden Persuaders*. New York: Van Rees Press.

Rothenberg, Randall. (1995). *Where the Suckers Moon: An Advertising Story*. New York: Knopf.

Vinikas, Vincent. (1992). *Soft Soap, Hard Sell: American Hygiene in an Age of Advertisement*. Ames, IA: Iowa State University Press.

White, Barton C. (1993). *The New Ad Media Reality*. Westport, CT: Quorum.

Notes

[1]Thomas, Pierre, and Farhi, Paul. (1995, November 16). Calvin Klein Ads Cleared. *The Washington Post*, p. D7.

[2]Parker, Cherie. (1995, October 22). Winning the Booby Prize: What the Wonderbra Election Reveals About America. *The Washington Post*, p. C1.

[3]Glassman, James K. (1996, December 3). Booze, Brews and the First Amendment. *The Washington Post*, p. A15.

14

PUBLIC RELATIONS, PUBLIC OPINION, AND MASS MEDIA

Have you ever smoked cigarettes, or have you ever been annoyed at breathing someone else's smoke? If so, you are part of an enormous public relations war. It is not against the law to smoke in most places, nor is it illegal to manufacture tobacco products, but smoking has become a major battleground in America. The "tobacco wars" are to some extent about legislation and scientific evidence, but far more important for us, they are wars of persuasion, using the techniques of public relations to influence public opinion through mass media. It is safe to say that hundreds of millions of dollars are being spent annually on public relations in the tobacco wars.

The combatants in these wars are advocacy groups on either side of the question, all fighting for our minds. On one side are many nonsmokers—government agencies such as the office of the Surgeon General, the Food and Drug Administration, and the National Cancer Institute; disease prevention organizations such as the American Cancer Society; and private advocacy groups such as the Campaign for Tobacco-Free Kids—all battling to legislate restrictions of all kinds. On the other side are tobacco companies—the Tobacco Institute (a public relations tool of the companies), prosmoking advocacy groups, and smokers—all fighting to preserve the right to smoke. The Tobacco Institute alone spends more than $20 million a year on public relations to lobby for laws sympathetic to smoking.

What is this business of public relations, and what role does it play in the world of mass communication? The practice is often misunderstood, partly because some of its practitioners operate behind the scenes, sometimes using questionable ethical judgment. *PR*, as it is often derisively called, is sometimes blamed for twisting the facts with half-truths and even lies in an effort to persuade and influence the public. This selective interpretation of facts has become known as *spin*, and its practitioners are *spin meisters* and *spin doctors*.

THE SCOPE OF PUBLIC RELATIONS TODAY

Despite criticism, public relations has become a well-defined and rapidly growing profession. According to the U.S. Bureau of Labor Statistics, it is practiced by nearly 200,000 professionals in America, with a 47 percent increase in the number of public relations jobs predicted for the 1994–2005 decade. (Table 14.1 lists the top public relations agencies.) Societies representing the profession have grown in the last half of the twentieth century; by the beginning of the twenty-first century, the Public Relations Society of America (PRSA) had nearly 20,000 members, and the International Association of Business Communicators (IABC) about 12,500.

The U.S. government employs about 15,000 people in public relations–related jobs, including about 3,000 in the Defense Department alone. An additional 8,000 or more work in the government's international public relations efforts—the U.S. Information Agency and the Voice of America. Compare the government's public relations efforts with the news media's efforts at covering government. In Washington, D.C., the city with the greatest concentration of both government employees and journalists, only about 5,000 journalists work regularly. Only about 300 regularly cover Congress, about 150 regularly cover the White House, and only about 30 regularly cover the Defense Department.

PR Newswire, an organization that claims to be the world's largest distributor of corporate, association, and institutional information to the news media and the financial community, has 19 offices in the United States and distributes more than 100,000 news releases a year to more than 2,000 newsrooms for more than 15,000 clients. The U.S. government sends hundreds of news releases every day to journalists and news media offices. These releases are distributed by fax machines and e-mail as well.

Today every institution or organization of any size—businesses, schools, religious organizations, activist groups, professional organizations—must have public relations representation to survive. Even the Queen of England now employs a team of public relations advisors to help with her relationships with her subjects.

Thirty years ago, the University of Maryland had one or two employees who served a public relations function for the university. By the end of the twentieth century, with no further growth in its faculty or student body, the university had to employ more than a hundred people who served some kind of public relations role. At the same time, only two newspaper reporters covered the university regularly, one for *The Washington Post* and another for the *Baltimore Sun*, and neither full-time. Public relations had become essential for the University to get its message out to its many publics. And at the beginning of the twenty-first century that is typical of most organizations in our society.

DEFINING PUBLIC RELATIONS

Public relations began as newspapers became powerful in the nineteenth century, with press agents for businesses and celebrities trying to get promotional items into the papers. Media relations is still a primary function of public relations, but the practice to-

TABLE 14.1

Top 25 Public Relations Firms, 1997, Based on Net Fees, of Those Firms Supplying
Information to O'Dwyer's *Directory of Public Relations Firms*

	Firm	Net Fees	Employees	Percent Change From 1996
1.	Burson-Marsteller (A)	$264,545,502	2,129	+13.5
2.	Shandwick	158,673,000	1,742	+6.9
3.	Porter Novelli International (A)	148,106,661	1,331	+22.0
4.	Fleishman-Hillard (A)	134,950,000	1,115	+25.0
5.	Edelman PR Worldwide	133,625,098	1,332	+19.7
6.	Ketchum PR Worldwide (A)	96,623,000	827	+29.0
7.	Manning, Selvage & Lee (A)	63,523,000	459	+32.5
8.	GCI Group (A)	62,037,966	645	+18.6
9.	BSMG Worldwide (A)	61,565,000	539	+40.2
10.	Weber PR Worldwide (A)	61,071,000	566	New Entity
11.	Ogilvy PR Worldwide (A)	55,339,000	500	+14.3
12.	Golin/Harris Communications	47,327,000	397	+11.8
13.	Ruder Finn	46,500,000	435	+11.1
14.	Rowland Worldwide (A)	34,200,000	308	+5.8
15.	Cohn & Wolfe (A)	30,216,000	248	+20.7
16.	Financial Relations Board	26,629,346	244	+31.7
17.	Gavin Anderson & Co.	25,300,000	180	+25.2
18.	Copithorne & Bellows (A)	21,597,553	203	+29.0
19.	Morgen-Walke Associates	19,606,544	110	+19.6
20.	Cunningham Communications	17,201,652	129	+9.8
21.	Powell Tate	15,556,820	99	+8.6
22.	The MWW Group	14,367,000	125	+37.2
23.	Lois Paul & Partners	13,193,716	106	+16.2
24.	Gibbs & Soell	11,451,000	99	+19.2
25.	Schwartz Communications	10,930,159	113	+75.9

Source: J. R. O'Dwyer Company, Inc. Copyright © 1998. Reproduced by permission.

(A) denotes firms related to advertising agencies

day includes relationships with many publics—employees, stockholders, labor
unions, government, and many more. For most practitioners today, the profession can
be succinctly described, as it was by Stan Sauerhaft and Chris Atkins (1989), vice
chairman and vice president respectively of Burson-Marsteller, one of the world's
largest public relations firms, as "the art and science of creating, altering, strengthening, or overcoming public opinion" (p. 13).

Other definitions seek to encompass a larger role for the profession. Rex Harlow (1975), after an exhaustive survey of writings about the field and in-depth interviews with more than 5 dozen leading practitioners, distilled the following:

> Public relations is a distinctive management function which helps establish and maintain mutual lines of communication, understanding, acceptance, and cooperation between an organization and its publics; involves the management of problems or issues; helps management to keep informed on and responsive to public opinion; defines and emphasizes the responsibility of management to serve the public interest; helps management keep abreast of and effectively utilize change, serving as an early warning system to help anticipate trends; and uses research and sound and ethical communication techniques as its principal tools. (p. 36)

We need to make it clear that public relations is different from journalism and that it is different from information, education, and persuasion. Public relations is an activity that furthers the purposes of communicators or their sponsors. It advocates a particular position. It may use all forms of communication to fulfill its purpose, including information, education, and persuasive communication. The journalist in American mass media culture is supposed to keep information and persuasion separate. News is supposed to be information, facts for their own sake, to be interpreted by each reader, listener, and viewer. Education, too, should be information for its intrinsic value, to be used by students for their own purposes, not to serve the purpose of teachers or schools. Public relations may use information and education to serve its purposes, but it does so to advocate and persuade, not to inform or educate.

In reality, advocacy and persuasion get into a lot of journalism and education, sometimes deliberately but most often incidentally. Much news, in fact, has a public relations basis. The amount of news that originates in public relations offices in one way or another has been estimated to be as little as 30 percent and as much as 80 percent in each day's mass media. Many news stories start as press releases from public relations offices; many newsworthy events are created and carefully staged for public relations purposes. A senior vice president for Hill & Knowlton, a major public relations counseling firm that has represented high government officials as well as key corporations, has said, "Most of what you see on TV is, in effect, a canned PR product. Most of what you read in the paper and see on television is not news" (Hiebert, 1999, p. 187).

Clearly, one of journalism's most important tasks today is to sort out real news from information manufactured to serve someone's interests. As readers, listeners, and viewers of mass media, we must be constantly aware of who wants us to have the information we receive, and why. Certainly, it is not possible to understand mass media in American society today without understanding public relations.

PUBLIC RELATIONS, DEMOCRACY, AND PUBLIC OPINION

Public relations in America grew up in the twentieth century. It came into existence as a profession mostly as a result of the growth of mass media. It developed because individuals and organizations outside the mass media wanted to give public expression to views that weren't being communicated in the mass media, or to defend themselves from criticism and attacks in the media. Public relations exists because everyone in a democracy has a right to express his or her own opinions. That right is not limited to the press or mass media or government or any other powerful interests.

In a democratic society, everyone should have an *equal* right to be heard, not just those few who own the means of mass communication or who have powerful resources to control mass media. Of course, not everyone has equal wealth. Effective public relations, like effective journalism, requires some resources. But the techniques of public relations can be used effectively with far less investment. No large printing presses or expensive transmitters are needed. Almost anyone who learns the techniques can afford to practice them. Without public relations, in fact, it would be harder to guarantee everyone such equal rights, harder to maintain democracy in a complex mass society where mass communication technology has become so expensive.

Furthermore, in a democracy supposedly everyone has a right to his or her own version of truth. Authorities can only enforce their version of the truth in authoritarian societies; in a democracy, the will of the majority must be accepted until someone can persuade the majority that it is wrong. Public relations is based on the notion that the truth or power of any opinion ultimately depends on its ability to be accepted by others in the marketplace.

In fact, public opinion is the most powerful force in a democracy, where laws cannot be passed unless people agree to them, where legislators cannot legislate unless they are put in office by a majority of the voters, where government cannot govern without the consent of the governed. These ideas were stated most powerfully in one of America's founding documents, the Declaration of Independence, in which Thomas Jefferson stated boldly what we have come to accept as our basic faith: that government exists to serve the governed, not the other way around.

This means that in democracy, public opinion is the real law, the ultimate authority. Public relations pioneer Ivy Lee told the American Railroad Guild in a 1914 speech, "The people now rule. We have substituted for the divine right of kings, the divine right of the multitude. The crowd is enthroned" (Hiebert, 1996, p. iv).

Opinions become powerful in a democratic society when they reach a critical mass; that is, when there are enough people expressing an opinion so that a law can be changed, or enough to elect a person to public office, or enough to give power to a political party, or enough to change a government. Public opinion can be institutionalized in a variety of ways: by the formation of pressure groups in society, by the use of lobbyists to seek specific legislation, and by the use of public relations techniques as a way of influencing mass communication.

TYPES OF PUBLIC OPINION AND PUBLICS

It is a mistake to think of public opinion as mass opinion. There are many different collections of opinion in society, and one job for public relations is to sort out the publics. Edward M. Block (1988), former vice president of AT&T, distinguished four different types of opinion publics:

1. A *general public*, which does not have much interest in the facts of public issues, or indeed, the issues themselves.
2. An *attentive public*, which at least knows that certain issues are before the public.
3. An *informed public*, which takes part in the discussion of public matters.
4. An *elite public*, which initiates and defines the issues, touching off public discussion. (Hiebert, 1988, p. 93)

Most experts agree that some people are more influential than others, and some have opinions that count more. Much analysis of mass communication effects is based on the two-step flow, namely influencing the influential opinion leaders who in turn influence the masses. Journalists who play a major role in the mass media are often considered the most influential people in our society and thus the prime targets of public relations.

Frank Mankiewicz (1989), vice president of Hill and Knowlton Public Relations, identified the 10 most influential persons for each decade from 1930 through the 1980s; only 4 nonjournalists were included in his list of 60: Eleanor Roosevelt, Emily Post (the writer on social etiquette), Fulton Sheen (Catholic Bishop popular on radio and early television), and Charles Schulz (the cartoonist and creator of "Peanuts").

Sociologist Herbert J. Gans (1989) describes two kinds of opinion makers: leaders and bystanders. Opinion leaders are influential people such as political and governmental officials, well-known intellectuals, doctors, teachers, ministers, priests, rabbis, media stars, and celebrities whose opinions are widely respected. Bystanders are normally politically uninvolved members of the general public, and they constitute the vast majority, according to Gans. They may not hold their opinions deeply, but they help shape public opinion in four ways:

1. They are the major creators of long-term public opinion.
2. They set the rough limits on what can and cannot be said and done by public figures on controversial issues, probably more so in the areas of religion and sex than in politics.
3. They force opinion makers to frame public rhetoric, legislation, and government budgets in such a way that they will be impressed.
4. At times bystanders are aroused in large numbers and express their opinions directly, and when they do so, opinion leaders must follow.

COURTING PUBLIC OPINION

Ivy Lee, one of the earliest practitioners of public relations, not only recognized that the public was king in a democracy, he went on to say in his 1914 speech that this "new sovereign has his courtiers, who flatter and caress precisely as did those who surrounded medieval emperors" (Hiebert, 1966, p. iv). He was speaking, of course, of the new public relations profession.

Walter Lippmann (1922), political philosopher and journalist in the first half of the twentieth century, in *Public Opinion*, one of the most important books on the subject, wrote that the general public had great difficulty in the modern age assimilating and assessing all the information needed to be responsible citizens. Even the press could not manage the process, he said. Lippmann believed that a new class of opinion managers—press agents, and publicity agents like Ivy Lee—would take over the task of making sense of a complex world, initially for the journalists and then, through the media, for the people.

Edward Bernays (1923), another early practitioner of public relations, wrote in his book *Crystallizing Public Opinion* that the public relations counsellor had to "isolate ideas and develop them into events so that they [could] be more readily understood and so that they may claim attention as news" (p. 171). Bernays claimed that "the conscious and intelligent manipulation of the organized habits and opinions of the masses is an important element in democratic society. Those who manipulate this unseen mechanism of society," he wrote, "constitute an invisible government which is the true ruling power of our country" (p. 171).

Since public opinion creates the laws by which a democracy operates, then democracy requires new kinds of lawyers. Regular lawyers are concerned with statutes. They advise their clients on what to do within the limits of the law, and they advocate their clients' positions before the court of law. Public relations counselors, on the other hand, practice before the court of public opinion. They advise their clients on what can be done within the limits of public opinion, and they advocate their clients' positions to the public. Public relations counselors cannot dictate public reaction, nor can lawyers dictate to the court. For both lawyers and public relations counselors, their work is a two-way proposition. Lawyers must interpret the laws to their clients and their clients to the court. Public relations counselors must interpret public attitudes and opinions to their clients and their clients to the public.

PUBLIC RELATIONS IN AMERICAN HISTORY: A CRITICAL ROLE

America, more than any other country, has led the way in the evolution of public relations to its modern worldwide practice. Perhaps that was because America was started with a sort of public relations activity. When the thirteen colonies were still ruled by the British monarchy, many in the New World chafed at their second-class status as British citizens, especially annoyed by the taxes they had to pay to the king.

A number of citizens seeking independence from the Crown were good writers (the Committee of Correspondence, for example), and they wrote essays that were printed in the little weekly 4-page newsletters published in capital cities of the colonies.[1] A leader among them was a fiery writer named Samuel Adams, sometimes called the first press agent. Their essays were read aloud in taverns and had great influence on the colonists, ultimately shaping opinion enough for the colonists to accept the startling Declaration of Independence and then become brave and bold enough to fight a revolution against one of the greatest armies in the world at that time.

After the colonists won independence, they had to choose a new form of government. Again, press agentry played an important role. A number of writers—especially John Jay, James Madison, and Alexander Hamilton—wanted the newly independent states to form a constitutional democracy, and they wrote essays for their local newspapers arguing for adoption of the drafted constitution. These essays became known as *The Federalist Papers*, and again they had enormous influence in shaping public ratification, giving America the form of government that still prevails. Historian Allan Nevins (1978) called *The Federalist Papers* the greatest example of public relations in American history.

In the nineteenth century, as the press became industrialized and powerful, press agentry became essential to success in many areas. Andrew Jackson was the first President to employ a press secretary to deal with reporters and editors. The antislavery movement used many press agentry tactics to promote abolition, including publishing antislavery newspapers and promoting antislavery books such as *Uncle Tom's Cabin*. When the Civil War became the first American war covered by reporters on the battlefield, their dispatches were sometimes published in newspapers before Lincoln received the news from his generals; the President was so disturbed by this that he proposed jailing reporters. He was not yet aware of public relations tactics that twentieth-century Presidents would employ to influence the media during wartime.

Industrialism in the late nineteenth century turned newspapers into mass media and big business, and that in turn made press agentry all the more important. When investigative reporters (the *muckrakers*) began exposing graft, corruption, greed, and abuse of power by big business and government, the natural tendency was to employ press agents to suppress the bad news and get a more sympathetic story into the press.

Ivy Lee, a reporter for *The New York Times* at the turn of the century, realized that helping big business interpret itself to the public through the press was an important undertaking, and he left journalism to start his own "publicity bureau" in New York. As a former journalist, he knew that he could win friends and influence among journalists by giving them facts. He also realized that big business needed to have good facts to tell. He viewed his work as maintaining good relations between the press and his clients. To succeed in maintaining good relations, he reasoned, one had to tell the truth and have a good truth to tell. Thus, press agentry became a more responsible undertaking, and public relations began an evolution into a profession.

THE RISE OF PUBLIC RELATIONS IN THE TWENTIETH CENTURY

When World War I started in Europe, Americans at first did not want to participate in a war they felt did not affect them. President Woodrow Wilson thought Americans should not isolate themselves from the world, so he wanted his country involved, a proposition that required an enormous amount of public persuasion. He became the first President to organize government publicity machinery for war. He formed the Committee on Public Information and named a Colorado newspaper editor to organize a national campaign to urge American involvement and support for the war. World War I thus became the first *information war*, where words were as important as bullets and bombs in defeating the enemy. Propaganda aspects have become paramount in all of America's subsequent wars.

A few years after Ivy Lee opened his publicity firm, in 1906, Edward Bernays became a theater press agent as a young man in New York. He went on to become one of the great practitioners and philosophers of public relations in the twentieth century. He worked for Wilson's Committee on Public Information and later on the President's efforts to get the American people to ratify the League of Nations (which they never did). Lee also worked for the war effort, directing the publicity of the American Red Cross in its emergency work. After the war, both Bernays and Lee turned their attention to clients in the business world, and public relations began to come of age. At the end of the 1920s, they were the only two public relations practitioners listed in the New York phone book. Today, as we have seen, more people work in public relations than in journalism.

PUBLICITY, ADVERTISING, AND CREDIBILITY

Public relations has come to be the communications umbrella in many organizations. Under public relations are placed all the means by which an organization communicates and maintains its relationships with its various publics, including marketing, advertising, publicity, and promotion. It is important to understand the distinction between publicity and advertising; both are useful tools, each for different purposes.

Advertising.   As we saw in the previous chapter, advertising is the purchase of time or space in the mass media to communicate a particular message. By purchasing time or space, the advertiser can exercise almost complete control over the message: what is said, how it is said, to whom it is said, how often it is said, and to some extent where it is placed in a publication or on the air.

Publicity.   Communication sent to mass media for their use as they see fit, without paying the media for its use, is publicity. Whoever writes it cannot control it at all once it is in the hands of the media. Editors control it; they can decide to use it or not, to use part of it, to change it, to add it to other messages; they decide when, where, how, and how often it might be used.

If one can exercise so little control over a communication, of what use is it to the persuader? It is not used because it might seem less expensive than advertising; in fact, its production could be just as costly as an ad. Much more important, if it appears as part of the medium's editorial or nonadvertising content, it is seen as a non-self-serving statement, whereas an advertisement on the surface clearly serves the interests of the advertiser. Publicity becomes a statement of the medium that carries it, providing an implicit endorsement of the medium itself. Publicity then can be perceived as objective news rather than as self-serving promotion, and that can give the message credibility.

Credibility.   This is perhaps the single most important ingredient in persuasion. Without credibility one's chances of persuading another are slim, as philosophers and communicators have long known. Aristotle put the proposition clearly 2,300 years ago when he wrote:

> We believe good men more fully and more readily than others; this is true generally whatever the question is, and absolutely true where exact certainty is impossible and opinions are divided. It is not true, as some writers assume in their treatises on rhetoric, that the personal

goodness revealed by the speaker contributes nothing to his power of persuasion; on the contrary, his character may almost be called the most effective means of persuasion he possesses.[2]

Many modern scientific studies have proved Aristotle's thesis. The importance of credibility cannot be overstated in persuasion. Public relations seeks credibility for its messages in a variety of ways, only one of which is by achieving the implicit endorsement of a third party through publicity. Another way is by having credible spokespersons. Research has confirmed that an attractive spokesperson seems to enhance credibility, that appearing to be non-self-serving makes a person seem more unbiased and trustworthy, that communication which does not seem to be trying to influence is more influential, that a frank answer to a tough question can make the answer seem more believable. These are some of the attributes that public relations practitioners commonly try to build into their messages.

THE PROCESS OF PUBLIC RELATIONS

The basic techniques of public relations are relatively simple, and they consist of three parts: understanding publics, managing communication, and monitoring results.

Understanding Public Perceptions and Opinions

The first step, *understanding the public*, is actually often ignored; sometimes it is understood through intuition rather than empirical research. But as the persuasive effort becomes more sophisticated, the understanding and the research to achieve it must be more precise, making serious research more common in today's public relations practice.

First it is important to understand that the public is actually many different publics. In his book on public relations, Fraser Seitel (1998) defines 20 different key publics for a typical multinational corporation: board of directors; workers; employee families; managers–supervisors; media; stockholders; investment community; competitors; suppliers; special interest groups (which may be subdivided further); community neighbors; international community; banks and insurers; trade associations; dealers–distributors; customers; federal, state, and local legislators; regulatory authorities; academic community; and labor unions (pp. 9–10). Other ways of describing publics can produce even longer lists. Persuasive messages must be stated somewhat differently for each public, because each has its own language, its own frame of reference.

Within those publics are other demographic factors to be considered: age, race, gender, ethnicity, socioeconomic status, education, geographic region, and political affiliation to name some. All these characteristics affect attitudes and opinions and influence the way in which audiences receive messages. Research is often important in helping persuaders learn not only what attitudes and opinions are held by the audience but also how and why those attitudes and opinions are held and what might change them. Often persuaders can know much about these things intuitively. Being an empathetic and attentive listener is a key attribute of an effective persuader and public relations practitioner, but it does not replace research.

Managing Communication

The second step and most creative aspect of the process, *managing communication*, is sometimes considered the only real work of public relations. One can separate communication management into four component parts:

1. Developing Acceptable Policies and Strategies.   Public relations works best when the practitioner is involved in helping determine the policies of the person or organization seeking to persuade the public. If public relations people have done their job of understanding perceptions and opinions of the public to be persuaded, they will be able to advise the organization on what policies and practices will be acceptable and to devise strategies to enable the organization to achieve its goals.

Every business has a marketing objective, for example, and public relations must develop appropriate public policies and strategies for achieving that goal. Sometimes those strategies may not be as simple as making a better product than the competitor's or selling it for less. Let's say that McDonald's corporate headquarters decides that one of its marketing objectives is to build its franchise business. The public relations office might decide that the strategy needed is to reinforce McDonald's community leadership and generate consumer trust, so an investor will feel secure in making an expensive investment in a franchise.

2. Exercising Self-Censorship.   In a democracy, one cannot censor the opinions or expressions of others; even the most powerful forces in government cannot do so, but we can censor ourselves. Every human being does this automatically in the course of daily living; we put on clothes that cover up what we don't want people to see, and we choose to wear clothes that will emphasize attributes and characteristics we most want others to know about us. Knowing what not to say can be as important to persuasion as knowing what to say.

It is not likely that McDonald's restaurants are going to reveal to all the world all the things they do to make hamburgers. To do so may be distasteful; it might even cause a loss of sales for those products, even though the processes may not be illegal or unhealthy. One has a right to emphasize some facts and deemphasize others in presenting a point of view to the world.

On the other hand, if McDonald's way of making hamburgers could cause even one person to become ill, to withhold that fact could end up as a public relations disaster for the company. The public relations office should provide counsel on what should and should not be withheld. The public has a right to know anything it wants to know; journalists have a right to find out what the public needs to know, and they are often pretty good at it. Withholding anything from the public that is a matter of health or safety or other public concern could be the worst of all strategies. Most public relations professionals advise that telling the truth about what the public wants to know is the best strategy, so having a good truth to tell is essential to success with the public.

3. Creating Interest Through Planned and Staged Events.   This is the most visible part of the public relations process, and in our world today almost everything that happens is planned and staged to get a message communicated. Clever events never seem as though they have been deliberately staged to send messages, yet very often that is exactly what has usually been the motive.

Consider the New Year's Day Rose Parade. It was created nearly a hundred years ago by a small group of businessmen in Pasadena, Calif., who wanted to promote their city as a good place to live. Even before television, the parade attracted tens of thousands of people to watch the event in person every year, and now with television millions can see it. That parade, and another staged event performed that same day—the Rose Bowl football game—played no small role in making southern California one of the most populated places in America. The parade also helps to promote dozens of businesses and organizations that sponsor floats carrying positive messages and images.

Much of every day's news comes from events that have been carefully staged by public relations personnel to make news. If the President wants to focus public attention on his elementary education program, he might schedule a visit to a model elementary school, where he will read a book to children or do nothing more than shake the hand of the principal. The President, of course, always has journalists and camera crews trailing him wherever he goes, so this *photo op* will probably get onto the evening network news. Most individuals and organizations do not have such automatic newsmaking power, so they have to be more creative with compelling events to capture the attention of their publics.

McDonald's uses a variety of promotional sponsorships, such as its All-American Band, its All-American Basketball, the Ronald McDonald House, and its sponsorship of Jerry Lewis's Muscular Dystrophy Telethon. These are all staged to support the public relations strategy of encouraging community involvement programs. The programs aid the marketing strategy of reinforcing the image of community leadership and generating consumer trust, both of which can help achieve the marketing objective of building investor interest in buying a McDonald's franchise.

4. Exercising Initiative in Putting Specific Messages on the Public Agenda.   Any communication vehicle can be used including programs, seminars, posters, billboards, publications, exhibits, shows, and mentions in books, movies, sound recordings, art, music, and drama, and in fact any other kind of communication one can imagine. But if the purpose is to get the message into the news media, some common techniques have been developed to do that. Public relations can build its public agenda by crafting messages in such a way that news media will use them in their news programs or editorial columns. And if they are used often enough, the messages acquire the status of being important and consequential and begin to take hold in the public psyche.

News releases, one of the most used and traditional methods, are usually written in the form of a news story and sent to newspapers by mail, fax, or e-mail, or on videotape as a news story sent to television stations. In fact, they may be overused, and so many are sent out that they have lost much of their power to command media gate-keepers' attention.

News conferences can be more effective, particularly if the head of the organization is powerful and newsworthy (and if he or she is able to answer tough questions quickly and easily, and if, in an age of television, he or she is telegenic). Presidents of the nation, governors, and leading political and public figures are best able to use the news conference. However, they should do so with great caution and must usually be carefully prepared and rehearsed for all possible questions.

A White House news conference for the President, for example, is a deliberately staged and carefully rehearsed drama. The President's aides prepare dozens of questions in advance that they think might be asked by reporters. Answers to all these questions are written out; many officials in government agencies are involved in anticipating the public's and the journalists' possible concerns and in shaping appropriate answers. The President is then carefully rehearsed. A President who is a skilled actor, who knows how to perform in front of a crowd and before cameras, who can memorize a script and thousands of details will be better in a news conference than someone who can't easily do these things. A president who can't do them should not hold news conferences. There is nothing in the law requiring anyone, even the President of the United States, to answer the questions of reporters. However, taking the initiative in getting information out is one of the keys to successful persuasion.

Briefings are another and in some ways safer way to take the initiative in releasing information. Briefings are usually done by public relations people or spokespersons rather than by the chief or the principal or the President. If the spokesperson makes a mistake, it usually causes less damage than if the top person makes a mistake. However, a spokesperson also has less impact than the principal. In places where journalists are constantly eager for news, briefings can be held regularly to get information published or broadcast to serve the organization's interests and still satisfy the journalists' need for timely and crucial developments. The White House normally holds a regular briefing at least once a day, as does the State Department. In times of war, the Defense Department may hold several briefings a day.

News conferences and briefings can often be more effective in gaining news coverage than news releases or even video news releases, because they allow reporters to ask tough questions, giving journalists the sense that they are actually digging up hard facts. Furthermore, when organizations appear to be answering tough questions, this seems less self-serving than statements in press releases or advertisements, so the message acquires more credibility. That credibility is usually well worth the risks involved in allowing journalists to probe and question.

Sound bites and photo ops are a major part of any public relations effort in making messages simple and vivid for mass media and mass audiences. In this endeavor, the public relations communicator often searches for the simple key phrase that will express an idea quickly, simply, and vividly, leading to the so-called *sound bite* (15- to 30-seconds worth of key words or phrases) that can be quoted in the news—especially the news on television and radio—and *photo ops* (staged opportunities for news cameramen and photographers), which allow them to capture the kind of picture that will put the person or thing in the best light. Syndicated columnist George Will called it "striking a pose useful in symbolizing an attitude or intimating a promise."[3]

Monitoring Results

Evaluation is the final step in the public relations process. Who received the messsage? How was it interpreted? How much did it influence? Did it achieve the intended results? These are crucial questions in the continual effort to persuade. Feedback providing answers to these questions is essential for any further efforts in order to know whether to repeat the message, refine the message, change the message, or stop communicating.

Politicians and public leaders constantly check the results of public opinion polls to see how they are doing. President Richard Nixon's public relations efforts to defend himself in the Watergate scandal were so inadequate to the task that his ratings fell the lowest point in his presidency. In his resignation speech, he said he could no longer lead the nation, because the public was no longer following him. Throughout his presidency and certainly during his impeachment ordeal, Bill Clinton followed the polls very deliberately and based much of his strategy on them.

Business organizations might monitor their public relations results by looking at sales figures, but those figures increasingly provide only a small part of what the successful business needs to know about public perceptions. In today's complex world, an organization that doesn't monitor results of its public communication will not likely last long.

DIFFICULT RELATIONS IN AN AGE OF MASS MEDIA

It may seem that public relations is the easy solution to anyone's public reputation, but the picture is more complex than that. Popular culture today is full of examples of people, products, and institutions whose reputations have been damaged by poor public relations efforts, or none at all, and that is true for the most powerful national leaders as well as the smallest public endeavor.

Use or misuse of celebrities can cause a variety of problems. Procter & Gamble came up with a publicity stunt that backfired when it used a list of least kissable celebrities to get publicity for its mouthwash, Scope. Celebrities on the list didn't appreciate being included. TV talk show host Rosie O'Donnell, who made the list, belittled the product on the air, saying, "If you're a dope, you use Scope," while she passed out samples of the competition's Listerine. Her tirades were extensively reported in *TV Guide* and other publications. Perhaps the publicity helped Procter & Gamble; only extensive monitoring after the fact could tell. Shoemaker Converse signed Dennis Rodman to promote its shoes, but the deal was announced the day after Rodman got national publicity for kicking a cameraman in the groin during a basketball game. Again, only sophisticated research could show the true consequences.

Failure to understand one's target public can lead to many problems. Sloan-Kettering, a medical research institution, sent surveys to black women featuring questions about voodoo, white racism, and stereotypical diets ("Do you ever eat chitterlings?"). The researchers said they were merely trying to find out why black women apparently do not trust the medical establishment. In another such failure, the Babe Ruth League in Boca Raton, Fla., insisted that 12-year-old Melissa Raglin wear a jockstrap and cup or else be removed as catcher. The league looked ridiculous when it told the Associated Press the rule was for Raglin's protection.

Underestimating a public also leads to gaffes. The president of Philip Morris said publicly that cigarettes were only minimally addictive, and then explained, "If they are behaviorally addictive or habit forming, they are much more like caffeine, or in my case, Gummi Bears .... I don't like it when I don't eat my Gummi Bears, but I'm certainly not addicted to them," he told the press. Another company, Eat Me Now Foods, produced a product it called Crave, which were glass tubes filled with white sugar, looking like vials of cocaine. When parents objected to the product, the company's president told the press the parents were just "constipated hypocrites .... It is their problem, not mine," he said. When that story got national coverage, the company had to kill the product.[4]

Failure to deal with journalists' serious questions can also lead to trouble. Corning Glass was asked by a reporter about the possible decline in its fiber optics business and refused to provide any answers. Using other sources, the reporter wrote a story for the local newspaper speculating that Corning's finances were worse than reported because of problems with the fiber optics segment of its business. The story got national coverage and Corning's stock plummeted overnight. Nike, as we saw in chapter 13, ignored questions about sweatshop conditions in its Southeast Asian shoe factories, brushing off reporters' inquiries by simply saying those workers were "better off than most and abuses are isolated." The story got national coverage, and cartoonist Garry Trudeau excoriated Nike repeatedly in his syndicated strip, "Doonesbury."[5]

ATTITUDES TOWARD PUBLIC RELATIONS

Although the concepts of public relations seem to make eminent good sense for a democratic society with a free press and mass media, the basic philosophical precepts as well as the individual techniques and often questionable practices have caused considerable debate. Thoughtful analysts have taken many sides on the issue.

Critics of Public Relations

Critics feel that the machinery of opinion management has become deeply entrenched and powerful, leaving little room for coherent opposition to come from ordinary citizens, making the meaning and realization of democracy more elusive.

Daniel Boorstin (1987), an American historian and Librarian of Congress Emeritus, wrote one of the most thoughtful critiques of public relations in the early 1960s as the age of television was reaching maturity. His book, *The Image: A Guide to Pseudo-Events in America*, maintains that the staging of events, which is at the heart of the profession, has overshadowed real and spontaneous events in American culture. His analysis is worth repeating here:

(1) Pseudo-events are more dramatic. A television debate between candidates can be planned to be more suspenseful (for example, by reserving questions which are then popped suddenly) than a casual encounter or consecutive formal speeches planned by each separately.

(2) Pseudo-events, being planned for dissemination, are easier to disseminate and to make vivid. Participants are selected for their newsworthy and dramatic interest.

(3) Pseudo-events can be repeated at will, and thus their impression can be re-enforced.

(4) Pseudo-events cost money to create; hence, somebody has an interest in disseminating, magnifying, advertising, and extolling them as events worth watching or worth believing. They are therefore advertised in advance, and rerun in order to get one's money's worth.

(5) Pseudo-events, being planned for intelligibility, are more intelligible and hence more reassuring. Even if we cannot discuss intelligently the qualifications of the candidates or the complicated issues, we can at least judge the effectiveness of a television performance. How comforting to have some political matter we can grasp.

(6) Pseudo-events are more sociable, more conversable, and more convenient to witness. Their occurrence is planned for our convenience. The Sunday newspaper appears when we have a lazy morning for it. Television programs appear when we are ready with our glass of beer. In the office the next morning, Jack Paar's [or any other star performer's] regular late-night show at the usual hour will overshadow in conversation a casual event that suddenly came up and had to find its way into the news.

(7) Knowledge of pseudo-events—of what has been reported, or what has been staged, and how—becomes the test of being "informed." News magazines provide us regularly with quiz questions concerning not what has happened but concerning "names in the news"—what has been reported in the news magazines. Pseudo-events begin to provide that "common discourse" which some of my old friends have hoped to find in the Great Books.

(8) Finally, pseudo-events spawn other pseudo-events in geometric progression. They dominate our consciousness simply because there are more of them, and ever more. (pp. 39–40)

Jurgen Habermas (1979), mid-twentieth-century German philosopher concerned with questions of public communication, is perhaps the most influential European theorist expressing a strongly negative position on public relations. He reasons that democracy takes place in what he calls "the public sphere," a place where private people come together as a public. Habermas argues that as mass media expanded in the nineteenth and twentieth centuries, they evolved from institutions for rational public discussion of political affairs into privately controlled, privately motivated organs, profit-making businesses in which editors became tools of proprietors and newspapers became "the gate through which privileged private interests invaded the public sphere" (p. 185).

Habermas maintains that, as advertising emerged to manage the process of commodity distribution, so public relations became the means by which politicians could be represented in the public sphere and gain access to the voting public. He concludes that the public relations industry, working on behalf of political actors, has transformed the public sphere from its original status as a forum for rational debate into an arena dominated by the values of entertainment and consumption.

Political parties have organized themselves as businesses, marketing and selling their ideas and programs in the name of the public interest. The style of a political performance, shaped and honed by public relations, has become more important than the substance of policy. "Important political decisions" in an age of public relations, Habermas (1979) wrote, are "made for manipulative purposes and introduced with consummate propagandistic skill as publicity vehicles into a public sphere manufactured for show" (p. 221).

A British communication scholar, Nicholas Garnham (1986), argues that "the rise of public relations [represents] the direct control by private or state interests of the flow of public information, not of rational discourse, but of manipulation" (p. 41).

An American, Stuart Ewen (1996), expresses this point strongly in his book, *PR: A Social History of Spin*. He feels that the development of public relations as a force in American society has undergone a consequential change. "The apparatus for molding the public mind and for appealing to the public eye," he wrote, has become so pervasive and sophisticated in its technology and expertise that "the free circulation of ideas and debate critical to the maintenance of an aware public" is harder to achieve (pp. 409–410).

Ewen brings his study of the history of public relations into the mid-1990s and concludes that "publicity becomes an impediment to democracy ... when the circulation of ideas is governed by enormous concentrations of wealth that have, as their underlying purpose, the perpetuation of their own power. When this is the case—as is too often true today—the ideal of civic participation gives way to a continual sideshow, a masquerade of democracy calculated to pique the public's emotions" (p. 410). Boorstin, Habermas, Garnham, and Ewen are representative of many current critics, reacting to the growth of powerful mass media controlled by fewer and fewer interests.

Defenders of Public Relations

Defenders tend to come from academics and critics who perhaps reflect attitudes about mass communication before its postmodernist, postcommunist economic and technological massiveness. Typical of this group is the American political scientist Stanley Kelley (1956). His book, *Professional Public Relations and Political Power*, presented a positive argument about the rise of public relations as the inevitable consequence of the process whereby mass media became ever more central to opinion formation and political decision making. For Kelley, mass participation in politics is only possible through the involvement with mass media through public relations.

Scott Cutlip, who coauthored a widely used public relations textbook, writes that the philosophy of public relations pioneer Bernays is the proper way to view public relations. Bernays (1923) described public relations as interpreting the public's view to the organization and interpreting the organization's policies and programs to its constituent publics, in order to arrive at an accommodation of mutual interests. Cutlip (1989) wrote that "this mature view of the function of public relations has taken hold slowly in management in the last 66 years. Where this concept is practiced," Cutlip concluded, "both the organization and the public are well served (p. 115).

Neutral Positions on Public Relations

Neutral positions on public relations are hard to come by. It seems that one either feels strongly for or strongly against the profession. Perhaps the best neutral expression about the field was made long ago by the British political philosopher J. A. R. Pimlott, who spent a year in the United States in 1947-1948, on a British Home Civil Service Fellowship, studying the American government's use of public relations practices. His study ended in the publication of an important book, *Public Relations and American Democracy.*

Pimlott's (1951) study led him to conclude that, like other tools, public relations can be misused. "It is most likely to be misused when the stakes are highest; and the dangers to society may be grave," he wrote. The remedy he suggests, however, is not "in doctoring the symptoms," though he suggests this might be desirable at times. He argues that abuse of public relations should not obscure its essential and constructive contribution. "This contribution should not be exaggerated—as is commonly done by public relations advocates," concludes Pimlott. "Neither should it be belittled" (p. 258).

The authors of this book, both experienced in journalism and public relations, agree with Pimlott. We think modern democracy could not exist in an age of mass communication without the professional support that public relations can provide to anyone who wants to communicate publicly. Even those without the financial means, with some public relations knowledge, can join forces with others of like mind, organize a grassroots communication effort, and get some publicity for their viewpoint.

But we also are concerned that the techniques can be used to manipulate publics. Therefore the most crucial point for citizens in a democracy is to be educated about the role of mass media and the practices of all those who would seek to use mass communication to manage public attitudes and opinions for their own gain.

Further Reading

Bernays, Edward L. (1923). *Crystallizing Public Opinion.* New York: Boni & Liveright.

Block, Edward M. (1988). In Hiebert, Ray Eldon, *Precision Public Relations* (pp. 86–99). New York: Longman.

Boorstin, Daniel J. (1987). *The Image: A Guide to Pseudo-Events in America.* New York: Atheneum.

Cantor, Bill, and Burger, Chester. (Eds.). (1989). *Experts in Action: Inside Public Relations* (2nd ed.). New York: Longman.

Cutlip, Scott M. (1995). *Public Relations History: From the 17th to the 20th Century.* Mahwah, NJ: Lawrence Erlbaum Associates.

Cutlip, Scott M. (1989, Spring). Public Relations: The Manufacture of Public Opinion. *Gannett Center Journal, 3*(2), 105–116.

Cutlip, Scott M., Center, Allen H., and Broom, Glen M. (1994). *Effective Public Relations* (7th ed.). Upper Saddle River, NJ: Prentice-Hall.

Ewen, Stuart. (1996). *PR! A Social History of Spin.* New York: Basic Books.

Gans, Herbert J. (1989, Spring). Bystanders as Opinion Makers: A Bottoms Up Perspective. *Gannett Center Journal, 3*(2), 97–104.

Garnham, Nicholas. (1990). *Capitalism and Communication: Global Culture and the Economics of Information.* London: Sage.

Grunig, James E., and Dozier, David E. (Eds.). (1992) *Excellence in Public Relations and Communication Management*. Mahwah, NJ: Lawrence Erlbaum Associates.

Habermas, Jurgen. (1979). *Communication and the Evolution of Society*. Boston: Beacon Press.

Harlow, Rex (1975). Defining Public Relations. *Public Relations Review, 2*(4), 34–42.

Hazen, Don, and Winokur, Julie. (Eds.). (1997). *We the Media*. New York: New Press and Norton.

Hiebert, Ray Eldon. (1966). *Courtier to the Crowd: The Life Story of Ivy Lee, Founder of Public Relations*. Ames: Iowa State University Press.

Hiebert, Ray Eldon. (1999). *Impact of Mass Media: Current Issues* (4th ed.). New York: Longman.

Hiebert, Ray Eldon. (1988). *Precision Public Relations*. New York: Longman.

Karlins, Marvin, and Abelson, Herbert I. (1970). *Persuasion: How Opinions and Attitudes Are Changed* (2nd ed.). New York: Springer.

Kelley, Stanley. (1956). *Professional Public Relations and Political Power*. Baltimore: Johns Hopkins University Press.

L'Etang, Jacquie, and Pieczka, Magda. (1996). *Critical Perspectives in Public Relations*. London: International Thomson Business Press.

Lippmann, Walter. (1922). *Public Opinion*. New York: Harcourt, Brace.

Mankiewicz, Frank. (1989, Spring). From Lippmann to Letterman: The Ten Most Powerful Voices. *Gannett Center Journal, 3*(2), 81–96.

Nevins, Allan. (1978, Fall). The Constitution Makers and the Public: 1785–1790. *Public Relations Review, 4*(3), 5–16.

Pimlott, J. A. R. (1951). *Public Relations and American Democracy*. Princeton, NJ: Princeton University Press.

Pratkanis, Anthony, and Aronson, Elliot. (1991). *Age of Propaganda: The Everyday Use and Abuse of Persuasion*. New York: Freeman.

Rourke, Francis E. (1961). *Secrecy & Publicity: Dilemmas of Democracy*. Baltimore: Johns Hopkins University Press.

Sauerhaft, Stan, and Atkins, Chris. (1989). *Image Wars: Protecting Your Company When There's No Place to Hide*. New York: Wiley.

Seitel, Fraser P. (1998). *The Practice of Public Relations* (7th ed.). Upper Saddle River, NJ: Prentice-Hall.

Notes

[1] Among them, in addition to Sam Adams, were Thomas Paine, Thomas Jefferson, John Adams, John Dickinson, Benjamin Franklin, and Richard Henry Lee.

[2] See Roberts, W. (Trans.). (1954). *Aristotle, Rhetoric, and Poetics* (p. 25). New York: Modern Library.

[3] Will, George. (1987). Afterword. In Daniel J. Boorstin (Ed.), *The Image: A Guide to Pseudo-Events in America* (25th Anniversary edition). New York: Atheneum.

[4] See St. John, Burton. (1998, February). Third Annual PR Blunders List Highlights 1997 Gaffes. *St. Louis Journalism Review*, p. 12.

[5] Ibid.

15

The Internet
and the Future of Mass Media

In the 1930s, the American family clustered around the radio console in the living room, mostly to be entertained. They computed family finances by hand or perhaps with the help of a mechanical adding machine with a noisy pull handle. They had a telephone, but they shared a single line with other neighbors, called a *party line*, which served several households. They wrote letters to distant relatives and mailed them with 2-cent stamps. All their news came from the local daily newspaper.

In the family of the 1960s, Mom and Dad watched their favorite programs on black and white TV while the kids watched theirs on the smaller set in an upstairs bedroom. They had four or five choices of stations to watch. There were three radios in the house and one in the car. One, a transistor radio, was so small it could fit into Dad's pocket. They computed their family finances on a battery-operated calculator. They occasionally talked to far-away relatives by telephone, but it was pretty expensive to make that kind of call. So they mostly wrote to relatives and sent their letters with 8-cent stamps. They got a lot of their news from radio and television, depended less on their local newspaper, and filled in the gaps in their news awareness with a weekly news magazine.

Things had changed even more by the 1990s. The family had three color and stereo TV sets hooked to the local cable television company, giving them access to 4 or 5 dozen different programs. They had two VCRs for recording programs off the antenna or cable and for playing movies and instructional videos. They had a video camera and made their own home videos on special occasions. The household had a stereo system with a CD player and a tape deck. The kids each had their own stereo in their rooms and a personal stereo that fit in their pockets. Mom had a cellular phone that, like the house phone, accepted phonemail.

But the big player in this electronic household was the personal computer (PC) in the den. Here, Dad dialed into his office to retrieve e-mail messages and to work on projects from home. Mom used the computer to write freelance articles, track the family finances, and interface with her bank to transfer funds between accounts and pay bills. Their son used the computer to duel with his buddies playing interactive video games and to do his homework. To write a school report critiquing the lyrics to a song for his music class, he listened to the music on the computer's CD-ROM drive and wrote the report on its word processing system. He consulted an online encyclopedia to get information about the composer. His sister got online to send an e-mail letter to their older sister away at college, attaching a file containing a short story she'd written and wanted her older sister to read.

Stamps were up to 33 cents and weren't getting used all that much except for packages, birthday and anniversary cards, and seasonal greetings. The family members increasingly turned to the Internet for the crucial news they needed each day, including weather reports, stock market quotations, and classified ads.

In the early years of the twenty-first century, home communications will have all those things but will change even more. Many homes will have media centers, with large-screen wall TVs and surround sound but, more important, almost every form of communication—radio, television, Internet, and phone calls—will probably come over one wireless digital signal into the TV set or pocket phone or car computer. All the hardware will be compressed into a gadget the size of a cell phone, and it will be a phone, a radio, and an Internet browser. Many household transactions, from shopping to security to banking to paying the bills, will be handled electronically.

Internet access in these homes of the future will enhance the role of multimedia for the whole family, allowing text, graphics, sound, and video to mix together. Most people will begin to take full advantage of the Internet's cornucopia—the world of news and information, knowledge and entertainment—with a few strokes of a keyboard. Most of society will use the Internet to send and receive messages, images, sounds, and even real-time videos of sender and receiver.

At the beginning of the twenty-first century, this is what new media are already accomplishing for individuals. The new media also have broad, exciting applications for business, education, journalism, and entertainment. In this chapter, we'll consider how the most influential new medium—the Internet—is reshaping communications, not just in the U.S. but everywhere.

CONVERGENCE AND NEW MEDIA

New media are developing so rapidly that it is difficult to provide any definitive list of what they are. Basically, however, in this book by *new media* we mean high-definition television, digital radio broadcasting, multimedia computers, the Internet, palmtop computers, wireless communications, CD–ROMs (compact disk–read only memory), videodiscs, direct broadcast satellites, advanced facsimile machines, intelligent telephones, consumer computer networks, and online news services. Each one of these would be worth a separate chapter, because each has something to add to or change our concepts, each with implications for the mass communication process as a whole.

Some of these have already been discussed in other chapters of this book. We concentrate on the most important one, the Internet.

As we indicated elsewhere, the "traditional" mass media are themselves changing and will be different in the future. Newspapers have added color, graphics, better paper and printing processes, satellite-transmitted regional editions, and online editions. Magazines are becoming even more specialized and can use computers to differentiate targeted audiences in order to include specialized content for individual subscribers. Newsletters, magazines, and books can be published more quickly and inexpensively with desktop publishing technologies, allowing a great many more publications to be produced.

Radio is being automated and digitized, but with consolidation of ownership, the future may see less specialized programming. Traditional network television is being upstaged by cable and by the rise of new networks. New technologies in the future, such as high definition TV, will bring changes to that medium. Cable TV will continue to crowd the field, as the 54-channel capacities of many local systems expand to 150 channels or more, and pay per view may well replace many programs we have traditionally thought were free. The movie industry, too, has changed drastically as a result of cable and videocassette recordings. The next step may be the delivery of movies through home computers via the Internet.

The convergence of audio, video, and Internet is rapidly turning interactive networks into a high speech digital distribution system in which every home and business will be a mail stop for magazines, e-mail, video entertainment, radio, and personal services such as banking and shopping.

The way in which the Internet is changing radio is a good example of the impact it will have on all media. Already, almost any standard computer can inexpensively become the ultimate radio, receiving stations for free from anywhere in the world. By the beginning of the twenty-first century, more than 1,500 radio stations were available online through the Internet. One can program an Internet radio to be one's own personal radio station, playing only country or classical or punk and, in time, even drive coast to coast listening to the same station playing one's own favorite tunes.

Even the act of broadcasting sound can and will change. A traditional radio transmitter is expensive, heavy, and unwieldy. A digital Internet station can be the size of a PC, creating the ultimate local or personal radio station without having to compete for frequency allocation or federal permission to be on a crowded AM or FM band. It can enable an individual, an office, a neighborhood, or a school to program the most relevant entertainment and information for its listener.

THE RISE OF THE INTERNET

The Internet, however, is the giant that looms over the future of the entire world of mass communication, changing not only itself but also the normal processing of information; the old notions of ownership and control; the traditional concepts of freedom, rights, and responsibilities; the usual creation and measurement of audiences; the understanding of effects; and the traditional uses and functions. In just a few years during the mid-1990s, it has become an entirely new mass medium. There has been nothing like it, and it has the potential for revolutionizing the entire communication process as much as the inventions of the alphabet, the printing press, and television. That is why we focus on it as we look at the new media and the future of communicating.

In the last few years of the twentieth century, the Internet burst on the scene as an entirely new mass medium. It moved from invention to mass communication far faster than any medium that preceded it. Even in the early 1990s, few people thought of it as anything more than a new postal system, a way of sending mail electronically. By the end of the century, it was clear that the Internet was a new mass medium, with new rules that would change almost every aspect of mass communication in the new millennium.

Books took nearly 400 years from their first appearance as a printed medium in the mid-fifteenth century to go from being an elite to a mass medium in the mid-nineteenth century. Newspapers took about 200 years, from the 1630s to the 1830s. Magazines required about 170 years, from 1700 to the 1870s. Sound recordings were transformed into a mass medium in about 60 years, from the 1880s to the 1940s. Motion pictures made the progression in about 50 years, from the 1870s to the 1920s; radio in about 40 years, from the 1890s to the 1930s; television in about 30 years, from the 1920s to the 1950s. The Internet took only 15 years, from the early 1980s to the mid-1990s.

DEFINING THE INTERNET

The Internet is simply a way of connecting all the computers of the world into new communities. It is not an entity in itself, but by connecting computers it creates an environment, a place to communicate, to conduct business, to share information and ideas. Some have called this new worldwide connection the global village, but, as Esther Dyson (1997) aptly suggested, it is more an environment in which a profusion of new and different villages, or online communities, can flourish. The Internet makes it easier for people to participate in a infinite variety of communities.

Online communities offer an opportunity for people to engage in conversations and other interaction through the medium of a particular *Web site* or through mailing lists or newsgroups—people linked together by text messsages and, increasingly, through multimedia virtual places that they enter from time to time. An example of a virtual community is ECHO, a New York-based online community founded by Stacy Horn (1998), who describes the community in her book *Cyberville*. ECHO is a place where people live much as they do in their own physical towns, experiencing the same joys, thrills, frustrations, and issues as members of every virtual gathering place—from small bulletin board systems to the giant America Online.

A **newsgroup** is a virtual bulletin board, which members post to or read on their own schedule. A **mailing list** (or **listserv**), is an active newsgroup; it sends regular messages to its members, but it also generally maintains archives for people to search.

Online **virtual places** can be anything from a **virtual room** where people communicate in text, to full-scale multimedia locations where people are represented by *avatars*, cartoon figures, images of themselves, or any other symbol they choose. Some of these places support voice or even video. **Buddy lists** enable users to see who is currently online and virtually tap them on the shoulder.

Domain names have been called both the real estate and the trademarks of cyberspace; they establish virtual identity and have become valuable properties in and of themselves. For example, the domain name *business.com* was sold for $150,000 in the mid-1990s. Generic top-level domain names include *.org* (for organizations), *.gov* (for government agencies and offices), *.com* (for commercial enterprises, including Internet service providers), *.edu* (for educational institutions), *.mil* (for military forces), and *.net* (for network service providers).

HISTORICAL BACKGROUND

The Internet concept dates from the 1950s when the Eisenhower administration created the Advanced Research Projects Agency (ARPA), funded by the Defense Department to link government computers for the exchange of information needed for the Cold War. It became a more public network in 1969 when four universities (Stanford, UCLA, UC Santa Barbara, and Utah) tapped into it because they wanted to keep current with the technology momentum but could not afford supercomputers; by embracing the *ARPAnet* they could all access time on a supercomputer without having to buy one.

The ARPAnet, of course, was designed for complex data analysis, but early in the 1970s its users discovered that they could create *mailing lists* to send messages through the ARPAnet to individual users, and one of the first big lists was *SF-LOVERS* to exchange science fiction among aficionados. This non-work-related activated was frowned on by many ARPAnet administrators, but it couldn't be stopped, and the germ of a new mass medium was born.

Thus, like many other mass media (especially movies, radio, and television), the Internet was started strictly for one business or educational purpose but ultimately became used by a mass public for completely different, more personal, more public information and for more entertainment purposes.

Becoming Affordable

The turning point in becoming a new mass medium probably came in 1975, when IBM decided it would start manufacturing personal computers. By the early 1980s, the price of an IBM PC had dropped to about $1,600, and in 1982 Timex started selling a drugstore model for $99.95, making computers affordable for the masses—the equivalent of the penny press, nickel magazine, dime novel, nickelodeon movies, and $99 TV set. This was followed shortly thereafter by the introduction of the Apple Macintosh, the PC that anyone could use without any technical knowledge of the workings of computers.

In 1981, 12 years after the first four universities connected with ARPAnet, the number of *hosts*, or individual computers linked in the network, had expanded to 213. This was not an earth-shaking number, but slowly, the network continued to grow. In 1987, the National Science Foundation established five supercomputing centers around the country, linked them with its own high-speed network known as NSFnet, and encouraged research institutions to form regional networks. This led to the basic structure of the Internet, with its multiple layers of networks.

In the 1980s, the Internet was still only a technical network of scientists and researchers. Over time this formal research network began to draw in a new group of less technically inclined users and commercial services. All over the United States and even worldwide, many users of those now affordable PCs joined together with scientists and researchers to push the Internet's evolution into becoming something much more powerful—a new medium of mass communication. In 12 years, from 1981 to 1993, the number of hosts expanded from 213 to 1.3 million.

Becoming a Mass Medium

Still by the early 1990s, the Internet had not yet become a mass medium. Like other mass media, especially those involving the use of complex technology, the Internet could not be used by the masses until its use no longer required mastery of the technology. People can watch television or use the telephone without understanding how they work. To become a mass medium, the Internet's technology had to fade into the background, and much of the innovation in the mid-1990s was inspired by that need.

One of the most important innovations was the introduction of the *World Wide Web*, (WWW) developed by Tim Berners-Lee at the European Center for Nuclear Research in Geneva. The WWW is a way of weaving together or linking information, using the idea of *hypertext*, highlighted words that link text documents to other text documents, allowing the user to jump to other information on the topic. This is accomplished through *HTML coding* (HyperText Markup Language) to connect subjects and headings on the World Wide Web.

Making It User Friendly

In 1992, the Internet was still largely the domain of specialists. New companies had been organizing to provide Internet services, such as CompuServe and Prodigy. In 1992, they launched a product called *Journalist* which would organize online information for the user, but it was too complicated to win a large following. In 1993, the first user-friendly *Web browser,* a function to help read and move through a hypertext document, was introduced. It was called *Mosaic*, developed by Marc Andreessen, and made available free to the public. Giving it away free, a surprise at first, turned into an enormously successful marketing ploy. In the next 3 years, 1993 to 1996, the number of hosts mushroomed from 1.3 million to 9.5 million. Mosaic was followed by *Netscape*, which became one of the most popular browsers.

In 1996, another innovation, *PointCast*, was launched with a new approach to customized news; it used a stream of tailored news blurbs that appeared as an attractive screen saver. It teamed with *The New York Times* and Cable News Network for content and sold ads interspersed with the content. More than a million users registered within 5 months. It brought the concept of broadcasting to the Web, allowing users to see colorful, animated ads automatically on the screen, much like television spots, without having to click on them.

Instead of having to search through Web sites for information, this technology, called *push*, allows users to select material they want and have it delivered automatically to their computer. As Andreessen said, "Information overload has become the Web's single biggest problem." The point of push software is to "simplify the way information is delivered on the Internet."[1] Many competitors have followed PointCast's lead.

Growth of a Mass Audience

In 1994, only 3 million people were using the Internet. By 1998, it was used by more than 100 million worldwide. They were sending more than 100 million messages a day by e-mail. More than 70 percent of American schools had access to the Internet.

By 1998, a survey by Computer Intelligence in California found that 45 percent of all U.S. households had a personal computer, an increase from 40 percent in 1996. Another 1998 survey, by IntelliQuest Information Group, found that 62 million adults were using the Internet in the United States, or 30 percent of the total adult population. The survey found that 15 million people, or 25 percent of the total population of online users, had first started accessing the Internet in 1997 alone.

By early 1999, the Internet in America was growing by 52,000 new users every day. A survey by the Pew Research Center for the People and the Press, released in January 1999, found that nearly half (46 percent) of Internet users started going online in 1998. The survey also found that the demographics of Internet use was changing. In the past, a relatively small and elite group, of mostly upper-middle-class educated males comprised the group. Pew reported that 40 percent of those who started going online in 1998 never attended college, and that 23 percent had household incomes below $30,000 a year. The survey also showed that women were more likely to be new users (52 percent) than men (48 percent).

OWNERSHIP AND CONTROL

The Internet is not an independent entity and is not owned by any particular business or group or country. It was created largely by the U.S. government, which until the early 1990s still owned most of it. However, an increasing proportion of the equipment it requires is owned by computer centers in universities, research organizations, and private companies. In addition, it uses existing phone lines owned by private companies and public utilities.

Although most of its operating costs were at first paid by the government, the Internet is increasingly subsidized by private computer centers, whose computers hold most of the Internet's content. *Internet service providers* (ISPs) have become the main property owners of cyberspace. They include such companies as America Online, Yahoo!, and Microsoft Network. (See Tables 15.1 and 15.2.) They manage or rent the physical assets, and they can control access to the system. Government control of cyberspace is increasingly limited to the kinds of regulation it exercises over other

TABLE 15.1

Top 10 Internet Service Providers, or Digital Media/Web Properties,
Based on Unduplicated Audience Reach

Rank	Properties*	Unique Visitors**
1.	AOL Network	37,956,000[1]
2.	Microsoft Sites	30,130,000
3.	Yahoo! Sites	29,495,000
4.	Lycos	28,513,000
5.	Go Network	22,771,000
6.	Geocities	19,257,000
7.	The Excite Network	18,225,000
8.	Netscape	18,001,000[2]
9.	Time Warner Online	12,180,000
10.	Altavista Search Service	11,237,000

Source: Media Metrix, Inc., January 1999 Audience Ratings. Reproduced with permission.

*Properties include the largest single Web site brands as well as consolidations of multiple domains that fall under one brand or common ownership.

**Unique visitors are the actual number of total users who visited the Web site once in the given month. All unique visitors are unduplicated (counted only once).

[1]Before merging with Netscape in 1999.

[2]Before merging with AOL in 1999.

TABLE 15.2

Top 10 Internet Domains, Based on Unduplicated Audience Reach

Rank	Domains	Unique Visitors*
1.	yahoo.com	29,198,000
2.	aol.com	28,990,000[1]
3.	msn.com	20,197,000
4.	go.com	19,871,000
5.	geocities.com	18,837,000
6.	netscape.com	18,001,000[2]
7.	excite.com	15,544,000
8.	lycos.com	14,999,000
9.	microsoft.com	14,238,000
10.	tripod.com	12,488,000

Source: Media Metrix, Inc., January 1999 Audience Ratings. Reproduced with permission.

*Unique visitors are actual number of total users who visited the Web site once in the given month. All unique visitors are unduplicated (counted only once).

[1]Before merging with Netscape in 1999.

[2]Before merging with AOL in 1999.

businesses, such as antimonopoly laws, minimum wage standards, and the like, although fierce arguments are raging about the need for government to exercise more control, even censorship, as we discuss later.

ISPs connect the physical and virtual worlds. Individual subscribers own their own PCs and their connections to the ISPs. The ISPs control the connection, however, and can charge a fee for the connection and the time spent using the connection. The ISPs also work with those authorities who register domain names for their customers—to give them identity in cyberspace.

Governance

The U.S. government originally allowed the interconnection of university and research center computers with its computers in order to further the work of science. It has continued to seek private involvement in the Internet to increase its benefits to all of society. Some control obviously was needed, but as the entity evolved, government often contracted out its control to private nongovernment organizations. For example, Network Solutions Inc. (NSI), a private subsidiary of a U.S. military contractor, was given a contract to establish the registration of domain names. NSI parcels the domain names to name registers that manage the registration and maintenance of domain names.

One central coordinating body is the Internet Assigned Numbers Authority (IANA). It is a vestige of the old academic and military sectors that gave birth to the Internet and remains under the authority and funding of the government. IANA oversees the Internet's infrastructure and sets policies that let addresses be translated into Internet protocol numbers used for routing digital traffic. Privately owned data networks that agreed to interconnect for mutual benefit have recognized the need for such an authority to make difficult decisions to allow the Internet to work and grow.

In 1994, the federal government withdrew even further from the Internet when it convened a National Information Infrastructure Advisory Council, composed of private citizens and other nonfederal government people, to guide the government in its efforts to use private enterprise to develop the Internet. These government actions should not be interpreted to mean that government will have no role to play in the Internet, but rather that power has naturally shifted to commercial entities, to multinational businesses and mass media conglomerates as well as to small businesses, small media, and small nongovernment organizations.

The ISPs themselves, although not regulating what their subscribers communicate among themselves, can to some extent govern external behavior. They can cut off service to customers who breach copyright laws, or send offensive messages, or otherwise misbehave. For example, senders of *spam*, the Internet's junk mail, could be refused service by an ISP and could eventually find their services blocked out by other ISPs. The ultimate restriction in cyberspace would be the refusal of an ISP to communicate with another ISP. In this way, ISPs can police their customers and one another, and this is starting to happen more frequently as the Internet grows. In other words, there are rules in the worldwide digital society, but those rules are derived and enforced in a decentralized, incremental way, not by one centralized governmental authority.

Economics

The Internet at first produced content as a relatively free public resource. Money was made by the producers of hardware and software, and by ISPs charging for access or connection, but not by the producers of content. By 1997, there were signs that the economic basis of the Internet was changing, that the selling of goods and services over the Internet could be enormously profitable. In that year, Amazon.com, an online bookstore, achieved gross sales of $148 million, an 838 percent gain over 1996. Advertising, as we will see, has come rushing to the Net, and charging for access to all content is the next step.

According to Forrester Research Inc., Internet commerce in 1998 amounted to about $17 billion, double that from 1997, but still only a fraction (0.2 percent) of the $11 trillion U.S. economy. By 2002, Internet transactions should be about $325 billion, or 2 percent of the gross economy. The price of many Internet stocks also soared in the late 1990s. America Online (AOL) stock grew by 304 percent in the first 10 months of 1998, and Netscape grew by 65 percent. At the end of 1998 AOL and Netscape merged to become a powerful Internet competitor to Microsoft, the world's biggest software company. These are just some of the indications of the new economics of the Internet.

RIGHTS AND RESPONSIBILITIES

Since access to the Internet is available to anyone, a host of new concerns have been raised about legal rights and moral responsibilities. A university student in Maryland, acting on hearsay, posted a public Internet message accusing a woman of mistreating her daughter and urging readers to call the family. The message generated threatening phone calls and other unwarranted abuse for the woman and her family. A student at a Washington, D.C., university, as part of a class project, proposed to use the Internet to launch a sperm bank business, complete with a sexually explicit approach to marketing.

These incidents, not unusual and rising in frequency, show how the power of the Internet can outpace its users' sense of responsibility. With older media, editors could act as gatekeepers to prevent inaccuracies and irresponsible reporting, but traditional checks do not apply to the Internet.

Current Concerns

A number of critical issues are at the heart of public discussion about the Internet in the first years of the new millennium. Increasing concern has been raised about Internet libel, patent infringement, gambling, and the rise of cyberwars. The Internet has been called a new battleground for refighting the wars that shape our culture, and we come back to this concern later in this chapter. Perhaps the key concerns are the following:

Sensationalism on the Internet, including gossip and rumor-mongering, has been rising. A prominent example is *The Drudge Report*, an Internet newsletter specializing in scooping traditional media, often with salacious gossip about celebrities and public officials. The author, Matt Drudge, was self-taught, without traditional training or experience in journalism. He got his information by listening to police scanners, monitoring online services, accessing unpublished underground Web sites, and receiving tips from online users. More important, he transmitted to his online readers instantaneously, with little or no checking of his facts or sources. As a result, he often beat the traditional media and achieved major scoops. However, he also made mistakes. One target of his work filed a $30 million libel suit against him. Others have defended his First Amendment rights.

Privacy is another major concern. Databases are filled with personal information that was once the domain of private investigators, investigative reporters, or government agencies. New companies are forming to profit from gathering and selling private and personal information. For example, Acxiom Corporation is a giant information service that electronically gathers and sorts information about Americans 24 hours a day. It has 350 trillion characters of consumer data, including credit card transactions, magazine subscriptions, telephone numbers, real estate records, car registrations, fishing licenses, consumer surveys, demographic details, credit reports, social security numbers, and much more, which it can sell to customers via the World Wide Web.

Pornography, sex, and obscenity have become a multibillion dollar business on the Internet in only a few years. An anaysis of the frequency that key words are searched revealed that most of the top ten *hits* had to do with sex. In fact, one critic called the Internet the world's largest dirty magazine.

Copyright infringement is a problem because computers and the Internet that connects them make it easy and almost cost-free to reproduce content and send or retrieve it anywhere in the world. One solution is to tag the content in some way so that its use can be electronically monitored and billed. *Playboy*, for example has started *watermarking* its images so one can detect whenever they may be copied on the Net.

Regulation

As a result of these and other growing concerns, the future will see continual attempts by governments to place restrictions and limitations on the Internet. In late 1995, Congress passed the U.S. Communications Decency Act aimed at the Internet. It would have outlawed the posting of indecent material on the Net, on the theory that it would corrupt and endanger helpless children. But in June 1997, in the case of *ACLU v. Reno*, the Supreme Court overruled the law in a landmark decision, saying it was too vague and that in seeking to protect children it trampled on everyone's rights.

Yet the Court's upholding the most stringent First Amendment protections in cyberspace in that case didn't resolve the underlying conflict between cultures that the Internet raises. In fact, many new bills were quickly introduced in Congress, including the Internet School Filtering Act of 1998, which would require libraries to block "harmful" content or face the loss of federal subsidies. Other federal bills, including one banning Internet gambling, as well as state and local laws, have multiplied. In Congress in 1998, more than 80 bills were introduced designed to exercise some restriction over the

Internet. In California alone between 1997 and 1998, the number of new Internet-related laws quadrupled to 34, with another 33 measures pending.

Another area of government encroachment has been *encryption*, the use of message-scrambling technology to protect the privacy of information on the Net. The government is opposed to the technology, claiming that it would give criminals and terrorists a cloak under which to hide their illegal activities. The federal government already prohibits the sale of strong cryptography products abroad, but in spite of this, the use of encryption is increasing internationally.

Ethics in Cyberspace

Because online media unlock a Pandora's box of ethical concerns, many professional organizations, such as the American Society of Newspaper Editors (ASNE), are deeply concerned about the problem. ASNE's Journalism Values Institute has admitted that online media create new ethical dilemmas as well as new solutions. In a summary of its concerns, it sought answers to a variety of key questions, as the following paragraphs show.

The Internet can actually enhance balance, fairness, and wholeness, because it can give unlimited time and space to a subject. But should journalists provide links to everything, including ads, hate groups, and opinionated material on any subject? What about readers who leave a comment, via links, before they have read all sides? How much actuality—photos and verbatim quotes and reports—should be used?

Online media have enough time and space to get all the facts with accuracy and authenticity. But in a medium that moves with such speed, chances for error are multiplied. In a medium that anyone can access, do journalists have an obligation to take a leadership role in deciding who should be heard the most? Internet accessibility means that anyone can get into the public communication stream. How can journalists maintain credibility of material they receive, especially leaked information from anonymous sources? Being online can improve news judgment, but can journalists keep up with the new wealth of information available fast enough to make proper judgments?

NEW THEORIES AND MODELS

In many respects, the Internet poses an entirely new model of the mass communication process. As Newhagen and Levy point out, the traditional mass media architecture has been a system where novel and relevant events were funneled into news media, which in turn compressed them into manageable forms and sent them out to mass audiences (Borden & Harvey, 1998, pp. 9–21). However, computer-based communication network architecture is quite different, with message-sender and message-receiver nodes all interconnected. "Because message production can take place at any node in the network," say Newhagen and Levy, "information distribution is a diffuse, parallel process, unlike the compressed, serial process of mass media" (p. 15).

The flow of information in the Internet is also interactive and nonlinear, with messages going back and forth between sender and receiver, more in the manner in which the brain and central nervous system might work rather than the traditional sender–receiver model. Newhagen and Levy point out that Marshall McLuhan, long before the Internet, suggested that technologies are extensions of human processes; the Internet comes closer to being an extension of the brain than any medium before it.

In *New Media Technology*, John Pavlik (1996) writes that electronic media technologies "are rapidly merging into a single digital communication environment," but final questions about their nature and impact are still unanswered "primarily because they are still developing both in their form and function" (p. xiv). But their basic model is that they are driven by computer technology, are interactive, and are accessible to mass audiences. However, they are different from traditional mass media in a number of ways, including production, distribution, display, storage, and the simultaneity of audience reception.

Production of online news and information services is not necessarily performed by professional communicators. Anybody can become a producer as well as a receiver. *Distribution* is based on the receiver's ability to use a particular technology, to search for information, and to negotiate a method of selection and delivery. *Display*, although limited to a screen, can be almost limitless in graphic design and content, but access is limited to individual hits. *Storage* is almost infinite in both time and space. *Simultaneous reception* possible in radio and television is not possible online.

Kevin Kawamoto says that the primary differences between traditional mass media and new media have to do with *space, time,* and *choice*. "New media are not confined by space or time restrictions the way traditional media are" (Borden & Harvey, 1998, p. 186). They do not have to fill a particular newshole or time slot nor be fragmented into smaller bits because of time or space limitations. Messages can be complete, and they can be put into context. Furthermore, by using hypertext links, the receiver can put together a nearly unlimited variety of related information, called *hypermedia*.

If users access information about an issue in the news—for example, the international community's political conflict with Iraq—they can also retrieve historical background on Iraq from any variety of sources, including encyclopedias, related articles, and related archive materials. They can bring up maps, diagrams, pictures, and graphic data about Iraq. They can access sound and video, and even a link to an online discussion group on various topics related to Iraq, all by clicking highlighted words, using hypertext. In hypermedia news environments, it is not self-evident where the content lies, and studying this development will require fundamentally new ways of thinking about media content.

AUDIENCES

One of the most important things about the new technologies is that they allow the message sender to get more information more quickly about the message receiver. Our demographics, our histories, our interests, our hopes, and our desires can all be learned by those who send us messages. This information allows those who want something from us to target us through appropriate media with effective messages. On the Internet, we know when receivers have *hit* our message, and we can find out who they are.

A 1998 survey by FutureScapes found that Internet users spent 60 percent more time surfing the Net than watching television, and the longer they had been online the less time they spent with TV. A similar study by the Strategis Group Inc. in 1998 asked 500 Internet users what they were doing less so they can surf the net more: 64 percent said watching TV or videos, 48 percent said reading, 28 percent said sleeping, 26 percent said family and friends, 22 percent said exercising, and 18 percent said working.[2]

Fragmented audiences are the obvious result of the Internet, where interactivity allows users to pursue almost an infinite number of messages. As with all new media, the Internet is part of an era of narrowcasting and niche publishing.

Homogeneous audiences, however, are also the norm. In other words, the Internet audience has been fragmented into groups with ideological if not demographic homogeneity, formed on the basis of very specific interests or belief systems. In fact, the Internet encourages the balkanization of audiences organized around specific political leanings, sexual orientation, occupations, and hobbies, to name just a few categories of self-selection.

Active audiences typify Internet users. The new media require a more active participant in the process, because the user must learn a particular new technology and then purposively search for information or find a way to negotiate a method of selection. Traditional mass media audiences are usually more passive participants in the mass communication process.

New and unusual audiences have also been formed. For example, the Internet has created a remarkable communication opportunity for disabled citizens who have fewer opportunities to interact with mainstream communication processes. Cyberspace offers a unique dialogue for the hearing impaired, who can exchange words on the screen with nearly the speed of spoken communication. Groups with viewpoints outside mainstream society's have found that the Net provides them with a unique opportunity to network. Cyberspace offers reticent people some comfort: A number of studies have shown that shy people prefer to communicate in cyberspace. Without question, the Internet will help make possible many more new ways for human beings to group together and organize in the future.

Elite audiences are one obvious result of the new technologies. Use of the Internet requires some technical know-how and fairly expensive equipment. At first, the only users of cyberspace were an elite group of scientists, intellectuals, specialists, and academics. Within a few years, its use spread to a broader spectrum of the middle class. However, there is no question that the new technologies could increase the difference between the *information rich* and the *information poor*. Wilson Dizard, Neil Postman, and other observers have suggested that the information poor will settle for the "hyped-up entertainment diversions the new channels will offer" (Dizard, 1994, p. 15), rather than data and information necessary to move them toward a more successful life. The couch potatoes of television could well become the nerds of cyberspace.

Economist Robert Reich argues that an economic imbalance has already come to U.S. culture, with the top fifth of working Americans earning more income than the other four-fifths of the population combined. He argues that the affluent group is composed largely of "symbol analysts," or professionals who create or deal with information, and they "inhabit a different economy from other Americans," linked by jet, modem, fax, and fiber-optic cable, "but not necessarily connected to the rest of the world."[3]

AUDIENCE USES AND INTERNET FUNCTIONS

A study by the Strategis Group Inc. in 1998 showed that most users were still using the Internet for research and product information, 63 percent; followed by headline news, 23 percent; entertainment, 20 percent; shopping, 17 percent; and chatting, 16 percent. When the question was asked in a somewhat different fashion by Emerging Technologies Research Group, they found the following breakdown for the percentages of adult Internet users of various content: news, 80 percent; hobbies and leisure, 68 percent; special interest group information, 66 percent; education and training, 57 percent; product information, 47 percent; health and medicine, 38 percent; and investment information, 32 percent.[4] Another survey, by Forrester Research, provides a more complex answer to Internet use, as shown in Table 15.3.

In other words, Internet usage depends largely on definitions. In some respects, it is not different from the uses of other mass media, and in other ways it allows the user to go well beyond the traditional functions. A closer look at Internet functions can help sort this out.

News and Information

The real birth of online news coverage, according to media critic Jon Katz, probably occurred in January 1994, when a subscriber to Prodigy noticed the earth was shaking in Los Angeles and used a wireless modem to post that news on the Internet. Well ahead of established media, Internet users were exchanging information about the earthquake's location and damage, providing details to specific users, helping notify relatives and organize rescue attempts.

By 1995, large media companies, including newspapers such as the *Boston Globe* and *The Washington Post* had launched online newspapers, using both journalists and computer personnel. At the *Star Tribune Online* in Minneapolis, the new service hired two Pulitzer Prize winners among the eleven recruited for its online product. In fact, within a short period more than 110 daily newspapers were available online, as were the texts of more than 5,000 magazines, newsletters, and newswires.

Online information quickly became essential to traditional journalism. A 1998 survey, "Media in Cyberspace," conducted with the cooperation of nearly 6,000 newspaper and magazine editors and broadcast journalists, found that journalists were increasingly turning to the Internet both to source stories and get new ideas for stories. In 1996 only 23 percent said they went online in search of news; in 1997 the number had risen to 33 percent; and by 1998 it was up to nearly half. A third of all newspapers who cooperated in the survey said their online editions had scooped their print editions on occasion. The report concluded that the Internet had irrevocably changed the face of traditional journalistic practice.[5]

TABLE 15.3

Top 25 Internet Uses

Rank	Activity	Percentage of Households
1.	Send e-mail	88.7
2.	Go to the World Wide Web	85.1
3.	Use search-engine sites	77.8
4.	Visit company or product sites	52.0
5.	Research product purchases	47.4
6.	Look up weather information	46.6
7.	Visit reference sites	40.7
8.	Read daily newspapers and magazines	33.8
9.	View stock quotes	27.7
10.	Make purchases	26.9
11.	Visit sports sites	23.8
12.	Participate in online chat	23.0
13.	Read product/entertainment reviews	21.6
14.	Play online games	20.7
15.	Request product service help	19.7
16.	Visit entertainment sites	18.0
17.	Use free Web-based e-mail	18.0
18.	Look up movie information	17.8
19.	Visit TV network sites	15.5
20.	Visit adult entertainment sites	15.3
21.	Visit family sites	15.1
22.	Visit financial sites	13.1
23.	Do financial transactions	9.7
24.	Receive financial advice	9.2
25.	Publish own Web pages	9.2

Forrester Research's Technographics 1999 study of 94,200 North American households that had been online at least three times in the previous three months (respondents could give multiple answers). Reproduced with permission.

But online journalism is a new world and raises new issues. Newhagen and Levy contend that journalism "now finds itself at ... a juncture, as it reflects on a set of mature norms and canons established during the reign of mass-circulation newspapers, and looks ahead to computer-based information network technologies" (Borden & Harvey, 1998, p. 9). They argue that the traditional standards of journalism may be "unnatural, unrealistic, and practically impossible to apply" (p. 10) when the participant is both message producer and message receiver. For one thing, they reason, the reporting and collecting of data is dispersed, with data collection conceivably occurring at any node on the Net. Second, and most important they say, in online journalism editors can lose control of the agenda.

Interpretation, Opinion, Gossip, and Rumor

Computer technology and the Internet have democratized information, making it no longer the sole province of journalistic organizations. "The Net is very much a part of the end of the 'official story,'" says cyber-visonary Esther Dyson.[6] "The Net also changes the balance of power ... between mass media and their audiences, who can now not only talk back but talk among themselves" (Dyson, 1997, p. 8).

Anyone can have a Web page, and news can come from "half-witted rumors from random strangers," as one *Washington Post* writer characterized the nonjournalists online. One result is a blurring of journalistic definitions and functions. In online journalism, marketing and advertising can merge with news, and the expression of opinion can merge with factual information, with the possible result that the public will be less able to distinguish between objective news and persuasive messages.

Online journalism can have serious impact on the news, as was demonstrated by the breaking of the Bill Clinton–Monica Lewinsky story in early 1998. The story, about the affair between the president and a White House intern, was first made public in a scoop by *The Drudge Report*. (As a consequence, this online "service" started getting 200,000 hits a day.) The result was that many newspapers rushed into print with aspects of the story that were still rumor, and even such newspapers as *The New York Times, The Wall Street Journal*, and *The Washington Post* all published stories that were incomplete, sometimes false, and often based on anonymous sources. Many news organizations traditionally have held to the notion that all news must be confirmed by at least two independent sources. The Internet and efforts such as *The Drudge Report* caused that rule to be abandoned in stories such as in the Clinton–Lewinsky case.

The lack of gatekeepers in the Internet communication process can become a serious problem in the future as the Internet user becomes overwhelmed with data and yet has little foundation for judging their rightness or wrongness, goodness or badness, accuracy or inaccuracy, truthfulness or falsity.

Entertainment

Although the Internet was originally started as a way to exchange data between computers, it has grown into a major entertainment medium. Dave Werthheimer of Paramount Digital Entertainment predicted in early 1998 that the Internet was more destined to become a forum for entertainment than a technological medium. By early 1998, developments in infrastructure and general technological improvements for the commercial Internet were beefing up the Internet's ability to deliver a myriad of entertainment functions to users. Already by that time, according to the president of Disney Online, Disney.com was receiving more than 1.6 million hits a day, more than visitors to its theme parks and stores.

By late 1997, AOL had established Entertainment Asylum, a site that united pop culture with the mass computer audience in what the company hoped would be the Web's top-rated show. "This could change the world. This could become interactive television. We're on the verge of a Golden Age," said the subsidiary's president.

According to *Time* magazine, the site would offer almost every content idea that was ever tried online, from interviews with stars and the usual news, reviews, and video clips, to "cool stuff like customizable TV listings. Members of the Screen Team, a handful of video-worthy young hosts, will report in from movie premieres, sitcom sets, and innumerable other shameless junkets while presiding over the site's message boards and chat rooms" (September 22, 1997, p. 39). Tabloid online had arrived.

Education

The Internet as an educational medium has great advantages but raises a few concerns as well. It can help connect teachers to one another, to school personnel, to parents and students. It can help connect children. Net-based rating services are being used to evaluate the performance of teachers and schools, and this can be a force from the outside for better schooling. With more information about their schools, parents and students can exercise greater choice over schooling, making the education market freer than ever before.

The Internet, with audio and video presentations, can also be an effective teaching tool, providing a dazzling array of facts. But some critics point out that the unnatural timescale of jump cuts and flashes in multimedia presentations can have a down side in education as well. They can attract student attention, says Esther Dyson (1977), but they might be not so good for mental discipline. Visual images with compelling sound may sell, but they don't enlighten with verbal logic. Multimedia presentations can make education entertaining, suggests Dyson, but not necessarily get students to think or assess consequences.

Advertising

When the Internet first came into being, it was envisioned as free public space for the exchange of information. People who wanted to make money from it at first couldn't figure out how. But by mid-1995, advertising companies were scrambling to take advantage of an arena that some predicted would do nothing less than change the nature of advertising itself. They were putting up video pages on the World Wide Web, buying space on electronic magazines, and frantically trying to figure out what interactive advertising was all about. An executive for Zenith Media, the media buying arm of Saatchi & Saatchi, called it "the Wild West out there ... a gold rush going on."

Two and a half years later, in early 1998, ads were almost ubiquitous online, and what had been a medium of text had become splashed with all the color and graphics of slick magazine ads. However, making money on the Internet was still a ways off. In early 1998, *Editor & Publisher* wrote that newspapers were still losing money on their online services. Knight Ridder's 32 Web sites cost $27 million and generated $11 million in ad sales. The Tribune Company spent $30 million and earned only $12 million. The New York Times Company lost between $12 million and $15 million. Some predicted a better future; analysts from Forrester Research estimated that classified ads alone would become a $1.5 billion annual business by 2001, while Jupiter Communications predicted the figure would be $1.9 billion.

Revenue from advertising had been the main form of income for most news Web sites through 1997, as most people didn't think of online news (or other Internet offerings) as something one might have to subscribe to, as one does to receive a hard copy of a publication. But media executives were already planning to start charging for access to their services as well. By early 1998, *Business Week, The Wall Street Journal, The San Jose Mercury News*, and *The Economist* were expecting readers to pay for at least some content.

Public Relations

In many ways, the Internet may be more adaptable for public relations than for news and advertising. Public relations is a persuasive function, not subject to the rules of objective journalism, and yet it is content given to the media free of charge, so buying time and space is not a problem. One merely has to get one's message somehow onto the Net. By 1995, public relations agencies were establishing a presence on the Internet and many were convinced that the new technology would drastically change the way people do public relations.

The public relations offices of many corporations put information bulletins onto the net for reporters (and other users) to use as they saw fit. As far as journalists were concerned, this was simply another way to get information for news stories. An editor for the *Boston Globe*, discussing IBM's information about its buyout of Lotus, which it had placed on the Web, called the information "useful. But critical reporting standards have to apply. There is plenty of junk out in cyberspace. We're going to be very careful about what we download and actually use in a story."[7]

EFFECTS OF THE INTERNET

So little time has passed since the advent of the Internet as a mass medium that we have little solid empirical evidence of its effects on users or on society as a whole, but many studies are underway and some are already indicating the direction of effects research.

Psychological Effects

Studies by psychologists at Stanford University show that heavy use of the Internet could cause social skills to atrophy and promote asocial behavior among already shy people.[8] An interesting study led a researcher to conclude that constant playing of video games actually prepared young people for careers in what she calls the modern "military-entertainment complex." J. C. Herz, in her book *Joystick Nation* (1997), showed how tank drivers in the Gulf War had been trained in "virtual reality pods," which enabled single tanks to destroy entire Iraqi armored brigades. The army later "took all the black boxes and satellite images from these tank wars and reconstructed the whole engagement, second-for-second, as a high-resolution 3D video game" to use for training of its armored personnel.[9]

Communication Effects

The Internet and new media are changing the mass communication process itself. The process will change because using it is less expensive than using other media, and because the message can span far greater distances. For instance, one can send e-mail messages around the world in the same timespan one can make a phone call and much faster than one can send "snail mail," but at a fraction of the cost. Furthermore, speed, channel diversity, and interactive communication will greatly increase. Internet communication can be almost instantaneous, certainly faster than even radio or television, if one factors in production time. Instead of a few channels or frequencies or publications, the diversity of originating messages can be nearly infinite. And all the messages can be returned with equal speed by their receivers.

Social Effects

This widespread availability of two-way electronic communication will change the lives of people as well. The ability to be heard across the world and the ability to find information about almost anything can give enormous power to individuals. The new strength this brings can sap some authority from central governments, reduce some influence of mass media, and decrease some pressures from big business.

Furthermore, the ability to be a mass communicator and a mass producer is now possible for any individual with a PC and an Internet connection. One no longer needs to own a printing press or a broadcast station or even a copy machine to get one's message to a widespread audience.

Decentralization

Perhaps the greatest structural impact of the Internet is decentralization. With users no longer dependent on a center to be connected, central authority can be undermined, whether for good or for bad. Decentralization can be a profound and destabilizing force, establishing a level playing field for everyone within an organization or unit, even a nation. For example, it can change the balance of power between mass media and their audience, giving the audience a great deal more say about message content. It can change the balance of power between employees and employers; workers can now not only talk back but also talk among themselves. It can help diverse and distant persons to act together, whether for good or for bad. In other words, says Dyson (1997), the Internet is a feeble tool for propaganda, but it is perfect for conspiracy.

Cyberwars and Fragmentation

One of the crucial effects of the Internet may be its role in fragmenting society into antagonistic forces, while giving opposing sides the platform and voice to attack. A riveting example is the use of the Internet by some foes of abortion. One hard-line radical antiabortion group has begun an Internet site called "The Nuremberg Files," named for the German city where Nazi leaders were tried after World War II. The site publishes names, photos, home addresses, and license plate numbers of doctors who perform abortions, making it seem as if they are war criminals. The doctors regard the site as a threat to their lives; some have moved their places of residence, unlisted their telephone numbers, and taken to wearing bulletproof vests. The doctors have sued, charging that the Internet site was a form of terrorism that was depriving them of their rights. The defendants claimed their site is a form of free speech protected by the First Amendment. In early 1999 the case was won by the doctors.

The Internet has had considerable effect in international political conflict as well. An example is the growing cyberwar in Burma. In that country, renamed Myanmar by the government in 1989 (a name disavowed by Burmese dissidents), despotic military juntas have ruled since 1962. Many Burmese have fled because of brutal repression of ethnic groups and junta critics. From their worldwide exile, the dissidents criticize the junta for drug trafficking, destroying the environment, and violating human rights, and would like to see the overthrow of the regime. They have turned to the Internet to organize and communicate their dissident activities. They use newsgroups, Web sites, listservs, and e-mail to keep in touch, spread information, and promote a coup d'etat of the Burmese military government.

Meanwhile, the military junta uses similar tactics to wage a war of words against the dissidents. And, of course, to keep the dissident message out of the country, they have strictly forbidden the use of the Internet by all Burmese citizens still in the country; so far, it has not been able to stop the worldwide flow of dissident information on the Internet.[10]

In 1996, when Serbian president Slobodan Milosevic jammed a Belgrade station, radio B92, because it was giving voice to a Serbian prodemocracy movement, a professor with computer skills and limited software used a phone connection to the Internet to tell the world what the Serbian dictator was doing. He used the Internet to rebroadcast what had been jammed, and the whole world could listen. The Internet rebroadcasts started public protests in the streets of Belgrade, and the outcry was heard worldwide. Milosevic had to back down. The episode demonstrates how new technologies have changed international politics. Anyone with a computer, modem, and some savvy could alter domestic political dynamics by exploiting the global character of the Internet.

The Case of China

At the beginning of this book, we described how China was changing its very language to enable mass communication and how that also allowed the Chinese language to be computerized, a major step forward in China's industrial development. The Communist Chinese government has supported the growth of the Internet, knowing that its widespread use will be essential to China's scientific and technological development in the twenty-first century. By 1998, there were 620,000 people surfing the Internet in China, and that figure was expected to rise to 2 million by the year 2000, soar to 7 million in the year after, and 10 million by 2003, according to Xinhua, the official Chinese news agency. The impact the government's support of the Internet will have on Chinese industry, economy, and politics in the future will be significant and worth watching.

However, the Communist Chinese government is so concerned about the power of the Internet as a threat to its stability that it keeps close watch on the new medium. By 1998, the government had begun an aggressive campaign to increase surveillance of the network. Shanghai police have trained computer users to keep their eyes and ears on the Internet. Arrests have been frequent. One case receiving international attention in 1998–1999 was the arrest and imprisonment of Shangai entrepreneur Lin Hai, who had used his Internet access to find e-mail addresses to promote his online personnel service. He was accused of inciting the overthrow of state power by allegedly providing part of his database to the Washington-based magazine *Chinese VIP Reference*, which advocates democracy and is sent to 120,000 e-mail addresses in China every 10 days. The cyberwar in China will likely have significant repercussions for that nation's development in the years ahead.

NEW MEDIA VERSUS OLD MEDIA

It would be a mistake to think that the new media described in this chapter, including the Internet, will at any time in the foreseeable future replace the older mass media described in this book. The long history of media proves quite conclusively that the development of new technologies bringing about new media do not cancel old technologies; they merely change them. Printing books changed the labor-intensive art of illustrating manuscripts by hand, but art in books continues. Newspapers changed books, magazines changed newspapers, radio changed newspapers, television changed radio and movies, videocassette recordings changed television and movies. That process will continue as long as human beings create and innovate.

Older media analysts are probably more likely to cling to older media than are the hip and young. As Richard Harwood, a retired *Washington Post* editor and an active media critic writes, "as a substitute for books, magazines, newspapers and many other printed materials, the Internet's future" is far from clear. He emphasizes that reading large bodies of text scrolled up on a computer screen is a tedious, inefficient, and probably unhealthy activity, "somewhat comparable to reading *War and Peace* on a microfilm machine."[11] The next generation undoubtedly will have different thoughts.

The more crucial question is how the new media will change the old. Newhagen and Levy conclude that the Internet "will probably not kill the mass media, but it will almost certainly reshape them" (Borden & Harvey, 1998, p. 21). And we should add, they will reshape the world, just as earlier media did.

The Medium Is the Message

We return to Marshall McLuhan, who wrote several decades before the Internet emerged and yet envisioned a world interconnected by media into a new global village. He was only partly right; the world has not been reshaped into one global village, but into an infinite number of global villages. He was right that it is the medium itself—in this case the Internet—that is producing that new decentralized world of global villages.

China is a good example of the effect of media on society, because in less than one century it has gone from a feudal, almost preprint culture, to a computerized age of the Internet. We saw in chapter 1 that as media have changed, social and cultural structures have had to reform, in some cases revolutionize, in order to accommodate them. To join the age of mass media, China had to making sweeping changes, even transforming the very nature of its language, the essence of a culture. Now the cyberage may force China to change yet again, to decentralize its highly centralized authoritarian structure to fit the new world of the Internet. Like many authoritarian cultures, the natural inclination is to resist new media and the changes they bring, including the decentralized and threatening world of cyberspace.

But the medium is stronger than the message. McLuhan was probably right—it *is* the message. Mass media have reshaped our lives and our minds and the way we experience the world. That is what this book has been about. We believe that in order to understand ourselves and our world today, we have to understand mass media. We have to become media literate, to understand what the message really is, so we can make it work for us.

As you finish reading this book, be aware that much lies ahead, for you, for mass media, and for the world. The more we know about mass media, the more we will be able to harness them to help us fulfill our own destinies. If we remain ignorant, we will live out the destiny that others set for us.

Further Reading

Abramson, Jeffrey B., Arterton, Christopher F., and Orren, Gary R. (1988). *The Electronic Commonwealth: The Impact of New Media Technologies on Democratic Politics.* New York: Basic Books.

Biocca, Frank, and Levy, Mark R. (Eds.). (1994). *Communication in the Age of Virtual Reality.* Mahwah, NJ: Lawrence Erlbaum Associates.

Borden, Diane L., and Harvey, Kerric. (1998). *The Electronic Grapevine: Rumor, Reputation, and Reporting in the New On-Line Environment.* Mahwah, NJ: Lawrence Erlbaum Associates.

Cook, Philip S., Gomery, Douglas, and Lichty, Lawrence W. (1992). *The Future of News.* Washington, DC: Woodrow Wilson Center Press.

Dizard, Wilson, Jr. (1994). *Old Media, New Media: Mass Communications in the Information Age.* New York: Longman.

Dupagne, Michel, and Seel, Peter B. (1997). *High Definition Television: A Global Perspective.* Ames: Iowa State University Press.

Dyson, Esther. (1997). *Release 2.0: A Design for Living in the Digital Age.* New York: Broadway Books/Bantam Doubleday Dell.

Federman, Joel, Carbone, Stephanie, Chen, Helen, and Munn, William. (1996). *The Social Effects of Electronic Games.* Studio City, CA: Mediascope.

Fredin, Eric S. (1997). *Rethinking the News Story for the Internet: Hyperstory Prototypes and a Model of the User*. Columbia, SC: Association for Education in Journalism and Mass Communciation, Journalism and Mass Communication Monographs, No. 163.

Groebel, Jo. (Ed.). (1997). *New Media Developments*. Amsterdam: Trends in Communication.

Harper, Christopher. (Ed.). (1998). *What's Next in Mass Communication: Readings on Media and Culture*. New York: St. Martin's.

Horn, Stacy. (1998). *Cyberville: Clicks, Culture, and the Creation of an Online Town*. New York: Warner Books.

Hudson, David. (1997). *Rewired: A Brief (and Opinionated) Net History*. Indianapolis: Macmillan Technical Publishing.

Levy, Mark R., and Gurevitch, Michael. (1994). *Defining Media Studies: Reflections on the Future of the Field*. New York: Oxford University Press.

Levy, Mark R. (Ed.). (1989). *The VCR Age: Home Video and Mass Communication*. Thousand Oaks, CA: Sage.

Neuman, W. Russell. (1991). *The Future of the Mass Audience*. Cambridge: Cambridge University Press.

Pavlik, John V. (1996). *New Media Technology: Cultural and Commercial Perspectives*. Boston: Allyn and Bacon.

Pearce, Celia. (1997). *The Interactive Book: A Guide to the Interactive Revolution*. Indianapolis: Macmillan Technical Publishing.

Platt, Charles. (1997). *Anarchy Online: Net Sex Net Crime*. New York: Harper Prism.

Reddick, Randy, and King, Elliot. (1995). *The Online Journalist: Using the Internet and Other Electronic Resources*. Fort Worth: Harcourt Brace.

Stepp, Carl Sessions. (1989). *Editing for Today's Newsroom: New Perspectives for a Changing Profession*. Mahwah, NJ: Lawrence Erlbaum Associates.

Swanson, Gillian. (Ed.). (1998, February). *Marketing on the Internet*. Queensland, Australia: Media International Australia: Culture and Policy, No. 86.

Thalhimer, Mark A. (Ed.). (1996). *Dollars and Demographics: News in the Next Century*. Washington, DC: Radio Television News Directors Foundation.

Thalhimer, Mark. A. (Ed.). (1996). *Digital Debate: Covering Government and Politics in a New Media Environment*. Washington, DC: Radio Television News Directors Foundation.

Wendlund, Mike. (1996). *Wired Journalist: Newsroom Guide to the Internet*. Washington, DC: Radio Television News Directors Foundation.

Zollman, Peter M. (1997). *Interactive News: State of the Art*. Washington, DC: Radio Television News Directors Foundation.

Notes

[1] Quoted in Chandresekaran, Rajiv. (1997, May 11). The Big Push? New Technology Could Change the Way the Web Is Used, *The Washington Post*, p. H1+.

[2] See Planning for the Internet Decade. (1999, March 1). *FutureScapes Executive Report*, Charleston, SC: Corporate Technology Research Corp. and *Internet User Trends*. (1998, June). Washington, DC: The Strategis Group.

[3] Reich, Robert. (1991, January 20). Secession of the Successful. *The New York Times Magazine*, p. 16.

[4] See Internet User Trends. (1988, June). Washington, DC: The Strategis Group. And *An Internet User Survey*. (1998). New York: Emerging Technologies Research Group, Cyber Dialogue.

[5] See Ross, Steven S., and Middleberg, Don. (1996, January 29). *Media in Cyberspace*. New York: Media Source, Middleberg and Associates.

[6] Dyson, Esther, in speech to the Washington, DC, chapter of the Association for Women in Communication, March 11, 1998.

[7] Quoted in *Jack O'Dwyer's Newsletter* (1995, July 12), p. 3.

[8] Pope, Justin. (1997, October). Computers Make Our Lives Easier—And Pull Us Further Apart. *Stanford Today*, pp. 36–37.

[9]Herz, J. C. (1997). *Joystick Nation: How Videogames Ate Our Quarters, Won Our Hearts, and Rewired Our Minds.* Boston: Little, Brown, p. 102.

[10]For an excellent analysis of the situation, see Hla, Aung, *Using the Internet in the Cyberwar Between Burma Activists and the Military Government in Burma.* University of Maryland, graduate thesis, 1998.

[11]Harwood, Richard. (1998, June 21). ... And a Slow Transition to the Internet. *The Washington Post,* p. A21.

Author Index

Subject Index